D0848387

Praise for *Foreign Corrupt Practices Act Compliance Guidebook*

"This book is a must for lawyers and any corporation that deals with global commerce. The chapter on Siemens shows how a large multinational can respond and reform under intense scrutiny. The Siemens chapter represents reform and transparency and will be seen as a model for a very long time."

—Michael G. Oxley, Of Counsel, Baker & Hostetler LLP

"An excellent FCPA guidebook! The Biegelmans' book makes it easy to understand the FCPA and includes fascinating case studies and interviews with compliance thought leaders. It should be required reading and a desktop reference for anyone committed to the fight against worldwide corruption or interested in creating a best practice anti-corruption compliance program within their organization."

—Cynthia Cooper, CEO of The CooperGroup LLC and one of *Time* magazine's Persons of the Year

"The *FCPA Compliance Guidebook* is an excellent and easy to use resource for companies doing business abroad and their lawyers. The book is full of practical guidance and compiles in one place an overview of the many issues a company and its counsel may face in effecting compliance and dealing with investigations. The book also provides a good overview of the law and lessons learned from many of the significant cases. A must read!"

—Karen A. Popp, Partner at Sidley Austin LLP, former federal prosecutor, and Associate White House Counsel to President Clinton

"As more organizations go global and the international lines of business blur, companies must understand their obligations under the Foreign Corrupt Practices Act. This book provides a highly relevant and invaluable guide for companies wishing to protect their assets and reputations from the menace of corruption. In addition to presenting a comprehensive discussion of the history, requirements, and importance of the FCPA, Martin and Daniel Biegelman offer insightful, in-depth examples and clear, practical guidance on compliance."

—James D. Ratley, CFE, President, Association of Certified Fraud Examiners

"Everyone in the compliance community will find what they need in this great new resource. It demystifies the FCPA and what it requires. The writing is crisp and lively, the examples and case studies are vivid and succinct, and the advice is rock solid. This is the best overall presentation of the FCPA between two covers that I have ever seen."

"The Biegelmans' *FCPA Compliance Guidebook* is a brilliant and crucial addition to FCPA literature. Any American company doing business overseas needs a copy. This will be a standard reference for many years."

"Martin and Daniel Biegelman have done it again. While the FCPA has been an issue for decades, it has taken center stage over the past few years and all signs point to it having an even greater impact on businesses going forward. The Biegelmans have built a comprehensive tool for all levels of interest—from the practitioner to the CEO, this is a book that should be mandatory reading for those touching international business."

"As the FCPA quickly becomes one of the world's true International Laws, compliance is essential for corporate accountability and integrity. The FCPA is a critical component of a free market system that rewards hard-working, honest individuals and companies, and strongly pursues violators. The Biegelmans' *FCPA Compliance Guidebook* isn't just about a regulation; it's about building a successful and compliant global economy."

"Martin, along with his son Daniel, have written the authoritative standard on the Foreign Corrupt Practices Act. It is a must read for Compliance or Ethics personnel looking to better understand this complex issue."

"Foreign Corrupt Practices Act violations are the current focus of regulators, investigators, and prosecutors, here and abroad. This exhaustive text explores the legal nooks and crannies with exacting precision, but it's most important contribution is the emphasis on compliance and prevention, areas that the authors know well. Through numerous illustrations of extraordinary crimes and splendid compliance and prevention techniques, the authors establish FCPA awareness and compliance as a *sine qua non* for doing business globally. A must-read for businesses wishing to avoid massive fines and/or imprisonment."

—George E. Curtis, J.D., Executive Director of the Economic Crime Institute, Utica College

"Martin and Daniel Biegelmans' work will go down in American corporate and financial lore as a comprehensive history of the series of train wrecks that have yielded the FCPA and its various progeny. It tells the fascinating story of how we got from the Lockheed disclosures of the mid-1970s to the hottest area of white collar practice today. It is required reading for those of us struggling to implement global compliance programs. Those unenlightened ones who remain committed to the dark side would also do well to read it, and take warning."

—Keith Hennessee, Associate General Counsel, Halliburton Company

"This book is a great compilation of information about the FCPA and practical guide that would have been incredibly useful to me when I was asked to be responsible for FCPA Compliance related matters. It is a much needed resource and it will be extremely valuable as a desk reference for anyone involved in business and who is accountable for FCPA compliance."

—Flora A. Francis, Counsel, Litigation, GE Oil & Gas

"Tackling corruption and insuring compliance with the Foreign Corrupt Practices Act makes this book a 'must read' for both current and future managers of today's global corporations. Increased global anti-corruption laws and efforts demand that corporate compliance and training programs are in place – this guidebook provides the 'how' and the 'why'! This book provides the 'wake-up call' and consequences of 'failure to act' that organizations can no longer ignore!"

—Joyce Barden, CPA, CBM, Senior Professor, DeVry University/Keller Graduate School of Management

Foreign Corrupt Practices Act Compliance Guidebook

*Protecting Your Organization from
Bribery and Corruption*

Martin T. Biegelman
Daniel R. Biegelman

JOHN WILEY & SONS, INC.

Published by John Wiley & Sons, Inc., Hoboken, New Jersey.
Published simultaneously in Canada.

For general information on our other products and services or for technical support, please contact our Customer Care Department within the United States at (800) 762-2974, outside the United States at (317) 572-3993 or fax (317) 572-4002.

Wiley also publishes its books in a variety of electronic formats. Some content that appears in print may not be available in electronic books. For more information about Wiley products, visit our web site at www.wiley.com.

Library of Congress Cataloging-in-Publication Data

Biegelman, Martin T.
  Foreign corrupt practices act compliance guidebook : protecting your organization from bribery and corruption / Martin T. Biegelman, Daniel R. Biegelman.
      p. cm.
  Includes index.
  ISBN 978-0-470-52793-1 (cloth)
  1. Fraud–Prevention. 2. Bribery–Prevention. 3. International trade–Corrupt practices–Prevention. 4. Corporations–Corrupt practices–Prevention. 5. Compliance auditing. I. Biegelman, Daniel R. II. Title.
  HV6691.B474 2010
  658.4'7–dc22

                                                                    2009047251

Printed in the United States of America

10 9 8 7 6 5 4 3 2 1

For Leonard Biegelman

Husband, father, grandfather, Navy veteran,
and a very special and good man.
His love and devotion, as well as
his integrity and character,
left an indelible mark on us.

Contents

Contents

Contents

Contents

Contents

Foreword

The biggest deterrent against unethical behavior is strong leadership. Controls alone do not do enough to create an ethical culture; strong leadership can make up for the absence of formal controls or policies, while weak leadership will amplify the effect of those absences. Nevertheless, controls are critical. Codes of conduct are important. Advice from companies that have failed to implement controls, test-run their controls, and investigate chinks in the armor are valuable lessons for companies and employees that want to make their company a great place to work.

Martin and Daniel have laid out those lessons in *Foreign Corrupt Practices Act Compliance Guidebook*. In the FCPA arena, fact is more compelling than fiction. Companies doing business outside U.S. shores have to constantly assess leadership, assess policies, and assess their reputation. Think about that for a second: Chief Executive Officers and Chairmen of the Board need to be concerned about the reputation their leaders are creating 12 time zones away at a facility that no executive leader of the company has ever planned to visit.

That is no easy task when you consider that companies are bigger, financially and in terms of headcount, than many developing countries. But companies enter into new markets and partnerships every day. The distributor agreement your team signed across the globe also brought along that agent's reputation; both good and bad. Moreover, customers will view your company's reputation through the behavior of the agent. Did your company do enough research into the ethical culture of the new partner? Does the familial relationship of the owner and current foreign government present a conflict of interest? How will success fees be calculated? These are all important questions which Martin and Daniel keenly delve into throughout the book and present practical experience from companies that have embedded "compliance programs" into their "business program" so that employees are speaking the same dialect regardless of their discipline or geography.

Most importantly, employees need to understand a company's expectations for integrity and for transparency. If the objective is to build a sustainable business, integrity must be at the core of corporate behavior; otherwise you will have a nice glossy Code of Conduct, with matching posters throughout campus, perhaps a few employees whose individual integrity impacts their team but for the vast majority of employees, integrity will be a marketing buzzword with no substance or context. Management has to be committed to integrity in all business operations. The only way to build a compliance culture is for every team to embed compliance into their daily business activity. You cannot depend on compliance officers, HR, lawyers, auditors, or corporate security to build this culture—the culture is built by employees, it is built by managers. Martin and Daniel have laid the blueprint to help you build your company's compliance program in this *Guidebook*.

Alfredo Avila
Assistant General Counsel
Business Conduct Office
Monsanto Company
December 2009

Preface

Watergate. The mere mention of the word invokes images and memories of a political scandal of huge proportion that brought down a president and left the man and his presidency disgraced. There were break-ins and burglaries, illegal wiretaps, slush funds, money laundering, hush money, and White House cover-ups, leading to the impeachment of Richard Nixon, and the indictment and conviction of his closest advisors and confidants. This was corruption at the highest levels of government. It severely rattled the American psyche and shook people's faith in government. But there was some good that followed. One beneficial outcome of the Watergate scandal would become a weapon against corruption in the corporate suites: the enactment of the Foreign Corrupt Practices Act (FCPA) in 1977.

In addition to the large-scale illegal contributions to Nixon's 1972 re-election campaign, the Watergate investigation revealed the existence of slush funds that corporations used for bribery of foreign government officials. The investigation found that this corruption and bribery to obtain and retain business was pervasive throughout corporate America. What's more, there was nothing illegal about this hidden and seamy practice. The outrage of good and honest public officials spurred Congress to act and the FCPA became law.

Fast forward to today and the FCPA is one of the fastest growing areas of law and corporate enforcement in both the civil and criminal arenas. It is now a major concern of businesses, be they public or private, large or small, foreign or domestic. The FCPA is of even greater importance now due to the globalization of business and the U.S government's commitment to enforcement. In short, the FCPA makes it a crime for a company in the United States, for U.S. citizens, or their agents, to obtain business by bribery of a government official of another country, or to conspire to do so from the United States, or for a publicly traded U.S. company to fail to record such a payment on the company books. The FCPA also impacts foreign companies that have business connections in the United States. The penalties for violating the FCPA can be severe.

There is a greater focus on corporate compliance and ethics than at any time in the past. The United States has also been joined by numerous other countries in the war on bribery and corruption and holding violators accountable. The fines and penalties for violators, both corporations and individuals, seem to get larger with each new case. All this makes a book on the FCPA both compelling and timely.

We have written about the FCPA in our prior books including *Executive Roadmap to Fraud Prevention and Internal Control: Creating a Culture of Compliance* and *Building a World-Class Compliance Program: Best Practices and Strategies for Success*. Our knowledge of the FCPA, the insidious nature of corruption, and the growing enforcement climate around anti-corruption and FCPA prosecution convinced us that a book dedicated to the subject was needed, and needed now.

This book provides an understanding of the critical importance of the FCPA in today's global environment. Readers will learn about the business, financial, legal, and reputational risks associated with bribery and corruption. An in-depth review of the FCPA statute with explanations of the various elements and how it applies to business operations is included. Throughout the book are lists of non-compliance red flags, mitigating controls, best practices, as well as numerous case studies of FCPA violators. One chapter focuses on a company involved in one of the most serious and large-scale bribery investigations ever conducted. Its recovery from corruption provides lessons and program models. A second chapter details a company that faced an FCPA prosecution as a result of the corrupt activities of a relatively low-level employee outside the United States and how the company subsequently responded by building a world-class anti-corruption compliance program.

Another chapter focuses on a company under investigation for alleged FCPA violations and the unique circumstances it faces while waiting to learn its fate. A discussion of the worldwide hotspots of corruption is included as well as trends, court decisions, government opinions, and guidance. A feature of the book is detailed strategies and insights on implementing an effective FCPA compliance program. We continually reinforce the critical importance of compliance with policies and program examples. Throughout the book are compliance insights that spotlight program enhancements as well as interviews with anti-corruption thought leaders who provide best practices and recommendations. The Appendix provides an overview of key Department of Justice (DOJ) Opinion Procedure Releases for further FCPA guidance.

While we can never completely eliminate corrupt behavior from the corporate suites and the halls of government, knowledge and understanding of the issues are powerful weapons in attaining and maintaining prevention and compliance. As Eleanor Roosevelt said, it's best to "learn from the mistakes of others." Use the material in this book, including the FCPA violations and compliance failures of companies and individuals, as powerful lessons to embrace and incorporate in your business planning and operations as well as enterprise risk management.

Let's not forget the growing impact of the FCPA as a weapon in the arsenal of federal prosecutors. As Seymour Glanzer, a former Watergate prosecutor, DOJ official, and current senior litigation and defense counsel has said, "Mail fraud, money laundering, and RICO were the darlings of federal prosecutors for many years. Now they're in love with the FCPA. And rightfully so."

Acknowledgments

With each book we write, the more we realize the arduous task it is to produce a definitive work that meets readers' expectations. We could not accomplish that without the generous assistance and wise counsel of the many people we acknowledge here. To all of them, we say thank you for sharing your experiences, stories, materials, and thought leadership. We are in your debt.

A special note of thanks to Tim Burgard, our executive editor at John Wiley & Sons, who again gave us a unique writing opportunity. Tim supported us from the initial concept of a book on the FCPA through to the finished product. We also want to acknowledge Helen Cho, Stacey Rivera, and Dexter Gasque at Wiley who have been invaluable in helping us navigate through issues large and small in the production process. They are true professionals.

Our sincere thanks to those who provided ideas, content, interviews, and assistance: George Stamboulidis, Marjorie Doyle, Richard Cassin, Karen Popp, Mark Kirsch, Scott Moritz, Jay Perlman, Joe Spinelli, David Seide, Seymour Glanzer, Leslie McCarthy, James Fitzmaurice, Gareth Elliot, Michael Horowitz, Dan Wachtler, Dennis Lormel, Jane Wexton, Russell Mokhiber, Ed Rial, and Wendy Schmidt.

Our deep appreciation to Dr. Andreas Pohlmann, Joel Kirsch, and Ariel Ramirez from Siemens and Alfredo Avila and Pete Sullivan from Monsanto Company who graciously gave us access to their world-class compliance programs so we could profile them in this book.

A special thank you to Amanda Massucci, Brian Loughman, Christopher Richardson, Ted Acosta, and Paul Harris from Ernst & Young's Fraud Investigation and Dispute Services Practice. They provided us with their rich knowledge and experience in FCPA and anti-corruption compliance and we are extremely grateful for their guidance.

When we wanted someone to read our draft manuscript and give us honest feedback and ideas, we again turned to our dear friend, DeWayn Marzagalli. DeWayn, a former federal agent extraordinaire, provided the constructive and thoughtful comments we needed. Writing a book without DeWayn's keen eye and recommendations would not seem right to us. As always, he offered advice and encouragement that was much needed and appreciated.

Although this work is solely ours and does not reflect the views or opinions of Microsoft Corporation or Baker Hostetler, we would like to thank our employers for supporting us in writing this book.

And, last but not least, our gratitude to Lynn, as wife and mother, she was indispensable as she spent countless hours reviewing the manuscript and providing insightful feedback. Lynn's constant encouragement, wisdom, and attention to detail were essential to our writing. Her patience, as we again spent all our free time engrossed in completing this book, is exceptional and much appreciated.

CHAPTER 1

Bribery, Corruption, and the Foreign Corrupt Practices Act

In the movie *Syriana*—a politically charged story of greed, self-interest, betrayal, and corruption in the oil and gas industry—one of the characters angrily learns he is under investigation by the U.S. Department of Justice (DOJ) for bribery to obtain drilling rights in Kazakhstan. "Corruption charges! Corruption? Corruption is government intrusion into market efficiencies in the form of regulations. . . . We have laws against it precisely so we can get away with it. Corruption is our protection. Corruption keeps us safe and warm. Corruption is why you and I are prancing around in here instead of fighting over scraps of meat out in the streets. Corruption is why we win." These contemptuous comments are what one would expect from people who have been caught up in bribery probes and prosecutions under the Foreign Corrupt Practices Act (FCPA).

The FCPA has long been an available weapon in the arsenal of federal prosecutors in the United States. Yet, the specter of the FCPA was one infrequently seen, so much so that companies and their employees came to believe they had nothing to fear. But how the times have changed. Now, the mere utterance of the acronym FCPA is enough to instill deep concern, and even fear, in corporate suites throughout the world. The FCPA is the U.S. law that makes bribery of foreign officials to obtain or retain business and the failure to maintain accurate books and records, as well as related internal controls, a very serious crime. The Act's provisions significantly impact business organizations through criminal and civil prosecutions and the collateral damage that comes with government enforcement of anti-corruption laws.

If there is a recent case that exemplifies the strong stance that government authorities are taking in pursuing FCPA violations, it is the prosecution of Control Components, Inc. (CCI). CCI is a California corporation that designs and manufactures control valves for the nuclear, oil and gas, and power generation industries throughout the world. Between 1998 and 2007, CCI, through its officers, employees, and agents, made more than 200 corrupt payments to employees of state-owned enterprises and private companies in 36 countries. These countries included China, Korea, Malaysia, and the United Arab Emirates. The bribes totaled $6.85 million and earned CCI $46.5 million in net profits.

Prosecutors used a variety of tactics to unravel the pervasive conspiracy, a move that is indicative of the new approach to fighting FCPA violations. Both the corporation and individuals were prosecuted. In fact, the eight CCI defendants is the single largest number of individual defendants in an FCPA case. There was cross-border law enforcement cooperation resulting in the prosecution of a UK official implicated in the bribery probe. Both government corruption and private company bribery were charged in this case. The Travel Act was used to charge commercial bribery. The Travel Act prohibits using interstate or foreign commerce to promote unlawful activity including bribery and corruption in violation of state law.

These tactics are part of the government's focused attack on FCPA violations. This strategy has had a visible impact on corporations. The $25 million fine against Lockheed Martin in 1994 held the record for many years until Titan Corporation paid $28.5 million in 2005. The $44 million fine levied against Baker Hughes in April 2007 was the largest ever at the time. That was eclipsed by the Siemens penalty. In December 2008, Siemens paid the largest fine ever handed down to settle the biggest FCPA case in the history of the statute. Siemens voluntarily paid $1.7 billion in fines, penalties, and disgorgement of profits to U.S. and German authorities. Of the $800 million to U.S. government authorities, $450 million was a fine and $350 million was in disgorgement of profits. In early 2009, Halliburton settled a bribery probe with a $559 million fine.

It seems inevitable that another case will come along soon with yet another record-high fine. The penalties for FCPA violations have skyrocketed of late, a trend expected to continue. Investigating and prosecuting corruption and bribery cases have become "a significant priority in recent years," according to Mark E. Mendelsohn, the DOJ's chief prosecutor for international bribery.[1]

GLOBAL CRACKDOWN

Like at no other time before, there is a growing global crackdown on corruption. The United States has been joined by other countries in this fight. There have been more investigations and prosecutions of both businesses and their employees than at any time in the past 30 years. "Crimes of official corruption threaten the integrity of the global marketplace and undermine the rule of law in the host countries," said Lori Weinstein, the Justice Department prosecutor who oversaw the Siemens case.[2]

Corruption and bribery are insidious elements of the dark side of business. Illegal payments by public and private corporations to foreign government officials to induce business dealings have long been an unscrupulous practice. These bribes, in the form of cash and a host of other means including gifts and gratuities, trips and entertainment, charitable contributions, forgiveness of debt, and more, are illegal and have been outlawed by the United States for many years. A rash of business corruption cases in the 1970s and a Congressional focus resulted in the enactment of the FCPA in 1977.

The FCPA prohibits individuals and companies from "corruptly making use of the mails or any means or instrumentality of interstate commerce in furtherance of an offer, promise, authorization, or payment of money or anything of value to a foreign official for the purpose of obtaining or retaining business for, or directing business to any person, or securing any improper advantage."[3] The FCPA also requires "issuers not only to refrain from making corrupt payments to foreign government officials, but also to implement policies and practices that reduce the risk that employees and agents will engage in bribery."[4] The books and records provision of the FCPA requires certain corporations to create and maintain books, records, and accounts that fairly and accurately reflect company transactions. The knowing falsification of company records is also prohibited.[5] Penalties include both civil and criminal sanctions against the company and culpable employees.

3

The Sarbanes-Oxley Act (SOX) was not the first federal law to require strict internal controls within publicly traded U.S. companies to prevent fraud. The FCPA mandated that corporate records contain accurate statements concerning the true purpose of all payments made by the company long before SOX was ever envisioned. Since the passage of SOX, there has been a renewed focus on investigations and prosecutions involving FCPA violations. Thus, compliance with the provisions of the FCPA is more important than ever.

Since the enactment of the FCPA, Nigeria has had the most prosecutions by country. Nigeria is followed by Iraq, China, Indonesia, India, Azerbaijan, Canada, Costa Rica, Rwanda, Egypt, Kazakhstan, and South Korea in number of cases. Countries in every region of the world have seen FCPA enforcement. By far, Asia has seen more cases than any other region with Africa a distant second.

What is not commonly known is that the FCPA was initially referred to as the "Lockheed Law," since the law was enacted as a result of the involvement of numerous corporations, including Lockheed, in making financial payments to foreign government officials in return for government contracts. As detailed later in this chapter, the Lockheed of the 1970s regularly paid bribes to foreign officials. The surprising disclosures of the size and scope of their payments in countries throughout the world did as much as anything to ensure that legislation such as the FCPA would become law.

DEVASTATING COST OF CORRUPTION

The sad fact is that corruption is pervasive and entrenched on a global scale. A culture of corruption is still embraced as a way of doing business in many parts of the world. "Each year one trillion U.S. dollars is lost in bribes and other forms of corruption around the world," said Alan Boeckmann, Chairman of the Board and Chief Executive Officer of Fluor Corporation. "Consider this: the trillion dollars lost each year to bribes could feed up to 400 million starving people for the next 27 years."[6] These impactful words reinforce the devastating cost of corruption and bribery on a global scale.

Corruption often occurs in the worst possible locales. They include developing and emerging countries and regions that suffer the most from corruption's evil consequences. Corruption fuels poverty, hunger, disease, illiteracy, contempt, and disillusion. It drains the funds necessary for the very programs that people in developing countries most need. Corrupt government officials in countries with rich natural resources such as oil, timber, and minerals "accumulate enormous personal wealth, taking millions in bribes from corporations looking to secure lucrative contracts" while the very poor live in abject poverty.[7] The resulting bribes and graft destroy honest government and business. The corruption ultimately turns the populace to distrust, ambivalence, acceptance, and ultimately, participation.

Corruption can only exist and flourish if it is tolerated. Businesses and governments need to step forward and fight corruption and bribery. This can only be done if people refuse to participate in corrupt activities. People have to take responsibility. The corruption chain can be broken if even one participant says no. Law enforcement does not have the ability to investigate every corrupt act or wrongdoer. "The answer to corruption is not necessarily at the end of handcuffs," says career federal prosecutor Patrick Fitzgerald. "People can't do this stuff without someone else knowing about it. The metric of whether or not you're doing a good job is not whether or not you get indicted."[8] Fitzgerald should know. His high-profile cases have included the World Trade Center bombings, the conviction of former vice-presidential advisor I. Lewis "Scooter" Libby, and the indictment of Illinois Governor Rod Blagojevich on numerous corruption charges.

President Obama tackled the issue of corruption in a speech he gave in Kenya in August 2008, aptly describing it as a worldwide problem.

Corruption is not a new problem. It's not just a Kenyan problem, or an African problem. It's a human problem, and it has existed in some form in almost every society. My own city of Chicago has been the home of some of the most corrupt local politics in American history, from patronage machines to questionable elections. In just the last year, our own U.S. Congress has seen a representative resign after taking bribes, and several others fall under investigation for using their public office for private gain.

It is painfully obvious that corruption stifles development—it siphons off scarce resources that could improve infrastructure, bolster education systems, and strengthen public health. It stacks the deck so high against entrepreneurs that they cannot get their job-creating ideas off the ground.

And corruption also erodes the state from the inside out, sickening the justice system until there is no justice to be found, poisoning the police forces until their presence becomes a source of insecurity rather than comfort.

Corruption has a way of magnifying the very worst twists of fate. It makes it impossible to respond effectively to crises—whether it's the HIV/AIDS pandemic or malaria or crippling drought.

5

Of course, in the end, one of the strongest weapons your country has against corruption is the ability of you, the people, to stand up and speak out about the injustices you see. The Kenyan people are the ultimate guardians against abuses.[9]

President Obama summed up his speech quite well by reinforcing the need for good people to stand up against corruption. Prosecutions can do only so much in preventing corrupt behavior. Law enforcement cannot arrest every bribe giver or recipient. Individuals and business organizations need to step up in stopping corruption. "The accomplice to the crime of corruption is frequently our own indifference," as former New York City Commissioner of Consumer Affairs Bess Myerson[10] once said. Yet, until this dream becomes a reality, the threat of business disruption, incarceration, and massive fines for violations of the FCPA and related criminal statutes will have to do.

GOVERNMENT'S COMMITMENT TO FCPA ENFORCEMENT

The DOJ and the Securities and Exchange Commission (SEC) are committed to holding individuals and organizations accountable for FCPA violations. One area of focus is whether internal control processes are designed but not implemented. Siemens had detailed anti-corruption policies and procedures but they were ineffective as they were ignored. The SEC considers this a core area for compliance and investigative attention. It is often said that the only thing worse than not having a compliance program, is having one that is simply a "paper program" and not followed. The DOJ has often commented on the risk of having a paper program and how that will play a significant role in determining whether the organization will be prosecuted for criminal violations.

The U.S. government has expanded their investigative approach to FCPA cases. While they still use self-disclosures of FCPA violations as a starting point, they have now embraced self-sourcing of cases. Self-sourcing is the proactive initiation of a new investigation using leads from an ongoing or recently concluded investigation. For example, when a corruption issue is discovered in a particular industry, the DOJ and SEC will start looking at other companies in that industry for similar violations. If a corporation has an FCPA issue, the investigators will look at their competitors as well. If one telecom company has corruption and bribery violations in China, it is reasonable to assume that the other telecom companies operating there may face similar issues.

This scrutiny of like companies will bear results for the government. An organization that self-discloses a violation will most likely tell the government about similar activities of their competitors. In fact, sources have advised that 60 percent of the FBI's current caseload is from self-sourcing. The SEC is also receiving information on violators from companies all too willing to tattle to potentially gain a competitive advantage. In addition, companies in trouble are readily sharing with the government any knowledge they may have of similar activity by their competitors.

FBI's Laser Focus on Anti-Corruption

In February 2008, the FBI created its International Corruption Unit based in the Washington, DC Field Office. Corruption is the number one target for the FBI's criminal program and there is zero tolerance for it. The unit's purpose is program oversight of corruption, bribery, and fraud investigations. There is a focus on FCPA, fraud, and corruption associated with the wars in Iraq and Afghanistan, defense contracting and procurement investigations, and antitrust cases. The unit has oversight of all FCPA investigations that the Bureau conducts.

The FBI has seen a significant growth in corruption cases in recent years. One estimate is at least a 300 percent increase since 2007. There are a number of factors contributing to this increase. Some of the reasons for increased cases include self-reporting of violations, cooperating defendants, whistleblowers, and competitors providing information. Disclosures have come from FBI investigations, disgruntled employees, foreign-based employees who have witnessed bribery, and corporate filings. There are other reasons. The FBI is providing better training to its agents on FCPA red flags. The many investigations of the past few years provided subject matter expertise to these investigators and they are sharing that thought leadership with others.

The close interaction of the International Corruption Unit with FBI legal attachés worldwide is also paying off. The FBI has over 200 special agents and support professionals in more than 60 overseas offices and embassies. While much of their work is related to terrorism, intelligence, and criminal threats, the global aspect and liaison has provided another dimension in investigating corruption and bribery. Legal attachés are briefed on the FCPA prior to deployment and as such increase the breadth and depth of FBI reach. The FBI is already teaming with investigators from the UK's Serious Fraud Office and the City of London Police to share intelligence and educate businesses on anti-corruption issues.

7

As for the future, there is a strong possibility that the Internal Revenue Service's Criminal Investigation Division may add troops to the war on bribery by assigning IRS agents to the FBI's International Corruption Unit. The IRS is already working on bribery cases, including the CCI case. The added resources of the IRS Criminal Investigation Division along with its expertise in tax evasion, undeclared income, money laundering, and other tax code violations would add further strength to FCPA enforcement efforts.

As one member of the FBI's International Corruption Unit said at a training conference on the FCPA, "we're here, we're there, we're everywhere, so beware." Based on the Bureau's results in recent years, this is not an idle threat. Business organizations, both in the United States and elsewhere, need to take notice.

WATERGATE AND THE BIRTH OF THE FCPA

It is a given that corruption and bribery have been a part of business dealings since time immemorial. In the years prior to 1977, bribery was the norm in all countries as a deal expeditor and closer. Not only was bribery of foreign government officials considered a legitimate business practice, in almost every country it was legal. Indeed, in many countries, particularly in the developing world, bribery was an accepted and encouraged business practice. That all changed in 1977 with the enactment of the FCPA.

The United States became the first country to outlaw bribery of foreign officials. The Act and its associated aspects would have far-reaching implications for U.S.-based companies and those throughout the world. In the years since its passage, the FCPA has had a significant impact on how the world deals with bribery. Just how the FCPA came to be is both fortuitous and prophetic for the change it would have in promoting anti-corruption programs in the corporate world.

The Watergate Special Prosecutor's 1973 investigations of illegal campaign contributions by public companies and their executives to Richard Nixon's 1972 reelection campaign opened a Pandora's box of other significant and pervasive criminality. What emerged was corporate America's dirty little secret: the existence of multimillion-dollar slush funds used to bribe foreign government officials and others to obtain lucrative business contracts. Slush funds are secret and often illegally obtained stashes of money used for corrupt activity such as bribes.

This corruption and bribery was extensive and long-standing and the wrongdoers made up a Who's Who of the movers and shakers in the corporate world. Their names included Northrop, Exxon, Mobil, Gulf Oil, United Brands, Ashland Oil, and Phillips Petroleum. The nation's largest defense contractor, Lockheed Aircraft Corporation, as it was then known, was identified as one of the worst offenders.

SECURITIES AND EXCHANGE COMMISSION ENTERS THE FIGHT

It wasn't long before the SEC got involved. Judge Stanley Sporkin, then Director of Enforcement for the SEC, started inquiries into how these corporate slush funds were created and whether they violated securities laws. Sporkin's staff dived into the investigation. "And before we knew it we had developed a horrendous situation where we found that out of those slush funds that were being used to give money to political parties, we went into them and we found that those monies were also being used for other and various activities, such as bribing officials in foreign countries to get business," said Sporkin years later.[11]

The expanding investigation determined that hundreds of American companies had been paying bribes to government officials in almost every region of the world. No foreign official was too big or too small to receive a bribe if it meant a business deal would close. "The public corporation is currently under severe attack because of the many revelations of improper corporate activity. It is not simple to assess the cause of this misconduct. Since it has taken so many different forms, the one dimensional explanation that . . . such conduct is a way of life, is simply not acceptable," said Sporkin in 1974 describing the many disclosures of bribes paid to foreign government officials.[12]

Not only were the bribes legal in foreign countries, they were an entrenched business practice. It was commonplace for companies to hide bribe payments on their corporate books. In European countries such as Germany and the United Kingdom, bribes could be deducted from corporate tax returns as a legitimate business expense. It was painfully obvious that no legal requirement existed for public companies to keep accurate books and records of their transactions.

Overwhelmed by the volume of bribery cases that sprung up, the SEC instituted a voluntary disclosure program in 1975 for companies to reveal both their slush funds and their foreign bribery schemes. Sporkin proposed the program to deal with the ever-growing number of subject companies

9

involved in bribery. Otherwise, it would be impossible to investigate and independently discover all the offenders. In a sense, the SEC granted unofficial deferred prosecutions to companies that stepped forward and fully cooperated with the government.

Under the program, any corporation which came forward and self-reported an illicit payment problem and fully cooperated with the Commission was informally assured that Commission enforcement action was unlikely to be taken against it. Full cooperation included conducting an independent internal investigation to determine the full extent of the company's worldwide bribery; sharing the results with the Commission, with the understanding they would be made public; and taking appropriate remedial steps to ensure that the problems were addressed and would not reoccur.[13]

Before it was over, more than 500 companies, including many of the Fortune 500, had disclosed more than $300 million in bribes to foreign officials to obtain or retain business.[14]

In response to the disclosures of widespread corporate bribery and to facilitate detection and investigation, on December 31, 1974, the IRS issued "Political Contributions" guidelines that covered political contributions made abroad. On August 29, 1975, they issued "Corporate Slush Funds" guidelines that included payments made through foreign subsidiaries. The IRS also began to more closely audit corporate tax returns for compliance.

SENATE INVESTIGATIONS

In May 1975, the Senate Committee on Foreign Relations opened its previously closed hearings on foreign bribery to the public. The committee was headed by Senator Frank Church, a strong advocate for fighting international corruption. Church had a thorough understanding of the problem from his many years of experience investigating clandestine CIA and FBI operations outside the country that had connections to bribery. In his opening remarks on the issue of bribery, Church said it was not a "question of private or public morality" but rather a "major issue of foreign policy for the United States.[15]

By June 1975, there was the expected backlash from other quarters in Washington. In a secret cable from June 2, 1975 that was declassified in 2006, a State Department Deputy Secretary warned that the Church Committee's public hearings would do more harm than good. "We hear that Senator Church is planning a week-long Saudi spectacular. . . . If members of the royal family are implicated, we will be in for a painful time. . . . We, the U.S. must recognize that we will take the brunt of whatever reaction there is. . . ."[16] It is ironic that similar logic was employed by British Prime Minister Tony Blair in his ordering his government to end a bribery investigation of BAE Systems and questionable connections to the Saudi government. A further discussion of the BAE case can be found in Chapter 8.

KISSINGER'S RESISTANCE

Secretary of State Henry Kissinger also weighed in, expressing his strong concern. In a declassified secret cable from June 4, 1975, Kissinger called the investigation into the systematic bribery of foreign officials "The Watergate of Private Industry" and recognized the "possible foreign policy repercussions."[17] The investigation intensified in the following months, leading Kissinger to attempt to stop public disclosure of Lockheed activities in foreign bribery. Fearing the fallout of public disclosure, Lockheed's outside counsel asked Kissinger to intercede and help quash the subpoena issued by the SEC for documents and testimony from Lockheed related to corporate bribery.[18] Kissinger responded in another declassified secret cable from December 19, 1975 where he stated:

> On November 19, 1975, Rogers and Wells, Counsel for Lockheed, wrote to me formally and requested the Department of State to file a suggestion of interest in the case. Accordingly, officers of the Department have examined some of the documents under subpoena which contain the names of officials of friendly foreign governments alleged to have received covert payments from Lockheed. As the Department has stated on many occasions, the making of any such payments and their disclosures can have grave consequences for significant foreign relations interests of the United States abroad. We reiterate our strong condemnation of any such payments, but we must note that premature disclosure to third parties of certain of the names and nationalities of foreign officials at this preliminary stage of the proceedings in the present case would cause damage to the United States foreign relations.[19]

Ironically, it was Kissinger's own actions that compelled Church to further his investigation. Church planned on seeking the Democratic nomination for president in 1976. Worried that a potential public backlash against a "post-Watergate frenzy of public disclosure and exposure" could hurt his chances, he ended the hearings early and did not push the inquiry as far as it could have gone.[20] Kissinger's behind the scenes maneuvers helped convince Church to hold more hearings and pursue culpable parties.[21]

Though Kissinger's attempts to stop the subpoenaed evidence and the ongoing investigation were fruitless, Lockheed continued to be defiant. In trying to stop the SEC from moving forward, Lockheed argued that the practice of bribery was good for its business and stopping it "could hurt its $1.6 billion backlog of unfilled foreign orders, presumably by causing embarrassed foreign governments to cancel contracts, and also damage prospects for future sales."[22] Lockheed further stated that bribes are "a normal and necessary feature of doing business in certain parts of the world, are essential to sales, and are consistent with practices engaged in by numerous other companies abroad."[23]

LOCKHEED'S DEFIANCE

There was a bigger question surrounding the whole issue of foreign bribery and how far the U.S. government was going to push the envelope. Was the government prepared for a full-fledged battle with corporate America over payments to foreign officials considering that at the time it was not a violation of any U.S. law? True, concealing the payments on a company's books and records was a violation but Lockheed and other companies didn't think much of that at the time. The question was moot as the SEC and Congress were steadfast and resilient in moving forward.

Lockheed was forced to admit in Congressional hearings in February 1976 that it had paid up to $24 million in bribes to government officials in at least 15 countries, including some very prominent leaders. Payoffs were funneled to the husband of then Queen Juliana of The Netherlands, the head of the then ruling political party in Japan, the Minister of the Interior in Italy, air force generals in Colombia, and to many others throughout the world.[24] Many of the bribes were made through agents and other third parties. Compounding the problems, the bribes were often large and made to the highest levels of government leaders.

Lockheed became the focal point for criticism not only from U.S. government regulators and legislators but also from other corporations. An unnamed corporate executive "condemned Lockheed for going beyond accepted practice in its payoffs" but admitted there was a "gray area in which American companies must accept the moral standards of the countries where they operate, like it or not."[25] The size of some of the Lockheed bribes stunned many and strangely, outraged other bribe givers.

12

The accepted practice for bribes was generally in the five percent range and Lockheed had clearly gone beyond those accepted standards. Just as disconcerting was the fact that although concealment of foreign bribes violated SEC reporting requirements, the penalties for disclosure were minor. The complaint from American companies was that if they didn't pay bribes, they would be at a competitive disadvantage as payoffs were pervasive worldwide. That defense held little water and soon there would be calls for passage of legislation to make bribery of foreign officials a crime. Yet, enacting antibribery laws will not be effective unless the moral fiber of any organization embraces corporate compliance. As a senior executive said at the time, "The top guy has to set the ethical standards" and without that support, no number of codes of conduct or laws will work.[26]

In February 1976, Kissinger again weighed in on the expanding issue of corporate bribes and cautioned that "The implications for the stability of other countries could be extremely serious."[27] But it was too late. Reform was coming.

QUESTIONABLE CORPORATE PAYMENTS TASK FORCE

In response to the chorus of people demanding reform, President Gerald Ford established the Task Force on Questionable Corporate Payments Abroad on March 31, 1976 and appointed then Secretary of Commerce Elliot Richardson as its chair. The task force would conduct a review of these payment practices and recommend additional policy steps as warranted. The President made it clear that the "purpose of the task force is not to punish American corporations but to ensure that the United States has a clear policy and that we have an effective, active program to implement that policy."[28]

On May 12, 1976, the SEC submitted the "Report on Questionable and Illegal Corporate Payments and Practices" to the Senate Committee on Banking, Housing and Urban Affairs. In the report, the SEC outlined the specific practices and necessary legislation to combat the rampant corporate bribery that had been discovered. The proposed legislation points would:

- Require issuers subject to the periodic reporting requirements of the Securities and Exchange Act to make and keep accurate books and records
- Require such issuers to devise and maintain a system of internal accounting controls meeting the objectives articulated by the American Institute of Certified Public Accountants

13

- Prohibit the falsification of corporate accounting records
- Prohibit the making of false, misleading, or incomplete statements to an accountant in connection with any examination or audit[29]

By June 1976, Richardson and his Task Force on Questionable Corporate Payments Abroad completed their review. On June 8, 1976, he submitted a memo to President Ford outlining the pros and cons of proposing legislation to address the issue of questionable payments abroad. The task force found clear and convincing evidence that a "significant number of America's major corporations, in their dealings with foreign governments, have engaged in practices which violated ethical and in some cases legal standards of both the United States and foreign countries."[30] Richardson identified problematic business practices and bribery consequences including:

- Falsified business records
- Lying to auditors
- Off-the-book slush funds
- Improper foreign payments unlawfully deducted as business expenses for income tax purposes
- Facilitation or grease payments
- Bribes as a "competitive necessity" to meet foreign competition
- Issue of extortion by corrupt foreign officials
- Adverse effect on foreign relations
- Adverse impact on multinational corporations
- Eroding public confidence in democratic institutions as a result of Watergate and subsequent investigations

Richardson discussed the pending legislation that was being proposed to address corporate bribery and whether it was needed. He also provided the President with a number of issues and options. Overall, Richardson commented that the SEC believed that "little if any business would be lost if U.S. firms were to stop these practices."[31]

FCPA ENACTMENT

The frenzied activity around corporate bribery had garnered the attention of Senator William Proxmire, who chaired the Senate Banking, Housing, and Urban Affairs Committee. The discoveries troubled Proxmire and he

14

asked Sporkin whether legislation was the answer. Sporkin advised the Senator "that all that was really necessary was a law that required all corporations to maintain accurate books and records, basically because not one of these companies booked these bribes and these other illegal payments correctly."[32] Sporkin added, "There is no provision that requires a company to keep accurate books and records."[33]

Senators Proxmire, Church, and others pushed through comprehensive legislation that included both antibribery provisions and a requirement to maintain accurate books and records of all transactions as well as the need for adequate internal controls. On December 19, 1977, President Jimmy Carter signed the FCPA into law. At the time, "the FCPA was decreed by some as the end of U.S. competitiveness in foreign markets."[34] In the beginning, there were few prosecutions and enforcement was inconsistent. Yet, Sporkin had no doubt that the FCPA would be a force to be reckoned with in the years to come. "It is clear that it has assumed a prominent place among our federal criminal laws," said Sporkin many years later.[35]

COMPLIANCE INSIGHT 1.1: FIRST FCPA PROSECUTION

Kenny International Corporation has the dubious distinction of being the first company prosecuted for violations of the FCPA shortly after its enactment. Finbar Kenny was chairman of the board, president, and the majority shareholder of Kenny International, a New York corporation. Kenny was a renowned philatelist and designed postage stamps for countries all over the world. He was also a very rich and powerful man.

Postage stamps and money got Kenny and his company entangled in the first FCPA prosecution. Kenny International became involved in the sale and distribution of Cook Islands postage stamps. Although the Cook Islands are a self-governing parliamentary democracy in the South Pacific, they are closely associated with New Zealand, which has responsibility for external affairs, defense, and other oversight. The population of the Cook Islands is relatively small but the sales of their postage stamps to tourists and stamp collectors are significant. The sale of postage stamps distributed by Kenny International provided over a million dollars a year in revenue shared equally with the government of the Cook Islands.

(continued)

(continued)

A representative of Sir Albert Henry, then Premier of the Cook Islands, solicited Kenny International for a bribe on behalf of the Premier "to ensure renewal of Kenny International's stamp distribution agreement with the government."[36] The payment would provide Kenny International with exclusive rights for the promotion, distribution, and sale of Cook Islands postage stamps worldwide. Kenny agreed to the corrupt act. The bribe turned out to be financial assistance worth 337,000 in New Zealand dollars to charter an aircraft to fly supporters of the reelection campaign of Sir Albert from New Zealand to the Cook Islands to vote in the general election. There were no provisions for absentee voting so voters needed to be physically present in the Cook Islands in order to vote for Sir Albert. A shell company was created to facilitate the transfer of funds for the purchase of the charter flight, and thus the bribe.

The disclosure of the FCPA violations in this case came from a tip to the U.S. government. The Cook Islands Superintendent of Police learned of the large payment made by Kenny to Sir Albert. He also learned of the recently enacted FCPA and immediately made the connection to possible violations of law. In May 1978, he visited the U.S. Consul's Office in Auckland, New Zealand to both obtain more information on the FCPA and alert them to the offense. The information was relayed to federal prosecutors in the United States and an investigation began.[37]

The investigation targeted Kenny and his company. Kenny hired prominent Washington, DC attorney Seymour Glanzer, one of the original Watergate prosecutors. Subsequently, Kenny International pleaded guilty to one count of violating the new FCPA and consented to a permanent injunction against further FCPA violations. The company paid a $50,000 fine as well as restitution to the government of the Cook Islands. Kenny was not charged criminally in the United States and consented to a civil injunction against further FCPA violations.[38] He also pleaded guilty before the High Court of the Cook Islands to a criminal charge of conspiracy to defraud the Cook Islands Government. He was fined and released with no jail sentence. His co-conspirator Sir Albert also pleaded guilty. Although Sir Albert won the rigged election as a result of Kenny International's help, once the conspiracy was discovered, the High Court disallowed the election results. The High Court ruled that Sir Albert be removed from office as a result of "unlawful votes tainted by bribery."[39]

Although this was the first prosecution under the newly enacted FCPA, it would definitely not be the last. The elements of the offense, including conspiracy, bribery of government officials, shell companies, and financial maneuvers to hide the payments and quid pro quo, would be repeated time after time in the years that followed. What comes to mind is the comment of the Harvard philosophy professor George Santayana who liked to say that those who do not remember the past are condemned to repeat it.

CRITICISM OF THE FCPA

In the few years after the enactment of the FCPA, there was still resistance and resentment in the corporate suites and in government. The Act was contemptuously called the "Accountants' Full Employment Act of 1977" for its onerous compliance requirements. Companies now had to increase their internal auditing departments, focus on internal controls, better police third-party agents, and carefully review all payments, especially those around commonplace grease payments that had now been outlawed. By 1981, there was already discussion to amend the FCPA. The Reagan administration signaled that it was not pleased with the legislation and that it would "cast a chill over the willingness of U.S. businessmen to push into foreign markets and thereby help boost U.S. exports."[40]

In March 1981, the General Accounting Office (GAO) released its report entitled "The Impact of the Foreign Corrupt Practices Act on U.S. Businesses." The report reaffirmed the Act's importance but also highlighted its "controversy and confusion over what constitutes compliance."[41] Much of the testimony mirrors what was heard after the enactment of the SOX legislation in 2002. Critics described the accounting provisions as "vague and causing business to incur unnecessary costs" and the antibribery provisions as "ambiguous and causing U.S. firms to forego legitimate export opportunities."[42]

The GAO report highlighted some positive changes but there was also a widespread call for changes in the legislation. Companies revised codes of conduct to reflect adherence to the FCPA and communicated this

17

to employees. In addition they reviewed the adequacy of their internal controls and improved documentation of internal control systems. The majority of firms that were polled by the GAO believed the Act was responsible for reducing corporate bribery but that the American companies would suffer financially as a result. Of note, "almost all the respondents who reported a decrease in business stated that the [A]ct had discouraged foreign buyers and agents from doing business with their firms."[43] The GAO report also reinforced that "without an effective international ban against bribery, unfair competitive advantage could be given to non-U.S. firms."[44] The report and subsequent related testimony before the Senate outlined a number of recommended changes around both the legislation and its implementation.

In August 1981, Attorney General William French Smith commented that the Reagan administration intended "to eliminate the more offensive provisions of our law that both harm our countries' ability to compete abroad and offend the business sensibilities of other countries."[45] There were few FCPA prosecutions in the Reagan years but there was a significant amendment in 1988. The most significant change was that the FCPA's jurisdiction now extended to foreign companies that committed related offenses within the United States. The 1988 amendment also directed the Executive Branch to "level the playing field by encouraging our trading partners to enact legislation similar to the FCPA."[46] The outcome was the creation of the Organisation for Economic Co-operation and Development (OECD) Convention on Combating Bribery of Foreign Public Officials in International Business Transactions. There is a more detailed discussion of the OECD and its Anti-Bribery Convention in Chapter 4.

A CULTURE OF COMPLIANCE

Watergate and the shocking disclosures that came out of that time in American history spawned the FCPA. The reaction to widespread corporate corruption and bribery has far-ranging implications for how organizations do business with integrity and honesty. With the FCPA, the law reaches around the world and covers the actions of U.S. corporations and their employees no matter where they are. Illegal actions relating to the FCPA can have major implications. There are harsh penalties for those who violate the Act. Financial and reputational risks abound.

Compliance goes beyond the borders of the United States with the globalization of business. International compliance is a necessity because of a confluence of several important factors. The global nature of

18

companies with subsidiaries, affiliates, and vendors all over the world provide great opportunity but also great risk. Third-party liability is another major concern as companies are liable for the actions of people it hires, be they direct employees or agents, as is successor liability in mergers and acquisitions. More than ever before, all organizations need a robust compliance program to ensure an enduring culture of compliance.

NOTES

1. Russell Gold and David Crawford, "U.S., Other Nations Step Up Bribery Battle," *Wall Street Journal*, September 12, 2008, B1.
2. Siri Schubert and T. Christian Miller, "At Siemens, Bribery Was Just a Line Item," *Frontline*, February 13, 2009, www.pbs.org/frontlineworld/ stories/bribe/2009/02/at-siemens-bribery-was-just-a-line-item.html.
3. Title 15, United States Code, Section 78dd-3.
4. *U.S. v. SSI International Far East, Ltd*, Criminal Information unsealed on October 16, 2006, United States District Court, District of Oregon, 24.
5. Ibid.
6. Alan Boeckmann (chairman of the board and CEO of Fluor Corporation), *Help Us Fight Against Corruption!*, comments in a YouTube video, World Economic Forum, December 8, 2008, www.youtube .com/watch?v=kesmuu0ERVw.
7. "Spotlight: The Victims of Corruption: The Human Cost of Bribery in the Developing World," *Frontline*, February 24, 2009, www .pbs.org/frontlineworld/stories/bribe/2009/02/spotlight-the-victims-of-corruption.html.
8. Mike Carter, "Fitzgerald Says Public Must Fight Corruption," *Seattle Times*, April 24, 2009, B1.
9. President Barack Obama, "An Honest Government, A Hopeful Future" (speech, University of Nairobi, Nairobi, Kenya, August 28, 2008), http://obamaspeeches.com/088-An-Honest-Government-A-Hopeful-Future-Obama-Speech.htm.
10. Bess Myerson is a former Miss America, television personality, frequent companion of former New York City Mayor Koch, and was appointed by him to various city positions. She is active in charitable work, and was eventually caught up in a corruption scandal.
11. Stanley Sporkin, interview by the Securities and Exchange Commission Historical Society, September 23, 2003, http://c0403731.cdn .cloudfiles.rackspacecloud.com/collection/oral-histories/sporkin092303 Transcript.pdf.

12. Stephen M. Cutler, "The Themes of Sarbanes-Oxley as Reflected in the Commission's Enforcement Program" (speech, UCLA School of Law, Los Angeles, CA, September 20, 2004), www.sec.gov/news/speech/spch092004smc.htm.
13. Linda Chatman Thomsen (director, Division of Enforcement, Securities and Exchange Commission), speech, Minority Corporate Counsel 2008 CLE Expo, Chicago, IL, March 27, 2008, www.sec.gov/news/speech/2008/spch032708lct.htm.
14. Ibid.
15. "Corruption in the Crosshairs: A Brief History of International Anti-Bribery Legislation," *Frontline*, April 7, 2009, www.pbs.org/frontlineworld/stories/bribe/2009/04/timeline.html.
16. Ibid.
17. State Department cable dated June 5, 1975, declassified on July 6, 2006, from Secretary of State Henry Kissinger to the U.S. Ambassador in Saudi Arabia, http://aad.archives.gov/aad/createpdf?rid=100565&dt=1822&dl=823.
18. State Department cable dated December 19, 1975, declassified on July 6, 2006, from Secretary of State Henry Kissinger to various U.S. ambassadors, http://aad.archives.gov/aad/createpdf?rid=228918&dt=1822&dl=823.
19. Ibid.
20. David Boulton, *The Grease Machine: The Inside Story of Lockheed's Dollar Diplomacy* (New York: Harper & Row, 1978), 267-68.
21. Ibid., 268.
22. "Lockheed's Defiance: A Right to Bribe?" *Time*, August 18, 1975, www.time.com/time/magazine/article/0,9171,917751-1,00.html.
23. Ibid.
24. "The Big Payoff," *Newsweek*, February 23, 1976, www.time.com/time/magazine/article/0,9171,918066,00.html.
25. Ibid.
26. Ibid.
27. Ibid.
28. President Gerald Ford, "Statement on the Task Force on Questionable Corporate Payments Abroad," March 31, 1976, www.presidency.ucsb.edu/ws/index.php?pid=5773.
29. Promotion of the Reliability of Financial Information and Prevention of the Concealment of Questionable or Illegal Corporate Payments and Practices, Securities and Exchange Commission Release

34-15570, February 15, 1979, http://content.lawyerlinks.com/library/sec/sec_releases/34-15570.htm.

30. Secretary of Commerce Elliot L. Richardson, "Questionable Corporate Payments Abroad," memorandum to President Gerald Ford, June 8, 1976. www.pbs.org/frontlineworld/stories/bribe/images/pdf/richardson_memo_1.pdf.

31. Ibid.

32. Sporkin, interview.

33. Ibid.

34. Thomsen, speech.

35. "Corruption in the Crosshairs."

36. Review of Implementation of the OECD Anti-bribery Convention and 1997 Recommendation, September 28, 2004, www.state.gov/e/eeb/rls/rpts/bib/36587.htm.

37. Howard Henry, *The Criminal Convictions of Albert Henry: Political Bribery, Corruption and Dishonour in the Cook Islands, 1978-79* (Auckland, NZ: Sovereign Pacific Publishing, 2003)

38. *U.S. v. Kenny International Corp.* (Cr. No. 79-372), D.D.C., 1979.

39. Alexandra Addison Wrage, *Bribery and Extortion: Undermining Business, Governments, and Security* (Santa Barbara, CA: Praeger, 2007), 64.

40. Gisela Bolte, Jonathan Beatty, and Christopher Byron, "Big Profits in Big Bribery," *Time*, March 16, 1981, www.time.com/time/magazine/article/0,9171,922462-5,00.html.

41. Donald L. Scantlebury (division director and chief accountant, Accounting and Financial Management Division, United States General Accounting Office) statement, before the Senate Committee on Banking, Housing, and Urban Affairs, Subcommittee on International Finance and Monetary Policy and Subcommittee on Securities on the Impact of the Foreign Corrupt Practices Act on U.S. Businesses, May 20, 1981, http://archive.gao.gov/f0102/115367.pdf.

42. Ibid.

43. Ibid.

44. Ibid.

45. "Corruption in the Crosshairs."

46. U.S. Department of Justice, International Anti-Bribery Act of 1998, Legislative History, www.usdoj.gov/criminal/fraud/fcpa/history/1998/amends/leghistory.html.

CHAPTER 2

Overview of the Foreign Corrupt Practices Act

This chapter and the following one focus on an understanding of the Foreign Corrupt Practices Act (FCPA) statute itself, as well as covering important case law and the role of government, specifically its enforcement policies and penalties. This chapter also covers the changes in the law over the years and important trends to be aware of in the FCPA arena. It is not just large, multinational companies that are violating the FCPA; it is also smaller, private companies and individuals who are employing the same corrupt practices. The best way to ensure anti-corruption compliance is to fully understand the FCPA statute and how it is applied.

FCPA PROVISIONS

The FCPA has two main parts: the antibribery provision and the accounting provision. The FCPA mandates that corporate records contain accurate statements concerning the true purpose of all payments made by the company. The law makes it a crime for American companies, domestic concerns, or foreign nationals doing business in the United States, as well as individuals and organizations acting on their behalf, to bribe any foreign government official in return for assistance in:

* Obtaining or retaining business, or directing business to any particular person
* Influencing a foreign government official to do or to omit an act in violation of his duty
* Influencing a foreign government official to affect an act or decision by a foreign government[1]

The FCPA not only makes it a crime to pay bribes to foreign officials, it also makes it a crime for publicly traded U.S. companies to make payments of any kind that are not on the books. Bribes are almost always disguised on the books as some other business expense rather than the true nature of the payments. This reduces the government's evidentiary burden because the very evidence the government will need in prosecutions can be found in the internal books and records. Government prosecutors do not have to prove a bribe, only that a payment was made and not recorded properly on the company's books.

In short, the FCPA makes it a crime for a company in the United States, for U.S. citizens, or their agents to obtain business by bribery of a government official of another country (or even conspire to do so from the United States), or for a publicly traded U.S. company to fail to record such a payment on its books. While the Department of Justice (DOJ) is responsible for bribery violations of the FCPA, the Securities and Exchange Commission (SEC) handles accounting violations of the FCPA. It is interesting to note that it is not a crime under the FCPA for an American company to pay bribes in a country where bribes are not illegal.

There are also specific exceptions granted in a 1988 amendment to the FCPA. American companies can pay facilitation fees to expedite permits, licenses, papers, visas, mail, and phone service, and to expedite the movement of perishable cargo. Further, it is not considered a bribe to reasonably reimburse public officials for expenses such as meals, travel, and lodging while the company is promoting, or demonstrating a product, or executing a contract. These expenses must not be excessive and must reflect bona fide charges. However, it must be kept in mind that these actions still may be illegal in the country where they occur.

The penalties for violating the FCPA can be severe. Enterprises can be fined $2 million for each violation, and individuals face five years in prison and a $250,000 fine. In addition, the company can be forced to abandon the business won by bribery through business debarments, face disgorgement of the profits obtained through bribery, be denied export licenses, or be disqualified from any U.S. government contracts.

U.S. companies can protect themselves with a compliance program that ensures all employees are specifically aware of which actions are prohibited by the FCPA. Companies can also protect themselves by including special clauses in their contracts whereby local agents and partners confirm that they will not violate the FCPA, as well as other anti-corruption laws. Many companies have tried to circumvent the FCPA by having local joint venture partners commit bribery while the U.S. companies are willfully blind. This use of third parties will not prevent an FCPA prosecution. The DOJ and the SEC expect U.S. companies and their foreign subsidiaries to comply with the FCPA.

LEVELING THE PLAYING FIELD

In the years after the FCPA's passage, Congress grew concerned that American companies faced a competitive disadvantage versus foreign companies who routinely paid bribes and were even allowed in some cases to deduct the cost of bribes as business expenses. This inequity spurred Congress to push forward on initiatives that encouraged other countries to follow the United States's lead in fighting corruption.

Accordingly, in 1988, the Congress directed the Executive Branch to commence negotiations in the Organisation for Economic Co-operation and Development (OECD) to obtain the agreement of the United States' major trading partners to enact legislation similar to the FCPA. In 1997, almost ten years later, the United States and thirty-three other countries signed the OECD Convention on Combating Bribery of Foreign Public Officials in International Business Transactions. The United States ratified this Convention and enacted implementing legislation in 1998.[2]

For more information on the OECD, see Chapter 4.

ANTIBRIBERY PROVISIONS

The FCPA prohibits individuals and companies from "corruptly making use of the mails or any means or instrumentality of interstate commerce in furtherance of an offer, promise, authorization, or payment of money or anything of value to a foreign official for the purpose of obtaining or retaining business for, or directing business to, any person or securing any improper advantage."[3] Furthermore, the FCPA also requires "issuers not only to refrain from making corrupt payments to foreign government officials, but also to implement policies and practices that reduce the risk that employees and agents will engage in bribery."[4] The Act has been amended and expanded over the years: "Since 1998, [the provisions] also apply to foreign firms and persons who take any act in furtherance of such a corrupt payment while in the United States."[5]

The law has several elements, which must be met in order for it to apply. While it may be complicated, in practice the application is somewhat straightforward, since corrupt payments to foreign government officials will be broadly construed. In general, if a similar action would be illegal in America there is a very good chance it would be illegal under the FCPA. "Bribery" encompasses offers, payments, promises to pay, authorizations of the payment of any money, or offer, gift, promise to give, or authorization of the giving of anything of value.

Section 78dd-1 of the FCPA covers "issuers" or companies that have registered with the SEC (i.e., companies with stock that is publicly traded in the U.S., and prohibits particular foreign trade practices). "An issuer is a corporation that has issued securities that have been registered in the United States or who is required to file periodic reports with the SEC."[6] The section affects the company as well as its directors, officers, employees, or any agents or third parties acting on behalf of the company.[7]

Section 78dd-2 covers domestic concerns and their officers, directors, employees, and agents. The definition of "domestic concern" encompasses an individual who is a citizen, national, or resident of the United States, as well as any corporation, partnership, association, joint-stock company, business trust, unincorporated organization, or sole proprietorship that either has its principal place of business in the U.S. or is organized under the laws of the U.S. or its territories.[8]

Section 78dd-3 prohibits foreign nationals from using the mails or any instrumentality of interstate commerce, while in the territory of the U.S., in furtherance of an FCPA violation. This section also covers foreign companies not registered with the SEC or that principally do business overseas.[9] All sections prohibit the same behavior and only differ in to whom they apply.

The law also applies when a bribe is offered to any foreign official, candidate for foreign political office, foreign political party, or anyone acting on behalf of one of the above categories. According to the statute's

26

definition, "foreign official" means "any officer or employee of a foreign government or any department, agency or instrumentality thereof, or of a public international organization, or any person acting in an official capacity for or on behalf of such government or department, agency, or instrumentality, or for or on behalf of any such public international organization."[10] In practice, "foreign officials" encompasses all government employees and employees of state-owned businesses. Recent cases have concluded that doctors in state-owned hospitals and journalists working for state-owned media fall under the definition. For purposes of this chapter, "foreign official" will refer to all foreign individuals covered under the statute.

It can be difficult to determine whether one is dealing with a foreign official, whether they are employed by a foreign government or a state-owned enterprise. Companies need to be aware of the business ownership structure of the country in which they are doing business, such as what industries are state-owned or under the control of the government. In countries with royal families, members can be highly influential and heavily involved in government agencies, even if the country is not a monarchy.

The law also applies when the bribe giver knows that the recipient will give at least part of the bribe to a foreign government official, even if they are not working for them.[11] It is common for bribes paid to government officials to be routed through family members, business associates, or designated businesses. In short, the law covers nearly anyone associated with government or politics, whether they are an elected official, a political party leader, or merely an employee of a state-run business. Subject to the statute's exceptions, it is difficult to envision a scenario where something of value is given to a person associated with a foreign government in connection to business where it would not fall under the FCPA's purview.

The person making the corrupt payment or instructing that it be made must have corrupt intent and the payment itself must be made for the purpose of causing the bribe recipient to abuse his or her position of authority within the government and to provide some type of commercial benefit to the bribe payer or the entity on whose behalf the bribe is being paid. A bribe does not have to be paid in order for there to have been a violation of the FCPA. There simply needs to have been an offer or promise to make a corrupt payment to a foreign official as an inducement to influence an official decision. For example, former Congressman William Jefferson faced FCPA charges for accepting bribe money which he intended to give to a foreign official, though he never did. For more on his case, please see the following chapter.

27

To violate the FCPA, one must "knowingly" do the corrupt act. This knowing requirement comes up most frequently in situations where the money is given to an intermediary. The government must prove that the bribe giver knew the money was for a bribe. To do so, the government can prove actual knowledge or knowledge that the outcome is substantially certain to occur.[12] Alternatively, "when knowledge of the existence of a particular circumstance is required for an offense, such knowledge is established if a person is aware of a high probability of the existence of such circumstances, unless the person actually believes such circumstance does not exist."[13] This second definition prevents the ostrich defense, where a person pleads ignorance after they have willfully ignored the facts and circumstances. Willful blindness in the face of a high probability of bribery will lead to an FCPA violation and conviction. Courts are strict when a defendant pleads ignorance. The defendant in *U.S. v. Bourke*, detailed in Chapter 7, tried this defense but was convicted.

The statute lists two different purposes for bribery; either one will satisfy the requirement. The bribe must be given with the intent of influencing an act or decision of a foreign official, or causing such foreign official to do or omit to do any act in violation of his or her lawful duty, or to secure an improper advantage. Otherwise, it must be given to induce such foreign official to use his influence to affect or influence an official decision, in order to assist in obtaining or retaining business, or directing business to any person. This later requirement must be tied to a business purpose in some manner.[14]

The bribe given to the government official must be connected with his official duty in some way. Hiring a government employee to sabotage a competitor's equipment, even though it is beneficial to the company, would likely not violate the antibribery provisions, as the act is not connected to the employee's official duties. However, this illegal payment would implicate the accounting provisions, which are discussed ahead.

Courts will interpret the "business purpose" requirement extremely broadly. While the FCPA originally applied mostly to obtaining and retaining government contracts, it has since been broadened. Even an indirect advantage will suffice; paying off customs officials to reduce taxes and duties on imported products is considered an FCPA violation. Furthermore, the bribe need not be tied to a specific contract. In the seminal case *United States v. Kay*, the court's theory was that the import taxes provided a competitive disadvantage for the company's products versus domestic competitors, and that reducing the cost disparities positively benefited the company's business, even if the competitive benefit

28

was indirect.[15] "Congress intended for the FCPA to apply broadly to payments intended to assist the payor, either directly or indirectly, in obtaining or retaining business for some person."[16]

Note that the statute of limitations for the FCPA is five years from the date the offense was allegedly committed. This period can be extended for up to three years upon request by a prosecutor and a finding by a court that additional time is needed to gather evidence located abroad.[17]

Jurisdiction

Jurisdiction to prosecute a domestic concern or issuer can be established on the basis of nationality or territoriality. Acts that occur on U.S. soil such as the use of the mails, interstate communications, or travel are territorial and establish prosecutorial jurisdiction in the United States. In addition, acts that occur entirely outside of the U.S. but are committed by or on behalf of domestic concerns or issuers can also be prosecuted in the United States by virtue of their nationality.

Until the 1998 amendments to the FCPA, foreign nationals, with the exception of issuers, were not subject to the FCPA. The amendments asserted "extraterritorial jurisdiction" over foreign nationals and entities. A foreign company or individual is subject to the FCPA if they directly or indirectly cause an act in the U.S. or its territories in the furtherance of a corrupt payment to a foreign official. U.S. parent companies of foreign subsidiaries can also be held liable under the FCPA if they are found to have directed the unlawful activities of their foreign subsidiaries.[18]

Facilitating Payments

The FCPA does present some exceptions and affirmative defenses to bribery. The Act expressly excludes what are known as "facilitating payments" or "expediting payments." They are also euphemistically called "grease payments." These are payments to officials to expedite or to secure the performance of routine and common government services and functions.[19] For a payment to be considered a facilitating payment, it must be something that is paid regularly to obtain a regular service. Typical examples include licensing fees, document processing fees, and government services such as police protection and customs inspections.

Generally, they are small payments made to low-level government officials, for simple actions. Note that these payments must be legal under the country's laws to qualify. The decision to award new business or to

29

continue business with a particular entity does not qualify as "routine governmental action." This exception will be narrowly construed; if the payments are solely intended to influence government action even if they otherwise meet the qualifications, they will fall outside this exception. Even though facilitating payments are allowed by statute, the trend is to not authorize them as a business practice. Many companies have instituted rules prohibiting their payments. Some countries, such as the United Kingdom, have banned them completely.

Affirmative Defenses

The Act provides affirmative defenses for those accused of FCPA violations. If the payment, gift, or offer was lawful under the foreign country's laws and regulations, it would be considered appropriate. These payments must be properly recorded by the company. It is not a defense to state the payment of bribes is a common and accepted practice in the country. Even in countries where bribes are expected they are usually against the law, even if the law is not enforced.

The statute also allows for reasonable and bona fide travel and lodging expenses incurred by or on behalf of foreign officials, provided they were directly related to the promotion, demonstration, or explanation of products or services, or the execution or performance of a contract with a foreign government or agency thereof.[20] If the expenses were not reasonable, a company will be on the hook. This situation happened to a Boston-based engineering firm while entertaining Egyptian officials. The expenses were determined to be unreasonable, the company was found guilty of FCPA violations, and was forced to implement a substantial FCPA compliance program. This company is profiled in Compliance Insight 2.1.

FCPA Elements Summary

The FCPA prohibits directors, officers, employees, or agents of registered companies or stockholders thereof, domestic concerns, or foreign nationals in the United States paying, or offering, or promising any payment, gift, or anything of value to any foreign official, or any foreign political party, or official thereof, or any candidate for foreign political office, or any person acting at least in part on their behalf, for purposes of:

- Influencing any act or decision of the official, party, or candidate, in his official capacity

- Inducing that person or entity to do or omit to do anything in violation of his lawful duty, or to secure an improper advantage
- Getting the recipient to use his influence with a foreign government or instrumentality to affect or influence any act or decision of such government or instrumentality, in order to assist the issuer in obtaining or retaining business for or with, or directing business to, any person

COMPLIANCE INSIGHT 2.1: METCALF AND EDDY CIVIL FCPA SETTLEMENT

Metcalf & Eddy International Inc., a Massachusetts-based environmental engineering firm, was convicted in 1999 of violating the FCPA for unlawfully providing travel and entertainment expenses to an Egyptian public official. The official was the chairman of a committee that was involved in contract negotiations for a sewage upgrade project in Egypt that Metcalf & Eddy wanted to secure. The official received, along with his family, trips to the United States and a per diem that amounted to 150 percent above the rate allowed by law. Metcalf & Eddy paid for the flights, including first-class upgrades, and almost all the travel and entertainment expenses, even though the official had already received the funds to pay for his expenses. Furthermore, Metcalf & Eddy failed to accurately record these transactions, furthering the prosecution's case that the company knowingly violated the law.[21]

The civil settlement in this case required Metcalf & Eddy to institute an FCPA compliance program. This case set the standard for what the government expects in such a program, and has been repeatedly followed in other cases. The standards laid out establish the minimum requirements that should be met when creating an FCPA compliance program.[22]

At minimum, an effective FCPA compliance program includes the following elements:

- Clear FCPA policy, establishing compliance standards and practices to be followed by employees, consultants, and agents. These standards and practices must be reasonably capable of reducing violations and ensuring compliance.

(continued)

31

(*continued*)

- Assignment of one or more senior officials to be responsible for oversight of the compliance program. The official shall have the authority and responsibility to implement and utilize monitoring and auditing systems to detect criminal conduct, and when necessary, bring in outside counsel and independent auditors to conduct investigations and audits. The officials should make any necessary modifications to the program to respond to detected violations and to prevent further similar violations.

- Creating and maintaining a committee to review the hiring of agents, consultants, or other representatives to do business in a foreign country, and the related contracts. The committee will also review all prospective joint venture partners, to ensure FCPA compliance, and the due diligence done in selecting the prospective partner. The committee has a continuing responsibility to ensure subsequent due diligence in retaining other agents and consultants by the joint venture. This committee should be independent and not be influenced by the company officials involved in the transactions at issue.

- Clear corporate policies to make sure that the company does not delegate substantial discretionary authority to individuals that the company knows or should know are likely to engage in illegal activities.

- Clear corporate procedures to assure that the necessary precautions are taken to make sure the company only does business with reputable and qualified individuals. The policy must require that evidence of the due diligence performed be maintained in the company's files.

- Communicating FCPA policies, standards, and procedures to employees; requiring regular training on the FCPA and other applicable foreign bribery laws to officers and employees involved in foreign projects. Agents and consultants hired in connection with foreign business should also be given appropriate training, as soon as is practicable.

- Implementation of appropriate discipline measures, including as necessary, discipline of individuals who fail to detect violations of the law or of the company's compliance policies.

- Establishing a reporting system whereby suspected criminal conduct may be reported, without fear of retribution, and without having to report directly to immediate superiors.
- Including in all foreign business contracts provisions banning foreign bribery. No payment of money or anything of value will be promised, offered, or paid, directly or indirectly to any foreign official, politician, political candidate, or similar individual, to induce them to use their influence or to obtain an improper advantage in a business deal. All contracts must include a provision that all prospective agents agree not to retain any subagents or representatives without prior written consent of a senior company official; any breach of this provision terminates the contract.

Furthermore, an effective FCPA compliance program should also include:

- Periodic review, at least once every five years, of corporate policies and the FCPA compliance program, to be conducted by independent legal and auditing firms retained for such purpose.
- Prompt investigation and/or reporting of any alleged violations of the FCPA or other applicable foreign bribery laws by the company, its officers, agents, or other personnel, and of any joint venture in which the company is a participant.

Case law has added an additional requirement:[23]

- The company, using objective measures, must determine the regions or countries in which it does business that pose higher risks of corruption, and then on a periodic basis, conduct rigorous FCPA audits of its operations in such areas. The audits shall include detailed audits of the operating unit's books and records, audits of selected agents, consultants, and joint venture partners, as well as interviews with relevant employees, consultants, agents, and so on.

BOOKS, RECORDS, AND INTERNAL CONTROLS PROVISION

The books and records provision of the FCPA requires certain corporations to create and maintain books, records, and accounts that fairly and accurately reflect company transactions. The knowing falsification of company records is also prohibited. Furthermore, the provision mandates a strong system of internal controls.[24] According to the DOJ:

> *The FCPA also requires companies whose securities are listed in the United States to meet its accounting provisions. . . . These accounting provisions, which were designed to operate in tandem with the antibribery provisions of the FCPA, require corporations covered by the provisions to make and keep books and records that accurately and fairly reflect the transactions of the corporation and to devise and maintain an adequate system of internal accounting controls.*[25]

While the antibribery provisions apply to a broad group, the books and records provision only applies to issuers. This is logical, as the financial records of individuals and private businesses are not subject to the same kind of scrutiny as public companies' are. This is similar to the Section 404 requirements of Sarbanes-Oxley (SOX). Note that violating the books and records provisions could also result in SOX violations. Covered companies must make and keep books and records that accurately and fairly reflect their transactions. Corporations must also devise and maintain an adequate system of internal accounting controls.

The statute lists several requirements for internal controls. These include:

- Companies must ensure that transactions are only executed in accordance with management's general or specific authorization.
- Transactions must be recorded in accordance with generally accepted accounting principles (GAAP).
- Access to assets must be limited to those with authorization.
- Internal audits must be done at reasonable intervals, comparing the records with the actual assets.

The requirement of limiting access to assets is to prevent the use of slush funds and off-the-books accounts, which are often used to facilitate bribery. The audits help to make sure that the books accurately reflect assets; for instance, a company must make sure that a sales contract with a company is that and is not a cover for questionable payments.

34

The accounting provisions are also broader in another way, as they cover all questionable payments, not just those made to foreign officials. Commercial bribery payments must also be recorded in a company's records or else it will be in violation. Of course, to do so would admit to violating the laws of the country in which the bribery occurred.

The purpose of the books and records provision is to put teeth into the statute. Logic tells us that companies probably will not accurately record bribe payments to foreign government officials but if they do, the evidence is there for the government to obtain. If companies omit or falsify transactions to hide the bribe payments, they also face legal peril. The strength of the FCPA gives great leverage to the government in investigating and prosecuting bribery and corruption schemes. Violators are damned if they do and damned if they don't. The best way to avoid punishment is not to do the crime in the first place.

Books and Records Elements Summary

Every issuer of stock publicly traded in the United States shall:

- Make and keep books, records, and accounts, which in reasonable detail, accurately and fairly reflect the transactions and dispositions of the assets of the issuer
- Devise and maintain a system of internal accounting controls sufficient to provide reasonable assurances that:
  - Transactions are executed in accordance with management's general or specific authorization
  - Transactions are recorded as necessary (i) to permit preparation of financial statements in conformity with GAAP and (ii) to maintain accountability for assets
  - Access to assets are permitted only in accordance with management's general or specific authorization
  - The recorded accountability for assets is compared with the existing assets at reasonable intervals and appropriate action is taken with respect to any differences

SARBANES-OXLEY AND THE FCPA

The enactment of SOX changed the course of governance by spotlighting and mandating the importance of compliance and ethics. SOX

35

strengthened corporate accountability and governance of public companies through rules covering conflicts of interest, financial disclosures, board oversight, and certification of financial statements and disclosures.[26] Like few laws in modern times, SOX required public companies to comply with its many requirements and implement heightened compliance. The focus on SOX soon brought renewed attention to the FCPA and anti-corruption compliance. The fact is that the FCPA should be understood and analyzed in conjunction with SOX and its disclosure requirements. Unlawful payments and the falsification of records are independently outlawed. Falsification of company records to cover up a bribe violates both the FCPA and SOX and can cause a company to quickly run afoul of the DOJ and SEC.

OPINION PROCEDURE

Under the DOJ Opinion Procedure, a company or individual can request an opinion on a proposed business transaction or conduct before undertaking it. This is a useful procedure whereby a company can ask the government to analyze a prospective course of action to see whether it would lead to any FCPA violations. "The Department of Justice has established a Foreign Corrupt Practices Act Opinion Procedure by which any U.S. company or national may request a statement of the Justice Department's present enforcement intentions under the antibribery provisions of the FCPA regarding any proposed business conduct."[27] Thirty days after receiving the request and related material information, the Justice Department shall issue an opinion. Failure to fully disclose material and relevant information will nullify the opinion and the requestor will be unable to rely on its contents as a defense.

Business conduct in conformity with an issued opinion will be granted a presumption of conformity with the FCPA. The request for or issuance of an FCPA opinion does not affect a company's responsibility to comply with the accounting procedures in any way. An FCPA opinion only binds the DOJ and does not affect any other agency or any entity not involved in the request.[28] That being said, issued opinions provide an excellent resource for FCPA compliance. (Please see the Appendix for more information and summaries of important DOJ Opinion Procedure Releases.)

When the DOJ issues the opinion, the conduct or transaction is presumed to be FCPA-compliant. "Over the years," former Assistant Attorney General Alice Fisher noted, "the FCPA opinion procedure has generally been underutilized, with only a handful of opinions being requested each year. But as Assistant Attorney General, I want the FCPA opinion procedure to be something that is useful as a guide to business."[29]

The opinion procedure may also be useful in the context of joint ventures, mergers, and acquisitions, "when the FCPA due diligence turns up potential problems with the foreign counterpart. Transactional due diligence in the FCPA context is good for business."[30]

PENALTIES

Violations of the FCPA can lead to major criminal and civil penalties and fines. Individuals can face jail time, while the company can be forced to pay millions, if not billions. Furthermore, a company can be forced to install costly new internal controls and business practices or even bring in an outside monitor as per agreement with the government. Monitors in particular can be very costly and intrusive to a company. A company also runs the risk of lawsuits from shareholders when FCPA violations are made public. The FCPA itself provides no private cause of action, but shareholders can use the underlying illegal activities as the basis for a derivative suit against the company.

The penalties for violations of the FCPA can be very severe and can include monetary fines of up to $25 million per violation against entities and $5 million per violation against individuals. Prison sentences can be for periods of up to 20 years. Other punishments can include:

- *Debarment:* The prohibition from doing business with or contracting with any agency of the U.S. government. Depending upon the industry and the defendant company's reliance on government contracts, debarment could result in a significant reduction in revenues.

- *Loss of export privileges:* Like debarment, loss of export privileges can be financially devastating for any company that manufactures goods for export.

- *Injunctive relief:* Companies may be barred from participating in a particular business or from engaging in certain practices by means of an injunction.

- *Appointment of a Monitor:* A conviction of an FCPA violation can cause a company to be subject to the court's continued oversight for many years. One way of enforcing the court's continued authority is the appointment of an independent monitor. Monitors typically have broad powers to oversee the company's continued operation and implementation of required changes to its compliance program, and can test to ensure that required changes are being followed. Monitors are typically law firms who also engage the services of forensic accounting and investigative firms to assist them in carrying out their duties, which often span several years. Monsanto had an independent monitor assigned for three years as part of its settlement with the DOJ for its FCPA violation. In addition to the monetary penalties of an FCPA violation, defendant companies must pay for the monitor's professional fees and travel expenses. Monitorships often cost many hundreds of thousands, or even millions, of dollars.

- *Loss of goodwill and reputational damage:* A company's reputation has intrinsic value. Companies who have been the focal point of negative news stories resulting from FCPA enforcement can sustain long-term damage to their reputations, sometimes resulting in a significant reduction of market capitalization when shareholder confidence results in large selloffs.

- *Other Potential Criminal and Civil Liabilities:* The facts that support an FCPA case may also be the basis for Mail/Wire Fraud, Securities Fraud, Money Laundering, Tax Evasion, Conspiracy, False Claims, Travel Act, and other criminal violations and civil liability.

Throughout the book, we profile various FCPA cases; the hefty penalties associated with many of these should more than illustrate the necessity of FCPA compliance. Chapters 6 and 7 in particular profile a number of cases that resulted in significant fines and jail sentences for participants, not to mention the compliance and monitorship requirements imposed in settlements and deferred prosecution agreements.

FCPA violations "may also give rise to a private cause of action for treble damages under the Racketeer Influenced and Corrupt Organizations Act (RICO), or to actions under other federal or state laws. For example, an action might be brought under RICO by a competitor who alleges that the bribery caused the defendant to win a foreign contract."[31]

Another law, the Travel Act, is also used in conjunction with the FCPA to prosecute offenders. The Travel Act prohibits interstate or foreign travel or use of the mail, with the intent to distribute the proceeds of any unlawful activity, commit any crime of violence to further any unlawful activity, or otherwise promote or facilitate the promotion of any unlawful activity.[32] The statute's definition of "unlawful activity" specifically includes bribery.[33] Thus bribery, which does not violate the FCPA but otherwise violates applicable state law, can be prosecuted under this Act. The Travel Act was used in the CCI case mentioned in Chapter 1.

THIRD-PARTY AND SUCCESSOR LIABILITY

Companies need to be aware that if they purchase or merge with a company that has committed an FCPA violation, the successor or purchasing company can be liable for the prior violation. The rules also apply to the use of third parties. Due diligence is of paramount importance here. Actions by foreign subsidiaries of American companies or the third parties they hire can also result in liability, even if the company is not aware of the actions or did not authorize them.

A number of legal theories support this vicarious liability. When the foreign subsidiary is majority or wholly owned by the parent company, the parent will be responsible for the actions of the subsidiary, under the theory that they are effectively the same entity. A parent company can also be found liable if it approves or ratifies the conduct at issue, meaning that it either directly approves of the actions or learns about them and fails to take appropriate action. A company should ensure that its compliance program also applies to its subsidiaries and third parties. Through agency principles, companies are vicariously responsible for the actions of agents that have been hired, whether they are independent contractors or foreign subsidiaries.

This liability is why the use of third parties is so fraught with potential risk. This liability is also not restricted to those parties that the company has formally engaged. Courts will look at the totality of the circumstances surrounding the involvement of the party in question to determine whether the company should be liable for the unlawful actions. The company's internal designation of whom it considers agents or not is not dispositive. This is particularly important in situations where the companies had knowledge of unlawful payments; the company's classification of the agent and its level of control will not matter. Companies must look into the behavior of third parties if it has reason to believe illegal payments are being made.

The internal controls provision has been used to impose responsibility for the conduct of distributors. Though companies do not generally maintain strict control over the actions of the entities responsible for distributing their products abroad, the SEC's position is that companies must be aware of their actions and exercise proper supervision.

Joint ventures present liability risks since the company shares responsibility for the actions taken by the other company or companies involved in the venture insofar as it is related to the joint venture. FCPA violations also often come to light during the due diligence phase of mergers and

39

acquisitions. By exercising appropriate due diligence and taking appropriate action for discovered violations, the company need not face any sanctions for the actions of the acquiring company. However, it must make sure it has discovered the violations and dealt with them appropriately. It must ensure that the behavior has ended and will not continue after the merger. The standard for acquisition due diligence is laid out in Opinion Release 08-02, contained in the Appendix. More discussion of third parties is contained in Chapters 9 and 10.

COMPLIANCE INSIGHT 2.2: SELF-DISCLOSURE FOLLOWS M&A ACTIVITY

On May 7, 2009, Sun Microsystems filed an SEC Form 10-Q that caught the investing public's attention. Under the risk factors section of the form, the company disclosed the following potentially serious FCPA violation:

We have identified potential violations of the Foreign Corrupt Practices Act, the resolution of which could possibly have a material effect on our business. During fiscal year 2009, we identified activities in a certain foreign country that may have violated the Foreign Corrupt Practices Act. We initiated an independent investigation with the assistance of outside counsel and took remedial action. We recently made a voluntary disclosure with respect to this and other matters to the Department of Justice (DOJ), Securities and Exchange Commission (SEC) and the applicable governmental agencies in certain foreign countries regarding the results of our investigations to date. We are cooperating with the DOJ and SEC in connection with their review of these matters and the outcome of these, or any future matters, cannot be predicted. The FCPA and related statutes and regulations provide for potential monetary penalties, criminal sanctions and in some cases debarment from doing business with the U.S. federal government in connection with FCPA violations, any of which could have a material effect on our business.[34]

The disclosure by Sun closely follows the April 20, 2009 announcement that Oracle Corporation had agreed to purchase Sun for $7.4 billion. Shortly after Sun's disclosure, Oracle acknowledged that it was aware of the potential violations and that it had been disclosed to them prior to both companies agreeing to the acquisition. There is strong speculation that the FCPA disclosure by Sun may have come about from the enhanced due diligence that often accompanies the acquisition process.[35] With the government spotlight on FCPA violations, robust vetting and self-disclosure are absolutely critical in protecting an organization.

Sun's self-disclosure of a potential FCPA violation may result in the government focusing more attention on the software, telecom, and information technology sectors. These typically are growing businesses that have interactions with the public sectors. Much of their business is in emerging markets that are high risk. Some companies have immature compliance programs and are focused on sales and marketing without factoring in the inherent risks.

The information technology sector on the West Coast of the United States may very well be an area of focus. There are several reasons for this:

- There is a large concentration of IT companies there, especially in Northern California.
- Many of these firms are start-ups and private entities.
- These companies may have less sophisticated compliance programs than older, more established companies in other industries.
- These companies are growth-oriented and may be willing to take risks to obtain and retain business.

WHY CORRUPTION MATTERS

Many mentions have been made thus far of the evil of corruption. It is what spurred Congress to enact the FCPA and it is that harm the Act intends to remedy. The harm of corruption seems self-evident; that it is bad is taken for granted. Corruption, bribery, and the like inspire a negative gut reaction. Yet, to understand the FCPA, it is necessary to better understand the harm that results from corruption. Transparency International defines corruption as "the misuse of entrusted power for private gain." This is further broken down into two types, "according to the rule" corruption and "against the rule" corruption. The former is the payment of a bribe to receive preferential treatment for something the recipient is required to do by law while the latter is a bribe paid to obtain services the receiver is prohibited from providing.[36] For example, paying a government official to curry favor during a bidding process would be "according to the rule" while paying a government official to ignore safety violations would be "against the rule."

Transparency International is a leading international nongovernmental organization fighting corruption. They have identified four costs of corruption:

1. *Political:* Corruption delegitimizes democratic institutions and presents a major obstacle to the rule of law. Institutional accountability cannot develop.

2. *Economic:* Corruption depletes national wealth. It transfers scarce public resources into projects that benefit only a small group of people while ignoring fundamental infrastructure. It distorts market forces and prevents competition while at the same time discouraging outside investment.

3. *Social:* Corruption undermines public trust, in leaders and government as a whole. Leaders ignore the needs of the many and focus solely on self-enrichment. Bribery and graft become the norm.

4. *Environmental:* Corrupt leaders ignore environmental harm caused, often by foreign businesses, since they directly benefit from the projects and are not accountable to the regions harmed. No heed is paid to long-term negative consequences as only short-term benefits matter to the leadership.[37]

For a deeper analysis into corruption's harm, Afghanistan serves as a useful case study.

COMPLIANCE INSIGHT 2.3: AFGHANISTAN: A CASE STUDY IN CORRUPTION

The Taliban emerged as the rulers of Afghanistan after its war against the Soviet Union in the 1980s. They were subsequently toppled by the American military following the government's refusal to hand over Osama Bin Laden and other al-Qaeda forces responsible for the terrorist attacks of September 11, 2001. The United States installed a democratic government in the war-torn country with former exile

---

Hamid Karzai as president. Many had great optimism for the development of Afghanistan following the removal of the oppressive Taliban regime. The country had suffered tremendously from near constant tribal warfare and the devastation of the Russian invasion, and in the wake of Operation Enduring Freedom, there was hope that the country's disparate tribes could unify into a coherent state. This hope would be short-lived.

Despite great promise after dismantling the Taliban, Afghanistan has become one of the most corrupt countries on earth. Even though many developing nations struggle with corruption, its scale and scope is unlike anything Afghanistan has ever seen before. Its rank in the Transparency International index has fallen from 117 out of 180 countries in 2005 to 179 in 2009. "Kept afloat by billions of dollars in American and other foreign aid, the government of Afghanistan is shot through with corruption and graft. From the lowliest traffic policeman to the family of President Hamid Karzai himself, the state built on the ruins of the Taliban government . . . now often seems to exist for little more than the enrichment of those who run it."[38]

Everything, no matter how mundane, requires a bribe: driving a truck, settling a lawsuit, resolving a property dispute, receiving an official job, and so forth. This has taken money out of the pockets of the poor and given it to the rich and powerful and deprived the country of money that could be used for improvements. The Afghan government is weak, focusing on selfish benefit rather than building the country; this has contributed to letting the Taliban reestablish a foothold. Despite their religious extremism and brutal repression, the Taliban represents an alternative to the overly corrupt government. Unlike the Afghan government, the Taliban takes fighting corruption seriously. It runs its own courts, which dispense justice quickly without the need for bribes, and has set up committees to give Afghanis a platform to complain about injustices.[39]

The failures of the Afghani government and growth of opium trafficking as a major money source has created tremendous instability in the region, leading to a reoccurrence of the conditions that allowed al-Qaeda to flourish there in the first place. President Barack Obama has pledged more troops and greater resources to combat this growing extremism and terrorism threat.

(continued)

(continued)

For example, police officials routinely steal funds from their departments and sell their equipment and supplies. These officials often do this to deliberately weaken police authority, to prevent an interference with their own corruption. This leaves the police dangerously underfunded and lacking needed items like ammunition or body armor. Judges and prosecutors ignore the law in favor of their own interests.[40] With no rule of law or an adequate body to police the area, the results have been predictable.

An American intelligence report, which casts serious doubt on the Afghan government's ability to restrain the Taliban, found that "the breakdown in central authority in Afghanistan has been accelerated by rampant corruption within the government of President Hamid Karzai and by an increase in violence by militants who have launched sophisticated attacks from havens in Pakistan."[41]

The public has lost faith in their government. Even President Karzai has publicly acknowledged the overwhelming corruption and the immense harm it has wreaked upon the country.[42] Even Karzai's family has been linked to opium smugglers. According to a former Afghan finance minister, "the government has lost the capacity to govern" and is completely in thrall to drug traffickers.[43]

Though it remains as one of their most pressing issues, the Afghani people have come to accept corruption as part of their daily lives. One contractor described "how the government is corrupt from A to Z: [t]he pressure . . . begins with 'suggestions' that he hire officials' relatives and friends and rent vehicles only from certain providers; it ends with the officials telling him exactly how big a cut of his profits they'll take to let the project continue."[44] In a province with an extremely high illiteracy rate, the local economy minister pushed to build a new university. Why? A big project like a university allows for plenty of opportunities for graft.[45]

Corruption was a major issue in the August 2009 Afghani election both as an election issue and in the campaign itself. It ranked as one of the major issues for voters and was addressed frequently by candidates. Widespread reports of voting fraud for Karzai overshadowed the election and drew negative attention worldwide. Though Karzai was eventually declared the winner, the fraud further tarnished his image and did little to inspire hope for Afghanistan's future.

INCREASED ENFORCEMENT

The increase in FCPA enforcement levels detailed throughout this book stems from corporate scandals of the early 2000s and the resulting corporate reform efforts. It has coincided with efforts from countries around the globe to fight bribery and corruption. This cumulative push has placed greater scrutiny on shady business practices and forced businesses to evaluate their practices and confront possible consequences. Companies have also uncovered more illegal payments as part of SOX-related financial reviews. Greater scrutiny on company record-keeping has helped to bring these issues to the forefront. Since penalties can be so high, many companies have voluntarily disclosed their violations to the government in a bid for leniency.

"Mark F. Mendelsohn, deputy chief of the DOJ's fraud section, says pursuing anti-corruption cases has become a 'significant priority in recent years.' He says: 'U.S. companies that are paying bribes to foreign officials are undermining government institutions around the world. It is a hugely destabilizing force.' "[46] Mendelsohn summarizes the government's effort against corruption and its global importance:

I do think that the global economic crisis that we're in presents a grave challenge in the fight against foreign bribery. I think it is very tempting for companies to divert resources, which are scarce, away from compliance. It is tempting for salespeople in the field who are trying to generate business, generate revenue, save their jobs, to cross the line and pay bribes. I think that companies need to be especially vigilant in this economic climate to not cut back. Our law enforcement efforts are not going to be scaled back, and so it would be, I think, a grave mistake for a company to take that path.[47]

Noting the ever-increasing amount of fines leveled, one school of thought has it that the enormous fines reflect the government's view of the FCPA as a profit center. The government can recover enormous sums of money from companies who have committed violations and are then resolved with a deferred prosecution agreement. This has led to a view of the government bullying companies who disclosed minor violations into paying large fines, for fear if they do not disclose, the punishment would be even worse.

Companies worry that paying for meals or the giving of seasonal gifts, common in many countries, could lead to serious trouble. Companies' overseas behaviors are dramatically changing. "For years, taking business associates to lavish dinners and giving them expensive holiday gifts, and

45

even outright cash, was expected and done in many countries."[48] These practices have been reevaluated and many companies have banned activities that are in the gray area of FCPA enforcement or could possibly be construed as illegal payments. They have hired consultants and have come forward with voluntary disclosures to the DOJ.

The government has responded to the increased FCPA focus by making enhancements to improve enforcement. The SEC plans to create dedicated divisions to focus exclusively on particularly specialized and complex areas of securities law. Of note, it will establish a new FCPA Unit. The unit will be proactive in its approach to identifying FCPA violations and will work closely with foreign counterparts for an even greater global approach.[49]

The year 2010 had barely begun before we had more evidence of the government's aggressive enforcement agenda. The DOJ announced on January 19, 2010 that it had arrested and indicted 22 individuals in Las Vegas and Miami as part of a major undercover FCPA sting. Using tactics more commonly associated with cases against drug cartels or the Mafia, FBI agents posed as representatives of an African country's Defense Ministry. They solicited a 20 percent "commission" as the fee to win a 15 million dollar contract to outfit the country's presidential guard. The defendants are 22 top-level executives from the arms industry. This case marked this first time the government has used an undercover operation to ferret out FCPA offenders, and it likely will not be the last.[50]

NOTES

1. Title 15, United States Code, Section 78dd-2(a).
2. Department of Justice, "Lay-Person's Guide to the FCPA," www .usdoj.gov/criminal/fraud/docs/dojdocb.html.
3. Title 15, United States Code, Section 78dd-1-3.
4. *U.S. v. SSI International Far East, Ltd.* Defendant, criminal information unsealed on October 16, 2006, (Dist. OR 2006), 24.
5. DOJ, "Lay-Person's Guide to the FCPA."
6. Ibid.
7. Title 15, United States Code, Section 78dd-1.
8. Title 15, United States Code, Section 78dd-2(h)(1).
9. Title 15, United States Code, Section 78dd-3(a).
10. Title 15, United States Code, Section 78dd-2(h)(2)(A).
11. Title 15, United States Code, Section 78dd-1.

12. Title 15, United States Code, Section 78dd-1(f)(2)(A).
13. Title 15, United States Code, Section 78dd-1(f)(2)(B).
14. Title 15, United States Code, Section 78dd-1(a)(1).
15. *U.S. v. Kay* 359 F.3d 738, 756 (5th Cir. 2004). This broad interpretation of "business purpose" does not negate the intent requirement of the statute. An intent to do the corrupt act must still exist.
16. Ibid., 748.
17. Title 18, United States Code, Section 3292(a).
18. Title 15, United States Code, Section 78dd-3.
19. Title 15, United States Code, Section 78dd-1(b).
20. Title 15, United States Code, Section 78dd-1(c).
21. "DOJ Obtains Injunction for FCPA Violations for Payment of Travel and Entertainment Expenses," *Wilmer Cutler & Pickering*, November 2, 2000, www.mondaq.com/article.asp?articleid=9249.
22. *U.S. v. Metcalf & Eddy, Inc.* (D. Mass No. 99CV12566-NG).
23. *U.S. v. Monsanto*, Deferred Prosecution Agreement (Dist. D.C. 2005), www.corporatecrimereporter.com/documents/monsantoagreement.pdf.
24. *U.S. v. SSI International Far East, Ltd*, 24.
25. DOJ, "Lay-Person's Guide to the FCPA."
26. Martin T. Biegelman and Joel T. Bartow, *Executive Roadmap to Fraud Prevention and Internal Control: Creating a Culture of Compliance* (Hoboken, NJ: John Wiley & Sons, Inc, 2006), 64.
27. DOJ, "Lay-Person's Guide to the FCPA."
28. Title 15, United States Code, Section 78dd-1(e)(1).
29. Alice S. Fisher (assistant attorney general, United States Department of Justice), speech at the American Bar Association's National Institute on the Foreign Corrupt Practices Act, Omni Shoreham Hotel, Washington, DC, October 16, 2006, www.justice.gov/criminal/fraud/docs/reports/speech/2006/10-16-06AAGFCPASpeech.pdf.
30. Ibid.
31. DOJ, "Lay-Person's Guide to the FCPA."
32. Title 18, United States Code, Section 1952(a).
33. Title 18, United States Code, Section 1952(b).
34. SEC Form 10-Q, Quarterly Report Pursuant to Section 13 or 15(d) of the Securities Exchange Act of 1934, filed by Sun Microsystems, Inc., May 8, 2009, 39, http://sec.gov/Archives/edgar/data/709519/000119312509103902/d10q.htm.
35. Don Clark, "Sun Discloses Misstep With Bribery Law," *Wall Street Journal*, May 9, 2009, B5.

36. Transparency International, "Frequently Asked Questions About Corruption," http://transparency.org/news_room/faq/corruption_faq.
37. Ibid.
38. Dexter Filkins, "Bribes Corrode Afghans' Trust in Government," *New York Times*, January 2, 2009, A1.
39. Richard Cassin, "The Taliban's Anti-Graft Program," FCPA Blog, December 1, 2009, www.fcpablog.com/blog/2009/12/1/the-talibans-anti-graft-program.html.
40. Richard A. Oppel, "Corruption Undercuts Hope for Afghan Police," *New York Times*, April 9, 2009, A1.
41. Mark Mazzetti and Eric Schmitt, "U.S. Study is Said to Warn of Crisis in Afghanistan," *New York Times*, October 8, 2008, A1.
42. Ibid.
43. Ibid.
44. Edward P. Joseph, "Not Even Afghans Know How to Fix It," *Washington Post*, February 15, 2009, B5.
45. Ibid.
46. Dan Slater, "And the FCPA Party Continues," *Wall Street Journal Law Blog*, September 12, 2008, http://blogs.wsj.com/law/2008/09/12/and-the-fcpa-party-continues.
47. Mark Mendelsohn (deputy chief of the Fraud Section, Criminal Division, U.S. Department of Justice), "Black Money," interview, *Frontline*, February 24, 2009, www.pbs.org/wgbh/pages/frontline/blackmoney/interviews/mendelsohn.html.
48. Ibid.
49. Robert Khuzami, "Remarks Before the New York City Bar: My First 100 Days as Director of Enforcement" (speech, New York, August 5, 2009), www.sec.gov/news/speech/2009/spch080509rk.htm.
50. Diana B. Henriques, "F.B.I. Charges Arms Sellers with Foreign Bribes," *New York Times,* January 21, 2010, A3; "Cracking Down on Misconduct By Corporate Officers—Can Corporate Liability Be Far Behind?," Baker Hostetler executive alert, January 21, 2010, www.bakerlaw .com/cracking-down-on-misconduct-by-corporate-officerscan-corporate-liability-be-far-behind-01-21-2010/.

CHAPTER 3

Government Guidance and Significant Cases

The Foreign Corrupt Practices Act (FCPA) gives the Department of Justice (DOJ) and the Securities and Exchange Commission (SEC) the power to enforce its provisions. Both the DOJ and SEC take this enforcement responsibility very seriously and vigorously pursue violators. Indeed, they have in effect supercharged prosecutions in recent years, indicting growing numbers of companies and collecting higher and higher amounts of fines. The fines collected based on FCPA violations have scaled tremendous heights, setting record after record in their amount.

Investigation of overseas corruption is a high priority for the DOJ. President Barack Obama's administration, with Attorney General Eric Holder at the helm, has continued trends begun during the Bush administration of strict FCPA enforcement and dramatic penalties. This priority is unsurprising considering Holder's involvement in fighting corporate crime as Deputy Attorney General in the Clinton administration. He authored the eponymous 1999 Holder Memo, formally called the Principles of Federal Prosecution of Business Organizations, which laid out the DOJ's corporate charging standards. These standards would continue to be refined and expanded in the subsequent 2003 Thompson and 2006

McNulty memos named after the Deputy Attorney Generals who subsequently revised the standards.[1]

FILIP MEMORANDUM

The DOJ's Filip Memorandum ("Filip Memo"), which sets forth the current guidance, lays out the standard for corporate federal prosecution and updates the government's stance on requests for privileged material. The Memo, released in August 2008 and now integrated into the DOJ's charging guidelines, supersedes the previous McNulty and Thompson memoranda. The Filip Memo retains much of its predecessors' principles. The factors used to decide whether to criminally charge a company have not changed significantly. The major changes have come with respect to the use of privileged materials and the requests for the same.

Under this guidance, the DOJ will not ask a company in the course of an investigation to waive the attorney-client privilege and disclose privileged material to the government. Instead, the government will seek the underlying facts of the putative misconduct under review. Information prepared by counsel, in the form of notes, memoranda, reports, and other documents created in the course of an internal investigation is protected by the attorney-client privilege, but the underlying facts are not privileged. These underlying facts, should they be relevant to the government's investigation and are not core work product—an attorney's mental impressions and legal theories—would need to be disclosed under the cooperation standard.

A company is free to waive the privilege in whole or in part as it sees fit, but the decision to do so should be the company's and the company's alone. Prosecutors should not ask for waivers. The critical factor in the government's analysis will be whether the corporation has timely disclosed the relevant facts about the events. This is the standard for receiving credit for cooperation. Failure to cooperate does not mean in and of itself that the company will be indicted; it merely means if charges are brought, it will not receive cooperation credit. In addition to the company itself, the DOJ will also strongly pursue charging individually culpable defendants. In fact, the Memo specifically states that charging only the company and not seeking charges against individuals should happen only in very rare circumstances.[2]

The Memo includes the standards used to hold a company liable for individual action, the legal concept of *respondeat superior*. *Respondeat superior*, the doctrine holding an employer or principal liable for the wrongful acts of an employee or agent committed within the scope of their duties, is a form of vicarious liability, which holds one party responsible

50

for the actions of another based on the relationship between the two. For the purposes of FCPA discussions in this book, the terms can be used interchangeably; they both mean that a company can be held responsible for the actions of those it contracts with or hires.[3]

To hold a corporation liable for the illegal acts of its directors, officers, employees, and agents, the government must establish that the individual's actions (i) were within the scope of his duties and (ii) were intended, at least in part, to benefit the corporation. The existence of an actual benefit to the company does not matter; all that matters is whether there was some intent to benefit.

The Filip Memo lists nine factors specifically to be considered by prosecutors when assessing the criminal culpability of corporations, in addition to the typical considerations, such as the strength of the evidence and the likelihood of conviction. In conducting an investigation, determining whether to bring charges, and negotiating plea agreements, prosecutors must consider:

1. The nature and seriousness of the offense, including the risk of harm to the public, as well as applicable policies and priorities, if any, governing the prosecution of corporations for particular categories of crime

2. The pervasiveness of wrongdoing within the corporation, including the complicity in, or condoning of, the wrongdoing by corporate management

3. The corporation's history of similar conduct, including prior criminal, civil, and regulatory enforcement actions against it

4. The corporation's timely and voluntary disclosure of wrongdoing and its willingness to cooperate in the investigation of its agents

5. The existence and effectiveness of the corporation's preexisting compliance program

6. The corporation's remedial actions, including any efforts to implement an effective corporate compliance program, or to improve an existing one, to replace responsible management, to discipline or terminate wrongdoers, to pay restitution, and to cooperate with the relevant government agencies

7. The collateral consequences, including whether there is disproportionate harm to shareholders, pension holders, and employees, and others not personally proven culpable, as well as impact on the public arising from the prosecution

8. The adequacy of the prosecution of individuals responsible for the corporation's malfeasance
9. The adequacy of remedies such as civil or regulatory enforcement actions[4]

FCPA COMPLIANCE PROGRAMS: CASE LAW GUIDANCE

The importance of having an effective FCPA compliance program is heightened by increased FCPA enforcement in the last several years, and the widening of its scope and the severity of its penalties. The DOJ and the SEC have attacked foreign corruption the same way they have confronted domestic corporate scandals. Court decisions have also furthered these efforts, by upholding the government's broad interpretation of the FCPA.[5] The government has wide latitude in enforcing the FCPA's provisions and can harshly punish violators as appropriate.

Illustrating the government's increased efforts is the case of the Monsanto Company. An employee of the agribusiness giant bribed an Indonesian official to induce him to repeal a law that Monsanto deemed burdensome. Even though the bribery appeared to result solely from the actions of a single employee operating without authorization, Monsanto's internal controls discovered the misconduct, stopped it, and disciplined those responsible. The company then voluntarily reported the incident to the government who proceeded with the case. However, because of the existence of Monsanto's compliance program and its cooperation, the company received a deferred prosecution agreement. For more on Monsanto and the major steps the company has taken to establish a best-in-class anti-corruption compliance program, please see Chapter 11.

Officials at the DOJ and the SEC have repeatedly dismissed the idea of a "rogue employee" defense. Regardless of the fact that an individual employee acting alone in contravention of company policy caused the violation, the company is still liable for the breach. The DOJ and SEC take the position that any FCPA problem must result from weaknesses in a company's internal controls. This position has engendered some criticism, as discussed ahead.

Even though the government has prosecuted companies that have working compliance programs and voluntarily reported misconduct, this still underscores the need for an effective compliance program. For one, compliance programs can always be improved and strengthened to increase their effectiveness. Additionally, the government's stepped-up prosecutions of FCPA violators have put corporations on notice that their wrongdoing will be found out and severely dealt with, particularly if they do not have a compliance program that meets the minimum standards and do not cooperate.

The complete lack of an FCPA compliance program can severely impact a company, as was the case with the Titan Corporation, a San Diego-based military intelligence and communications firm. An SEC complaint alleged, among other FCPA violations, that "Titan funneled approximately $2 million, via its agent in Benin, towards the election campaign of Benin's then-incumbent President. . . . Titan made these payments to assist the company in its development of a telecommunications project in Benin and to obtain the Benin government's consent to an increase in the percentage of Titan's project management fees for that project."[6] After consenting to the entry of final judgment, Titan agreed to pay $28.4 million, at the time the largest FCPA penalty ever, which included disgorgement of profits stemming from the illicit payments. A merger deal with Lockheed Martin also fell through after the discovery of the violations.[7] Most importantly, the SEC took the company to task for its failure to have any sort of compliance program or to even make any sort of substantial compliance effort at all.

In its 23 years of existence prior to 2004, Titan has never had a FCPA compliance program or procedures. Titan's only related "policy" is a statement in Titan Corporation's Code of Ethics, which all Titan employees were required to sign annually, stating "employees must be fully familiar with and strictly adhere to such provisions as the Foreign Corrupt Practices Act. . . ." Titan did not enforce that policy nor did it provide its employees with any information concerning the FCPA.[8]

This complete absence of compliance efforts undoubtedly factored into the harsh penalties that Titan suffered. The government treats harshly those companies that make no efforts at compliance, and will take that into account when punishing them.

Opinion Release 04-02 contains more information on the DOJ's expectations of compliance program standards and practices. Please see Chapter 9 for further detail.

A Lesson in Overseas Compliance

The mere presence of a compliance program, even a functioning one, will not alone serve to preclude prosecution. The case of Faro Technologies

COMPLIANCE INSIGHT 3.1: ROGUE EMPLOYEE DOES THE CRIME, COMPANY DOES THE TIME

A Criticism of American Corporate Criminal Liability

A major criticism of FCPA enforcement is the application of the respondeat superior doctrine to corporate liability. As the company is liable for the acts of its subsidiary companies, all of its employees, and its agents, there exists the great possibility that the act of a single individual could result in dire consequences.

A 2009 case, *U.S. v. Ionia Mgmt. S.A.*, led to a discussion on the appropriateness of respondeat superior in this context. Ionia was prosecuted for pollution violations stemming from the illegal disposal of waste oil by employees and subsequent falsification of records, though they acted in contravention of explicit company policy. Ionia, along with a number of "friend of the court" briefs, "argued that the court should revisit its long-standing rule that a company can be held criminally liable for any criminal acts of even its low-level employees."[9] It was unquestioned that the criminal acts by Ionia employees were directly contrary to company directives and were done in spite of the company's compliance program. The court rejected Ionia's appeal and upheld its conviction.

While the government would be unlikely to prosecute for limited, isolated actions by rogue employees, it does have the ability to do so, and this gives it tremendous leverage. "Therefore, when confronted with a federal investigation, a company has no choice but to agree to a deferred-prosecution or non-prosecution agreement, with heavy fines, collateral civil consequences, and even the imposition of monitorship."[10] As one article states, "a company literally is powerless to avoid criminal sanctions when any of its employees violate the law, regardless of how conscientiously the company acts to prevent such misconduct."

This article's authors suggest limiting liability for respondeat superior by allowing the corporation to demonstrate that "the criminal acts were those of a truly rogue employee, who was acting in violation of a robust compliance program." Offering this as defense would strongly incentivize the establishment and maintenance of effective compliance programs under the guidelines of the U.S. Sentencing

Guidelines, as well as encourage strong corporate monitoring and due diligence to ensure wrongdoing is not widespread. This would also not give corporations an escape hatch to avoid liability for criminal acts involving management participation or acquiescence. As attorney and FCPA commentator Richard Cassin made the point in his popular FCPA Blog, "To give organizations the best possible reason to have an effective compliance program, give them a defense based on their efforts to comply."[11]

underscores just how important an effective compliance program is. Faro's Chinese subsidiary hired an individual who indicated that he wished to do business "the Chinese way," meaning offering kickbacks to potential customers.[12] Faro sought legal advice and after determining such payments would violate Chinese law, particularly where the customer was a state-owned enterprise, issued a directive against making any such payments.

Faro's Sales Director for China disregarded the order and authorized illegal cash payments in order to obtain contracts. The individual, hired to be Faro's Chinese Country Manager, stated in an e-mail "that to have a good relationship with customers in China" you have to give them "money."[13] From 2004 to 2006 the illegal payments continued and Faro-China's staff altered account entries to hide the payments. The payments were made despite direct warnings from corporate officers in the United States to always observe U.S. law in dealings in China. After that, Faro-China continued with its bribery, but used third parties to avoid detection.[14] Once the company discovered the illegal payments, it voluntary disclosed them to the government.

The government determined that the company's internal controls did not detect the improperly recorded payments. Crucially:

During the period of the improper payments . . . Faro provided no training or education to any of its employees, agents, or subsidiaries regarding the requirements of the FCPA. Faro also failed to establish a program to monitor its employees, agents, and subsidiaries for compliance with the FCPA.[15]

The government faulted the company not for the absence of a compliance program as a whole but rather that it did not provide FCPA training, or monitor for FCPA violations.

Some facts in this case are sympathetic to the company, but it is important to understand why the government still penalized them. The company did its due diligence to determine that the kickbacks violated Chinese law. The violators were rogue employees who operated in contravention of express rules and directives from the company's officers. This case would have been much different, however, if the company could have shown the rogue employees operating despite robust FCPA training and compliance.

The presence of an effective FCPA compliance program and cooperation with the government, while it will not preclude prosecution, will help to reduce the penalties faced by a company. In dealing with self-reporting of FCPA violations, the government gives companies the potential for leniency. By voluntarily reporting and cooperating with the investigation, a company stands a much greater chance of escaping with a deferred prosecution agreement and lessened penalties than otherwise could have been achieved. Designing and implementing effective anti-corruption compliance programs are discussed in Chapters 9 and 10.

COLD CASH: *U.S. V. JEFFERSON*

Ninety thousand dollars found in a Louisiana Congressman's freezer, stuffed inside packages of frozen pie crusts. While this incident provided fodder for countless late night monologue jokes, it also goes to the heart of an important FCPA case. A federal grand jury indicted Congressman William Jefferson in June 2007 on bribery and corruption charges. The indictment alleged he used his position and influence to garner business for companies in Africa in return for bribes for himself and family members as well as bribed foreign officials to advance the business ventures. "The schemes charged are complex, but the essence of the case is simple: Mr. Jefferson corruptly traded on his good office, and on the Congress . . . to enrich himself and his family through a pervasive pattern of fraud, bribery, and corruption that spanned many years and two continents," said U.S. Attorney Chuck Rosenberg.[16]

Jefferson made trips to Africa, arranged by his congressional staff, to meet with foreign officials to promote the business venture for which he received bribes. He was charged with offering bribes to those officials and for meeting with other official contacts to secure more business. He got caught when a disgruntled associate working with the FBI gave him $100,000 to be used to bribe Nigerian Vice President Atiku Abubakar. It was this money, which never made it to Abubakar, which was found in the

56

freezer, neatly wrapped in aluminum foil and hidden in frozen food containers. Though he denied all accusations of illegal activity, Jefferson never explained the freezer money.[17]

This case is also important, as it marked the first prosecution of a member of Congress for FCPA violations. Of course, it should be noted that Jefferson is no longer a current member of Congress, losing his bid for re-election in November 2008. The case also had foreign repercussions, as the ties to the Jefferson scandal contributed to Abubakar's loss in his re-election campaign.[18] Jefferson's legal team defended him, stating that many of his actions, if true, would not be considered officials acts and therefore can't be the basis for the corruption charges, and also denying that he intended to bribe anyone. The case also featured a high-profile search of the Congressman's office, the first of its kind, and one on Abubakar's Maryland house, also the first-ever raid on the American residence of a foreign elected official. President Bush interceded in the case and secured the papers in Jefferson's office without giving prosecutors access to them. This touched off a firestorm, particularly when it was rumored Bush was going to return them to Jefferson.[19]

Jefferson's prosecution was a prominent test for the government's enforcement strategy, as it attracted heavy media attention, and its commitment to public integrity. The trial began in June 2009. The government presented substantial evidence against Jefferson, including multiple videos of him accepting the bribe money from the agent, photos of the money in the freezer, taped conversations, and testimony from co-conspirators.[20] Throughout, the prosecution portrayed Jefferson as the consummate shakedown artist. As Assistant U.S. Attorney Rebeca Bellows put it in her closing, "[Jefferson] never let an opportunity to demand a bribe payment pass him by."[21]

After the prosecution rested, the defense's case only lasted two hours, with the defense boiling down to convincing the jury that Jefferson's actions put him in an ethical gray area but were not illegal. Without presenting a credible alternate explanation for the government's evidence, the jury, unsurprisingly, was not swayed. They convicted Jefferson on 11 of 16 counts, including conspiracy to violate the FCPA, racketeering, and solicitation of bribes but not of violating the FCPA itself.[22] Since the money did not make it from the freezer to Abubakar's hands and the prosecution could not prove what exactly was said between Jefferson and Abubakar, it was difficult to prove that charge beyond a reasonable doubt.

The jury still convicted Jefferson on numerous substantive charges and the evidence behind the FCPA charge provided the foundation for other convictions. Even though they did not receive a direct FCPA conviction, this undoubtedly serves as a major victory for the government and a demonstration of their ability to wield the FCPA at trial. Following his conviction, the judge sentenced Jefferson to thirteen years in prison.[23]

VOLUNTARY DISCLOSURE

To avoid hefty penalties, criminal and civil, financial and penal, many companies have elected to voluntarily disclose violations to the DOJ. Companies are not required to report discovered violations, but they are generally granted leniency in prosecution for doing so. Cooperation is highly valued by the DOJ. As noted in the Filip Memo, the federal government will not request a waiver of attorney-client privilege by the company in order to access privileged materials. What the government is after is a full accounting of the facts. If the only way to understand what happened is through privileged material and the company elects to not turn it over, the decision not to waive privilege will not be held against them, but the fact that the company did not fully disclose the facts will be considered. Again, the federal government seeks the full facts, not a waiver of privilege.

This should be taken into account when deciding whether or not to voluntarily disclose. A company should decide what it is willing to turn over when it discloses. The company should also evaluate the seriousness of the violation as well as the likelihood that it will be discovered. A further discussion of voluntary disclosure is contained in Chapter 12.

EVALUATING THE SEABOARD CRITERIA IN MITIGATING ENFORCEMENT ACTIONS

Like the DOJ, the SEC encourages self-reporting by companies. The self-reporting is promoted by a strong possibility of reduced liability, or in some cases, no action being taken against either the culpable company or official. That was the case with the SEC's investigation of Seaboard Corporation.

In late 1999, Seaboard began an investigation of a division controller for booking improper entries in the financial statements that overstated deferred costs and understated expenses. A concern raised over these unusual entries by other employees resulted in an inquiry by the internal audit department. The controller subsequently confessed to her manager in

July 2000 that she had been making these false accounting entries for five years resulting in over $7 million in accounting discrepancies.

Seaboard's management quickly notified the board of directors of the incident and that its financial reports had been misstated due to the controller's actions. The board retained an outside law firm to conduct a thorough investigation of the entire matter. In short order, the controller was fired as were two other employees who failed to adequately supervise her. Seaboard issued a public statement that it would be restating its financial statements for a five-year period due to the controller's action, and self-reported the matter to the SEC.[24]

The SEC conducted its own investigation and confirmed the findings of Seaboard's internal investigation that the controller had violated securities laws, but noted that Seaboard fully cooperated and assisted in the SEC investigation. As a result, the SEC decided not to take any action against Seaboard. The SEC explained how the company's swift and transparent actions including self-reporting, benefited investors and the SEC's enforcement program. As a result of this case, the SEC issued four key factors and related criteria that they would consider in determining whether or not to "credit self-policing, self-reporting, remediation, and cooperation" in deciding whether to take reduced action or no action against others in future enforcement actions.[25] The following are the SEC's four key factors in this regard:

1. *Self-policing:* The establishment and ongoing maintenance of an effective compliance program strongly supported by executive management and the board of directors where issues and allegations are properly escalated and fully investigated.

2. *Self-reporting:* As a result of effective self-policing and determination of violation of the code of conduct, the organization then promptly and effectively discloses the violation(s) to the public, government regulators, and law enforcement as appropriate.

3. *Remediation:* The appropriate disciplinary process for those found to have violated the organization's code of conduct as well as the strengthening of internal controls to mitigate repeat misconduct or other violations.

4. *Cooperation:* Full and complete cooperation with the SEC and other law enforcement agencies including providing all relevant documentary and testimonial evidence related to the violations and investigation at hand.

The following are the SEC's related criteria and questions to be asked and answered by an organization:

- What is the nature of the misconduct involved? Did it result from inadvertence, honest mistake, simple negligence, reckless or deliberate indifference to indicia of wrongful conduct, willful misconduct, or unadorned venality? Were the company's auditors misled?
- How did the misconduct arise? Is it the result of pressure placed on employees to achieve specific results, or a tone of lawlessness set by those in control of the company? What compliance procedures were in place to prevent the misconduct now uncovered? Why did those procedures fail to stop or inhibit the wrongful conduct?
- Where in the organization did the misconduct occur? How high up in the chain of command was knowledge of, or participation in, the misconduct? Did senior personnel participate in, or turn a blind eye toward, obvious indicia of misconduct? How systematic was the behavior? Is it symptomatic of the way the entity does business, or was it isolated?
- How long did the misconduct last? Was it a one-quarter, or one-time event, or did it last several years? In the case of a public company, did the misconduct occur before the company went public? Did it facilitate the company's ability to go public?
- How much harm has the misconduct inflicted upon investors and other corporate constituencies? Did the share price of the company's stock drop significantly upon its discovery and disclosure?
- How was the misconduct detected and who uncovered it?
- How long after discovery of the misconduct did it take to implement an effective response?
- What steps did the company take upon learning of the misconduct? Did the company immediately stop the misconduct? Are persons responsible for any misconduct still with the company? If so, are they still in the same positions? Did the company promptly, completely, and effectively disclose the existence of the misconduct to the public, to regulators, and to self-regulators? Did the company cooperate completely with the appropriate regulatory and law enforcement bodies? Did the company identify what additional related misconduct is likely to have occurred? Did the company take steps to identify the extent of damage to investors and other corporate constituencies? Did the company appropriately recompense those adversely affected by the conduct?

- What processes did the company follow to resolve many of these issues and ferret out necessary information? Were the Audit Committee and the Board of Directors fully informed? If so, when?
- Did the company commit to learn the truth, fully, and expeditiously? Did it do a thorough review of the nature, extent, origins, and consequences of the conduct and related behavior? Did management, the Board, or committee consisting solely of outside directors oversee the review? Did company employees or outside persons perform the review? If outside persons, had they done other work for the company? Where the review was conducted by outside counsel, had management previously engaged such counsel? Were scope limitations placed on the review? If so, what were they?
- Did the company promptly make available to our staff the results of its review and provide sufficient documentation reflecting its response to the situation? Did the company identify possible violative conduct and evidence with sufficient precision to facilitate prompt enforcement actions against those who violated the law? Did the company produce a thorough and probing written report detailing the findings of its review? Did the company voluntarily disclose information our staff did not directly request and otherwise might not have uncovered? Did the company ask its employees to cooperate with our staff and make all reasonable efforts to secure such cooperation?
- What assurances are there that the conduct is unlikely to recur? Did the company adopt and ensure enforcement of new and more effective internal controls and procedures designed to prevent a recurrence of the misconduct? Did the company provide our staff with sufficient information for it to evaluate the company's measures to correct the situation and ensure that the conduct does not recur?
- Is the company the same company in which the misconduct occurred, or has it changed through a merger or bankruptcy reorganization?[26]

The SEC's approach in the Seaboard case underscores the importance of an effective compliance program and the rewarding of good behavior. Ultimately many aspects of Seaboard's compliance program worked well beginning with the escalation of questionable accounting practices by vigilant employees, the response of internal audit, involvement of management, an internal investigation, referral to the board, disciplinary action for those culpable, self-reporting, cooperation with the government, and then correcting deficiencies and enhancing internal controls. There is no guarantee that this approach and result will happen in all instances of compliance failures but the precedence is there. The SEC's four key factors and related criteria are additional tools in the compliance toolkit to be used by every organization in enhancing compliance.

Though the SEC issued this report in 2001, Seaboard remains the standard. In an August 2009 speech, Robert Khuzami, the SEC's director of its Division of Enforcement, indicated the SEC would pursue creating a Seaboard standard to evaluate cooperation of individuals.[27]

COMPLIANCE INSIGHT 3.2: APPOINTMENT OF CORPORATE MONITOR RESULTS IN CHARGES OF CRONYISM

Who would have thought that the appointment of independent monitors would become a political campaign issue with primetime media spots accusing a candidate of impropriety in their selection and calling for Congressional inquiries? Yet that is exactly what occurred in the 2009 gubernatorial race between incumbent Jon Corzine and challenger Christopher Christie, the former U.S. Attorney for New Jersey. The firestorm started when a New Jersey congressman called into question the appointment of monitors in corporate fraud prosecutions by Christie alleging nepotism, backroom deals, and the awarding of tens of millions in legal fees.

In the fall of 2007, then U.S. Attorney Christie "awarded the Ashcroft Group LLC, a lobbying and consulting firm formed and headed by [former Attorney General] John Ashcroft, with a no-bid government contract monitoring Zimmer Holdings."[28] Zimmer is a medical devices company that received a deferred prosecution agreement by Christie's office after a criminal investigation into kickbacks to doctors. As part of the deferred prosecution agreement, Zimmer agreed to the appointment of an independent monitor to oversee the terms of the agreement. The firm was reported to have "paid Ashcroft's firm between $28 million and more than $52 million for 18 months' work" and that resulted in the allegations of cronyism and impropriety.[29]

Christie defended himself by stating that while he recommended the former Attorney General who was his boss at the Justice Department, he did not negotiate the fees and Zimmer agreed to

Ashcroft's appointment. Congressman Bill Pascrell, who made the public complaint against Christie, responded, "Under the continued threat of prosecution, any party being investigated seemingly has little choice but to agree to the selection of these federal monitors and their exorbitant fees."[30] The congressman called for greater transparency in the selection of federal monitors. A bill was introduced that would provide oversight over the appointment process. These and other similar concerns by Congress resulted in the DOJ issuing the Morford Memorandum in March 2008. The memo provided new guidelines for the selection of corporate monitors in criminal cases. That probably was no consolation for Zimmer Holdings who at one point complained about the exorbitant fees they were to be charged but Christie declined to intervene.[31] Corruption was a major subject in the election but this issue did not seem to harm Christie, as he bested Corzine to become governor.

SELECTING A MONITOR: THE MORFORD MEMO STANDARDS

Cases brought by the DOJ often are resolved through deferred prosecution agreements (DPAs) or nonprosecution agreements. These agreements will resolve a criminal case without resulting in a conviction, as distinct from a plea bargain. These agreements sometimes include a provision for the appointment of an independent corporate monitor. "A monitor's primary responsibility is to assess and monitor a corporation's compliance with the terms of the agreement specifically designed to address and reduce the risk of recurrence of the corporation's misconduct, and not to further punitive goals."[32] Monitors are appropriate in circumstances where the lack of internal controls or insufficient controls led to the violation. The monitor would be able to ensure the sufficiency of future compliance.

With the controversy surrounding the monitor appointment process and the possibility of congressional involvement, then Acting Deputy Attorney General Craig S. Morford issued the first official standards to guide the monitor appointment process, which became known as the Morford Memo. These guidelines addressed the lack of transparency and lack of specific guidance with respect to the monitors and DPAs in general. The memo aimed to standardize monitor appointments throughout the DOJ.

63

Given the wide variety of circumstances that prosecutors may encounter, a prosecutor should be flexible in the consideration of whether to appoint a monitor.

"In negotiating agreements with corporations, prosecutors should be mindful of both: (1) the potential benefits that employing a monitor may have for the corporation and the public, and (2) the cost of a monitor and its impact on the operations of the corporation."[33] The Memo lays out eight principles to govern monitors:

1. Monitors should be highly qualified and selected only on the basis of merit, and the selection process should serve to avoid any potential and actual conflicts of interests.

2. Monitors are independent third parties, not employees or agents of the corporation or government.

3. A monitor's primary responsibility is to assess and monitor a corporation's compliance with the terms of their agreement that are specifically designed to address and reduce the recurrence of the corporation's misconduct, including evaluating (and where appropriate, proposing) internal controls, and corporate ethics, and compliance programs.

4. A monitor's responsibilities should be no broader than necessary to address and reduce the risk of recurrence of the corporation's misconduct.

5. Communication among the government, corporation, and the monitor is in the interest of all parties.

6. The monitor should report refusal by the corporation to adopt the monitor's recommendations, but the corporation has the right to explain its refusal in order to determine whether it is fulfilling its obligations under its agreement.

7. The agreement should clearly identify any types of previously undisclosed or new misconduct that the monitor will be required to report directly to the government. The agreement should also provide that as to evidence of other such misconduct, the monitor will have the discretion to report the misconduct to the government or corporation or both.

8. The duration of the agreement should be tailored to the problems that have been found to exist and the types of remedial measures needed for the monitor to satisfy his or her mandate.[34]

THOUGHT LEADER IN CORPORATE COMPLIANCE: GEORGE STAMBOULIDIS

Best Practices in Managing Independent Monitors

George A. Stamboulidis is Managing Partner of Baker Hostetler's New York office, one of the largest of the firm's ten offices. Based in part on the strength of its New York office, Baker Hostetler was named Counsel to the Court-appointed trustee in the liquidation of Bernard L. Madoff Investment Securities LLC.

Stamboulidis joined the firm with the opening of the New York office after an illustrious 13-year career as a federal prosecutor in New York and New Jersey. He has been selected as an independent monitor on five separate occasions, more than any other attorney. In addition to having served as the U.S. DOJ-appointed corporate monitor for Merrill Lynch, The Bank of New York, Mellon Bank, and others, Stamboulidis and the firm's white collar team have conducted monitoring work and internal investigations for leading corporations.

While with the U.S. Attorney's Office in the Eastern District of New York, Stamboulidis served in a variety of supervisory positions, including Chief of the Long Island Division. In that capacity, he investigated and prosecuted cases involving complex business, bank, health care, accounting, securities and bankruptcy fraud, tax, public and labor corruption, extortion, racketeering, environmental, and money laundering offenses. Stamboulidis successfully prosecuted Mafia boss Vincent "Chin" Gigante, the boss of the Genovese crime family. After a nationwide search, former U.S. Attorney General Janet Reno selected Stamboulidis to take over and successfully resolve the Wen Ho Lee nuclear weapons secrets prosecution. Three times Reno presented Stamboulidis with the DOJ Director's Award.

Over the last eight years at Baker Hostetler, Stamboulidis has served as Litigation Coordinator for the office, is a current member of the firm's Policy Committee and Operating Group, and co-heads the firm's White Collar Defense and Corporate Investigations Practice Group, which has become one of the preeminent such practices in the country.

(*continued*)

65

(*continued*)

Here Stamboulidis provides his perspectives, recommendations, and thought leadership for implementing independent monitors:

Independent monitors have long been used to oversee the government's negotiated settlements with corporations and other organizations either convicted of corporate fraud violations or those receiving deferred prosecution and nonprosecution agreements. Now monitors are being used to oversee enforcement of newly-instituted compliance programs including those related to FCPA violations. With the government's intensified prosecutions of corruption and bribery, they have become more important than ever.

There are many best practices in finding the most qualified and experienced monitor. For example:

- *Make the selection process transparent.*
- *Use a Request For Proposal.*
- *Publish a notice in a widely read legal newspaper such as the* New York Law Journal *requesting submissions for consideration.*
- *New DOJ policy requires the subject corporation and the government to agree to the necessary qualifications and expertise needed for the monitor role.*
- *Conduct interviews of the best-qualified candidates and select a final group of three.*
- *The subject corporation should be able to reject one candidate for good reason with the assigned federal judge making the final decision as to appointment.*

When selecting a monitor, several important qualities must be considered in any prospective candidate:

- *Independence, both in lacking a past or present association with the company, and in having the courage and conviction to operate independently in fulfilling necessary duties*
- *Sense of integrity, fairness, and the judgment to solicit management's input*
- *Prior experience and involvement in monitoring compliance, such as a former government lawyer or other government official*

- *Industry background, though a lack of particularized experience can be ameliorated by the hiring of subject matter experts and consultants*
- *Appointment should be merit-based. Avoid the appearance of cronyism in the appointment and make sure there are no conflicts of interest in the appointment.*

To ensure a monitor's success, consider designating one person in the organization, such as the general counsel or employee selected by the general counsel, as the central point person. This point person will be the primary contact person for the monitor, fielding information requests, facilitating access, and receiving regular progress reports. This is beneficial for both sides: the monitor has a dedicated contact, while the company gets oversight and can ensure that the monitor gets all necessary access.

Of course, giving a monitor access is easier said than done. Leaders in an organization may have understandable concerns about a monitor's presence at internal meetings and disruptions to the business. The wrong approach is to bar the monitor from compliance-related meetings or to unnecessarily challenge the scope of the monitor's purview. A spirit of openness and cooperation can be very beneficial in the end. Remember that voluntary disclosure breeds trust, whether it is accurate information on employee misconduct, or letting the monitor sit in on meetings related to the subject matter of the review.

The more access the company provides to the monitor, the more readily the monitor will accept the company's representations about the progress of its compliance program, and report back favorably to the government. An effective way to demonstrate commitment and to make the monitor's job easier is to prepare a comprehensive remediation plan before the monitor arrives, and have it ready to go upon arrival. This plan should comprehensively review business ethics or compliance issues, anticipate potential problems and concerns, and create an infrastructure to address problems and handle training. The responsibility for this falls on the directors to ensure that management carries it out.

The corporation's directors and officers need an open and trusting relationship with the monitor. This includes disclosing any crimes or other misconduct that occur during the monitor's tenure before the monitor discovers it. Trust ensures a better outcome for the organi-

(continued)

> *(continued)*
> *zation and a more effective compliance program. A respectful and collaborative approach between the company and the monitors will be beneficial in accepting and implementing the monitor's recommendations.*
>
> *There are benefits to having a productive relationship between the company and the monitor. There have been times when the company will ask the monitor to stay on to do additional remedial or compliance work outside the scope of the original monitor role. Even when the monitor relationship has ended, there may be a future need for a compliance enhancement review, independent attorney review, or legal advice focused on a particular issue.*

GOVERNMENT PROCUREMENT FRAUD AND THE FCPA

Government contracting fraud has long been a serious problem for both businesses and the government. In the early 1980s, the media reported on numerous stories detailing questionable and highly inflated defense contracts. The U.S. military had purchased outrageously priced $300 hammers, $600 toilet seats, and other such items from defense contractors. Ultimately, billions of dollars of the defense budget were lost as a result of waste, fraud, and abuse.

Federal Acquisition Regulations Disclosure Requirements and the FCPA

Contracting fraud continues to be a major problem today, especially with the billions of dollars in reported fraud related to the wars and reconstruction efforts in Iraq and Afghanistan. In response to these and other cases of contractor fraud, the DOJ decided to step up its enforcements efforts. The DOJ signaled its strong intent in a letter from then Assistant Attorney General Alice Fisher to the General Services Administration on January 14, 2008. Fisher commented on proposed modifications to the Federal Acquisition Regulations (FAR) to require mandatory reporting to the government whenever a government contractor becomes aware of a material overpayment or fraud relating to the award or performance of either a contract or subcontract. In the letter, Fisher wrote:

> *The Justice Department continues to believe that mandatory disclosure of material overpayments and fraud is necessary and appropriate, and that government contractors should be held to the same disclosure standards as those in the healthcare and banking industries. We recognize that many government contractors have taken steps and are now required to establish corporate compliance programs, but our experience suggests that few have actually responded to the invitation of the Department of Defense (DOD) that they report or voluntarily disclose suspected instances of fraud.*[35]

The FAR amendment was approved in a final rule issued on November 12, 2008 by the Civilian Agency Acquisition Council and the Defense Acquisition Regulations Council, effective December 12, 2008. The amendment establishes mandatory disclosure requirements for certain violations of federal criminal law and/or the False Claims Act as well as requirements for government contractors to establish and maintain specific internal controls to detect, prevent, and disclose improper conduct related to the awarding or performance of any government contract or subcontract. The government's message is clear that contractors must now self-disclose violations when they learn of them rather than wait for the government to discover them, or not, at a later date. The emphasis for compliance now shifts even more to contractors. The implication for corruption and related FCPA violations is also clear.

The FAR disclosure requirements mandate the reporting of certain violations of criminal and civil law to the Office of Inspector General of the U.S. Department of Commerce. Federal Acquisition Rule 52.203-13 requires:

> *a government contractor to timely disclose, in writing, to the agency Office of Inspector General whenever the contractor has credible evidence that a principal, employee, agent, or subcontractor of the contractor has committed a violation of the Civil False Claims Act or a violation of Federal criminal law involving fraud, conflict of interest, bribery, or gratuity in connection with the award, performance or closeout of a government contract or any related subcontract. The individual making the report must be an officer or manager empowered to speak for the company. A copy of the disclosure report must also be sent to the government contracting officer for the contracting office for the contract. The disclosure requirement continues until at least three years after final payment on the contract.*

Knowing failure on the part of a contractor to make such a required disclosure could be a cause for suspension and/or debarment until 3 years after final payment on the contract.[36]

Business Ethics Awareness and Compliance Program

Besides the requirement of self-disclosure, the FAR amendments include the creation of a business ethics awareness and compliance program and internal control system designed to detect and prevent fraud and other violations of law. These program elements mirror the seven steps to an effective compliance as detailed in the Federal Sentencing Guidelines for Organizations. Key provisions of the FAR amendments include:

- Contractor will promote an organizational culture that encourages ethical conduct and a commitment to compliance with the law.
- Contractor Code of Business Ethics and Conduct:
  - Each contractor will have a written code of business ethics and conduct.
  - Provide a copy of the code to each employee engaged in the performance of the contract.
- Business Ethics Awareness and Compliance Program and Internal Control System:
  - Ongoing compliance program that includes reasonable steps to communicate periodically and in a practical manner, the Contractor's standards and procedures and other aspects of the Contractor's business ethics awareness, and compliance program, and internal control system. This includes conducting effective training and disseminating appropriate information appropriate to an individual's respective roles and responsibilities.
  - The training conducted under this program shall be provided to the Contractor's principals and employees, and as appropriate, the Contractor's agents and subcontractors.
  - Establish standards and procedures to facilitate timely discovery of improper conduct in connection with Government contracts.
  - Ensure corrective measures are promptly instituted and carried out.
  - Assignment of responsibility at a sufficiently high level and adequate resources to ensure effectiveness of the business ethics awareness and compliance program, and internal control system.

- Reasonable efforts not to include an individual as a principal, whom due diligence would have exposed as having engaged in conduct that is in conflict with the Contractor's Code of Business Ethics and Conduct.
- This same focus by contractors in excluding certain principals extends to selecting its subcontractors.
- Periodic reviews of company business practices, procedures, policies, and internal controls for compliance with the Contractor's Code of Business Ethics and Conduct and the special requirements of Government contracting, including monitoring and auditing to detect criminal conduct; periodic evaluation of the effectiveness of the business ethics awareness and compliance program and internal control system, especially if criminal conduct has been detected; and periodic assessment of the risk of criminal conduct, with appropriate steps to design, implement, or modify the business ethics awareness and compliance program and the internal control system as necessary to reduce the risk of criminal conduct identified through this process.
- An internal reporting mechanism, such as a hotline, which allows for anonymity or confidentiality, by which employees may report suspected instances of improper conduct, and instructions that encourage employees to make such reports.
- Disciplinary action for improper conduct or for failing to take reasonable steps to prevent or detect improper conduct.
- Timely disclosure, in writing, to the agency Office of Inspector General, with a copy to the Contracting Officer.
- Contractors are responsible to ensure that the substance of these compliance standards are passed down to subcontracts exceeding $5 million and 120 days.
- This requirement does not apply to small businesses or commercial item contracts.
- Full cooperation with any Government agencies responsible for audits, investigations, or corrective actions.
- Display of government agency hotline posters in common areas of contractor.
- Whistleblower protections under the American Recovery and Reinvestment Act of 2009.[37]

As a result of the FAR Amendments, there are serious implications for federal government contractors with regards to the FCPA. Besides the new and imposing requirements for these contractors, the specter of the FCPA looms. Any FCPA violations that a covered contractor discovers are connected to the FAR disclosure requirements must be disclosed in a timely manner to the government. The failure to self-disclose FCPA violations, as well as any other criminal and civil violations, opens the contractor to prosecution, litigation, program suspension, and/or debarment. These risks need to be considered and addressed as part of an effective FCPA compliance program.

To compound the quandary that companies may find themselves in, some of the FAR requirements language is ambiguous. For example, there is no definition as to what "timely disclosure" is when reporting a violation. Does that allow for an internal investigation that could take months prior to disclosure? Similarly, there is no definition as to what constitutes "credible evidence" as the standard for when to disclose or what a "significant" overpayment means. Agency interpretations and guidance will be needed and can be expected as FAR is implemented and violations are discovered.

NOTES

1. For more information on the Thompson and McNulty memoranda: see Martin T. Biegelman with Daniel R. Biegelman, *Building a World-Class Compliance Program: Best Practices and Strategies for Success*, (Hoboken, NJ: John Wiley & Sons, 2008), 54–61.
2. Department of Justice, "Principles of Federal Prosecution of Business Organizations," 2, www.usdoj.gov/opa/documents/corp-charging-guidelines.pdf.
3. Distinguishing it from pure vicarious liability, *respondeat superior* requires that the wrongful act be committed within the scope of the employee or agent's duty. Since an act that violates the FCPA must be done to benefit the business in some way, *respondeat superior* will necessarily be invoked in FCPA cases. Thus, both terms can be accurately used interchangeably in this context.
4. DOJ, "Principles of Federal Prosecution of Business Organizations," 3–4.
5. For an example, see *U.S. v. Kay*, 359 F.3d 738 (5th Cir. 2004) (holding that when Congress enacted the FCPA, it intended to cast a "wide net over foreign bribery").

72

6. *SEC v. The Titan Corporation*, Complaint, Civ. Action No. 05-0411 (JR) (Dist. DC March 1, 2005), 1–2.
7. Fred Shaheen and Natalia Geren, "Penalties Get Tougher for FCPA Violations," *National Defense*, September 1, 2005, 50.
8. *SEC v. The Titan Corporation*, 16.
9. Stanley A. Twardy Jr. and Daniel E. Wenner, "One Rogue Worker Can Take an Entire Company Down," *National Law Journal*, July 16, 2009, www.law.com/jsp/ihc/PubArticleIHC.jsp?id=1202432285270.
10. Ibid.
11. Richard Cassin, "Getting Loud For Justice," FCPA Blog, July 27, 2009, www.fcpablog.com/blog/2009/7/27/getting-loud-for-justice.html.
12. *In the Matter of Faro Technologies, Inc.*, June 5, 2008, 2, www.sec .gov/litigation/admin/2008/34-57933.pdf.
13. Ibid., 3.
14. Ibid., 4.
15. Ibid.
16. Department of Justice, "Congressman Williams Jefferson Indicted on Bribery, Racketeering, Money Laundering, Obstruction of Justice, and Related Charges," Press Release, June 4, 2007, www.usdoj.gov/ opa/pr/2007/June/07_crm_402.html.
17. Bruce Alpert, "Oft-Delayed Trial of William Jefferson Finally About to Begin," *New Orleans Times-Picayune*, June 7, 2009, www.nola .com/news/index.ssf/2009/06/oftdelayed_trial_of_william_je.html.
18. Ibid.
19. Ibid.
20. Bruce Alpert and Jonathan Tilove, "William Jefferson Guilty on 11 of 16 Corruption Counts; Sentencing is Oct. 30," *New Orleans Times-Picayune*, August 5, 2009, www.nola.com/news/index.ssf/2009/08/ william_jefferson_guilty_on_11.html; Jonathan Tilove, "William Jefferson Case Will Always be Remembered for Cash in the Freezer," *New Orleans Times-Picayune*, August 5, 2009, www.nola.com/news/ index.ssf/2009/08/william_jefferson_case_will_al_1.html.
21. Alpert and Tilove, "William Jefferson Guilty."
22. Ibid.
23. David Stout, "Ex-Louisiana Congressman Sentenced to 13 Years," *New York Times*, November 13, 2009, A14.
24. Jonathan G. Katz, *In the Matter of Gisela de Leon-Meredith, Respondent*, Securities and Exchange Act of 1934 Release No. 44970, October 23, 2001, United States Securities and Exchange Commission, www.sec.gov/litigation/admin/34-44970.htm.

25. Securities and Exchange Act of 1934 Release No. 44969, Report of Investigation, United States Securities and Exchange Commission, www.sec.gov/litigation/investreport/34-44969.htm.

26. Ibid.

27. Robert Khuzami (director, SEC's Division of Enforcement), "Remarks Before the New York City Bar: My First 100 Days as Director of Enforcement," speech, August 5, 2009, www.sec.gov/news/speech/2009/spch080509rk.htm.

28. D'Angelo Gore, "Corzine on Christie: Contracts for Cronies?" FactCheck.org, July 13, 2009, www.factcheck.org/2009/07/corzine-on-christie-contracts-for-cronies/.

29. Ibid.

30. Laura Craven, "Congressman Calling for Inquiry into Ashcroft Deal," *Star Ledger*, November 26, 2007, www.nj.com/news/index .ssf/2007/11/pascrell_seeks_inquiry_into_fr.html%20.

31. Gore, "Corzine on Christie."

32. Craig S. Morford (acting deputy attorney general, Department of Justice), "Selection and Use of Monitors in Deferred Prosecution Agreements and Non-Prosecution Agreements with Corporations," memorandum, March 7, 2008, 2, www.justice.gov/criminal/fraud/docs/dag-030708.pdf.

33. Ibid.

34. Ibid., 3–8.

35. Alice Fisher (assistant attorney general, Criminal Division, U.S. Department of Justice), letter to General Services Administration, Washington, DC, regarding Comments on FAR Case 2007-006, January 14, 2008. www.usdoj.gov/criminal/npftf/pr/statements/2008/01-14-08faag-statement-farcase.pdf.

36. Federal Acquisition Rule Disclosure Requirements, U.S. Department of Commerce, Office of Inspector General, www.oig.doc.gov/oig/FAR_Disclosure_Req.html.

37. Federal Acquisition Rule 52.203-13, www.acquisition.gov/far/cur rent/html/52_200_206.html.

CHAPTER 4

Global Anti-Corruption Efforts

Olusegun Obasanjo, the former President of Nigeria, who fought bribery and corruption during his years in leadership, called corruption "the greatest single bane of our society today." He should know as Nigeria has faced the effects of entrenched corruption since its formation as a country and rule by a succession of corrupt dictators. Corruption is a way of life in Nigeria as it is in many parts of the world. While it's much too early to say that society has turned the corner on this massive problem, anti-corruption activities and initiatives have taken hold and are making a difference. A multitude of countries and organizations such as the United Nations, the World Bank, Transparency International, and many others are united in the fight against corruption. This focused effort has brought needed changes in laws and how business operates throughout the world.

It is as if the rest of the world is finally realizing the evil of corruption. We are seeing more anti-corruption activities in the last few years than at any other time. That is a very good development. Global anti-corruption initiatives are a result of a number of converging factors. There is a different regulatory environment as a result of the corporate scandals of Enron, WorldCom, Adelphia, and other companies. These massive frauds spawned the enactment of Sarbanes-Oxley (SOX) in 2002 and increased scrutiny and regulation.

GLOBALIZATION OF LAW ENFORCEMENT COOPERATION

The globalization the world has witnessed has extended beyond business and into the world of law enforcement. Anti-corruption activity is being given the worldwide attention it so desperately needs. Police and prosecutors are working together to prosecute corruption like never before. While there was a time police authorities did not fully share intelligence or cooperate in investigations, there has been a sea change in fighting corruption and bribery. This transformation has resulted in a significant improvement of cross-border cooperation and investigative successes.

There are several reasons for this change. Governments are recognizing that corruption is a destabilizing force that impacts their standing in the world community. In addition, developing countries want to create a level playing field for business competition, no matter where they do business.[1] The United States' increasing enforcement of the Foreign Corrupt Practices Act (FCPA) has sent a strong message to other countries. Other countries are slowly adopting FCPA-like statutes and enforcement. "International harmonization of antifraud and anti-corruption regulation will lead to more parallel investigations, with the likely consequence of increased penalties."[2] This quote from a July 2009 PricewaterhouseCoopers report on anti-corruption compliance sums it up very well.

The Department of Justice (DOJ) and Securities and Exchange Commission (SEC) have become more focused on FCPA enforcement than at any time since the act's enactment. Self-disclosure of FCPA violations has been extraordinary and has caught the attention of foreign regulators and prosecutors. More and more countries are embracing the tenets of the Organisation for Economic Co-operation and Development (OECD) Anti-Bribery Convention. The OECD is increasing pressure on convention signatories to heighten visibility around anti-corruption enforcement. The increasing interactions and cooperation among international enforcement agencies has helped U.S. prosecutors bring record numbers of cases and settlements. Cross-border and collaborative investigations in other countries have grown and will continue to do so. Germany, Brazil, France, Nigeria, Korea, and other countries are increasingly focused on anti-corruption efforts.

Another contributing factor is that over the last two decades, there has been a significant increase in both the adoption of international antibribery agreements and the creation of anti-corruption organizations. The many agreements, organizations, and efforts are focused on reducing bribery and corruption through increased legislation, interactions and cooperation, and awareness, as well as prevention.

INTERNATIONAL ANTIBRIBERY EFFORTS

OECD Convention on Combating Bribery

The OECD was established in 1961 to bring together the governments of member countries in an effort to improve democracy and the world economy. The OECD commitments encompass economic development and growth, increasing employment and living standards, maintaining financial stability, and world trade. There are 30 member countries including Australia, Japan, Korea, Germany, France, Turkey, United Kingdom, Mexico, Canada, and the United States.[3]

Although the United States enacted the FCPA in 1977 to attack bribery and corruption, the rest of the world did not apply the same level of urgency to this issue. Through many years of efforts by the United States and other interested countries, the OECD decided to act. In November 1997, the 29 member countries unanimously agreed on principles to combat bribery of foreign government officials in international business dealings. On December 17, 1997, the OECD members and nonmember nations signed the OECD Convention on Combating Bribery of Foreign Public Officials in International Business Transactions.

The signatory nations agreed to enact legislation similar to the FCPA outlawing bribery of public officials, and to create a legal basis for extradition and international cooperation. The OECD details its stance on fighting corruption in the following anti-corruption overview from their web site:

Corruption threatens good governance, sustainable economic development, democratic process, and fair business practices. The OECD has been a global leader in the fight against corruption for over a decade. Our multidisciplinary approach addresses corruption in business, taxation, development aid, and governance in member countries and beyond.

In today's interconnected world, corruption's damaging effects spread far beyond where the corrupt act is committed, throughout the global economy and society. Technological advances have made acts of corruption easier to commit and harder to detect.

In order to effectively fight corruption—both at home and internationally—transparency, accountability, and integrity in the public and private sectors are necessary.

77

The OECD has been a key player in the fight against corruption for more than a decade, and the Organisation continues to take the lead in setting and promoting international anti-corruption standards and principles by:

- *Combating the "supply side" of bribery*
- *Preventing bribery through export credits*
- *Denying tax deductibility of bribes*
- *Promoting responsible business conduct*
- *Preventing corruption in the public sector*
- *Improving governance through development assistance*
- *Initiatives with non-member economies[4]*

The OECD Convention has been signed by 38 countries and its influence is growing. There is no doubt that the OECD Convention has had an impact on anti-corruption activities and legislation. Signatories have a requirement to pass legislation that makes bribery and corruption a criminal offense. This includes individuals or corporate entities that "intentionally offer, promise, or give any undue pecuniary or other advantage, whether directly or through intermediaries, to a foreign public official, for that official or for a third party, in order that the official act or refrain from acting in relation to the performance of official duties, in order to obtain or retain business, or other improper advantage in the conduct of international business."[5] A foreign public official is defined as "any person holding a legislative, administrative, or judicial office of a foreign country, whether appointed or elected; any person exercising a public function for a foreign country, including for a public agency or public enterprise; and any official or agent of a public international organization."[6]

Yet, there are some key weaknesses in the OECD Convention language as noted by Transparency International:

- Excludes coverage of facilitation payments (also known as "grease" payments)
- Inadequately covers foreign subsidiaries
- Inadequately covers foreign political parties and party officials
- Does not cover private sector bribery (private-to-private)
- Does not include preventive measures, except for the accounting provisions
- Contains no provisions on whistleblowers or witness protection[7]

Prior to the signing of the convention, 11 OECD members including Germany, France, and the United Kingdom, allowed tax deductions for bribery of foreign officials as a legitimate business expense. Pressure from other OCED members has helped to enhance both enforcement and antibribery legislation. Still, much work needs to be done. According to a 2009 Transparency International report on the enforcement of the OECD Convention, only 15 member countries, including Korea, France, Germany, and the United States, were either actively or moderately enforcing the principles of the OECD Convention on Combating Bribery. The report found that the other signatory countries including Australia, Brazil, Canada, and Ireland have little or no enforcement.[8]

Inter-American Convention Against Corruption

On March 29, 1996, the member states of the Organization of American States (OAS), met in Caracas, Venezuela to ratify the OAS Inter-American Convention Against Corruption. This was the first international anti-corruption legal instrument to detect and deter corruption throughout the Americas. It criminalized specified acts of corruption, designed provisions for extradition, seizure of assets, mutual legal agreements, and technical assistance among Member States. The purpose of the Convention was twofold:

1. *To promote and strengthen the development by each of the States' Parties of the mechanisms needed to prevent, detect, punish, and eradicate corruption*
2. *To promote, facilitate, and regulate cooperation among the States' Parties to ensure the effectiveness of measures and actions to prevent, detect, punish, and eradicate corruption in the performance of public functions and acts of corruption specifically related to such performance.*[9]

The Preamble of the Convention reads as follows:

The member states of the Organization of American States,

CONVINCED that corruption undermines the legitimacy of public institutions and strikes at society, moral order and justice, as well as at the comprehensive development of peoples;

CONSIDERING that representative democracy, an essential condition for stability, peace and development of the region, requires, by its nature, the

79

combating of every form of corruption in the performance of public functions, as well as acts of corruption specifically related to such performance;

PERSUADED that fighting corruption strengthens democratic institutions and prevents distortions in the economy, improprieties in public administration and damage to a society's moral fiber;

RECOGNIZING that corruption is often a tool used by organized crime for the accomplishment of its purposes;

CONVINCED of the importance of making people in the countries of the region aware of this problem and its gravity, and of the need to strengthen participation by civil society in preventing and fighting corruption;

RECOGNIZING that, in some cases, corruption has international dimensions, which requires coordinated action by States to fight it effectively;

CONVINCED of the need for prompt adoption of an international instrument to promote and facilitate international cooperation in fighting corruption and, especially, in taking appropriate action against persons who commit acts of corruption in the performance of public functions, or acts specifically related to such performance, as well as appropriate measures with respect to the proceeds of such acts;

DEEPLY CONCERNED by the steadily increasing links between corruption and the proceeds generated by illicit narcotics trafficking which undermine and threaten legitimate commercial and financial activities, and society, at all levels;

BEARING IN MIND the responsibility of States to hold corrupt persons accountable in order to combat corruption and to cooperate with one another for their efforts in this area to be effective; and

DETERMINED to make every effort to prevent, detect, punish and eradicate corruption in the performance of public functions and acts of corruption specifically related to such performance.[10]

In January 2002, the OAS Member States established the Mechanism for Follow-Up on the Implementation of the Inter-American Convention against Corruption (MESICIC) to evaluate the performance of the Inter-American Convention Against Corruption. MESICIC promotes the implementation of the Inter-American Convention Against Corruption (ICAC) to ensure its goals are met, including the exchange of best practices around such areas as conflicts of interest, procurement activities, obligation of public officials to report acts of corruption, systems for protecting whistleblowers, and classification of acts of corruption. The OAS Anti-Corruption Portal of the Americas provides additional

80

information on the ICAC, the MESICIC framework, anti-corruption activities, policy development, and technical cooperation efforts.

European Union Convention on the Fight Against Corruption

The European Union (EU) Convention on the Fight Against Corruption was adopted on May 26, 1997 in Brussels by the Member States of the European Union. The EU Convention was enacted to fight corruption involving both government officials and corporate employees within the Member States or European communities. Judicial cooperation in criminal matters, asserting criminal liability to business leaders for the acts of their employees, and classifying the types of corruption are hallmarks of the EU Convention. Passive corruption is defined as the direct or indirect request or receipt of a bribe for requester or a third party. Active corruption is defined as the direct or indirect promise of a bribe to a government official or other third party. Each Member State must criminalize this corrupt conduct.[11]

African Union Convention on Preventing and Combating Corruption

Bribery and corruption have been endemic throughout Africa and have impacted the growth and development of the region. Recognizing that, the African Union came together after years of debate and meetings to adopt anti-corruption principles. On July 11, 2003, the African Union Convention on Preventing and Combating Corruption (AU Convention) was adopted in Maputo, Mozambique. All but eight African member countries have signed the AU Convention. Those eight include Botswana, Central African Republic, Cape Verde, Egypt, Eritrea, Sahrawi Arab Democratic Republic, Democratic Republic of Sao Tome and Principe, and Tunisia. Morocco is not a member of the African Union.

The five principles of the Convention are as follows:

1. *Respect for democratic principles and institutions, popular participation, the rule of law, and good governance.*

2. *Respect for human and peoples' rights in accordance with the African Charter on Human and Peoples Rights and other relevant human rights instruments.*

3. *Transparency and accountability in the management of public affairs.*

4. *Promotion of social justice to ensure balanced socio-economic development.*

5. *Condemnation and rejection of acts of corruption, related offences, and impunity.*[12]

The AU Convention covers bribery, illicit enrichment, diversion of property, concealment of bribery proceeds, and conspiracy as acts of corruption and related offenses. It mandated the criminalization of these acts, the creation and maintenance of public anti-corruption agencies, measures to create and strengthen internal accounting and auditing functions, protection of informants and whistleblowers, measures to improve reporting of corruption, and education and awareness activities. Other areas covered include preventing corruption in the private sector, cooperation and mutual legal assistance among AU member countries, extradition, and international cooperation.

Council of Europe Criminal Law Convention on Corruption

The Council of Europe Criminal Law Convention on Corruption (COE Convention) was an additional instrument adopted in the fight against corruption in the European Union. It was clear that the prior EU Convention on the Fight Against Corruption did not go far enough, especially in enforcement and monitoring functions. The COE Convention includes both criminal and civil articles and is similar to other conventions enacted elsewhere in the world. It was signed by the member and nonmember States of the Council of Europe on January 27, 1999 and went into effect on July 1, 2002. The United States signed the COE Convention on October 10, 2000.

The COE Convention is wide-ranging in scope. It criminalizes a significant number of corrupt practices. It includes increased cooperation, not only among COE members but improved international cooperation in prosecutions. The COE Convention specifically prohibits trading in influence and the use of local agents specifically for their ability to influence public officials. The following corrupt acts are covered:

- Bribery of domestic and foreign public officials
- Bribery of national and foreign parliamentarians and of members of international parliamentary assemblies
- Bribery in the private sector
- Bribery of international civil servants
- Bribery of domestic, foreign, and international judges and officials of international courts
- Trading in influence
- Money-laundering of proceeds from corruption offenses
- Accounting offenses connected with corruption offenses[13]

82

The COE Convention covers monetary sanctions for both civil and criminal offenses. It incorporates penalties for aiding and abetting corruption, protocols for immunity, protection of witnesses and others cooperating with investigations, establishing anti-corruption agencies, as well as seizure and forfeiture of criminal proceeds. Similar to other conventions, the COE Convention provides for enhanced international cooperation including mutual legal assistance, extradition, and sharing of information in investigations and prosecutions.[14]

The introduction to the Explanatory Report of the COE Convention contains an interesting overview of corruption from a historical standpoint, how the acceptance of corruption has changed, and how anti-corruption enforcement is now critical.

Corruption has existed ever since antiquity as one of the worst and, at the same time, most widespread forms of behavior, which is inimical to the administration of public affairs. Naturally, over time, customs as well as historical and geographical circumstances have greatly changed public sensitivity to such behavior, in terms of the significance and attention attached to it. As a result, its treatment in laws and regulations has likewise changed substantially. In some periods of history, certain "corrupt" practices were actually regarded as permissible, or else the penalties for them were either fairly light, or generally not applied. In Europe, the French Napoleonic Code of 1810 may be regarded as a landmark at which tough penalties were introduced to combat corruption in public life, comprising both acts which did not conflict with one's official duties and acts which did. Thus, the arrival of the modern State-administration in the 19th century made public officials' misuse of their offices a serious offence against public confidence in the administration's probity and impartiality.

Notwithstanding the long history and the apparent spread of the phenomenon of corruption in today's society, it seemed difficult to arrive at a common definition and it was rightly said "no definition of corruption will be equally accepted in every nation." Possible definitions have been discussed for a number of years in different fora but it has not been possible for the international community to agree to on a common definition. Instead international fora have preferred to concentrate on the definition of certain forms of corruption, e.g. "illicit payments" (UN), "bribery of foreign public officials in international business transactions" (OECD), "corruption involving officials of the European Communities or officials of Member States of the European Union" (EU).

Even if no common definition has yet been found by the international community to describe corruption as such, everyone seems at least to agree that certain political, social, or commercial practices are corrupt. The qualification of some practices as "corrupt" and their eventual moral reprobation by public opinion vary however from country to country and do not necessarily imply that they are criminal offences under national criminal law.

More recently, the deepening interest and concern shown in such matters everywhere have produced national and international reactions. From the beginning of the 90s corruption has always been in the headlines of the press. Although it had always been present in the history of humanity, it does appear to have virtually exploded across the newspaper columns and law reports of a number of States from all corners of the world, irrespective of their economic or political regime. Countries of Western, Central, and Eastern Europe have been literally shaken by huge corruption scandals and some consider that corruption now represents one of the most serious threats to the stability of democratic institutions and the functioning of the market economy.

This illustrates that corruption needs to be taken seriously by Governments and Parliaments. The fact that corruption is widely talked of in some States and not at all in others, is in no way indicative that corruption is not present in the latter because no system of government and administration is immune to corruption. In such countries corruption may be either non-existent (which seems in most cases rather improbable), or so efficiently organised as not to give rise to suspicion. In some cases silence over corrupt activities is merely the result of citizen's resignation in face of widespread corruption. In such situations corruption is seen no longer as unacceptable criminal behavior, liable to severe sanctions, but as a normal or at least necessary or tolerated practice. The survival of the State is at stake in such extreme cases of endemic corruption.[15]

United Nations Convention Against Corruption

The United Nations Convention Against Corruption was created in 2003 and fully adopted on December 14, 2005 after ratification by the 30th state. As described in the related United Nations press release announcing the ratification, the Convention "is the first global instrument designed to assist Member States to fight corruption in both the public and private sectors, and given the inclusion of a mechanism that allows countries to recover billions in stolen assets, is considered a landmark achievement."[16] Some of the relevant articles of the Convention Against Corruption include:

- *Article 5:* Each State Party shall establish and promote effective practices aimed at preventing corruption. They will also evaluate the legal and administrative measures currently in existence, determining their effectiveness.

84

- *Article 8:* Create a code of conduct for public officials including the reporting of corrupt acts.
- *Article 9:* Develop appropriate systems of procurement based on transparency, competition, and objective criteria in decision-making that will prevent corruption.
- *Article 10:* Enhance transparency in public administration, protection of privacy and personal data, simplifying administrative procedures to facilitate public access to decision-making authorities, and public reporting on the risks of corruption in public administration.
- *Article 11:* Strengthen the integrity and prevention of corruption among members of the judiciary and prosecution agencies.
- *Article 12:* Enact measures to prevent corruption in the private sector, enhancing accounting and auditing standards, and appropriate civil, administrative, as well as criminal penalties for violations. These measures should include:
  - Closer interaction and cooperation between law enforcement agencies and the private sector
  - Codes of conduct for the private sector
  - Preventing conflicts of interest
  - Promoting ethical business practices
  - Improved corporate governance
  - Strengthened regulatory oversight to detect and deter corruption and bribery[17]

In order to prevent corruption, each State Party shall take such measures as may be necessary, in accordance with its domestic laws and regulations regarding the maintenance of books and records, financial statement disclosures, and accounting and auditing standards, to prohibit the following acts carried out for the purpose of committing any of the offences established in accordance with this Convention:

- Establishment of off-the-books accounts
- Making of off-the-books or inadequately identified transactions
- Recording of non-existent expenditures
- Entry of liabilities with incorrect identification of their objects
- Use of false documents
- Intentional destruction of bookkeeping documents earlier than foreseen by the law[18]

United Nations Global Compact

The United Nations Global Compact is a strategic policy initiative advanced by the United Nations to strongly support and encourage corporate citizenship on a worldwide level. The Global Compact's intent is to encourage businesses in "aligning their operations and strategies with ten universally accepted principles in the areas of human rights, labour, environment, and anti-corruption."[19] The Anti-Corruption Principle is asserted as Principle 10 and states that "Businesses should work against corruption in all forms, including extortion and bribery."[20] Principle 10 was included in the Global Compact on June 24, 2004 to reinforce the message that the private sector is also responsible for eliminating corruption. The Anti-Corruption Principle is an extension of the legal principle and work of the United Nations Convention Against Corruption.

The Global Compact embraces the OECD definition of extortion as "the act of asking or enticing another to commit bribery [that] becomes extortion when this demand is accompanied by threats that endanger the personal integrity or the life of the private actors involved." They also embrace Transparency International's definition of bribery as "an offer or receipt of any gift, loan, fee, reward, or other advantage to or from any person as an inducement to do something which is dishonest, illegal, or a breach of trust, in the conduct of the enterprise's business."[21]

The Global Compact recommends that businesses employ the three elements of Principle 10 in fighting corruption. These steps are as follows:

1. *Internal: As a first and basic step, introduce anti-corruption policies and programs within their organizations and their business operations*
2. *External: Report on the work against corruption in the annual Communication on Progress; and share experiences and best practices through the submission of examples and case stories*
3. *Collective: Join forces with industry peers and with other stakeholders*[22]

Canada's Corruption of Foreign Public Officials Act

Canada has been active in anti-corruption initiatives, both inside the country and throughout the world. The OECD is but one of the various international forums they have been involved in. Canada ratified the OECD Convention on December 17, 1998 and enacted their Corruption of Foreign Public Officials Act on February 14, 1999. The Corruption of Foreign Public Officials Act contains three separate offenses. They

86

include bribing a foreign public official, laundering property and proceeds, and possession of stolen property and proceeds of criminal activity.

The bribery offense states that "Every person commits an offense who, in order to obtain or retain an advantage in the course of business, directly or indirectly gives, offers or agrees to give or offer a loan, reward, advantage, or benefit of any kind to a foreign public official or to any person for the benefit of a foreign public official; as consideration for an act or omission by the official in connection with the performance of the official's duties or functions; or to induce the official to use his or her position to influence any acts or decisions of the foreign state or public international organization for which the official performs duties or functions."[23]

Canada has jurisdiction if the offense occurs in whole or in part in its territory. There is a five-year maximum prison sentence upon conviction for individuals. Corporations face fines for violations. Facilitation payments are allowed under the Act as long as they are made "to expedite or secure the performance by a foreign public official" of any "act of a routine nature" that is part of the foreign public official's duties or functions.[24] The Royal Canadian Mounted Police investigates violations of the Corruption of Foreign Public Officials Act. They have established International Anti-Corruption Units to investigate related allegations involving Canadian individuals and businesses bribing foreign public officials.

COMPLIANCE INSIGHT 4.1: INTERPOL FIGHTS CORRUPTION

The International Criminal Police Organization (INTERPOL) is actively involved in the war on corruption. INTERPOL is the world's largest international police organization. With 187 member countries as partners, INTERPOL's mission is to facilitate cross-border cooperation to prevent and combat international crime. Fighting corruption worldwide is one of INTERPOL's six priorities related to crime. Reducing the impact of corruption has been an INTERPOL focus area since 1998. The organization understands how corruption plays a role in terrorism and other international criminal activity and the importance of a global response to investigate and prevent it.

INTERPOL has implemented a number of anti-corruption initiatives that include:

(continued)

(*continued*)

- Creation of Global Standards to Combat Corruption in Police Forces/Services that was adopted in September 2002 to promote high standards of honesty, integrity, and ethics in the world's law enforcement agencies. The standards also provide a framework to prevent corruption and promote anti-corruption measures for each member. These standards mirror those of the United Nations Convention Against Corruption

- Adoption of a Code of Ethics and Code of Conduct for all law enforcement officers

- Establishment of a collection of best practices to assist corruption investigators in their work. This Library of Best Practices includes anti-corruption strategies and structures, undercover investigations, operatives and techniques, witness protection, anti-corruption legislation, prevention, training, and education

- Design of a Police Integrity Survey to benchmark the capacity of INTERPOL member countries to combat corruption

- Sharing of international contact points so law enforcement agencies in different countries can quickly connect and jointly work together in cross-border corruption investigations[25]

In October 2008, INTERPOL joined forces with the United Nations Office on Drugs and Crime (UNODC) to establish a ground-breaking International Anti-Corruption Academy that will be located just outside Vienna, Austria. The Academy is expected to be a center of excellence in anti-corruption education, research, and training for anti-corruption professionals. "This partnership agreement between INTERPOL and UNODC to establish the world's first and only International Anti-Corruption Academy demonstrates our common resolve and commitment to educate and train police, government officials, and others to fight this serious criminal conduct which threatens the security and safety of citizens around the world," stated INTERPOL Secretary General Ronald K. Noble.[26] This new training academy will further the sharing of investigative expertise, best practices, research, as well as improve cross-group collaboration among the world's anti-corruption professionals. Partnerships such as this demonstrate a strong commitment to combating corruption and we can expect beneficial outcomes.

INTERNATIONAL ANTI-CORRUPTION ORGANIZATIONS

Transparency International

Transparency International (TI) is a leading international non-governmental organization fighting corruption through awareness and practical solutions. Its members include thought leaders from government, civil society, business, and the media to promote transparency in business, procurement, public administration, and elections. TI was founded in 1993 to be politically nonpartisan and to bring together like-minded people with one common mission: a world without corruption. The organization has grown into a global network of more than 90 chapters around the world. It has been instrumental in widely communicating the damaging impact of corruption, defined as the misuse of entrusted power for private gain, through a variety of references, materials, and tools.

TI has five global priorities in the war against corruption:

1. Corruption in politics
2. Corruption in public contracting
3. Corruption in the private sector
4. International anti-corruption conventions
5. Poverty and development

TI does not conduct investigations but they will work with organizations that do to share their knowledge, skills, and abilities. The organization's global network of chapters and associated contacts evangelize the importance of anti-corruption and use advocacy campaigns to lobby governments to implement anti-corruption reforms. TI is involved in ongoing regional and global initiatives to fight corruption.[27]

Corruption Perceptions Index

TI may be best known for its annual *Corruption Perceptions Index* (CPI) that has been published since 1995. The CPI ranks 180 countries by the perceived levels of corruption believed to exist among public officials and politicians. The scoring is determined through expert assessments and opinion surveys. For the index, TI defines corruption as the abuse of public office for private gain. CPI scores range from 10 (least corrupt) to 1 (most corrupt). Several factors are present in those nations that have high CPI scores: accountability, political stability, effective government regulations, and rule of law. The fewer of these factors present, the lower, and worse, the CPI score will be.[28] Compliance Insight 4.2 lists the top 20 countries with the least amount of perceived corruption. Compliance Insight 4.3 lists the bottom 20 countries with the greatest amount of perceived corruption.

COMPLIANCE INSIGHT 4.2: 2009 CORRUPTION PERCEPTIONS INDEX: TOP 20 COUNTRIES

Country Rank	Country	2009 CPI Score	Surveys Used	Confidence Range
1	New Zealand	9.4	6	9.1 – 9.5
2	Denmark	9.3	6	9.1 – 9.5
3	Singapore	9.2	9	9.0 – 9.4
3	Sweden	9.2	6	9.0 – 9.3
5	Switzerland	9.0	6	8.9 – 9.1
6	Finland	8.9	6	8.4 – 9.4
6	Netherlands	8.9	6	8.7 – 9.0
8	Australia	8.7	8	8.3 – 9.0
8	Canada	8.7	6	8.5 – 9.0
8	Iceland	8.7	4	7.5 – 9.4
11	Norway	8.6	6	8.2 – 9.1
12	Hong Kong	8.2	8	7.9 – 8.5
12	Luxembourg	8.2	6	7.6 – 8.8
14	Germany	8.0	6	7.7 – 8.3
14	Ireland	8.0	6	7.8 – 8.4
16	Austria	7.9	6	7.4 – 8.3
17	Japan	7.7	8	7.4 – 8.0
17	United Kingdom	7.7	6	7.3 – 8.2
19	United States	7.5	8	6.9 – 8.0
20	Barbados	7.4	4	6.6 – 8.2

Source: 2009 Corruption Perceptions Index, Transparency International.

This universally used tool has grown in popularity each year as an indicator of the level of corruption in countries of the world. More and more organizations use the CPI in enterprise risk management for their operations in the countries surveyed. The countries perceived as the most corrupt have earned that designation for good reason and companies that do business there need to be especially vigilant.

COMPLIANCE INSIGHT 4.3: 2009 CORRUPTION PERCEPTIONS INDEX: BOTTOM 20 COUNTRIES

Country Rank	Country	2009 CPI Score	Surveys Used	Confidence Range
158	Tajikistan*	2.0	8	1.6 – 2.5
162	Angola	1.9	5	1.8 – 1.9
162	Congo Brazzaville	1.9	5	1.6 – 2.1
162	Democratic Republic of Congo	1.9	5	1.7 – 2.1
162	Guinea-Bissau	1.9	3	1.8 – 2.0
162	Kyrgyzstan	1.9	7	1.8 – 2.1
162	Venezuela	1.9	7	1.8 – 2.0
168	Burundi	1.8	6	1.6 – 2.0
168	Equatorial Guinea	1.8	3	1.6 – 1.9
168	Guinea	1.8	5	1.7 – 1.8
168	Haiti	1.8	3	1.4 – 2.3
168	Iran	1.8	3	1.7 – 1.9
168	Turkmenistan	1.8	4	1.7 – 1.9
174	Uzbekistan	1.7	6	1.5 – 1.8
175	Chad	1.6	6	1.5 – 1.7
176	Iraq	1.5	3	1.2 – 1.8
176	Sudan	1.5	5	1.4 – 1.7
178	Myanmar	1.4	3	0.9 – 1.8
179	Afghanistan	1.3	4	1.0 – 1.5
180	Somalia	1.1	3	0.9 – 1.4

*Cambodia, Central African Republic, and Laos also tied for 158th place.

Source: 2009 Corruption Perceptions Index, Transparency International.

Other Transparency International Resources

TI also publishes other excellent resources and tools on corruption and bribery. They include:

- The Progress Report: Enforcement of the OECD Anti-Bribery Convention
- Global Corruption Barometer
- Transparency in Reporting on Anti-Corruption: Report on Corporate Practices

- Bribe Payers Index
- Anti-Corruption Handbook
- Corruption Fighters' Tool Kit

The Progress Report: Enforcement of the OECD Anti-Bribery Convention is an especially useful tool in comparing the progress that the OECD signatories have made in anti-corruption enforcement. Compliance Insight 4.4 provides the level of enforcement activities in OECD Convention signatory countries. Compliance Insight 4.5 lists foreign bribery cases in OECD signatory countries. Compliance Insight 4.6 lists the status of foreign bribery cases in OECD signatory countries.

COMPLIANCE INSIGHT 4.4: FOREIGN BRIBERY ENFORCEMENT IN OECD CONVENTION COUNTRIES

Category	Countries
Active Enforcement (4 Countries)	Germany Norway Switzerland United States
Moderate Enforcement (11 Countries)	Belgium Denmark Finland France Italy Japan Korea (Republic of) Netherlands Spain Sweden United Kingdom
Little or No Enforcement (21 Countries)	Argentina Australia Austria Brazil Bulgaria Canada Chile

Czech Republic
Estonia
Greece
Hungary
Ireland
Israel
Mexico
New Zealand
Poland
Portugal
Slovak Republic
Slovenia
South Africa
Turkey

Source: 2009 Progress Report on Enforcement of the OECD Convention, Transparency International.

COMPLIANCE INSIGHT 4.5: FOREIGN BRIBERY CASES AND INVESTIGATIONS

		Enforcement		
		Cases		Investigations
Country	2008	2007	2008	2007
1. Argentina	1	1	0	0
2. Australia	6	1	1	s
3. Austria	0	0	2	2
4. Belgium	3	2	s	s
5. Brazil	1	u	4	s
6. Bulgaria	3	3	1	0
7. Canada	1	1	1	s
8. Chile	0	0	0	0
9. Czech Republic	0	0	4	1
10. Denmark	13	13	1	0
11. Estonia	0	0	0	0
12. Finland	2	1	4	3
13. France	17	17	9	16
14. Germany	110	>43	>150	>88
15. Greece	0	0	0	1 or 0

(continued)

93

(*continued*)

16.	Hungary	24	23	>1	1
17.	Ireland	0	0	4	4
18.	Israel*	0	—	0	—
19.	Italy	2	2	s	3
20.	Japan	2	1	2	u
21.	Korea (Republic of)	9	9	u	1
22.	Mexico	0	0	0	0
23.	Netherlands	7	7	4	3
24.	New Zealand	0	0	6	s
25.	Norway	5	4	u	u
26.	Poland	0	0	0	0
27.	Portugal	0	u	2	u
28.	Slovak Republic	0	0	u	0
29.	Slovenia	0	0	1	0
30.	South Africa*	0	—	1	—
31.	Spain	3	2	2	0
32.	Sweden	2	1	6	15
33.	Switzerland	16	16	s	36
34.	Turkey	0	0	0	1
35.	United Kingdom	4	0	approx. 20	20
36.	United States	120	103	110	69

*First year covered in report.
u = unknown
s = some

Source: 2009 Progress Report on Enforcement of the OECD Convention, Transparency International.

COMPLIANCE INSIGHT 4.6: STATUS OF FOREIGN BRIBERY CASES

Country	Total Cases	Major Cases	Recent Major Cases	Minor Cases	Significant Penalties
Active Enforcement					
Germany	110	>10	2008	Many	yes
Norway	5	≥3	2008	Some	yes
Switzerland	16	>3	at least 2007	Many	yes
United States	120	>10	2008	Many	yes
Moderate Enforcement					
Belgium	3	≥1	2008	≥1	no
Denmark	13	some	2008	Some	No concluded cases
Finland	2	1	2009	1	unknown

France	17	some	2008	Some	no
Italy	2	1	2004	1	unknown
Japan	2	1	2008	1	no
Korea (Republic of)	9	≥ 1	2004	9	unknown
Netherlands	7	7	2007	0	no
Spain	3	2	2008	1	yes
Sweden	2	1	2009	1	unknown
United Kingdom	4	2	2008	2	yes
Little or No Enforcement					
Argentina	1	1	2006	0	—
Australia	6	6	2008	0	—
Austria	0	0	—	0	—
Brazil	1	unknown	—	1	—
Bulgaria	3	0	—	3	no
Canada	1	0	—	1	no
Chile	0	0	—	0	—
Czech Republic	0	0	—	0	—
Estonia	0	0	—	0	—
Greece	0	0	—	0	—
Hungary	24	unknown	—	unknown	unknown
Ireland	0	0	—	0	—
Israel	0	0	—	0	—
Mexico	0	0	—	0	—
New Zealand	0	0	—	0	—
Poland	0	0	—	0	—
Portugal	0	0	—	0	—
Slovak Republic	0	0	—	0	—
Slovenia	0	0	—	0	—
South Africa	0	0	—	0	—
Turkey	0	0	—	0	—

Source: 2009 Progress Report on Enforcement of the OECD Convention, Transparency International.

World Bank

The World Bank (Bank) is an institution that provides financial and technical assistance to developing countries around the world. Their mission is to reduce poverty by assisting developing countries through economic growth and improving the business environment. A key factor in achieving this is by reducing the impact of corruption and bribery. A culture of corruption limits basic services to the people who most need them: the poor, the sick, and the disabled. Restoring services, employment opportunities, and free enterprise is vital in fighting corruption. The Bank has global partnerships to fight corruption and help countries recover stolen assets while strengthening public sector governance and anti-corruption.[29]

In 2001, the Bank created an Integrity Vice Presidency (INT) as an internal group to investigate fraud and corruption, both inside and outside the organization. Since 1999, INT has investigated numerous cases resulting in the debarment of 351 companies and individuals.[30] Investigative results are referred as appropriate to law enforcement authorities for potential prosecution. There is an international hotline for the reporting of fraud, corruption, and other misconduct in Bank-financed projects. Case findings are shared with operational units in the Bank to improve anti-corruption measures.

Under former Bank President Paul Wolfowitz, anti-corruption became a key priority. On April 11, 2006, in Jakarta, Wolfowitz outlined his strategy for fighting corruption. He attacked corruption as "one of the biggest threats to development in many countries," saying that it "weakens fundamental systems, it distorts markets, and it encourages people to apply their skills and energies in nonproductive ways."[31] Wolfowitz responded with a Bank strategy focused on several fronts including using governance specialists within country offices to review outreach project design in order to reduce bribery incentives, while enhancing country corruption prevention efforts, and partnering with the private sector. Wolfowitz's aggressive campaign against corruption included suspension of loans for projects in Argentina, Bangladesh, Chad, Kenya, India, and Uzbekistan due to allegations of corruption.[32]

The suspension of hundreds of millions in loans and contracts for these countries created a backlash. Numerous critics, both at the Bank and officials outside the United States, said "that developing countries are being threatened with arbitrary punishment in a way that jeopardizes the Bank's longtime mission to reduce poverty."[33] Wolfowitz responded by saying that he has tried to rebut the myth that combating fraud is "somehow at odds with development or becomes an excuse not to provide assistance."[34] The criticism became moot when Wolfowitz resigned under pressure in May 2007 over a scandal involving lavish pay raises for his girlfriend who was also a Bank employee.

The new leadership of the Bank has continued to focus on eliminating corruption. They maintain strong global relationships with numerous stakeholders, private sector companies, civil society groups, as well as multilateral and bilateral development partners. They work closely with Transparency International as well as actively promoting the OECD

Convention on Combating Bribery of Foreign Public Officials, United Nations Convention Against Corruption Treaty, and other anti-corruption initiatives.

International Monetary Fund

The International Monetary Fund (IMF) is an international organization of 186 member countries, "working to foster global monetary cooperation, secure financial stability, facilitate international trade, promote high employment and sustainable economic growth, and reduce poverty around the world."[35] The organization is a specialized agency of the United Nations with its own charter, governing structure, and finances. Its member nations are represented through a quota system broadly based on their relative size and characteristics in the world economy.

The IMF has been concerned about the impact of corruption on its member nations and the world since 1996. At that time, the IMF stressed the importance of "promoting good governance in all its aspects, including by ensuring the rule of law, improving the efficiency and accountability of the public sector, and tackling corruption, as essential elements of a framework within which economies can prosper."[36] This continues as core policy. The IMF understands that most of the causes and consequences of corruption are economic in nature and this is factored into their lending decisions. They look for abuse and fraud, and promote fiscal transparency. They also conduct and publish research on governance and corruption although most of their papers are several years old. *Corruption Around the World: Causes, Consequences, Scope, and Cures* was published in 1998 and provides an interesting view of the rise of worldwide corruption in the 1990s.[37]

Asian Development Bank

The Asian Development Bank (ADB) is an international finance institution that assists its 67 member countries in reducing poverty and improving the quality of life for their citizens. It was established in 1996 and is located in Manila. The ADB's partners include government and non-government organizations, private sector, foundations, and development agencies. ADB's mission includes providing loans, technical assistance, grants, and thought leadership to its member countries.

In 2001, the ADB, OECD, and other member countries prepared the Anti-Corruption Action Plan for Asia and the Pacific to combat corruption in the region. It was designed as a legally nonbinding document that contained governance principles and standards for voluntary implementation. The plan contains three pillars of action:

1. Developing effective and transparent systems for public service
2. Strengthening antibribery actions and promoting integrity in business operations
3. Support active public involvement[38]

The implementation plan includes identifying country priorities, reviewing progress in the reform process, providing assistance to the reform process, and other mechanisms.

The ADB's Integrity Division is an independent unit that investigates fraud and corruption involving ADB-financed projects or ADB employees. Allegations of wrongdoing can be reported through a variety of channels including e-mail, facsimile, mail, telephone, or in person, and confidentiality and anonymity are practiced. The Integrity Division has investigated hundreds of firms and individuals resulting in sanctions, debarments, and program exclusion. This information is published on their web site.

The ADB also publishes numerous anti-corruption policy and procedures guides including:

- *Anti-Corruption and Integrity: Policies and Procedures*
- *Procurement Guidelines*
- *Guidelines on the Use of Consultants by ADB and its Borrowers*
- *Integrity Principles and Guidelines*
- *Harmonized Definitions of Corrupt and Fraudulent Practices*
- As well as many others.[39]

World Trade Organization

The World Trade Organization (WTO) is an international organization dealing with the rules of trade between nations. Their stated goal is to help producers of goods and services, exporters, and importers conduct their business by reducing obstacles to international trade and ensuring a level playing field that results in global economic growth and development. It was established in 1995 and is headquartered in Geneva. The WTO states that the "procurement of goods and services by government agencies for their own purposes is a core element of the operation of governments" and "government procurement is also an important aspect of international trade."[40]

The WTO recognizes that corruption is inherent in procurement and a well-regulated government procurement system must encompass the principles of transparency and nondiscrimination. Their procurement principles include limiting corruption and bribery through fair opportunities for suppliers to compete for government contracts. In 1997, the WTO created the Working Group on Transparency in Government Procurement to examine the transparency-related provisions in existing international instruments and national practices. There is also the Committee on Government Procurement that works to increase transparency in the awarding of government contracts.

Partnering Against Corruption Initiative

In an effort to fight global corruption, the World Economic Forum created the Partnering Against Corruption Initiative (PACI) in January 2004. PACI is committed to using the influence of chief executives to develop principles and practices that create a competitive business environment based on integrity, fairness, and ethical conduct. PACI's two overarching principles are zero tolerance for bribery and the development of a practical and effective anti-corruption program. Thus far, 140 companies have signed the PACI Principles for Countering Bribery.

PACI works closely with other organizations also focused on anti-corruption. They include the OECD, Transparency International, United Nations Global Compact, Basel Institute on Governance, International Chamber of Commerce, and other development banks and financial institutions. PACI, in conjunction with its partners, has published *Clean Business is Good Business: The Business Case Against Corruption* as a monograph on anti-corruption compliance.[41] In May 2009, PACI, again in collaboration with its partners, launched a practical tool for international companies to use in fighting corruption. The tool is named RESIST (Resisting Extortions and Solicitations in International Transactions) and is used in employee training to respond to and resist corruption and extortion demands. The guide contains 21 real-life scenarios of solicitation and extortion demands. *Resisting Extortion and Solicitation in International Transactions: A Company Tool for Employee Training* is an excellent example of how collaboration between the private sector and other organizations and institutions can effectively address corruption and bribery.[42]

THOUGHT LEADER IN CORPORATE COMPLIANCE: ALAN BOECKMANN

Innovative CEO Leading the Fight Against Corruption

"A company that discovers corruption and deals with it is an ethical company."[43] These are the words of Alan Boeckmann, Chairman and Chief Executive Officer of Fluor Corporation, who has made fighting corruption an important focus, both at his company and in his industry leadership roles. An organization's leadership sets the tone and culture for its employees. Boeckmann is an exceptional example of a chief executive with the right tone at the top. He believes that companies can have a major impact in reducing corruption through their business role and leading by example. "Companies represent the supply side of corruption," Boeckmann commented. "It is companies and individuals within those companies that pay the bribes that are demanded by corrupt officials."[44]

Boeckmann believes in the importance of a level playing field for all companies. He knows that corruption and bribery pervert honest business practices, although they may at first appear to be the easy way of winning business. Boeckmann believes that his company has been affected by competitors who were able to undercut its bids after receiving information through payoffs. "There were times when we just knew someone had paid someone off or obtained information through bribery that gave them an advantage over us," he remarked.[45] This made Boeckmann realize that companies needed to work together in fighting corruption to adopt a zero tolerance approach. Every organization needs to embrace ethical business practices and he was committed to doing that. Boeckmann reinforces that belief whether he is speaking to employees or external audiences.

Corruption has been around and accepted for centuries, and many argue that it's not possible to stop it or even slow it down. However, my thinking was crystallized from the start. I had a four-word response to that view: Do not believe it! When I became Fluor's CEO in 2001, I had already formed strong convictions on this subject.

I was sick and tired of losing business to overseas competitors who played by different rules. The engineering and construction sector has an especially large exposure to corruption, and I was frustrated that our employees were pressured occasionally to pay up. I did not want our industry—and especially Fluor—to wind up as the 'poster child' for world bribery.[46]

Boeckmann decided to get personally involved. He was invited to chair an industry group at the World Economic Forum in 2003 and then took on a more active role in the organization to attack corruption. When he learned that the construction industry was ranked as the second worst industry for corruption worldwide, this really hit home for him. Construction is a core business for Fluor and he further realized how his company, employees, and shareholders were adversely impacted by corruption. By 2004, he and other CEOs launched the World Economic Forum's PACI. Boeckmann is a strong advocate for PACI and is constantly evangelizing its benefits.

Boeckmann joined with three other CEOs of global companies, who are all members of the PACI board and PACI signatories, in the first ever anti-corruption campaign using YouTube. The video was entitled "Help Us Fight Against Corruption!" and was made at the World Economic Forum on December 8, 2008. The video appeal emphasized the work of the World Economic Forum and PACI as well as the need for the public to be engaged in fighting worldwide corruption. This video further reinforced Boeckmann's commitment to ending corruption. "With our considerable resources, practical experience, and front line position, international business must take a stand, for it is no longer enough to simply be against corruption or other unethical business practices. Global business leaders must be fully engaged in eradicating them and leveling the competitive playing field for all," said Boeckmann.[47]

Boeckmann has also reinforced the importance of robust anti-corruption policies and procedures at Fluor. The company has an Antibribery and Corruption Policy that strictly prohibits the payment of bribes. The policy states that no employee will suffer any adverse consequences for refusing to pay bribes even if this results in Fluor losing business. The policy details the risk when using third

(continued)

(*continued*)
parties and agents as well as the requirement for enhanced due diligence and monitoring in regard to agents, joint ventures, suppliers, and subcontractors. There are no exceptions to Fluor's anti-corruption policy. Employees are also trained annually in the company's Code of Business Conduct that covers the FCPA and ethical business conduct. Boeckmann believes that zero tolerance for corruption and bribery is the hallmark of an ethical company.

Boeckmann and Fluor continue to fight global corruption. The company partnered with the American Society of Civil Engineers and donated funds to create and distribute a comprehensive anti-corruption training program targeted to those who design and build capital projects. Boeckmann encourages chief executives, compliance officers, and others to take a more active role in anti-corruption activities. He wants those in responsible positions to be better trained and knowledgeable about corruption and its detrimental effects. He advocates that people find a particular corruption issue and focus on mitigating it. He is constantly enlisting all who listen to become foot soldiers in the fight against corruption and bribery.

The road to compliance starts at the top of an organization. The right tone at the top exhibited by senior management is a strong deterrence and prevention factor. In fighting corruption and the risk of FCPA prosecutions, strong and effective anti-corruption leadership like Boeckmann's needs to be emulated by all chief executives and organizations.

GLOBAL ANTI-CORRUPTION ENFORCEMENT TRENDS

The many global anti-corruption efforts, initiatives, and partnerships over the last several years are beginning to make a real difference. The increased cooperation between U.S. and international law enforcement authorities in corruption and bribery investigations has yielded very positive results. Incriminating evidence obtained from the many FCPA prosecutions is being used by anti-corruption agencies all over the world for their own investigations. While the collaboration between the DOJ and German authorities in the Siemens case is probably the best known example, there are others and we can expect to see more. The Siemens case is explored in detail in Chapter 5.

THE GOOD FIGHT AGAINST CORRUPTION

Frank Serpico, the hero New York City Police Department cop who blew the whistle on pervasive police corruption in the early 1970s, said, "The fight for justice against corruption is never easy. It never has been and never will be. It exacts a toll on our self, our families, our friends, and especially our children. In the end, I believe, as in my case, the price we pay is well worth holding on to our dignity."[48] Serpico's timeless commentary on the impact of bribery and corruption reinforce the need for a global anti-corruption commitment.

NOTES

1. Pricewaterhouse Coopers, *Corruption Crackdown: How the FCPA is Changing the Way the World Does Business*, July 27, 2009, 3.
2. Ibid.
3. The complete list of OECD member countries includes: Australia, Austria, Belgium, Canada, Czech Republic, Denmark, Finland, France, Germany, Greece, Hungary, Iceland, Ireland, Italy, Japan, Korea, Luxembourg, Mexico, Netherlands, New Zealand, Norway, Poland, Portugal, Slovak Republic, Spain, Sweden, Switzerland, Turkey, United Kingdom, and United States.
4. Organisation for Economic Co-operation and Development, The OECD Fights Corruption, www.oecd.org/document/44/0,3343,en_2649_37447_42217196_1_1_1_1,00.html.
5. Organisation for Economic Co-operation and Development, OECD Convention on Combating Bribery of Foreign Public Officials in International Business Transactions, Article 1, Section 1, www.oecd .org/document/4/0,3343,en_39048427_39049497_43131524_1_1_1_1,00.html.
6. Ibid.
7. Transparency International, "Combating Bribery of Foreign Public Officials," www.transparency.org/content/download/2558/14830/OECDSummary.doc.
8. Transparency International, *Progress Report 2009: Enforcement of the OECD Convention on Combating Bribery of Foreign Public Officials in International Business Transactions*, 10, www.transparency .org/publications/publications/conventions/oecd_report_2009.
9. Organization of American States Inter-American Convention Against Corruption, March 29, 1996, www.oas.org/juridico/english/corr_bg.htm.

10. OAS Inter-American Convention Against Corruption.
11. European Union Convention on the Fight Against Corruption, http://europa.eu/legislation_summaries/fight_against_fraud/fight_against_corruption/l33027_en.htm.
12. African Union Convention on Preventing and Combating Corruption, www.africa-union.org/Official_documents/Treaties_%20Conventions_%20Protocols/Convention%20on%20Combating%20Corruption.pdf.
13. Council of Europe Criminal Law Convention on Corruption, July 1, 2002, http://conventions.coe.int/Treaty/en/Summaries/Html/173.htm.
14. Ibid.
15. Council of Europe Criminal Law Convention on Corruption, report, January 27, 1999, www.usdoj.gov/criminal/fraud/fcpa/intlagree/related/explainrpt.html.
16. United Nations "Convention Against Corruption Ratified by 30th State, Will Enter Into Force 14 December 2005," press release L/T/4389, September 15, 2005, www.un.org/News/Press/docs/2005/lt4389.doc.htm.
17. United Nations Convention Against Corruption, 2004, 9–15, www.unodc.org/documents/treaties/UNCAC/Publications/Convention/08-50026_E.pdf.
18. Ibid., Article 12.
19. United Nations Global Compact, "Overview of the United Nations Global Compact," www.unglobalcompact.org/AboutTheGC/.
20. United Nations Global Compact, "The Ten Principles," www.globalcompact.org/AboutTheGC/TheTenPrinciples/index.html.
21. United Nations Global Compact, "Principle 10," December 14, 2005 www.unglobalcompact.org/AboutTheGC/TheTenPrinciples/principle10.html.
22. Ibid.
23. Canada Department of Justice, "The Corruption of Foreign Public Officials Act: A Guide," May 1999, www.justice.gc.ca/eng/dept-min/pub/cfpoa-lcape/index.html.
24. Ibid.
25. INTERPOL, "Additional resources for anti-corruption professionals," www.interpol.int/Public/Corruption/corruption.asp.
26. INTERPOL, "International Anti-Corruption Academy Established in Austria," media release, October 13, 2008, www.interpol.int/Public/ICPO/PressReleases/PR2008/PR200857.asp.
27. Transparency International, www.transparency.org/about_us.

28. Martin T. Biegelman and Joel T. Bartow, *Executive Roadmap to Fraud Prevention and Internal Control: Creating a Culture of Compliance* (Hoboken, NJ: John Wiley & Sons, 2006), 324.
29. The World Bank, "Governance and Anti-Corruption," http://web.worldbank.org/WBSITE/EXTERNAL/NEWS/0,contentMDK:20040922~menuPK:34480~pagePK:34370~theSitePK:4607,00.html.
30. The World Bank, "World Bank Debars Seven Firms and One Individual for Collusive Practices Under Philippines Roads Project," Press Release, January 14, 2009, http://web.worldbank.org/WBSITE/EXTERNAL/NEWS/0,contentMDK:22034560~pagePK:64257043~piPK:437376~theSitePK:4607,00.html.
31. Bank Information Center, "Wolfowitz announces World Bank anti-corruption strategy," April 12, 2006, www.bicusa.org/en/Article.2724.aspx.
32. Ibid.
33. Steven R. Weisman, "Wolfowitz Corruption Drive Rattles World Bank," *New York Times*, September 14, 2006, www.nytimes.com/2006/09/14/business/14wolf.html.
34. Ibid.
35. International Monetary Fund, www.imf.org/external/about.htm.
36. International Monetary Fund, "International Monetary Fund Approach to Promoting Good Governance and Combating Corruption—A Guide," www.imf.org/external/np/gov/guide/eng/index.htm.
37. Vito Tanzi, "Corruption Around the World: Causes, Consequences, Scope, and Cures," International Monetary Fund, May 1998, www.imf.org/external/pubs/ft/wp/wp9863.pdf.
38. Asian Development Bank, "Anti-Corruption Action Plan for Asia and the Pacific," www.oecd.org/dataoecd/38/24/35021642.pdf.
39. Asian Development Bank, "Anti-Corruption Policy and Procedures," www.adb.org/Integrity/policy-procedures.asp.
40. World Trade Organization, "Government Procurement," www.wto.org/english/tratop_e/gproc_e/gproc_e.htm.
41. Partnering Against Corruption Initiative, *Clean Business is Good Business: The Business Case against Corruption*, June 27, 2008, www.weforum.org/pdf/paci/BusinessCaseAgainstCorruption.pdf.
42. Partnering Against Corruption Initiative, *Resisting Extortion and Solicitation in International Transactions*, www.weforum.org/pdf/paci/PACI_RESIST.pdf.

43. Lisa Roner, "Choose Honesty, And Get More Business," *Ethical Corporation Magazine*, June 5, 2007, www.ethicalcorp.com/content .asp?ContentID=5135.
44. Jennifer Warren, "Fluor CEO Talks About the Challenges and Rewards of Going Global," *D Magazine*, July/August 2007, www .dmagazine.com/Home/2007/06/07/Fluor_CEO_Talks_about_the_ Challenges_and_Rewards_of_Going_Global.aspx?p=1.
45. Roner, "Choose Honesty, And Get More Business."
46. Alan Boeckmann (speech, Ethics and Compliance Officer Association 2007 Annual Business Ethics & Compliance Conference, Los Angeles, CA, September 26, 2007), www.fluor.com/SiteCollectionDocuments/ in_ECOA_speech.pdf.
47. Alan Boeckmann, "Clean Business Is Good Business: The Business Case against Corruption" (remarks, July 17, 2008), www .unglobalcompact.org/docs/news_events/8.1/clean_business_is_good_ business.pdf.
48. Official Frank Serpico web site, www.frankserpico.com/bio_message .html.

CHAPTER 5

Siemens: A New Commitment to a Culture of Compliance

"The key message is that only clean business is Siemens business."[1] With those strong words, CEO Peter Loescher reinforced the new rules and principles of the Siemens Business Conduct Guidelines. This declaration from October 2007, constantly repeated, is a striking difference from the way Siemens operated just a few years earlier. The fact is that for almost two decades, some Siemens employees engaged in a pervasive scheme to bribe foreign government officials on a worldwide basis to obtain and retain business.

For a company with a proud and innovative history dating back to 1847, nothing is more painful and embarrassing than to be connected to the largest bribery investigation and prosecution ever conducted. That was the predicament that German engineering giant Siemens AG, a member of the Fortune Global 500, found itself in. The damaging revelations were outlined in government charging documents released to the public in December 2008. "From the 1990s through 2007, Siemens engaged in a systematic and widespread effort to make and hide hundreds of millions of dollars in bribe payments across the globe."[2]

Yet, as Siemens had embraced a culture of bribery and corruption as a practice for many years, they just as quickly realized the error of their ways and took profound steps to rectify the wrongdoing. As the U.S. Department of Justice (DOJ) emphasized, Siemens cooperated extensively with authorities, accepted full responsibility for their actions, conducted an exhaustive internal investigation, and provided law enforcement with significant evidence of illegality. This chapter will detail both the entrenched corruption and the birth of a culture of compliance.

COMPANY OVERVIEW AND HISTORY

Siemens AG is a recognized global leader in electronics and electrical engineering, operating in the industry, energy, and health care sectors. Its extensive products and services range from design and construction of some of the world's most sophisticated power plants and trains to the manufacture and sale of light bulbs. The company has over 430,000 employees in more than 190 countries. As stated on its web site, for over 160 years, Siemens has stood for technical achievements, innovation, quality, reliability, and internationality. In 2001, the company was listed on the New York Stock Exchange (NYSE). In fiscal year 2008, Siemens had revenue of $110.82 billion.

Siemens was founded by Werner von Siemens in Berlin in 1847 with a focus on the then new technology of telegraphy. The prolific inventor and his innovative company are credited with transforming Germany from an agricultural economy to one of the world's leading industrial powerhouses. The company opened with a major invention in its first year; that of a telegraph key that was the most advanced device of its day. In 1848, Siemens built the first telegraph line between Berlin and Frankfurt.

The innovation and inventions continued. The company built the first telegraph network in Russia in 1853 followed by an unprecedented telegraph line from London to Calcutta in 1870. In 1866, von Siemens discovered the dynamoelectric principle that opened the door for the unlimited use of electricity. In 1879, came the world's first electric locomotive and then the first electric streetcar in 1881. The inventions and industry leadership have continued through to today.

THE ROAD TO CORRUPTION

By the early twentieth century, Siemens was a global company with offices and employees worldwide. Although initially crippled by the

108

devastation of World War II, the company began to rebuild with a focus on emerging markets. Asia Pacific, the Middle East, Africa, South America, and Central and Eastern Europe were ripe markets for development. By 1997, Siemens had 45,000 employees in Asia Pacific with 70 joint ventures and 60 plants in the region. There was immense expansion in other world regions as well. Globalization was indeed paying off and by year 2001, sales growth reached a record high.

Siemens' financial success was aided by a largely unregulated business environment where questionable business practices were looked upon as the norm. Prior to 1999, German companies were able to deduct bribes paid to foreign government officials as a business expense in their tax returns. In practice, this did not always occur as the deduction required documentation evincing the fact that the bribe was a necessary part of the business transaction. In 1999 Germany implemented the Organisation for Economic Co-operation and Development (OECD) Convention on Bribery of Foreign Public Officials in International Business Transactions that required signatory countries to enact laws similar to the Foreign Corrupt Practices Act (FCPA). Even after the implementation of the OECD Convention requirements, Siemens continued to pay bribes.

Corruption and payoffs were entrenched in many of the emerging markets in which Siemens operated. Siemens was not alone as a company in paying bribes in these countries and it was an accepted and expected practice. It was so routine that Siemens' books and records reflected the words "*nützliche aufwendungen,*" a common German tax term that translates as "useful expenditures" but in reality means bribes.[3] Siemens employed a variety of corrupt practices that enabled the collection of corporate funds to be distributed as bribes to foreign government officials and others to win business. Included was the use of off-books accounts to maintain slush funds. Much of the distribution of these bribes was done through third-party business consultants.

When Siemens was first listed on the NYSE in 2001, it then came under the issuer requirements of that stock exchange. These issuer requirements included compliance with securities laws and the FCPA, but the company continued to pay bribes and conceal their existence even after joining the NYSE. Still, company officials began to address corruption with policies and procedures. An anti-corruption clause was included in all contracts with agents and other third parties that reads:

The agent shall strictly comply with all laws and regulations regarding the performance of the activities applicable to the agent. Without limitation, the

Agent agrees to comply with the requirements of the anticorruption laws applicable to the Parties.[4]

Another anti-corruption provision found in the 2001 Siemens Business Conduct Guidelines reads:

No employee may directly or indirectly offer or grant unjustified advantages to others in connection with business dealings, neither in monetary form nor as some other advantage.[5]

Despite these policies, the company continued to learn of wrongdoing by employees and not take appropriate action. In April 2004, an investigating judge in Milan, Italy issued a written opinion in an ongoing investigation that Siemens saw bribery "at least as a possible business strategy" and that bank accounts had been "disguised deliberately" to conceal the true purpose of the accounts as slush funds.[6] The judge also found that Siemens was not cooperating with the investigation. Employees were not disciplined for failing to cooperate with the investigation. The company subsequently learned of numerous corruption investigations in various countries and failed to adequately investigate the allegations. Unfortunately, Siemens' compliance program was the proverbial "paper program," ineffective in stopping corruption.

MUNICH PUBLIC PROSECUTOR'S OFFICE INVESTIGATION

The worst corruption scandal in the long history of Siemens threatened to shake the company to its foundation when serious revelations hit the headlines in November 2006. It was then that the Munich Public Prosecutor's Office announced that they had uncovered $257 million in suspicious transactions after searching the homes and offices of numerous Siemens' employees, including that of the then CEO. As a result of the searches, 36,000 incriminating documents were seized. In addition, six suspects were arrested and held in jail. The scheme involved secret bank accounts to funnel bribes to foreign government officials to obtain business deals. Corruption allegations like these were not supposed to happen in a country like Germany with a record as one of the least corrupt places in the world to do business.[7]

Within a few weeks of the raid and arrests, word leaked that one of those arrested was talking to the German prosecutors. The former sales official detailed the existence of slush funds, bribes to government officials in

110

Africa, Russia, and the Middle East, and the involvement of senior company officials. Although there were ongoing investigations of Siemens on fraud and corruption allegations in other countries, this investigation was proving to be the one that threatened to expose a myriad of criminal and civil violations. And as is often the case, a cooperating defendant who knows all about the conspiracy is the one to blow the whistle on the others.

SELF-DISCLOSURE AND SUBSEQUENT INTERNAL INVESTIGATION

As the government investigation picked up steam, Siemens realized the need to quickly respond to the growing crisis. On November 29, 2006, the Chairman of Siemens' Audit Committee, CFO, Chief Compliance Officer, other senior executives, and representatives of the outside auditor, KPMG, met and pledged to cooperate with the authorities. It began its own investigation. Siemens soon announced that it had discovered $556 million in possibly corrupt payments, an amount that was twice as much as German prosecutors had found. The slush funds were believed to have been used for bribes all over the world. Siemens contacted the DOJ and the Securities and Exchange Commission (SEC) to disclose additional information. Adding fuel to the fire, a United Nations investigative panel had previously "accused three Siemens subsidiaries of paying $1.6 million in kickbacks tied to the U.N.'s oil-for-food program in Iraq."[8]

To ensure the independence of the investigation and to prove to regulators the legitimacy of the results, Siemens chose one of the premier law firms in the world to lead the investigation. In December 2006, Siemens' Audit Committee announced that it had retained international law firm Debevoise & Plimpton, LLP to conduct an internal investigation and evaluate the existing compliance program. They were joined by forensic accountants from Deloitte & Touche. Together, they devoted large amounts of resources to the investigation. Debevoise was given a charter "to conduct an independent and comprehensive investigation to determine whether anti-corruption regulations have been violated and to conduct an independent and comprehensive assessment of the compliance and controls systems at Siemens."[9]

Siemens wanted the investigation to be comprehensive to determine how far-reaching and pervasive the corruption was in the various business operations worldwide. The investigation would focus on areas of the business with the highest risk of corruption including "operations with significant amounts of government business, large infrastructure projects, work in countries notorious for corruption, contracts procured with the assistance of outside business consultants, and projects where existing compliance files contained preliminary indications of possible bribery."[10] An important aspect of the investigation would be the past conduct of senior management and the Audit Committee, as well as their knowledge and involvement in bribery.

Legal and Fair Internal Investigation

Siemens knew that its internal investigation would be closely scrutinized by the various authorities. The company took extraordinary precautions to ensure that the investigation would comply with the laws of Germany, the United States, and other countries where the investigation would be conducted. This included the enhanced privacy and data protection laws in Germany, the European Union, and elsewhere. It also wanted an investigation that was fair to its employees. Interviews were conducted in the native language of employees. Siemens provided professional foreign-language translators when necessary. Independent outside counsel was made available to current and former employees to both prepare them for interviews and later be present in the actual interviews.

Debevoise worked closely with labor representatives to ensure the processes were followed for interviews, collecting documents and data, in addition to protecting workers' rights. There were also strict procedures to protect confidential information and other intellectual property using controls, data encryption, and security. The investigation took almost two years and included:

- *1,750 interviews with Siemens employees and other individuals*
- *800 informational briefings with employees to obtain background information*
- *82 million documents electronically searched to identify potentially relevant material*
- *14 million documents reviewed*
- *38 million financial transactions analyzed*
- *10 million bank records reviewed[11]*
- *300+ lawyers, forensic accountants, and support staff*
- *1.5 million billable hours of work*
- *$1.4 billion in fees for outside counsel and forensic accountants*
- *Investigative work in 34 countries*

112

The investigation "could not identify legitimate business purposes for approximately $1.4 billion in expenditures and concluded that approximately $805 million of the $1.4 billion was intended, in whole or in part, to bribe foreign officials."[12]

Project Office Compliance Investigation

Shortly after the internal investigation started, Siemens established a Project Office Compliance Investigation (POCI) to ensure the success of the investigation. POCI was led by senior in-house counsel and other Siemens personnel. Sixteen full-time employees were assigned to the POCI. It provided exceptional assistance in a number of ways, including scheduling interviews, providing technical support for document and data collections, and retaining local counsel to obtain requested information regarding local laws and regulations in countries involved in the investigation.

Amnesty and Leniency Programs

In October 2007, Siemens established a unique amnesty program for current and former employees to gain additional information and evidence. The program protected current or former employees who fully cooperated with the investigation and provided truthful information. The program was strongly supported by the Audit Committee and senior management. A key feature of the program was that "qualifying current and former employees would not face civil damages claims or, in the case of current employees, involuntary termination" but the company "reserved the right to impose lesser disciplinary sanctions."[13] The amnesty program did not include certain senior executives and managers; it distinguished between employees such as regional CEOs and CFOs who may have had more culpability in decision-making than lower level ones who may have been simply following the instructions of higher ups. Fairness was a key element in Siemens' amnesty program to separate those who may have been pressured to participate in inappropriate activities from those most responsible for misconduct.

In April 2008, Siemens then created a leniency program that provided specific disciplinary decisions for employees deemed significant to the internal investigation. Amnesty was used for those who lied in earlier interviews and now wanted to correct their statements. Unlike the amnesty program that excluded senior management, the leniency program included them. Both programs were very successful in furthering the Debevoise

113

investigation. More than 171 Siemens employees took advantage of the amnesty or leniency programs to provide information to the company. Previously unknown information was disclosed that led to new areas for investigation.

Cooperation with Law Enforcement

At the very beginning of the internal investigative process, Siemens made it policy that it would be fully cooperative in all phases of the government investigation. They realized that in order to benefit from any plea agreements, complete cooperation was a requisite. While the internal investigation would coincide with the government investigation, there was no question that the government investigation would take precedence. Nothing would be done to interfere or impede any public investigation. The cooperation paid off. "A substantial mitigating factor was that, during the investigations, Siemens AG cooperated extensively with the investigators and assisted them in clarifying the allegations."[14]

The Debevoise internal investigation uncovered significant evidence of corruption and bribery at Siemens operations throughout the world. Debevoise and Deloitte, as directed by Siemens, provided ongoing and extensive reports of investigative findings to the DOJ, SEC, and Munich Prosecutor's Office. There is no doubt that due to the extent of the violations, much of what was disclosed to the government investigators would not have been easily discovered if not for the comprehensive internal investigation, total cooperation, and voluntary disclosures.

Siemens knew that the outcome of both its internal investigation and that of German and U.S. prosecutors would be a corporate plea acknowledging the company's wrongdoing. Fighting any criminal charges would be imprudent given the growing volume of evidence against it. Siemens made a business and legal decision to resolve the matter and they fully believe that they achieved a substantial benefit from cooperation with authorities as well as from its revitalized compliance efforts. Siemens knew that resolving the criminal investigation with respect to the company with both German and U.S. prosecutors would help them from both reputational and financial perspectives.

Compliance Comeback

Siemens began its "compliance comeback" in November 2006 in conjunction with the internal investigation and self-disclosures. The company realized that their self-inflicted wounds would need a long and extensive rebuilding effort. The words of Warren Buffett resonated at the company: "It takes 20 years to build a reputation and five minutes to ruin it. If you think about that, you'll do things differently." The compliance efforts involved a three-phased approach. First, there was the immediate response with the selection of external experts to conduct an independent investigation, the appointment of an ombudsman, tone at the top town hall meetings and communications from the CEO and other senior leaders, restrictions on the use of business consultants, and centralized payments and bank accounts.

The second phase involved creating and implementing a comprehensive compliance program called "Prevent–Detect–Respond" that encompassed all three of these elements. Prevent included new policies and procedures, program communication, creation of a compliance helpdesk, centralization and global expansion of the compliance function, and training. Anti-corruption training was conducted for all managers and those employees in sensitive functions. Detect included worldwide compliance investigations to address the many allegations and issues being escalated, compliance reviews, and newly created compliance controls. Respond included disciplinary actions and consequences for misconduct, global case tracking of all issues received and investigated, and monitoring for compliance effectiveness and continuous improvement. Tone at the top and the overall compliance organization resonated across these three elements.

The third and ongoing phase of Siemens' compliance rebuilding focuses on becoming a "recognized leader" in corporate compliance. These efforts include elimination of material weaknesses in financial controls, robust compliance tools and simplification of business processes, compliance in incentive compensation, as well as strong policies and controls around third parties. All three phases are intended to build compliance and a "culture of integrity" into the framework of the company. Compliance Insight 5.1 provides the key elements of the Prevent–Detect–Respond Program.

CRIMINAL CHARGES, PLEA AGREEMENTS, AND FINES

The DOJ agreed to a plea agreement and penalties that while strong could have been far more punitive. The mitigating factors included the exceptional cooperation, acceptance of responsibility, and sweeping compliance

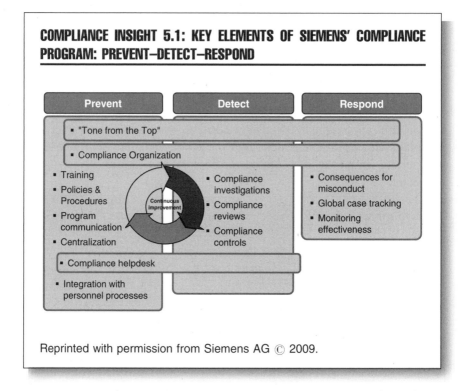

COMPLIANCE INSIGHT 5.1: KEY ELEMENTS OF SIEMENS' COMPLIANCE PROGRAM: PREVENT–DETECT–RESPOND

Reprinted with permission from Siemens AG © 2009.

enhancements. The explanation is further described in the DOJ Sentencing Memorandum:

> In accordance with the Department's Principles of Federal Prosecution of Business Organizations, the Department considered a number of factors in its decisions regarding the overall disposition. Those factors included, but were not limited to, Siemens' cooperation and remediation efforts, as well as any collateral consequences, including whether there would be disproportionate harm to the shareholders, pension holders, employees, and other persons not proven personally culpable, and the impact on the public, arising from the prosecution. The Department's analysis of collateral consequences included the consideration of the risk of debarment and exclusion from government contracts. In considering the overall disposition, the Department also considered related cases of other government authorities.[15]

On December 15, 2008, in a federal courthouse in Washington, DC, Siemens and three of its subsidiaries pleaded guilty to violations of the FCPA.

Specifically, Siemens pleaded guilty to two criminal counts involving the internal controls and books and records provisions of the FCPA. Subsidiaries in Argentina, Bangladesh, and Venezuela each pleaded guilty to one conspiracy count to violate the FCPA.

The criminal information charging document filed by the DOJ contained a section entitled "Siemens' Systematic Efforts to Circumvent Internal Controls and Falsify Books and Records." As detailed in the Information, between the mid-1990s and 2007, Siemens used the following techniques to falsify its corporate books and records:

- *Using off-books accounts for corrupt payments even after compliance risks associated with such accounts were raised at the highest levels of management*
- *Entering into purported business consulting agreements with no legitimate business purpose, sometimes after Siemens had won the relevant project*
- *Engaging former Siemens employees as purported business consultants to act as conduits for corrupt payments to government officials*
- *Justifying payments to purported business consultants based on false invoices*
- *Mischaracterizing corrupt payments in the corporate books and records as consulting fees and other seemingly legitimate expenses*
- *Limiting the quantity and scope of audits of payments to purported business consultants*
- *Accumulating profit reserves as liabilities in internal balance sheet accounts and then using them to make corrupt payments through business consultants as needed*
- *Using removable Post-it notes to affix signatures on approval forms authorizing payments to conceal the identity of the signors and obscure the audit trail*
- *Allowing third party payments to be made based on a single signature in contravention of Siemens' "four eyes principle," which required authorization of payments by two Siemens managers*
- *Drafting and backdating sham business consulting agreements to justify third party payments*
- *Changing the name of purported business consulting agreements to "agency agreements" or similar titles to avoid detection*[16]

In the period 2001 to 2007, Siemens made corrupt payments totaling $1.36 billion through a variety of payment mechanisms as detailed in Department of Justice criminal information:

117

- *Direct payments to business consultants: Business groups and regional companies made payments directly to business consultants with the knowledge that some or all of the funds would be funneled to foreign government officials.*

- *Cash desks: These were unofficial in-house banking offices that Siemens maintained for Communications Operating Group employees to withdraw large sums of cash for corrupt payments. Employees literally brought in empty suitcases to fill with cash for bribes.*

- *Barschecks: Barscheck is German for check. These were special checks from the accounting department given to managers in the Communications Operating Group who would then deposit the checks in Austrian off-books accounts. Money was then transferred to foreign government officials. The use of Barschecks stopped after the Austrian public prosecutor seized the off-books accounts as a result of an investigation they were conducting.*

- *Bearer checks: Bearer checks were created to replace the Barschecks system. Communications Operating Group employees authorized its bank in Germany to issue bearer checks to managers. These checks were cash equivalents and were deposited into off-books accounts. The managers then transferred funds from these accounts to business consultants.*

- *Payment intermediaries: Various operating groups entered into agreements with intermediaries for the purpose of transferring money to business consultants. The business consultants then used the funds for bribes to government officials. The intermediaries created phony invoices and submitted them to Siemens to generate the corrupt payments. The intermediaries kept a percentage of the funds as payment for facilitating the bribes to government officials. While Siemens used thousands of business consultants all over the world, they used a very small number of intermediaries, less than a dozen. While business consultants interacted directly with the government officials, the intermediaries did not.*

- *Slush funds: Various operating groups and a Siemens regional company in South America created slush funds controlled by Siemens managers and other non-employees at off-shore banks. These funds were pooled over time and used for corrupt payments rather than the project-specific invoices generated by payment intermediaries.*

- *Confidential payment system: This was a system outside the normal accounts payable process used to generate bribes without creating invoices. With no evidence of the corrupt payments in the accounts payable detail, there was no audit trail to follow. Funds were available to be used for any number of payments to government officials.*

- *Internal Commission Accounts: The Medical Solutions Operating Group and various regional companies created pools of money in balance sheet accounts called Internal Commission Accounts. They reserved percentages of customer prices from a variety of projects and moved them to the internal commission accounts as liabilities. The funds were later disbursed to business consultants for bribes.*
- *Other methods of payments: Besides the above listed mechanisms for corrupt payments, other methods were employed including sham supplier agreements, sham resale transactions, and receivables manipulation.*[17]

Siemens paid a $450 million criminal fine, the largest such fine in FCPA enforcement history. Siemens agreed to revamp its compliance program and retain an independent monitor for a period of four years to ensure compliance with enhanced internal controls and program development. Also, on December 15, 2008, Siemens resolved the criminal charges with the Munich Public Prosecutor's Office with the imposition of a €395 million fine. Siemens and its subsidiaries paid a combined $1.7 billion in criminal and civil penalties in the United States and Germany, including $350 million in restitution to the SEC.

NEW CORPORATE COMPLIANCE PROGRAM

As part of Siemens' acceptance of responsibility for the corporate wrongdoing and subsequent guilty plea to the violations of the FCPA's internal controls and books and records provisions, the company agreed to implement an effective corporate compliance program as follows:

Defendant Siemens Aktiengesellschaft (Siemens AG) on behalf of itself and its subsidiaries and affiliates (collectively, Siemens) represents and agrees, as a condition of the plea agreement, that its internal controls system and compliance code will include, but not be limited to, the following ten minimum elements:

1. A compliance code with a clearly articulated corporate policy against violations of the FCPA, including its antibribery, books and records and internal controls provisions, and other applicable counterparts (collectively, the anti-corruption laws).
2. A system of financial and accounting procedures, including a system of internal accounting controls, designed to ensure the maintenance of fair and accurate books, records, and accounts.

119

3. Promulgation of compliance standards and procedures designed to reduce the prospect or violations of the anti-corruption laws and Siemens' compliance code. These standards and procedures shall apply to directors, officers, and employees and, where necessary and appropriate, outside parties acting on behalf of Siemens in foreign jurisdictions, including agents, consultants, representatives, distributors, teaming partners, and joint venture partners (collectively referred to as agents and business partners).

4. The assignment of responsibility to one or more senior corporate officials of Siemens AG for the implementation and oversight of compliance with policies, standards, and procedures regarding anti-corruption laws. Such corporate official(s) shall have the authority to report matters directly to the Audit or Compliance Committee of Siemens AG's Supervisory Board.

5. Mechanisms designed to ensure that the policies, standards, and procedures of Siemens regarding the anti-corruption laws are effectively communicated to all directors, officers, employees, and, where necessary and appropriate, agents and business partners. These mechanisms shall include: (a) periodic training for all such directors, officers, employees, and where necessary and appropriate, agents and business partners; and (b) annual certifications by all such directors, officers, employees, and, where necessary and appropriate, agents and business partners, certifying compliance with training requirements.

6. An effective system for reporting suspected criminal conduct and/or violations of the compliance policies, standards, and procedures regarding the anti-corruption laws for directors, officers, and, as necessary and appropriate, agents and business partners.

7. Appropriate disciplinary procedures to address, among other things, violations of the anti-corruption laws or Siemens' compliance code by directors, officers, and employees.

8. Appropriate due diligence requirements pertaining to the retention and oversight of agents and business partners.

9. Standard provision in agreements, contracts, and renewals thereof with all agents and business partners which are designed to prevent violations of the FCPA and other applicable anti-corruption laws, which provisions may, depending upon the circumstances, include: (a) anti-corruption representations and undertakings relating to

120

compliance with the anti-corruption laws; (b) rights to conduct audits of the books and records of the agent or business partner to ensure compliance with the foregoing; and (c) rights to terminate an agent or business partner as a result of any breach of anti-corruption laws, and regulations or representations, and undertakings related to such matters.

10. Periodic testing of the compliance code, standards, and procedures designed to evaluate their effectiveness in detecting and reducing violations of the anti-corruption laws and Siemens' internal controls systems and compliance code.[18]

CORPORATE COMPLIANCE MONITOR

As part of its plea agreement, Siemens agreed to retain an independent compliance monitor for a four-year period to oversee the ongoing implementation and continuous evaluation of its compliance program and system of corporate governance. The monitor would evaluate "the effectiveness of the internal controls, record-keeping, and financial reporting policies and procedures of Siemens as they relate to Siemens' current and ongoing compliance with the books and records, internal accounting controls, and antibribery provisions of the FCPA and other applicable anti-corruption laws and take such reasonable steps as, in his or her view, may be necessary to fulfill the foregoing mandate."[19]

Siemens agreed to cooperate fully with the monitor. That included access to any and all documents, resources, facilities, and employees. There would be no attorney-client relationship between Siemens and the monitor regarding privileged information. The monitor would conduct ongoing assessments and report to Siemens and the DOJ. Siemens agreed to adopt all recommendations from the monitor and there is a process for alternative proposals. Any evidence that corrupt payments or related false books and records entries have occurred after the plea agreement date will be reported to the DOJ.

Dr. Theodor Waigel, a lawyer, judge, and former German Minister of Finance, was appointed as the monitor and will serve in that position through December 2012. Attorney F. Joseph Warin of Gibson, Dunn & Crutcher, LLP was assigned as legal counsel to Dr. Waigel. Mr. Warin is a former federal prosecutor who currently leads the litigation practice at his law firm. He has extensive experience in FCPA investigations for clients.

121

SIEMENS' REMEDIAL EFFORTS

Siemens' remedial efforts were rapid and extensive once the extent of the bribery became public.[20] Just as the company's cooperation with government authorities was exceptional, its efforts to fix the pervasive corruption were extensive. As Acting Attorney General Matthew Friedrich stated on the day Siemens took responsibility and settled the case with the DOJ and SEC, they "implemented real reforms."[21] Siemens' remedial efforts included:

- Extensive internal investigation
- Preservation, collection, testing, and analysis of evidence
- Replacing much of the senior leadership
- Enhanced tone at the top
- Reorganization of Audit Department
- Significant increase in size and responsibilities of the new compliance department

Replacement of Top Management

Siemens has changed much of its senior management including CEO, General Counsel, Chief Audit Officer, and Chief Compliance Officer. It brought in industry leaders with strong corporate governance and compliance backgrounds as well as reputations of integrity and accountability. In July 2007, the company named Peter Loescher as new CEO. He was previously an executive at Merck and General Electric (GE). Peter Solmssen was hired as General Counsel and was also given a position on the Vorstand management board to signify the importance of the role. Mr. Solmssen was previously a corporate officer with GE and General Counsel of GE Healthcare.

In September 2007, Dr. Andreas Pohlmann was named Chief Compliance Officer. Dr. Pohlmann is the former Executive Vice President and Chief Administrative Officer at Celanese Corporation where he was also responsible for legal matters, corporate governance, compliance, and risk management. Hans Winters, former Partner in PricewaterhouseCoopers' Advisory and Securities Litigation Practice specializing in forensic investigations, was named Chief Audit Officer, heading up a reorganized internal audit function. All of these leaders have extensive anti-corruption experience and that was a key factor in hiring them.

The company reorganized its operating groups into three sectors—Industry, Energy, and Healthcare—and the CEO of each sector was also appointed to the Vorstand. They are also responsible for compliance oversight within their sectors. All finance officers now report to the CFO and all legal counsel report to the General Counsel. There is also a new Compliance Committee within the Supervisory Board, with a focus on the compliance function.

Comparison of Old and New Compliance Programs

Siemens first established a compliance function in 2001. By 2004, there were several lawyers assigned to compliance in Germany. Besides working on compliance initiatives, they also had other responsibilities that limited full-time proactive compliance work. That work included defending the company against allegations and conducting internal investigations. The company had Regional Compliance Officers and Group Compliance Officers who were ostensibly responsible for compliance activities in the various business regions and operating groups. The problem was that compliance was a collateral duty for these employees who had other noncompliance responsibilities that took up much of their time. In addition, they received minimal training and direction regarding compliance.

Until late 2006, the compliance department consisted of one part-time chief compliance officer and five or six other compliance attorneys. There were 75 compliance officers in the various operating groups and regional subsidiaries but they reported to local management and were not independent or effective. The compliance office was not empowered or appropriately resourced. It had to request assistance from the audit function or other groups in order to investigate allegations as it did not have the staff or expertise. Senior management was made aware of the insufficiency of resources but did nothing. In fact, a benchmarking analysis of the compliance program at GE, requested by a Vorstand member, pointed out the severely lacking program at Siemens as compared to the comprehensive program at GE. No action was taken to supplement compliance resources.

The internal investigation by Siemens documented why the existing compliance program failed to effectively protect the company from the pervasive culture of corruption. The company did not implement suitable anti-corruption policies and procedures. It also failed to appropriately investigate and remediate allegations of corruption. Discipline of employees involved in corrupt activities was often nonexistent. The compliance department was not empowered or competent to fully address corruption.

Siemens did not candidly report to the Audit Committee the full extent of corruption and bribery at the company. Most importantly, there was a clear lack of tone at the top that should have evangelized the importance of anti-corruption policies and practices. Had Siemens communicated "that the Company would rather forego business opportunities and miss performance targets than win business corruptly," there might have been a different outcome.[22]

In stark contrast to its prior program, Siemens' expanded and enhanced global compliance organization now had the compliance function represented on the Managing Board. Strong corporate governance was now the foundation of the company and embedded in every business unit in every worldwide region.

Clear Reporting Lines

The company created clear reporting lines for the compliance function with a direct reporting to the top of the management chain. The Corporate Compliance Office was reorganized with a direct reporting relationship between the various business sectors, the regional compliance officers, and the Chief Compliance Officer. The new Chief Compliance Officer now reports to the General Counsel and the CEO.

The legal and compliance departments were combined under the leadership of the General Counsel. The Corporate Compliance Office created four new departments to develop and support company-wide compliance efforts. As Siemens noted, this "new structure offers much-needed support, clarity, and accountability for the compliance function."[23] The newly restructured Legal Department added lawyers and legal support personnel from both inside and outside the company. "Most importantly, the lawyers have been empowered to participate actively in the businesses to which they are assigned and instructed to be proactive in addressing potential compliance issues," Siemens stressed.[24]

Siemens went from fewer than 100 compliance employees to more than 600 compliance professionals worldwide today. The company created a compliance investigative unit headed by a former INTERPOL officer and a forensic audit unit headed by a former professional services firm investigations leader. The units have significantly increased the number of investigators and forensic auditors worldwide to address compliance issues and other allegations of misconduct and policy violations. The forensic audit investigators who are based in internal audit are highly skilled with forensic accounting expertise.

Training and Communication

Training and communication of compliance requirements has been a hallmark of Siemens' compliance program. The CEO is highly visible in communicating through a variety of media and messages to employees. Ongoing communications are sent to management, the global compliance organization, and all employees using e-mail, intranet, and the internal television network. Specialized training is tailored for target groups including senior management, managers, and those who interact with government officials, employees with signing authority, and new compliance officers.

Senior management includes executive leadership, supervisory board, board of management, CEOs and CFOs of divisions, subdivisions, and regional companies, and members of group boards. Training for senior management is delivered in-person in four-hour blocks by either compliance personnel or outside counsel. Managers and those who interact with government officials include personnel involved in sales and project management with regular interactions with government entities. Their training is live, in four -to eight-hour blocks delivered by local compliance officers and in-house counsel.

Employees with signing authority include employees in management positions and those with customer-facing and controller functions. Their training is one-hour Web-based sessions available in 15 languages. New compliance officers from regions, sectors, divisions, and business units receive a four-day compliance course. All employees receive anti-corruption training using a variety of in-person and Web-based training. Employee surveys are also used to evaluate the effectiveness of compliance program activities, tone at the top, learn best practices or problem areas, and receive feedback on the compliance perception at the company.

Anti-Corruption Training Program

Beginning in November 2006, Siemens developed a robust anti-corruption training program. By December 2008, more than 180,000 employees, representing over one-third of the company's global workforce, received training on compliance issues including the FCPA and other antibribery laws. It instituted ongoing meetings and conferences "designed to bring the Company's compliance officers together to discuss important anti-corruption challenges."[25]

Anti-Corruption Handbook

Siemens issued a new compliance handbook for all employees that incorporated its clear global anti-corruption policy. The company also grasped that local managers in the various subsidiaries and regions are the ones best situated to demonstrate the appropriate tone at the top and enforce the compliance culture. Full compliance with enhanced internal controls and the anti-corruption program was required in over 1,400 Siemens entities and managers are being held accountable. The company created a 24/7 compliance hotline and online compliance helpdesk for employees to both report compliance violations and ask for assistance in addressing compliance issues.

Ombudsman Program

Siemens created an Ombudsman Program to handle complaints regarding questionable business practices for people who do not want to contact the company directly. The company retained an attorney from a prominent Nuremberg law firm to act as an external ombudsman and provide yet another channel for employees or others outside the company to report business irregularities. Employees and third parties can contact this independent professional on a confidential and anonymous basis if they observe any inappropriate business practices in the company and do not want to contact Siemens directly. Communications with the Ombudsman are confidential and can be made anonymously.

Strengthened Internal Audit Function

Siemens' internal audit was consolidated from a number of separate units and functions into one 450-employee unit. The company's new Corporate Finance Audit (CFA) is part of the Corporate Finance Department and is under the auspices of a former partner of PricewaterhouseCoopers who has extensive international anti-corruption experience. The Chief Audit Officer now reports to the CFO and has an independent reporting line to the Audit Committee. The CFA has added hundreds of highly qualified internal audit staff to beef up the function. The company has made a commitment that only the most qualified and capable employees will be employed in the audit function.

The new CFA "has redesigned the internal audit methodology at Siemens, taking into consideration financial reporting integrity, effectiveness of risk management and internal control systems, and adherence to compliance."[26] All audits are now directed by the CFA and reported centrally. The recently developed Enterprise Risk Management (ERM) process is incorporated in all audit planning and strategy. The ERM process at Siemens assesses "on an enterprise-wide basis the strategic, operational, financial and compliance risks and opportunities faced by Siemens."[27] Company auditors regularly audit the compliance program on a worldwide basis for implementation and effectiveness. Siemens has mandated that all managers continuously review internal controls within their areas of responsibility with a focus on compliance with antitrust and anti-corruption laws.

Enhancing Internal Controls

Siemens has taken strong steps to enhance its internal controls to both prevent a reoccurrence of the bribery and improve its business operations and effectiveness. An interdisciplinary task force conducted an extensive review and addressed weaknesses "in controls over the use of funds, bank accounts, and the IT-based accounting systems, which contributed to improper use of Siemens' funds."[28] In addition, the new management issued new policies and procedures "designed to centralize the process of managing all bank accounts and tighten control over cash and cash equivalents."[29] The new rules and guidance include:

- Reducing the number of bank accounts held by Siemens entities and instituting rules and processes designed to ensure that all bank accounts are centrally registered and monitored at Siemens Financial Services, which is the Siemens central treasury function
- Clarifying prohibitions on Siemens' funds being held in bank accounts registered in the name of a Siemens employee or third party
- Enhancing the rules governing signature authorization for payments and other transactions
- Further centralizing and automating processes for payments to third parties
- Strengthening the restrictions on cash advances to employees and on Siemens entities keeping and disbursing cash

- Establishing a process to ensure that intercompany accounts are reconciled
- Instituting data assurance processes and additional controls over payment systems
- Updating approval processes for project management so as to address corruption risks in bidding for and performing projects[30]

Enhanced Policies and Procedures

Siemens realized that new and revised policies and procedures were needed to ensure that the past compliance failures and misconduct would not reoccur. These standards and procedures would address the specific risks that resulted in the criminal violations, evangelize anti-corruption policy creation, and reinforce ethics and values. The new policies covered high risk areas including third parties, business consultants and intermediaries, mergers and acquisitions, gifts and entertainment, and business partner due diligence. Siemens also restated its values and vision so that all policies and procedures were closely aligned with effective compliance goals. Compliance Insight 5.2 is an overview of Siemens' enhanced policies and procedures.

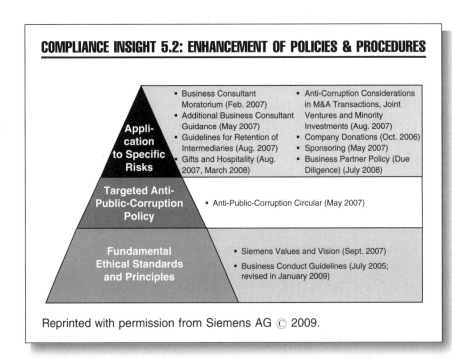

COMPLIANCE INSIGHT 5.2: ENHANCEMENT OF POLICIES & PROCEDURES

Application to Specific Risks
- Business Consultant Moratorium (Feb. 2007)
- Additional Business Consultant Guidance (May 2007)
- Guidelines for Retention of Intermediaries (Aug. 2007)
- Gifts and Hospitality (Aug. 2007, March 2008)
- Anti-Corruption Considerations in M&A Transactions, Joint Ventures and Minority Investments (Aug. 2007)
- Company Donations (Oct. 2006)
- Sponsoring (May 2007)
- Business Partner Policy (Due Diligence) (July 2008)

Targeted Anti-Public-Corruption Policy
- Anti-Public-Corruption Circular (May 2007)

Fundamental Ethical Standards and Principles
- Siemens Values and Vision (Sept. 2007)
- Business Conduct Guidelines (July 2005; revised in January 2009)

Reprinted with permission from Siemens AG © 2009.

Compliance Helpdesk

Siemens established a confidential communications channel for employees and others outside the company to report a variety of business issues including violations of the Siemens Business Conduct Guidelines. Siemens realized that there must be a mechanism for people to both report misconduct and to ask for guidance in business processes and operations. The Helpdesk provides the ability for people to ask questions and reinforces both accountability and transparency. The Helpdesk can be contacted 24/7 by e-mail, telephone, and other means in 150 languages and provides confidentiality and anonymity if asked. A professional third-party provider of hotline services maintains the Helpdesk.

The Compliance Helpdesk has five communication platforms. They include:

1. *Tell Us* function provides global, 24/7 intake for allegations of non-compliance with Siemens policies and procedures
2. *Ask Us* function answers questions about compliance and other issues
3. *Find It* function allows users to search for compliance-related information, policies, and training material
4. *Approve It* function is the platform for approvals of gifts and hospitality
5. *Improve It* function is the virtual suggestion box where people can provide ideas and recommendations to improve the compliance program

Anti-Corruption Toolkit

Siemens also established a unique compliance and financial controls program called the Anti-Corruption Toolkit that incorporates over 100 controls to fully implement its new compliance initiatives. The toolkit provides management worldwide with clear steps and deliverables to ensure implementation of Siemens anti-corruption compliance program at the local level.[31] The toolkit and its guidelines identify specific control activities that are required in each identified entity in ten designated areas. It includes examples for each activity to ensure compliance is fully understood.

The company formed a working group of numerous employees from the Finance and Compliance Departments along with 75 professionals from PricewaterhouseCoopers to develop the step-by-step guide. "The

Anti-Corruption Toolkit and its accompanying guide contain clear steps and timelines required of local management in the various Siemens entities to ensure full implementation of the global anti-corruption program and enhanced controls."[32] The team went worldwide to evaluate existing controls at select high risk entities. The information learned from these visits was incorporated into the toolkit. The cost for these remedial efforts alone exceeded $150 million.

The Anti-Corruption Toolkit includes various components including tone at the top, the overall compliance organization, case tracking, training and communication, monitoring effectiveness, and implementation of policies and procedures. The toolkit identifies control activities that must be put into practice at each business entity for overall compliance. Compliance Insight 5.3 is an overview of the ten focus areas for implementation of the Anti-Corruption Toolkit.

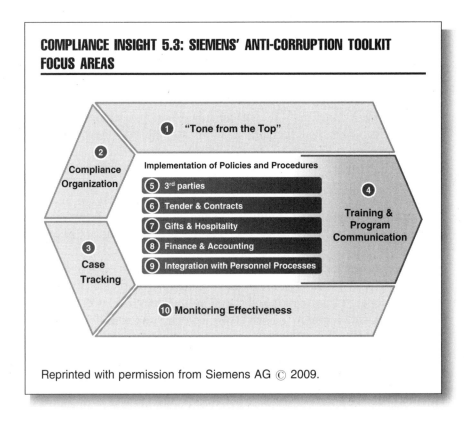

COMPLIANCE INSIGHT 5.3: SIEMENS' ANTI-CORRUPTION TOOLKIT FOCUS AREAS

1. "Tone from the Top"

2. Compliance Organization

Implementation of Policies and Procedures
- 5 3rd parties
- 6 Tender & Contracts
- 7 Gifts & Hospitality
- 8 Finance & Accounting
- 9 Integration with Personnel Processes

4. Training & Program Communication

3. Case Tracking

10 Monitoring Effectiveness

Reprinted with permission from Siemens AG © 2009.

The Anti-Corruption Toolkit incorporates the following controls to implement a comprehensive compliance program:

Prevent

- Communicate commitment to compliance from highest levels of management—both internally and externally
- Maintain a Compliance Review Board to centralize information and provide direction
- Maintain compliance infrastructure through appropriate staffing selection, training, assessment of competencies, and adequate budget
- Continuously assess compliance risks
- Communicate and train on policies and expectations
- Conduct due diligence in advance of engaging with business partners, conducting a merger, or acquisition, or entering a joint venture

Detect

- Facilitate reports of, and investigate, allegations of noncompliance
- Monitor bank accounts
- Open accounts with appropriate approvals
- Compare internal and external transaction records
- Sample payments and confirm appropriate approvals for payments to Business Partners and potentially high-risk entities and payments for gifts, hospitality, sponsorship, and donations
- Sample changes to Master Data and confirm appropriate approvals

Respond

- Impose appropriate penalties for substantiated noncompliance
- Integrate compliance and Human Resources records and objectives
- Reward management support for compliance initiatives
- Conduct background checks prior to appointing senior leaders

Business Partner Review and Approval

Business partners, consultants, agents, and suppliers helped facilitate the bribes and corrupt payments that significantly contributed to Siemens' criminal conduct. Siemens knew that it needed to effectively address this corruption risk to prevent it from reoccurring in its business. Shortly after the corruption disclosures, Siemens took a number of remedial actions to correct its compliance failures. The DOJ reported on the responsive steps taken by Siemens in mitigating third-party risk in its December 2008 Sentencing Memorandum:

> *Siemens imposed a moratorium on entering into new business consulting agreements or making payments under existing business consulting agreements until a complete collection and review was undertaken of all such agreements. Siemens also initiated, and has nearly completed, a review of all third party agents with whom it has agreements. This has resulted in a significant reduction in the number of business consultants used by Siemens. Siemens also significantly enhanced its review and approval procedures for business consultants, in light of the past problems. The new state-of-the-art system requires any employee who wishes to engage a business consultant to enter detailed information into an interactive computer system, which assesses the risk of the engagement and directs the request to the appropriate supervisors for review and approval. Siemens has also increased corporate-level control over company funds and has centralized and reduced the number of company bank accounts and outgoing payments to third parties.*[33]

Siemens established a new policy with best practices to evaluate and manage all third-party relationships. This risk-based approach includes "a risk assessment and rigorous due diligence review supported by an online tool that provides assistance, transparency, and accountability across the process."[34] Compliance Insight 5.4 is an overview of the Business Partner Review and Approval Process.

Supplier Code of Conduct

Siemens established a code of conduct for its suppliers to ensure that those who do business with the company share similar values and compliance requirements. The code "defines the basic requirements placed on Siemens' suppliers of goods and services concerning their responsibilities towards their stakeholders and the environment."[35] The supplier code specifically requires compliance with all applicable laws including a corruption and bribery prohibition. The code reinforces that Siemens will "tolerate no form of and not engage in any form of corruption or bribery, including any payment or other form of benefit conferred on any government official for the purpose of influencing decision making in violation of law."[36]

COMPLIANCE INSIGHT 5.4: BUSINESS PARTNER REVIEW AND APPROVAL PROCESS

During the Due Diligence phase, the first 3 steps are performed by the Business Unit. The fourth step (Approval Process) is conducted by management and the Compliance Organization.

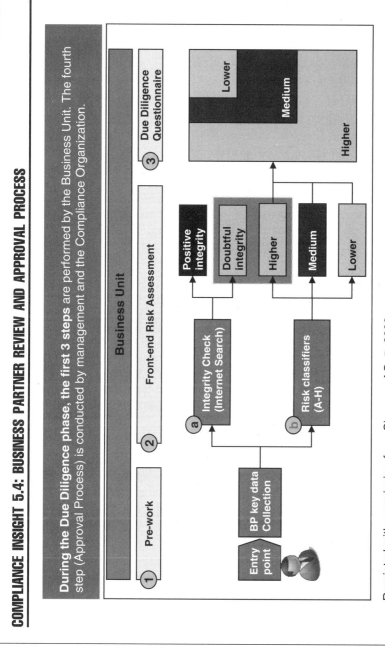

Reprinted with permission from Siemens AG © 2009.

133

Corporate Disciplinary Committee

Siemens' Corporate Disciplinary Committee (CDC) was established in 2007 and evaluates allegations of misconduct and determines appropriate disciplinary actions. The CDC is made up of the General Counsel, Labor Director, Chief Compliance Officer, Compliance Operating Officer, head of Human Resources, and the head of the relevant business unit where the violation occurred. The CDC also establishes disciplinary action precedents for the various business regions and sectors.

Compliance Element of Senior Management Compensation

Siemens has established compliance as a central management responsibility for a culture of integrity and compliance. Leading by example and enhanced tone at the top are critical actions for leaders and this compensation program provides incentives to embrace that. Senior managers can be measured in many ways. This can include how strongly they support the compliance and ethics program, how responsive they are to requests for investigative support, whether they give out appropriate disciplinary action, and how they work with legal and human resources. These measurements provide a good indicator of tone at the top. Of note, the Ethics and Compliance Officer Association has previously reported that fewer than ten percent of U.S.-based corporations tie executive compensation to the measurement of ethics and compliance.[37] Siemens wants its senior managers to live the compliance program and communicate the message that compliance is not rewarded, but expected.

Compliance Progress Report

Siemens wants its corporate compliance program and its results to be transparent and indicative of the progress they are making to become world class in compliance. On a quarterly basis, Siemens publishes information on its web site as to the status of its corporate compliance program using the three elements of Prevent, Detect, and Respond. Under Prevent, they report on training participation and Helpdesk questions received. Under Detect, they report on the number and type of allegations of business conduct violations received. Under Respond, they report on the disciplinary actions resulting from investigations and the growth of the compliance staff worldwide. Compliance Insight 5.5 is the Compliance Progress Report from Q2 FY 2009.

134

SIEMENS

Compliance – Progress Report Q2 FY 2009

Prevent

Training
- ☐ Participation in person training
- ■ Participation web-based training

in thousands; cumulative

Helpdesk
"Ask Us"

Detect

Helpdesk
"Tell Us" & Ombudsman
- ☐ Not substantiated
- ■ Substantiated

Helpdesk
Q2 topics "Tell Us"
- Other misconduct
- Conflict of interest
- Working conditions
- Embezzlement
- Fraud
- Corruption
- Other topics

Respond

Disciplinary Sanctions

243 infringements resulting in disciplinary sanctions
- Dismissal / Separation
- Others [1]
- Warning

Compliance Staff Worldwide

1) Forfeiture of variable payment elements, transfer to another position, suspension 2) Compliance only one area of responsibility
3) Including Implementation Management

© Siemens AG 2009

Reprinted with permission from Siemens AG © 2009.

135

Becoming a Recognized Leader in Compliance

Siemens' goal is to go beyond just establishing high compliance standards within the company and to become a recognized leader in transparency and compliance externally. The company wants its program to be the standard that others will want to emulate by sharing internal policies, experiences, best practices, and success stories. Siemens will achieve this by something they call Collective Action. The company does, and will continue to, reach out to industry peers and initiate joint activities to fight worldwide corruption. Compliance Insight 5.6 contains the company's objectives for 2009 to reach a gold standard of compliance.

COMPLIANCE INSIGHT 5.6: SIEMENS' COMPLIANCE OBJECTIVES FOR 2009

- Create a culture of integrity
  - Move toward a value-based culture
  - Act as change agents ("tone from the middle")
  - Make compliance a competitive advantage
- Look beyond Siemens
  - Benchmark with the best
  - Participate in Collective Action Projects. Show our commitment
  - Support the Compliance Monitor
- Become more efficient
  - Improve and simplify policies and control processes to minimize business disruption while continuing to accomplish compliance objectives

Reprinted with permission from Siemens AG © 2009.

PARTNERING WITH THE WORLD'S ANTI-CORRUPTION COMMUNITY

Siemens is doing more than just taking responsibility for its prior actions and building a culture of compliance within the company. It is committed to being an external thought leader in fighting corruption throughout the world. Siemens' corporate responsibility is furthered by its memberships and partnerships in various organizations, including those focused on anti-corruption. The company has also embarked on a number of collective action initiatives, including one with the World Bank that seeks to ensure that other multinational companies commit themselves to abide by anti-corruption principles in their worldwide businesses.

Partnering Against Corruption Initiative

The World Economic Forum's Partnering Against Corruption Initiative (PACI) was launched in January 2004 by CEOs from various industries in an effort to combat global corruption. As detailed on the PACI web site, the organization's mission "is to develop multi-industry principles and practices that will result in a competitive level playing field, based on integrity, fairness, and ethical conduct. PACI places the private sector in a unique position to guide governments' and international organizations' strategies and policies on anti-corruption and has built strong relationships with the key players and institutions from the global anti-corruption landscape."[38]

Siemens President and CEO Peter Loescher signed the PACI principles in December 2007. In February 2009, the company was made an official member of PACI. "In granting us full membership, PACI has rewarded our efforts over the last two years to effectively implement our internal compliance program. This is an important step. It shows that we've significantly improved our reputation and that people have confidence in us once again—a key prerequisite for business success," said Andreas Pohlmann, Siemens' Chief Compliance Officer.[39]

Business Guide on Fighting Corruption

Siemens partnered with a coalition of businesses, NGOs, and international organizations lead by the World Bank Institute to produce a practical business-oriented guide and Web portal to fight corruption. *Fighting Corruption through Collective Action: A Guide for Business*, released on June 19, 2008, details proven methods and strategies to fight corruption, principles of effective compliance programs, best practices, case studies from various world regions, contract templates, and lists of anti-corruption coalitions.[40]

137

THE ROAD FORWARD

Siemens corporate leadership has been very public in discussing the compliance failures at the company. While the company had policies and procedures, "the rules were not practiced, the values were not embraced, and leadership failed."[41] The company voices the costs of noncompliance in billions of dollars in fines and related costs for external consultants. Siemens' senior leaders reinforce the strong correlation between corruption and poverty, how it slows economic growth by siphoning off foreign investment, and that seven percent of the global economic product is lost to corruption. Siemens dispels the four myths of corruption:

1. Everybody does it; it's simply part of the culture in some countries
2. I did it for the company, I didn't put any money in my own pocket
3. We're having these problems only because Siemens is listed on the New York Stock Exchange
4. The U.S. government supports Siemens' competitors, especially General Electric[42]

The company's rebuilding efforts around corporate compliance has been unprecedented. The development of a new culture of compliance is on track. "The reorganization and remediation efforts of Siemens have been extraordinary and have set a high standard for multi-national companies to follow."[43] Much has been done but it will take time to ensure that the program does not weaken to just a paper program. The effort and commitment of the company strongly supports that it will not. Some of the many compliance program enhancements include:

- Top management replaced and more than 900 disciplinary actions taken against employees
- Reorganization of the compliance organization and significant increase in staff, reporting lines, and direction
- Compliance presentations to top management in over 50 countries
- 180,000 employees trained in compliance requirements
- Compliance helpdesk available 24/7 in more than 100 languages
- Compliance is a strong component of compensation of senior managers[44]

On December 15, 2008, Siemens issued a 26-page press release discussing in painstaking detail the extensive investigation and findings related to the corruption investigation and prosecution. The release also reinforced all that Siemens had done and would be doing to rebuild both its compliance program and its reputation. The last paragraph sums up quite well what the company went through and its vision for the future:

> *These last two years have not been easy ones for Siemens. But it is gratifying that so many of the Company's investors, employees and customers have remained loyal to Siemens, and that through prodigious effort and unprecedented self-examination the Company has begun to rebuild the trust of authorities in some of the most important places where Siemens does business. The Company looks forward to a future in which it is again recognized as a leader, not just in the business sectors where the Company competes, but also in corporate governance and compliance.*[45]

Effective compliance is not an option for Siemens; it's a mandate and an absolute requirement. As Joel Kirsch, Vice President and Chief Compliance Officer, Siemens Corporation, headquarters for U.S. Operations, has said, "The fact is, we will not get a second chance and another major compliance failure would likely be disastrous."[46]

NOTES

1. Siemens Business Conduct Guidelines, January 2009, 2, http://w1.siemens.com/responsibility/pool/cr-framework/business_conduct_guidelines_e.pdf.
2. Department of Justice, "Transcript of Press Conference Announcing Siemens AG and Three Subsidiaries Plead Guilty to Foreign Corrupt Practices Act Violations," press release, December 15, 2008, www.usdoj.gov/opa/pr/2008/December/08-opa-1112.html.
3. *U.S. v. Siemens, Aktiengesellschaft*, information filed December 12, 2008, United States District Court for the District of Columbia, 9.
4. Ibid., 11.
5. Ibid., 11–12.
6. Ibid., 16.
7. Mike Esterl, "Corruption Probes Threaten Germany's Image," *Wall Street Journal*, November 24, 2006, A3.
8. Mike Esterl, "Corruption Scandal at Siemens May Derail Restructuring Drive," *Wall Street Journal*, December 18, 2006, A1.
9. Siemens, "Statement of Siemens Aktiengesellschaft: Investigation and Summary of Findings with respect to the Proceedings in Munich

and the US," press release, December 15, 2008, http://w1.siemens.com/
press/pool/de/events/2008-12-PK/summary-e.pdf.
10. Ibid.
11. Ibid.
12. Marjorie Doyle, "Meet Joel Kirsch, JD, Vice President and Chief
Compliance Officer, Siemens AG, U.S. Operations," *Compliance and
Ethics Magazine*, Volume 6, Number 2, April 2009, 16.
13. Siemens, "Statement of Siemens Aktiengesellschaft."
14. Ibid.
15. *U.S. v. Siemens Aktiengesellschaft*, Sentencing Memorandum filed
December 12, 2008, United States District Court for the District of
Columbia, 11.
16. Ibid., 22–23.
17. Ibid., 24–27.
18. *U.S. v. Siemens Aktiengesellschaft*, Statement of Offense filed December 15, 2008, Cr. No. 08-367-RJL, United States District Court for
the District of Columbia, Attachment 1.
19. Ibid., Attachment 2.
20. The material in this section and elsewhere in this chapter was
graciously provided by Siemens AG.
21. Department of Justice, "Transcript of Press Conference Announcing
Siemens AG and Three Subsidiaries Plead Guilty to Foreign Corrupt
Practices Act Violations."
22. Siemens, "Statement of Siemens Aktiengesellschaft."
23. Ibid.
24. Ibid.
25. Ibid.
26. Ibid.
27. Ibid.
28. Ibid.
29. Ibid.
30. Ibid.
31. Siemens Compliance Program Anti-Corruption Toolkit.
32. *U.S. v. Siemens Aktiengesellschaft*, Sentencing Memorandum, 23.
33. Ibid., 24.
34. Siemens, "Statement of Siemens Aktiengesellschaft."
35. Code of Conduct for Siemens Suppliers, www.smed.com/Supplier
Standards/01_00_Code%20of%20Conduct%20for%20Siemens%20
Suppliers%20V2%201%20July%2031%202008.pdf.
36. Ibid.

37. Martin T. Biegelman with Daniel R. Biegelman, *Building a World-Class Compliance Program: Best Practices and Strategies for Success* (Hoboken, NJ: John Wiley & Sons, 2008), 100.
38. Partnering Against Corruption Initiative, www.weforum.org/en/ initiatives/paci/index.htm.
39. Siemens Corporate Responsibility Memberships and Partnerships, http://w1.siemens.com/responsibility/en/stakeholders/memberships .htm#toc-3.
40. World Bank Institute, *Fighting Corruption through Collective Action: A Guide for Business*, www.unglobalcompact.org/docs/news_events/ 8.1/fighting_corruption_through_collective_action.pdf.
41. Peter Y. Solmssen, "Fighting Corruption at Siemens" (presentation, University of Passau, Passau, Germany, October 11, 2008 (www .wiwi.uni-passau.de/fileadmin/dokumente/lehrstuehle/lambsdorff/ Economics_of_Corruption_2008/Peter_Y_Solmssen.pdf.
42. Ibid.
43. *U.S. v. Siemens Aktiengesellschaft*, Sentencing Memorandum, 24.
44. Solmssen, "Fighting Corruption at Siemens."
45. Siemens, "Statement of Siemens Aktiengesellschaft."
46. Doyle, "Meet Joel Kirsch."

CHAPTER 6

Worldwide Hotspots for Corruption: UK, Russia, Africa, the Middle East, and Latin America

This section, split into two chapters, aims to give the reader an overview of critical areas around the world that present a concern for Foreign Corrupt Practices Act compliance. Our intent is to highlight particular areas of significance and cases of interest in high-risk locations. One cannot hope to cover every possible issue, much less in two chapters. These chapters will look at various places around the world to assess their risk for bribery and corruption. Doing business in these countries and regions should raise a red flag for the risk of possible FCPA violations.

Different factors influence the risk levels. Cultural norms, political structures, economic pressures, and recent history all influence them. It is not just the level of corruption, but also the volume of business done in these locations. A heavily corrupt country with little international trade would create fewer FCPA risks than a medium corrupt country with a large amount of trade. For example, Somalia is ranked as the most corrupt country in the world but because of its lawlessness, the lack of a permanent national government, and very little international trade, the FCPA risk level is low. Other countries with more stable governments but where bribery is a way of doing business pose a more significant risk.

This does not mean that these areas should be avoided at all costs. In fact, many are fast growing and present numerous economic and investment opportunities. It is this growth and development that has contributed to and exacerbated corruption. On the one hand, the amount of money flowing in has far outstripped the ability (or the will) of the government to properly regulate transactions. Despite the increased revenue, the enforcement infrastructure cannot compete with the pace of the economic development. Antibribery laws and enforcement in many countries have not been modernized to reflect growth and the current worldview, and practically, they cannot handle the volume of transactions. Concurrently, bribes give corrupt officials the opportunity to enrich themselves at the expense of foreign businesspeople.

Perhaps in far-off locales companies feel more secure in paying bribes, in the sense that they are less likely to get caught, or "that's just how they do business over there." They may feel that corrupt payments are necessary to level the playing field in competing with other companies who historically use bribes to win and retain business. Conversely, companies may be less familiar with the customs of that country and would be more likely to pay bribes to move recalcitrant government officials or fall prey to local hustlers acting as third parties to broker the deals.

This chapter examines the United Kingdom, Russia, Africa, the Middle East, and Latin America. The following chapter covers Asia including China, Central Asia, India, and Asia Pacific. Along with the hotspots, we have also highlighted anti-corruption efforts from around the world. The exclusion of North America, Australia, and the rest of Europe from the list of hotspots does not mean that there are no risks associated with these countries. Nevertheless, they have mature enforcement structures, strong oversight, and a relative lack of corruption and minimal history of graft expectations.

OVERVIEW

In general, the hotspots fall into what was generally termed the third world; that term has now been superseded by the terms "developing world," the

BRICs,[1] and the Next 11.[2] However, one should not generalize from one country to another. Each country should be examined individually. What works in one would not necessarily work in another country. That being said, certain regional trends and tendencies emerge.

One trend of particular note is the link between abundant natural resources and deeply rooted corruption. This is discussed in further detail in the following section. The implementation of anti-corruption programs in emerging market economies is also a major challenge. For example, although no society openly *approves* paying or accepting bribes, in countries where government employees receive lower than subsistence-level pay, "expediting fees" (also known as "grease" or "facilitating payments") often become unapproved but *accepted* behavior under local custom. In such countries, bribery is so common that even law enforcement officials pay bribes to gain their positions.[3]

As mentioned already, one should not ignore FCPA red flags in countries not listed. The German truck manufacturer MAN paid millions in bribes between 2002 and 2005 in an effort to increase sales across Europe. The bribes went to employees and customers inside and outside the country, often paid through shadow companies in Malta, the Bahamas, Cyprus, London, and New York.[4] MAN has cooperated with the German investigation and brought in an outside auditor to determine the extent of the corrupt payments. Investigators focused on the marketing and sales divisions and have not implicated senior management. The internal investigation determined that MAN paid €52 million in payments to advisors and agents to win business. Twenty employees were fired and MAN paid €150 million in court-ordered fines to resolve the investigation.[5] The company has seemingly learned lessons from the Siemens scandal and is now working diligently to root out corruption.

THOUGHT LEADER IN FCPA COMPLIANCE: SCOTT MORITZ

Understanding the Corruption Risk in Worldwide Hotspots

Scott Moritz is an Executive Director with Daylight Forensic & Advisory, a global regulatory compliance, forensic accounting, and *(continued)*

(*continued*)
investigative consulting firm that advises financial institutions, Fortune 500 companies, law firms, and government agencies on regulatory and investigative issues worldwide. He also leads Daylight's
FCPA and Investigative Due Diligence practice and is widely recognized as an authority on investigative due diligence and international
investigations. Prior to joining Daylight, he has held executive positions at other major accounting firms and global investigative firms.
For nearly ten years, Scott served as an FBI Special Agent where he
was nationally recognized for his expertise in money laundering and
asset forfeiture investigations. Here he gives his perspectives on
corruption hotspots around the world:

> *Brazil, Russia, India, China, Korea, and Mexico are rapidly growing
> economies whose growth is based in part to a huge influx of foreign
> investment. These governments have made and continue to make
> sizable investments in the infrastructure required to sustain their
> economic growth. Highways, hydro-electric plants, international
> airports, telecommunication systems, Internet backbone, and other
> infrastructure projects are often awarded to outside companies
> which must deal directly with various government agencies from
> the bid process through to the completion of the projects that often
> take many years and cost many millions of dollars. These countries
> are listed on Transparency International's Corruption Perceptions
> Index (CPI) as among the world's most corrupt.*
>
> *In addition, the economies of sub-Saharan Africa are also growing
> rapidly. U.S., EU, and Chinese companies are all very active in
> Africa. Nigeria has been perhaps the most frequently mentioned
> country in FCPA enforcement actions. It is an oil-rich nation, is
> highly populated and is one of the most corrupt nations in the world.
> Nigeria is in good company on most authoritative lists with many sub-
> Saharan countries rounding out the bottom of the CPI.*
>
> *While Russia is given a great deal of attention in anti-corruption
> circles, most of the Commonwealth of Independent States ("CIS") are
> rife with corruption and have scored badly on the CPI. Kazakhstan,
> Poland, Serbia, the Czech Republic, Ukraine, and Uzbekistan are
> frequently the focus of corruption investigations. Rounding out
> the lower half of the Planet Earth is South and Central America.
> Argentina, Mexico, Venezuela, Chile, Bolivia, Guatemala, Colombia,
> Peru, Panama, and Honduras are all characterized by high degrees*

> *of corruption, unstable governments, narcotics trafficking, and money laundering.*
>
> *Certain industries are more susceptible to FCPA risk than others. The oil and gas industry for example operates in some of the world's most corrupt countries and often has to partner with the government where the oil drilling and pipelines are located. They are also heavily reliant on freight forwarders, customs brokers, ports, and intermodal logistics companies both in getting their equipment to drilling operations and in transporting crude oil and natural gas to market. Defense contractors are likewise susceptible to FCPA risk by their role in direct sales of high value contracts to foreign governments. While certain industries such as those mentioned previously have garnered a great deal of regulatory attention over the years, any company that is doing business in high corruption countries is at risk. What is key, is understanding where the company intersects with the government in each of these jurisdictions.*

THE NATURAL RESOURCE-CORRUPTION LINK

Why is it that some of the world's most resource-rich countries are also some of its most corrupt? A theory, popularized as the Sachs-Warner theory, posits that countries with greater natural resources suffer from lower rates of economic development. This theory is also known as the *"resource curse."* It refers to the paradox that resource-rich countries tend to have less growth and less economic development than countries without significant natural riches.[6] The mere fact that a country has abundant resources does not cause it to have lower development. Rather, the resources give the country a crutch on which to earn money, lowering the incentive to modernize or to develop alternative industries. Outside influences become prominently involved in the country's affairs.

Given the amount of personal gain that can be had, the government will attract individuals who seek only to benefit themselves and those around them, at the expense of the governed. Access to the resources makes being in power very attractive. This weakens government institutions and their authority. As the rule of law is openly flouted and graft becomes the norm, corruption spreads endemically throughout a society.

These countries often have a dictatorial government or one that is a democracy more or less in name only. The governing structure is common because the will of the people is irrelevant in terms of governmental

147

accountability. Leaders do not need the support of the people to maintain power; they can use resources to pay off those whose support is needed, such as the military or corporate interests. These leaders, once in power, siphon off the country's resources for personal benefit, thereby impoverishing the country. They can act with impunity because there is little to no accountability. The only accountability is to those who require bribes.

The natural resources attract foreign businesses, which are often happy to pay off leaders to extract and export the resources. Extractive resources give little benefit to local population when foreign companies are involved; without governmental pressure, they have little incentive to build infrastructure beyond what is necessary to get to the resources and get them out of the country. In short, the apparatus of government is designed to enrich participants and ensure the maintenance of their power.[7]

UK TACKLES INTERNATIONAL CORRUPTION

It is evident that more and more countries are joining the United States in aggressively prosecuting corruption. The United Kingdom is but one example of a country embracing this trend. Serving as the host for the July 2005 Gleneagles G8 Summit in Scotland, UK Prime Minister Tony Blair made a strong statement in fighting corruption and bribery when he said "African leaders and the heads of the G8 countries were united in identifying the importance of fighting corruption to help reduce poverty in Africa and worldwide. The UK has a responsibility to tackle money laundering and bribery where it stems from our own shores, and to support developing countries in fighting corruption."[8] Blair followed on his words with the establishment of the Overseas Anti-Corruption Unit in June 2006.

This dedicated task force of police officers from both the City of London Police and the Metropolitan Police Service was created to focus on "investigating international corruption, including money laundering in the UK by corrupt politicians from developing countries, and bribery by UK businesses overseas."[9] The unit works closely with the UK's Serious Fraud Office (SFO) and other international law enforcement agencies in investigating corruption. Backing up the unit was a change in the law. A 2001 amendment to UK corruption statutes made prosecutions more likely. It reinforced the rule of law that the bribery of foreign public officials and agents was a crime and gave the courts jurisdiction for offenses committed outside the United Kingdom by UK nationals or organizations incorporated under UK law.

The first successful prosecution coming from the Overseas Anti-Corruption Unit occurred in 2008 when the Danish head of a UK security company was convicted for bribing Ugandan officials. The security firm specialized in training to detect and counteract chemical, biological, radioactive, and nuclear threats and provided training and equipment to the Ugandan army. The Ugandan government official who received the illegal payments was also convicted and sentenced to a year in prison.

The celebration of this landmark case was diminished by "the 2006 decision to scrap a probe into alleged bribery in [defense contractor] BAE Systems' Saudi Arabian arms deals."[10] The reputational impact to the UK government after Blair ended the probe of BAE Systems for national security reasons was still on everyone's minds. It would take more than one successful prosecution to restore the faith in the government to effectively investigate and prosecute corruption and bribery. More information on the BAE Systems bribery investigation can be found in Chapter 8. Yet, some very positive signs are coming from the UK that needed change is coming.

COMPLIANCE INSIGHT 6.1: WEAK INTERNAL CONTROLS LEADS TO FINE FOR INSURANCE GIANT

In January 2009, Aon, Ltd, the UK unit of insurance broker Aon Corp., was fined $7.9 million by a UK financial markets regulator for weak internal controls resulting in dozens of suspicious payments that may have been used for bribes. Aon Ltd. is one of the largest insurance and reinsurance brokers in London. The investigation by the Financial Services Authority (FSA) found that between 2005 and 2007, Aon made 66 suspicious payments totaling $7 million to several overseas companies and individuals in Bahrain, Bangladesh, Bulgaria, Indonesia, Myanmar, and Vietnam.[11]

Aon was found to have ineffective internal controls that failed to detect or prevent potentially corrupt payments to win or retain business in high risk countries. These payments related to Aon's business sectors of aviation and energy. Aon's payment processing program did not factor in the risk that its business was exposed to in countries with a high incidence of bribery and did not provide training to its employees about the risks of bribery and corruption.

(continued)

(*continued*)

The company also failed to question the nature and purpose of these suspicious payments.[12] Had they done so, these payments might have been stopped sooner or never occurred in the first place.

The accounting firm hired by Aon to audit all overseas payments between 2002 and 2007 discovered the suspicious payments. They then conducted an in-depth internal investigation of these issues and delivered appropriate discipline. Aon then disclosed the results of its investigation to the FSA who in turn conducted its own investigation. Since Aon cooperated fully and quickly agreed to resolve the investigation, they qualified for the FSA's early settlement plan. Aon received a 30 percent reduction in the fine levied. Aon also agreed to implement a robust anti-corruption compliance program that includes the following elements:

- New procedures to review all existing and proposed third-party relationships
- A global third-party policy controlling and restricting the use of third parties, especially those in high-risk countries
- Prohibiting the use of third parties if their only service is making client introductions to obtain business[13]

Aon should have been aware of this risk well before this most recent incident. Two Aon predecessor companies were fined in 2000 by the UK for bribing government officials in Ghana, Nigeria, and the Philippines.[14] The report at the time found that these companies failed "to have adequate systems and procedures in place to prevent the matters . . . from occurring or to discover them when they did occur. The procedures for the authorization of payments were defective, and the checks carried out by those signing the authorization forms were inadequate."[15]

This settlement, although not criminal in nature, portends increased scrutiny of corrupt practices and holding violators accountable in the United Kingdom. "This reflects a new wave of enforcement by regulatory authorities across Europe, and reflects the approach the U.S. authorities have been taking for some years in clamping down on bribery and corruption."[16]

150

UK Bribery Bill

The UK's criminal law for bribery dates back to the turn of the twentieth century and needed updating to meet the requirements of the modern age. Not only was a strong statute necessary to hold those involved in giving and accepting bribes accountable but also to ensure that the long arm of the law can reach those who commit bribery in both the public and private sectors, in the United Kingdom or abroad, and ensure a culture of compliance. As a result, the UK draft Bribery Bill was published on March 25, 2009 and is intended to reform existing criminal law "to provide a new, modern, and comprehensive scheme of bribery offences that will enable courts and prosecutors to respond more effectively to bribery at home or abroad."[17]

The Bribery Bill covers both active and passive forms of bribery. Active bribery is the giving of bribes and passive bribery is the receipt of bribes. The bill includes both public and private sector bribery. It will be the first anti-corruption statute in the United Kingdom to include penalties for commercial bribery and governmental corruption. There is a specific offense involving bribery of foreign public officials that incorporates the strict anti-corruption compliance requirements of the *OECD Convention on Combating Bribery*. A corporate offense for companies that negligently fail to detect and prevent bribery is also included. The bill holds senior corporate officials accountable for corrupt activities at their companies. There is a defense available if the organization can demonstrate that an effective compliance program was previously in place and the corrupt activity was not carried out by senior officers or agents acting on their behalf.

Conventional wisdom is that the bill is sorely needed and certain to be passed into law. Some key provisions of the bill include:

- *Extra-territorial jurisdiction to prosecute bribery committed abroad by persons ordinarily resident in the United Kingdom as well as UK nationals, and UK corporate bodies*
- *A maximum penalty of ten years imprisonment for all new offences, save the corporate offence, which will carry an unlimited fine*[18]
- *Providing a more effective legal framework to combat bribery in the public or private sectors*
- *Providing clearer compliance with international obligations*
- *Simplifying legislation covering two general offences: offering, promising, or giving of an advantage, and requesting, agreeing to receive, or accepting an advantage*

- Creating a discrete offence of bribery of a foreign public official
- Creating an offence of negligent failure by commercial organizations to prevent bribery
- Supporting high ethical standards in UK businesses
- Tackling the threat that bribery poses to economic progress and development around the world.[19]

The bill covers offenses committed in England, Wales, and Northern Ireland but not Scotland. A previous anti-corruption act remains in effect for corrupt acts committed there. Third-party risk is also addressed by including language on the corrupt offer, promise, or gift made to a foreign public official through a third party. Unlike the FCPA, this bill does not contain a books and records provision.

Mabey & Johnson Prosecution

Mabey & Johnson, Ltd. may become best known for being the first corporate prosecution brought in the United Kingdom for corrupt activity outside the country. Mabey & Johnson is a British engineering firm that designs and manufactures steel bridges throughout the world. In February 2008, the company self-disclosed to the SFO that it sought to corruptly influence government officials in public contracts in Jamaica and Ghana between 1993 and 2001.[20] The ensuing prosecution also involved corruption in contracts in the United Nations "Oil-for-Food" program.[21] Furthermore, the investigation determined that the company paid additional bribes to government officials in Madagascar, Angola, Mozambique, and Bangladesh. In July 2009, the company agreed to plead guilty to the charges and correct their compliance failures.

Since the disclosure to the SFO, Mabey & Johnson brought in new management and replaced five of its eight directors. The company enhanced its corporate compliance program and implemented extensive anti-corruption training. An independent monitor was appointed to oversee and report on the effectiveness of the new compliance program. "We deeply regret the past conduct of our company, and we have committed to making a fresh start, wiping the slate clean of these offences," said Peter Lloyd, Mabey & Johnson's new Managing Director. "We and our lawyers have worked intensively with the SFO to enable these charges to be brought and a prosecution obtained: as a result, the case will be dealt with as quickly and as efficiently as possible. This approach we believe could act as a template for others facing a similar situation as we believe it secures the interest of justice in the most proper and effective way for all parties in terms of sentence, time, and expenditure," added Lloyd.[22]

The SFO used this first such prosecution to send a message to the business world that self-disclosure of bribery and corruption would be expected from all violators. "These are serious offences and it is significant that Mabey & Johnson has cooperated with us to get to this landmark point. This has enabled this case to be dealt with in just over a year and is a model for other companies who want to self-report corruption and have it dealt with quickly and fairly by the SFO," said Director Richard Alderman of the Serious Fraud Office.[23]

Strong Message from the SFO

Seizing the moment from both the release of the draft Bribery Bill and the plea agreement from Mabey & Johnson, the SFO announced on July 21, 2009, an intensified effort to detect and prosecute overseas corruption. The SFO released a nine-page memo entitled "Approach of the Serious Fraud Office to Dealing with Overseas Corruption" and reinforced their standing as the lead agency in the United Kingdom for investigating and prosecuting cases of overseas corruption. The SFO stated their responsibility for enforcing the current law and Bribery Bill once it is enacted and their intention to have a staff of 100 focused on anti-corruption enforcement.

The SFO also reinforced the importance of self-reporting in order to mitigate the impact of a bribery prosecution. They made it clear that self-disclosure of corruption violations was the preference for offenders. They also made it clear that they would use all available law enforcement tools to identify and prosecute any individual or corporation, whether or not there was self-disclosure involved. The following are highlights of the SFO public notice on self-reporting of overseas corruption:

Discussions with business and professional advisers have revealed a lot of interest in a system of self-reporting cases of overseas corruption to us. We have been asked for any additional guidance we can give with respect to our policies on this and in particular on the benefits to be obtained from self-reporting.

As will be seen from this Guide, the benefit to the corporate will be the prospect (in appropriate cases) of a civil rather than a criminal outcome as

153

well as the opportunity to manage, with us, the issues and any publicity proactively. The corporate will be seen to have acted responsibly by the wider community in taking action to remedy what has happened in the past and to have moved on to a new and better corporate culture. Furthermore, a negotiated settlement rather than a criminal prosecution means that the mandatory debarment provisions under Article 45 of the EU Public Sector Procurement Directive in 2004 will not apply.

For the SFO, such a system would have the effect of crafting effective and proportionate sanctions for this type of case and of helping to produce a new corporate culture. This will bring about behavioural change within businesses themselves and will create corporate cultures in which no form of corruption is tolerated.

This is the key to the outcome we are set on achieving. Self-referral under this Guide leading to a civil outcome in appropriate cases is one tool for this: criminal prosecution and confiscation in other cases is another vital tool we shall be using. We expect to conduct more criminal investigations and prosecutions in the future (particularly if the Bribery Bill becomes law). This tough approach is needed as part of the SFO toolkit to ensure that appropriate cases are brought before the Criminal Courts.

Many corporates have welcomed what they have heard about self-reporting at conferences. They have asked for a document setting out the issues covered in speeches and the approach we are likely to take. This Guide is a first attempt to set this out. It will be revised following feedback and in the light of experience.[24]

The full SFO announcement contains more detailed information along with recommendations on approaching the SFO to self-report violations and acknowledge a legal problem, follow-up actions by the SFO, scope of any further SFO investigation, settlement discussions, potential global settlement relating to other jurisdictional investigations, and other guidance. Interestingly enough, the SFO indicated they have been asked by companies to offer opinion research similar to that provided by the U.S. Department of Justice (DOJ) and they are considering that request.

RUSSIA

With its overreliance on oil wealth, authoritarian government cloaked in the mantle of democracy, extreme corruption at all levels of the government and judiciary, and violence against those who attempt reform, Russia far more closely resembles a less sophisticated country than the growing economies of India and China to which it is often compared. Estimates place the size of the Russian corruption market at close to $300 billion, which would be 20 percent of Russian Gross Domestic Product (GDP).[25] The average bribe has risen from $10,000 to $130,000 over the past decade. Beyond being a facet of everyday life, most Russians, especially the young, do not even consider bribery a crime. The Russian language does distinguish, however, between offering a reward to a bureaucrat to make life easier and the forcible extraction of a bribe by a bureaucrat.[26]

The Russian judicial system strongly resembles the Soviet-era one in that prosecutors and judges have tremendous power, only now that power is unchecked by Soviet bureaucracy. A common trend now is the use of legal power for personal gain, in the form of "raiding," the takeover of businesses through court orders or other ostensibly legal means. The "state" seizes the business on trumped up or outright phony charges, reaping the profits for the individuals involved and then often quietly transferring the business into the hands of allied private interests. Local Russian media reports peg the raiders' fees as $10,000 to alter a corporate registry, $50,000 to open a criminal case, or $300,000 for a court order.[27] "A U.S. Justice Department official in Moscow has described [raiding] as 'a new and sophisticated form of organized crime' that 'poses a serious threat to foreign investors. . . .' "[28]

The most infamous case of raiding came in 2004 when Russia arrested Mikhail Khodorkovsky, the head of the Yukos oil company and the richest man in Russia at the time. Subsequently, the company was broken up and sold to a close ally of Vladimir Putin. This case marked a turning point in Russian corruption. Prior to this, officials were content to merely collect a percentage of businesses' profits. Afterward, they began to take the entire businesses themselves. Bribes must now be paid as a matter of survival.[29]

Even lawyers who defend companies from raiding and similar practices face major risk. Of the three lawyers defending investment fund Hermitage Capital's Russian subsidiaries from illegal takeover, one was jailed and died in prison while the other two fled the country. They faced arrest because they were so bold as to defend themselves and the company and were able to identify some of the culprits.[30] This sadly is not an isolated incident and one that companies must be aware of when operating in Russia.

At the behest of President Dmitry Medvedev, Russia enacted new anti-corruption laws in 2008. Unfortunately, they will likely make no difference. The law only criminalizes completed acts of bribery, not the demanding or offering of bribes. Furthermore, the law does nothing to address the widespread judicial corruption.[31]

155

Doing Business in Russia

Even with its corruption problems, as an emerging market, Russia commands the world's attention for investment and growth opportunities. In July 2009, PepsiCo announced that it would boost its investment in Russia with another $1 billion. This brings their already huge investment in Russia to $4 billion. PepsiCo's Chairman and CEO Indra Nooyi reinforced this business strategy by stating, "This investment reflects very clearly our great confidence in Russia and our long-term commitment to this very important market."[32] Other companies are following PepsiCo's lead. Farm equipment manufacturer Deere & Company has announced plans to expand its manufacturing operations in Russia. Boeing has opened an engineering design site in Moscow and will be buying almost $1 billion in aircraft parts from a Russian manufacturer.

Yet, doing business in Russia is fraught with peril. One key factor is corruption's impact on business operations. In June 2009, Swedish retailer IKEA announced that it was putting the brakes on further investments in Russia. The official statement from IKEA's management stated the decision was "due to the unpredictability of the administrative processes in some regions."[33] Construction on 30 new stores that had been planned for the country has been postponed. This about face is disconcerting given that IKEA has invested $4 billion in Russia since 2000. The real reason for the change of business strategy is most likely the challenge of corruption and bribery. "While IKEA hasn't said so directly, company officials have implied they're tired of corruption in Russia."[34]

IKEA has faced numerous project delays when regional authorities impose ever-changing building code standards and cite the company for violations of untold safety regulations. In one example, IKEA was given a requirement that the mall they were building in Samara "be able to withstand near-hurricane force winds, even though there's no history of such weather conditions there."[35] A local government recommended that IKEA use a specific construction company and this would resolve the issue. A skeptic might say this was a shakedown. But what is one to do? Russia has huge potential and as one of the BRIC countries is a powerhouse for business opportunity. The saying that "you have to be in it to win it" is especially true for Russia and other emerging markets. Abandon the market and a company risks losing billions of dollars over time. Competitors will not hesitate to fill the void left by a company's decision to leave Russia. Doing business in countries where corruption abounds is like navigating land mines. You have to be prepared, careful, and willing to take big risks.

156

AFRICA

The African Union estimates that corruption costs Africa $160 billion annually. That is roughly 25 percent of sub-Saharan Africa's total GDP.[36] Endemic corruption has stunted Africa's growth potential, leaving it behind many other parts of the developing world. It is home to many of the world's poorest countries and some of its most war-torn. Foreign companies have had a major hand in fueling this corruption. Weak central governments, with even weaker internal oversight, have often had no qualms with letting those companies set up shop and operate as they see fit. This arrangement has enriched both the companies and the leadership but impoverished the African people themselves.

As a region, Africa is emblematic of the resource curse. Despite natural resources such as oil, timber, precious metals, and diamonds, many governments cannot or will not meet the daily needs of their citizens. Government instability and internecine warfare, particularly of the ethnic variety, are hallmarks of the region. Pollution, deforestation, and the forced movement of indigenous peoples from their land have all been consequences of unchecked and unregulated operations by foreign companies.

Outside money wields great influence, including in recent years, greatly increased Chinese investment. As its investment has grown, China's influence in the region has risen concomitantly. Chinese companies have built major industrial works and have supplied weapons and military equipment to the region.

Anti-corruption efforts in the region have found some success. Not long after starting a major initiative against official corruption, Namibia uncovered a large-scale bribery effort by a prominent Chinese company. The company, Nuctech Company Limited, through its African representative and two Namibian nationals concocted a bribery scheme that netted the company a lucrative $55.3 million contract to install its scanning devices at customs inspections points throughout Namibia. The Chinese loaned most of the money to the Namibian government at below market rates. "Namibia's government paid about $12.8 million to Nuctech in February [2009]. But prosecutors allege that most of the money was quickly transferred to a Namibian company listed as a Nuctech consultant" and was quickly spent by the defendants in an incredible spending spree.[37] Further complicating matters, Chinese president Hu Jintao's son headed Nuctech until 2009. No evidence has been released tying Hu's son to the case, but it has been embarrassing for the Chinese government and resulted in the censoring of Internet searches for anything related to this case.[38]

This also shows why some companies choose to pay bribes. They are competing against companies like Nuctech, which can offer soft loans from its government to countries soliciting business. One can understand why a company pays bribes in such a competitive market, but of course that does not change its illegality.

Nigeria

Nigeria has had the highest number of FCPA prosecutions of any country. It's infamous for its criminal activity and corruption, which has ravaged the country. Transparency International ranks it tied for 130 out of 180 countries, better than what it used to be but still among the worst in the world. One estimate places the cost of corruption in Nigeria since its independence in 1960 at more than $380 billion dollars.[39]

The oil-rich country, despite its resources, has major energy problems. Power outages are frequent. "Despite low labor costs, Nigeria has little manufacturing due to the high price of energy, among other factors. Across Lagos, Nigerians blame their notoriously corrupt government for the electricity problems, saying their leaders steal funds earmarked for the country's generators."[40] Government neglect and corruption leads to derelict infrastructure, which leads to shortages of necessities like electricity and gasoline, which leads to poverty and stagnant economic development. Bribery from foreign companies doing business in Nigeria is a major influence. "If bribe money has brought anything in the [Nigerian] Delta, it is a culture of pervasive, profound neglect."[41]

Willbros employees paid bribe money to officials at the Nigerian Natural Petroleum Corporation to secure a lucrative gas pipeline contract and to ensure their success, spread the wealth among lower levels of government, such as tax agencies and the courts. The bribes totaled approximately $6 million.[42] The employees pleaded guilty and faced jail time, while the company cooperated with the investigation and agreed to a deferred prosecution agreement (DPA) for its FCPA violations. Willbros paid a $22 million penalty to the DOJ plus they agreed to disgorge $10.3 million in profits to the Securities and Exchange Commission (SEC).[43]

Willbros' efforts were nothing but small change when compared to the scandal involving Halliburton and its subsidiary KBR. The case resulted in one of the largest FCPA penalties of all time. KBR's chief executive Albert "Jack" Stanley stood at the center of the allegations and acted as point man for the widespread bribery. A fearsome competitor, "Stanley

158

spent nearly his entire career in the oil business, a globe-trotting high-level roustabout who made a specialty of dealing with governments in resource-rich, accountability-poor countries."[44] He ran M.W. Kellogg until Halliburton bought out its parent company in 1998, whereupon Dick Cheney appointed him to run the newly formed KBR subsidiary.[45]

In Nigeria, Stanley channeled approximately $180 million in illicit payments to government officials to land some $6 billion worth of contracts between 1994 and 2004. "[T]he payments were vital to a KBR-led consortium securing a succession of construction projects related to a liquefied natural gas plant at Bonny Island, on the Atlantic Coast of Nigeria."[46] Stanley and others met with high-ranking Nigerian officials to arrange the bribe payments, with Stanley then approving sham contacts with "agents" to funnel the money to its intended recipients.[47] A consultant from the United Kingdom would pay off the high-level officials while a Japanese consultant handled the lower-level ones. The primary recipient of the bribes was the late Nigerian President Sani Abacha, who was frequently cited for human rights violations.[48]

Stanley pleaded guilty to FCPA violations in September 2008 and agreed to cooperate with prosecutors. He was sentenced to seven years in jail and a $10.8 million restitution payment. This assistance contributed to the major penalty Halliburton paid to settle the charges against its subsidiary. Halliburton agreed to pay a total of $559 million, $382 million to the DOJ and $177 million to the SEC.[49] Stanley also had involvement in numerous other projects in Egypt, Yemen, and Malaysia. Since it stands to reason that Nigeria was not his first brush with corruption, these projects are also being investigated. Stanley's prosecution does highlight one positive trend. His case is a major example of enhanced cross-boundary investigation and collaboration. Enforcement agencies in the United Kingdom, France, Switzerland, and Nigeria were all involved in the investigation besides U.S. authorities.

Unfortunately for Nigeria, the positives in this case have not been reflected elsewhere. The Nigerian government forced out its top anti-corruption official in January 2008 in a blatant case of retaliation. Nuhu Ribadu headed the Economic and Financial Crimes Commission, starting in 2003. He accomplished much during his time in the position, recovering more than $5 billion in stolen assets and scoring major victories against e-mail scammers and corrupt politicians. He even indicted and prosecuted the inspector general of police, who had embezzled $150 million. Regrettably, Ribadu's effectiveness led to his downfall.[50]

After Ribadu arrested a powerful governor on corruption and money laundering charges, the head of Nigeria's police ordered Ribadu removed from his position and reassigned him to take a training course. Much of the pressure came from Nigeria's president and his ruling party, as Ribadu's investigations exposed corruption in the administration.[51] After being pushed out, Ribadu then survived two assassination attempts, forcing him to flee the country. Since his removal, corruption investigations have ground to a halt.[52] In November 2009, Nigerian authorities issued a warrant for Ribadu's arrest, alleging he failed to properly declare assets while in office, a charge he vehemently denies.[53]

These two cases represent only a small sample of the corruption cases emerging from Nigeria and West Africa as a whole. Prominent companies including Chevron, BP, Titan, and Siemens have all been involved in corruption cases there. Unsurprisingly they include many natural resource companies. Remember also that Congressman Jefferson's freezer money was intended to be paid to the Vice President of Nigeria.

MIDDLE EAST

As the region with the earth's largest oil reserves, the Middle East has attracted tremendous amounts of foreign investment and involvement, to put it mildly. When combined with powerful, repressive governments, this is a recipe for corruption. Moreover, opportunities for civic participation, whether through the media, political participation, or protest, are far more limited than in other developing regions. With little to no accountability, corruption is to be expected.

Corruption in the Middle East is not limited to authoritarian regimes. Israel has faced numerous corruption scandals over the years, including one that has snared former Prime Minister Ehud Olmert. The country has dropped from 15th overall in Transparency International's 1997 rankings to 32nd in 2009.[54]

Iraq has become one of the most corrupt countries in the world; according to Transparency International's 2009 study, only Somalia, Afghanistan, Myanmar, and Sudan ranked higher in corruption. In terms of a strong central government, Iraq has only begun to recover from the removal of Saddam Hussein and American actions in Operation Iraqi Freedom. The Oil-for-Food scandal resulted in heavy FCPA prosecutions by DOJ. Note that the bribery and other schemes on which these cases are based occurred during Saddam Hussein's rule.

160

The Oil-for-Food Scandal

When Saddam Hussein ruled Iraq with an iron fist, few companies invested in the country. Economic sanctions put in place by the United Nations, with the intent of isolating the country, prevented outside trade, subject to some exceptions. This one exception was the Oil-for-Food Program begun in 1996. This program allowed Iraq to sell its oil on the world market, then to use a portion of the proceeds to purchase humanitarian aid. However, this program was rife with corruption. The United Nations provided only minimal supervision; Iraq chose to whom it sold oil and from whom it purchased supplies, negotiating with these entities directly. As has been seen many times in this book, and will be seen further, mixing large amounts of money with minimal oversight invariably leads to corruption.

Companies receiving Iraqi oil contracts had to pay a special "surcharge" of ten to thirty cents a barrel. Suppliers deliberately overcharged Iraq for goods while paying kickbacks to get the contracts in the first place. The overcharged amount made its way into the hands of the government and high-level officials. This money, estimated to be over a billion dollars, helped to sustain a government on the verge of toppling.[55] Had Hussein not been able to maintain his government through these illegal surcharges and kickbacks, the war in Iraq may very well not have happened. By giving Iraq the ability to choose the recipients of its oil contracts, Iraq took full advantage of its position and gave most of them to Russian, French, and Chinese companies. This meant that these countries, United Nations Security Council members, had little incentive to approve tighter oversight and further sanctions.

The scandal's revelation caused a major controversy around the world. Critics aimed a large portion of the furor at the United Nations for its poor oversight, and at then-Secretary General Kofi Annan in particular. Much of this criticism was later echoed by the official report issued in 2005 by the Independent Inquiry Committee, headed by former Federal Reserve Chairman Paul Volcker. The U.S. government opened numerous investigations, including ones by the Senate, the SEC, a federal grand jury in the Southern District of New York, and the Manhattan D.A.'s Office. Compliance Insight 6.2 contains a list of some of the companies involved in this corruption scandal.

Several companies, including El Paso Corp., Textron, York International, Ingersoll-Rand, Chevron, Akzo Nobel, AB Volvo, Fiat, and Novo Nordisk have settled with the government. As of summer 2009, the SEC

161

and DOJ have entered into eleven DPAs or settlement agreements.[56] Interestingly, nearly every DPA did not include a monitor requirement as part of the settlement. This is likely due to the unique circumstances surrounding the violations.

In June 2009, Iraq filed suit in the Southern District of New York against dozens of companies for bribery it claims occurred as part of the program. Iraq claims that New York is the proper court for the case as the United Nations headquarters is located in the city. The suit is still pending.

COMPLIANCE INSIGHT 6.2: COMPANIES IMPLICATED IN OIL-FOR-FOOD SCANDAL*

AB Volvo
Akzo Nobel
Beckman Coulter
Chevron
DaimlerChrysler
El Paso
Fiat
Flowserve
GlaxoSmithKline
Ingersoll-Rand
Johnson & Johnson
Novo Nordisk
Siemens
St. Jude Medical
Textron
Tyco
Valero Energy
Weatherford International
Wyeth
York International

---

*This is a partial list of companies that have admitted involvement in the Oil-for-Food scandal, signed DPAs with the U.S. government, or have been otherwise implicated.

Iraq Today

Unfortunately for the people of Iraq, the corruption has only gotten worse since the American-led invasion of 2003. Some strides have been made in attempting to stabilize the country, such as reducing the levels of violence, but little headway has been made in reducing corruption. "Endemic graft is seen as a significant threat to Iraq's progress and stability as it begins to emerge from the years of bloodshed unleashed by the 2003 U.S.-led invasion."[57]

Baghdad has passed good anti-corruption laws, but as yet it has not staunchly enforced them. Iraqis are bitterly resigned to the unchecked malfeasance they face from every level of government, from the lowest official to the highest.[58] Corruption is one of the toughest challenges Iraq faces. According to Deputy Prime Minister Rafie al-Esawi, "widespread corruption is at the root of Iraq's persistent, destabilizing lack of basic services."[59] One can hope that with continued development and democratic progress, Iraq will be able to make progress against the formidable foe of corruption and the other ills plaguing its society.

LATIN AMERICA

According to Transparency International, "the fight against corruption in North America has been marked primarily by accounting, financial, and political scandals; Latin American countries continue to suffer from structural problems that affect the region's economic and democratic development."[60] These structural problems which have lead to corruption in Central and South America can be traced to the governmental structure of these countries.

For much of the twentieth century, the United States had sponsored and supported dictatorships in the region, ignoring rampant corruption and human rights abuses so long as they kept communists and socialists out of power. Latin American countries have made admirable strides toward democracy as long-serving dictators have died or been removed from power. Even Venezuelan President Hugo Chavez, often vilified in the United States, is a democratically elected leader. As an indicator of the region's increasing stability, the June 2009 coup in Honduras was the first such coup in 20 years.

The influence of drug money is behind a large part of official corruption in many countries. Colombia has been called a narco-state due to the power the cocaine cartels wield there. Mexico has tried, with only limited success, to remove corrupt police officers, judges, and government officials

163

who are beholden to the drug cartels. In fact, the level of corruption, kidnapping, drug-related violence, and murder has reached epidemic proportions in the country. Corruption has had devastating consequences elsewhere in the region as well. Much of the destruction from the January 2010 earthquake in Haiti can be attributed to the infamously corrupt government to properly enforce building codes and regulate construction.

A survey conducted by Transparency Mexico, the Latin America Chapter of Transparency International, found that Mexicans paid an amazing $2.58 billion in bribes in 2007. That was 42 percent more than was paid out in 2005. The study learned that while the number of bribes is increasing, the average amount paid was smaller: approximately $13 as compared to $17 in 2005.[61] The great majority of bribes are paid to government workers to avoid traffic tickets, get trash collected, have water delivered to homes, and to get goods through customs. This environment of corruption extends to business dealings as well, and is not limited to Mexico.

Cases of Corruption

The oil and gas driller Helmerich & Payne paid the U.S. government $1 million in criminal penalties to resolve FCPA violations committed between 2003 and 2008. The company, which sells oil and gas drilling equipment, paid bribes to customs officials in Argentina and Venezuela to avoid having to pay customs charges on equipment it imported and exported.[62] The company paid approximately $185,673 to the officials in the two countries, most through third-party customs brokers. The payments let the company avoid delays associated with moving its equipment in and out of the country as well as avoiding approximately $320,604 in costs.[63]

These payments were not facilitating payments; the company paid the officials to act in violation of their duty and responsibility, namely help the company unlawfully expedite the customs process and avoid paying required fees. As is often the case, the FCPA violations wound up costing the company far more than if it had simply paid the customs fees at the outset.

One of the region's major cases was the prosecution of Alcatel, a French telecommunications company. As it does business in the United States, it is subject to the FCPA even though it is a foreign corporation. Tired of losing out on government contracts in Costa Rica, an Alcatel executive conspired with Alcatel's senior country official in Costa Rica and others to set up an elaborate bribery scheme to win business for the company. They made more than $2.5 million in bribe payments between 2000 and 2004, funneled

164

through consultants, to government officials, including a director of the Instituo Constarricense de Electricidad, the state-run telecommunications company. This director shared his payments with a senior government official and they used their influence to rig the bidding process and award Alcatel a $149 million cell phone contract in August 2001.[64]

The Alcatel executive pleaded guilty to FCPA violations in 2008, receiving 30 months in prison, and must forfeit $261,500. He also agreed to cooperate in the investigation and is expected to testify against his co-conspirators.[65] Two former Costa Rican presidents have also been connected to the scandal. Former president Miguel Angel Rodriguez was forced to step down from his position as Secretary General of the Organization of American States after he was alleged to have received part of the cell phone payoff. He is currently awaiting trial on corruption charges. Former president Abel Pacheco is alleged to have taken $100,000 from Alcatel despite a ban on political donations by foreign entities.[66]

The case spurred Alcatel, now Alcatel-Lucent, to take some dramatic steps to prevent future occurrences. The company severely reduced its usage of outside consultants to obtain customer deals. An internal memo stated "that [the company's] strategy will no longer rely on the services of agents and consultants."[67] Some Alcatel managers, upon hearing the news, complained that the company will have a difficult time obtaining business, given the competitive advantage consultants often provide.[68] This is a bold strategy; Alcatel is to be commended, as agents are often at the center of bribery allegations. This will be interesting to monitor to see how Alcatel-Lucent can continue to successfully maintain their business under this new policy.

Multinational Company As Victim

Bribery and corruption is not always about paying off government officials to win contracts. Sometimes it is the large multinational that is the victim of bribery. In August and September of 2009, Chevron released evidence of what it says is a bribery plot against the company. These charges stem from a $27 billion environmental damages case that the company is defending in Ecuador. Surreptitious video and audio recordings turned over by Chevron to Ecuadorean authorities show the judge in the suit stating that Chevron is guilty and he will rule against them, even though the trial was ongoing at the time, and that any appeal would be merely a formality. A separate recording, during which the judge was not present, appears to implicate him as the recipient of a million-dollar bribe.[69]

165

An official in the president's political party refers to a $3 Million bribe, to be split equally between the judge, the plaintiffs in the case, and the presidency. The legal advisor to the president, who is himself mentioned on the tapes but otherwise not implicated in any wrongdoing, has attacked Chevron and called for an investigation into the company's conduct while dismissing the contents of the recordings. After the tapes' revelation, the judge recused himself; the case is still ongoing.[70]

NOTES

1. Goldman Sachs first used the BRIC acronym in 2001 to refer to the fast-growing economies of developing countries Brazil, Russia, India, and China, www2.goldmansachs.com/ideas/brics/index.html.
2. Goldman Sachs' Next 11 Report, issued on December 12, 2005, cited 11 emerging markets that would fuel the next wave of economic growth: Bangladesh, Egypt, Indonesia, Iran, Mexico, Nigeria, Pakistan, Philippines, South Korea, Turkey, and Vietnam.
3. Martin T. Biegelman with Daniel R. Biegelman, *Building a World-Class Compliance Program: Best Practices and Strategies for Success* (Hoboken, NJ: John Wiley & Sons, 2008), 127.
4. Judy Dempsey, "German Truck Manufacturer MAN in Bribery Investigation," *New York Times*, May 13, 2009, B8.
5. Vanessa Fuhrmans and David Crawford, "Probe Finds Millions in 'Suspicious Payments,'" *Wall Street Journal*, December 11, 2009, B3.
6. Michael Strauss, "The Growth and Natural Resource Endowment Paradox: Empirics, Causes & the Case of Kazakhstan," *Praxis*, vol. xvi, 2000, http://fletcher.tufts.edu/praxis/archives/xvi/Strauss.pdf.
7. For a jaundiced, tell-all account of this phenomenon, see John Perkins, *Confessions of an Economic Hitman* (New York: Penguin, 2005). Perkins alleges many misdeeds done by him and others to entice and coerce foreign leaders into giving up their natural resources to Western interests and corporations.
8. Slaughter & May, "*Corruption?!*" April 2008, www.slaughterand may.com/media/760542/corruption.pdf.
9. City of London Overseas Anti-Corruption Unit, www.cityoflondon .police.uk/CityPolice/ECD/anticorruptionunit/aboutus.htm.
10. Michael Peel, "Guilty Plea to Bribery Sets Legal Landmark," *Financial Times*, August 23, 2008, www.ft.com/cms/s/0/ff993ec6-70ad-11dd-b514-0000779fd18c.html.

11. Kerry E. Grace, "UK Fines an Aon Unit $7.9 Million," *Wall Street Journal Online Europe*, January 9, 2009, http://online.wsj.com/article/SB123145324985265811.html.
12. Ibid.
13. Aon Corp., "Aon Limited Confirms a Settlement of £5.25M with FSA," news release, January 8, 2009, http://aon.mediaroom.com/index.php?s=43&item=1434.
14. Caroline Binham, "U.K. FSA Fines Aon $7.9 Million Over Suspect Payments," *Bloomberg News*, January 8, 2009, www.badfaithinsurance.org/reference/General/0840a.htm.
15. Financial Services Authority, "Aon Ltd. Final Notice on Requirement to Pay a Financial Penalty," January 6, 2009, www.fsa.gov.uk/pubs/final/aon.pdf.
16. Binham, "U.K. FSA Fines Aon."
17. United Kingdom Ministry of Justice, Draft Bribery Bill, www.justice.gov.uk/publications/bribery-bill.htm.
18. United Kingdom Ministry of Justice, Presented to Parliament by the Lord Chancellor and Secretary of State for Justice by Command of her Majesty, "Bribery Draft Legislation," March 2009, www.justice.gov.uk/publications/docs/draft-bribery-bill-tagged.pdf.
19. UK Ministry of Justice, Draft Bribery Bill.
20. Serious Fraud Office, "Mabey & Johnson Ltd Prosecuted by the SFO," press release, July 10, 2009, www.sfo.gov.uk/press-room/latest-press-releases/press-releases-2009/mabey–johnson-ltd-prosecuted-by-the-sfo.aspx.
21. "Firm Admits Overseas Corruption," *BBC News*, July 10, 2009, http://news.bbc.co.uk/2/hi/business/8144361.stm.
22. Mabey & Johnson, "Mabey & Johnson Resolves SFO Probes with Guilty Pleas," press release, July 10, 2009, www.mabey.co.uk/english/docs/press%20release%20issued%20Friday%2010%20July%202009.pdf.
23. Serious Fraud Office, "Mabey & Johnson Ltd Prosecuted."
24. Serious Fraud Office, "Approach of the Serious Fraud Office to Dealing with Overseas Corruption," July 21, 2009, www.sfo.gov.uk/media/28313/approach%20of%20the%20sfo%20to%20dealing%20with%20overseas%20corruption.pdf.
25. "Grease My Palm," *The Economist*, November 27, 2008, www.economist.com/specialreports/displaystory.cfm?story_id=12628030.
26. Ibid.

27. Philip P. Pan, "'Raiding' Underlines Russian Legal Dysfunction," *Washington Post*, August 13, 2009, www.washingtonpost.com/ wp-dyn/content/article/2009/08/12/AR2009081203359.html?hpid= sec-world.
28. Ibid.
29. "Grease My Palm."
30. Ibid.
31. Carol Matlack, "The Peril and Promise of Investing in Russia," *BusinessWeek*, October 5, 2009, 52.
32. Emily Fredrix, "PepsiCo Bets Big on Russia," *Seattle Times*, July 7, 2009, A9.
33. Jason Bush, "Ikea in Russia: Enough is Enough," *BusinessWeek*, July 13, 2009, 33.
34. Ibid.
35. Ibid.
36. "Corruption Cop: A Conversation with Nuhu Ribadu, Anti-Corruption Crusader," *Washington Post*, May 24, 2009, www.washingtonpost .com/wp-dyn/content/article/2009/05/22/AR2009052202025.html.
37. Michael Wines, "Graft Inquiry in Namibia Finds Clues in China," *New York Times*, July 21, 2009, A6.
38. Ibid.
39. "Corruption Cop: A Conversation with Nuhu Ribadu."
40. Edward Harris, "Corruption Leaves Nigeria in the Dark," *Associated Press*, March 2, 2007, accessed via www.washingtonpost.com/wp-dyn/content/article/2007/03/02/AR2007030200673.html.
41. Sam Kennedy, "Nigeria: The Hidden Cost of Corruption," *Frontline World*, April 24, 2009, www.pbs.org/frontlineworld/stories/bribe/ 2009/04/nigeria-the-hidden-cost-of-corruption.html.
42. Ibid.
43. Department of Justice, "Willbros Group Inc. Enters Deferred Prose-cution Agreement and Agrees to Pay $22 Million Penalty for FCPA Violations," press release, May 14, 2008, www.usdoj.gov/opa/pr/ 2008/May/08-crm-417.html.
44. "Bribery Scandal Rocks Big Oil," ProPublica and PBS' *Frontline*, September 8, 2008, http://articles.moneycentral.msn.com/Investing/ Extra/bribery-scandal-rocks-big-oil.aspx?GT1=33002.
45. Ibid.
46. Stephen Foley, "Cheney Colleague Admits Bribery in Halliburton Oil Deals," *The Independent (UK)*, September 4, 2008, www.independent

.co.uk/news/world/americas/cheney-colleague-admits-bribery-in-halliburton-oil-deals-918133.html.

47. Ibid.
48. "Bribery Scandal Rocks Big Oil."
49. Anna Driver, "Halliburton to Pay $559 Million to Settle Bribery Probe," *Reuters*, January 26, 2009, www.reuters.com/article/ousiv-Molt/idUSTRE50P5ZE20090126.
50. "Corruption Cop: A Conversation with Nuhu Ribadu."
51. Craig Timberg, "Under Pressure, Anti-Corruption Official in Nigeria Steps Down," *Washington Post Foreign Service*, January 5, 2008, www.washingtonpost.com/wp-dyn/content/article/2008/01/04/AR20 08010403511.html.
52. "Corruption Cop: A Conversation with Nuhu Ribadu."
53. "Nigeria Warrants for el-Rufai and Ribadu a 'Witch-Hunt,'" *BBC News*, December 10, 2009, http://news.bbc.co.uk/2/hi/africa/8405818.stm.
54. Transparency International's Corruption Perception Index, www .transparency.org/policy_research/surveys_indices/cpi/2009/cpi_20 09_table.
55. "Report on the Manipulation of the Oil-for-Food Programme," October 27, 2005, www.iic-offp.org/story27oct05.htm.
56. Richard Smith, William Jacobsen, and Kimberly Walker, "Novo Nordisk A/S Agrees to Pay Over $18 Million to Resolve Oil for Food Allegations," Fulbright & Jaworski, May 13, 2009, www.fulbright .com/index.cfm?fuseaction=publications.detail&pub_id=3872&site_ id=494&detail=yes.
57. "Iraq Leader Vows to End Corruption Amid Scandal," *Reuters*, May 27, 2009, www.reuters.com/article/worldNews/idUSTRE54Q53X20 090527?feedType=RSS&feedName=worldNews.
58. "Corruption Seen at Root of Iraq's Lack of Services," *Reuters*, May 7, 2009, www.reuters.com/article/latestCrisis/idUSL7411402.
59. Ibid.
60. Transparency International, The Americas Department, www.trans parency.org/regional_pages.
61. Associated Press, "Mexico's Graft Bill Up Sharply," *Seattle Times*, April 17, 2008, A7.
62. Department of Justice, "Helmerich & Payne Agrees to Pay $1 Million Penalty to Resolve Allegations of Foreign Bribery in South America," press release, July 30, 2009, www.usdoj.gov/criminal/pr/press_ releases/2009/07/07-30-09helmerich-pays.pdf.

63. In the Matter of Helmerich & Payne, Order Instituting Cease-and-Desist Proceedings, July 30, 2009, 2-3, www.sec.gov/litigation/admin/2009/34-60400.pdf.

64. Department of Justice, "Former Alcatel CIT Executive Sentenced for Paying $2.5 Million in Bribes to Senior Costa Rican Officials," press release, September 23, 2008, www.usdoj.gov/opa/pr/2008/September/08-crm-848.html.

65. Ibid.

66. "Cell Phone Bribery Figure Gets 30 Months in U.S. Prison," *A.M. Costa Rica*, www.amcostaricas.com/092408.htm.

67. Carol Matlack, "Alcatel-Lucent Says 'No Thanks' to Middlemen," *BusinessWeek*, January 7, 2009, www.businessweek.com/globalbiz/blog/europeinsight/archives/2009/01/alcatel-lucent.html.

68. Ibid.

69. Chevron has posted the recordings and other relevant information at www.chevron.com/ecuador.

70. Simon Romero and Clifford Krauss, "Chevron Offers Evidence of Bribery Scheme in Ecuador Lawsuit," *New York Times*, September 1, 2009, A4; Patrick Markey, "Chevron says gives Ecuador evidence in bribery case," (sic), *Reuters*, September 7, 2009, www.reuters.com/article/rbssEnergyNews/idUSN0744380520090907.

CHAPTER 7

Worldwide Hotspots for Corruption and Bribery: China, Central Asia, India, and Asia Pacific

Of all the worldwide hotspots for FCPA violations, corruption, and bribery, perhaps none is hotter than China. This is not to say that China is the most corrupt country on earth, far from it in fact. China ranks 79 out of 180 countries in Transparency International's 2009 corruption survey. China's prominence in corruption and bribery issues and as a major locus for FCPA violations results from several factors. Bangladesh, for instance, easily trumps China in terms of corruption levels, but China's volume of international business crushes that of Bangladesh many thousands of times over. The greater the amount of business, and the greater the competition for said business, will invariably lead to higher corruption risks. Among FCPA prosecutions, China ranks third after Iraq and Nigeria.[1]

China remains officially a Communist country. Nearly all major enterprises and industries are state-run enterprises or are heavily involved with the government. As noted earlier, an employee of a state-run company may be considered a government official for FCPA purposes. Many companies have subsidiaries based in Asia, particularly in China and India. Growing companies there are also prime acquisition targets for Western companies. That region, particularly China, presents opportunities for economic growth even in the face of global recession. Economic downturns in other countries have further encouraged companies to look for opportunities elsewhere, to lower costs by shifting operations or as new markets for their products.

Beyond China, this chapter examines the rest of Asia, specifically Central Asia, India, and Asia Pacific. These other regions and countries are very important and should not be ignored, as they are the sites of many FCPA prosecutions.

CHINA

The primary FCPA compliance issue for China is that most industries are state-owned enterprises. As the FCPA's antibribery provisions do not cover commercial bribery, paying a bribe to another company to facilitate business would not subject one to FCPA liability, though they may still be liable under the books and records provisions, the Travel Act, or local bribery laws. However, the employees of state-run business are considered "foreign officials" for the purposes of the FCPA; bribing them would subject a business to liability under the antibribery provisions. In the case of AGA Medical Corporation, the company got in trouble for paying kickbacks to doctors in state-run Chinese hospitals. The doctors then directed the hospitals to purchase medical devices from AGA.[2] The doctors were found to be "foreign officials" for purposes of the FCPA. A similar case, *United States v. Diagnostics Products Corporation Co. Ltd.*, involved bribes disguised as commissions paid to doctors and laboratory workers.[3]

Some of the difficulties come from the combination of cultural divides and the physical distance. The Faro Technologies case, discussed in Chapter 3, involved a company that specifically instructed its employees not to bribe but did so anyway. The company was faulted for lack of rigorous training. Yet, despite being told not to, the employees broke the rules anyway. They made the "referral fees" as their way to get business.

The Dangers of Agents: Avery Dennison

Companies doing business in China are well aware of the risks they run if they engage in corrupt behavior, thanks to aggressive FCPA enforcement.

172

If they are not, they have no excuse. "U.S. firms are widely considered to operate with higher ethics than Chinese and Western competitors—in large part because of stringent laws such as the FCPA . . . and the Sarbanes-Oxley Act of 2002."[4] They are also well aware of the rampant corruption and cutthroat competition for business. "Faced with the choice between bribing officials and losing business, some U.S. firms have turned to middlemen, often from Hong Kong or Taiwan, to grease the wheels for them."[5]

Avery Dennison ("Avery") was one of those companies. The company is best known for its labels and other self-adhesive products. It has done business in China since 1995 when it began making the labels for various products, such as Tsingtao beer. Avery aspired to grow its business when, after acquiring another company, it entered the market for reflective film used in traffic safety applications. This was a market dominated by 3M and Avery Dennison needed an edge to gain a foothold.

In 2003 and 2004, Avery employed multiple consultants to obtain contracts for the company in exchange for a cut of the proceeds. In one lucrative deal, Avery hired a marketing representative whose wife was one of the officials in charge of awarding the deal. After finalizing the deal, Avery sold the finished product to a company owned and operated by the China Public Safety Commission and then returned part of the proceeds to government officials as a "commission." The company spent lavishly on entertainment for clients. Sales nearly tripled over a two-year period. The arrangement of a government agency owning a profit-generating business is not unusual in China. Nevertheless, the business structure, its finances, and relationship with the government are often murky and are likely to breed corruption.[6]

Avery wanted to grow its Chinese operations and did what it could to achieve this goal. "In building relations and cutting deals with Chinese officials, local employees said they took their cues from management in Pasadena, which wanted to rapidly expand in China, retaining high-level consulting help and spending extensively on entertainment."[7] As a former employee pointed out, entertaining was a major way of attracting Chinese customers. As he put it, "You cannot just do PowerPoint presentations."[8]

By the summer of 2004, things began to change in Avery's practices. Outside counsel conducted an internal investigation. Senior management ordered the removal of employees and the consultants involved in the corruption. The company then self-reported the FCPA violations. Unfortunately for Avery, this decision had consequences. Sales in the affected unit plunged as the company lost its lucrative arrangement. Avery Dennison pushed out at least eight employees and managers, and several other senior staff members quit in frustration. Some of those employees had warned the company about the use of local consultants and their questionable behavior in obtaining contracts.[9]

Avery wound up settling with the SEC, disgorging profits, and paying a penalty of $200,000. The settlement encompassed its bribes, sightseeing trips, and gifts to Chinese officials, plus the actions of an acquired company which failed to end its preacquisition practices of off-the-books payments.[10] Since then, the company has ramped up its ethics training and monitoring in China while ending the lavish parties and corrupt payments.

HEIGHTENED ANTI-CORRUPTION ENFORCEMENT EFFORTS IN CHINA

The People's Republic of China (PRC) has become increasingly focused on enforcing anti-corruption laws. Governmental corruption has long been a serious problem in the region. The violent Tiananmen Square protests of 1989 grew out of the public's demand that government stop the widespread corruption problem. A 2007 study estimated that corruption cost China $86 billion in a single year,[11] a figure that has likely only risen since then. In recent years, the country has had a renewed focus on fighting the pervasive bribery and corruption culture. As China gains greater acceptance into the mainstream of global business, it has pledged to embrace improved business practices and governance. There has been a marked increase in anti-corruption arrests and convictions that is expected to continue in the coming years.

Like most countries, the PRC has a number of laws that address corruption and bribery issues. But there is a very significant difference that cannot be ignored. Serious cases of fraud and corruption can be prosecuted as capital crimes in China. A large number of those convicted for these capital crimes have been executed over the years. For those avoiding a death penalty, life imprisonment is the norm. In addition, and unlike the statutes and laws in the United States and other countries, Chinese statutes can be very general in nature and lack definitions of the various elements of the crime.

In July 2009, the former chairman of Sinopec Corp., the second-largest oil company in China was convicted for receiving $28 million in bribes over an eight-year period ending in 2007. Chen Tonghai was one of the highest-ranking executives of a state-owned enterprise ever prosecuted for corruption. When he resigned in June 2007, the announcement only gave "personal reasons" for his departure. While normally a crime of this magnitude would result in execution, his remorse, a full confession, and extensive cooperation resulted in a suspended death sentence, which will be changed to life imprisonment if he does not commit another crime for two years.[12] Chinese officials hope that this sentence will serve as a warning to other offenders and encourage officials to resist corruption. This will be easier said than done, as "Senior officials in state firms have many opportunities to ask for bribes in a system that lacks checks and balances and in which money has become the driving force in society."[13]

This lack of accountability and official restrictions will be a major hurdle to overcome. Much of China's efforts so far have been at the national level; however, most corruption happens at the local level, such as with local Communist party bosses. This makes it difficult to fight, as it requires significant amounts of effort and manpower. This sort of corruption is also less visible and less likely to embarrass China. National corruption stories, on the other hand, can prove very damaging globally. Newspapers around the world carried the story of the former head of China's State Food and Drug Administration Zheng Xiaoyu's bribery conviction. He took payments in return for approving substandard food and drugs. The tainted products were linked to dozens of deaths and China executed him for his crimes.[14]

China also sentenced two men to death and a third to life imprisonment for their roles in the 2008 tainted milk scandal.[15] Zheng was seen as a scapegoat for China's regulatory failings. The death sentences for those involved sent a very strong message with how seriously China takes these crimes, but it remains to be seen whether the institutional changes needed to prevent these types of incidents will be made.

In a similar vein, China executed two people for running Ponzi schemes and defrauding investors out of more than $100 million. "Though usually reserved for violent crimes, death sentences are also applied for non-violent offenses that involve large sums of money or are seen to threaten social order."[16] This fraud " 'seriously damaged the country's financial regulatory order and social stability,' " said the official Xinhua News Agency.[17]

Following the law of unintended consequences, these tough sentences have caused another phenomenon in China: suspects accused of corruption fleeing the country. Fearful of receiving the death penalty and well aware that many countries will not extradite fugitives back to China, roughly 800 or more government officials have fled.[18]

Corruption and Societal Discontent

These issues remain at the forefront of China's policy agenda. China has put a focus on fighting corruption because a failure to do so could have dramatic consequences. Rampant corruption is seen as a source of public discontent. Corrupt local governments and an overriding sense of societal unfairness have sparked unrest and riots, including the 2009 riot involving thousands of Han Chinese and Muslim Uighurs. "The violence underscores how unfair China seems to many Chinese. . . . As standards of living have risen, so have aspirations—and frustrations when outside factors like kickbacks and nepotisms further unlevel the playing field."[19] Furthermore, government officials have used anti-corruption laws to settle personal scores and eliminate rivals. Though many prosecutions are genuine, this highlights one of China's major contradictions: "the government regularly publicizes an astounding number of corruption cases, yet little progress seems to be made in uprooting corruption."[20]

One Chinese lawmaker warned that unless China institutes better regulation and tighter supervision, state-owned enterprises will face extensive corruption risks. These enterprises have access to tremendous amounts of capital but inadequate oversight. When combined with the power given to their executives, this equals a recipe for corruption.

A rash of incidents has led many to stress that China is in need of more anti-corruption efforts and personnel. Local procuratorates, or people's courts, usually only have three or four officials fighting corruption, while the number of cases a year averages 30,000. Whistleblowers also face risks from retaliation, particularly from corrupt judicial and law enforcement officials. They also may not receive adequate protection from higher authorities.[21]

Criminal Law of the People's Republic of China

The Criminal Law of the PRC defines numerous crimes and was amended in 1997 to include corruption offenses. The anti-corruption provision is the most comprehensive antibribery law in effect and covers bribes given to and received by government officials and employees of private businesses. Bribery requires the intention to derive an improper benefit or when the value is excessive. Unfortunately, there are no guidelines as to what excessive means. Criminal liability for bribery can start with receipt of a few hundred dollars but a death penalty sentence usually requires very large amounts of money exchanging hands.

176

The law does not clearly differentiate between gifts and bribes. In China, gifts, meals, travel and entertainment, donations, and commissions could easily be used as bribes and law enforcement is very aware of this. Government officials, including those employed by state-owned enterprises, are generally prohibited from accepting meals, gifts, entertainment, and overseas trips. Unless there is a legitimate business need for providing these benefits, they are usually considered violations of law. Small promotional giveaways are unlikely to be considered bribes. Under the law, giving a bribe is less severe than accepting a bribe. The possession of significant assets without a legitimate source of income can be prima facie evidence of bribery.

One must also be aware of creative forms of bribery that are hard to detect. One example can occur when a government official is a gambler. The bribe giver intentionally loses when playing with the official and these intentional losses form the beneficial bribe. Another is paying for educational costs for children of officials. Generally, the thresholds for prosecution depend on the extent of the bribery scheme, the seniority and positions of those receiving bribes, the amounts, and degree of criminal intent. China is particularly problematic due to the large numbers of state-owned enterprises whose officers, directors, managers, and employees are considered government employees. The same is true with officials in Communist Party committees within state-owned enterprises whose employees are considered government employees.

Company Law of the People's Republic of China

The Company Law of the PRC regulates the "organization and operation of companies, protecting the legitimate rights and interests of companies, shareholders, and creditors, maintaining the socialist economic order, and promoting the development of the socialist market economy."[22] Companies are defined as any limited liability or joint stock company that is established to do business within the PRC. Under the Company Law, a director, supervisor, or manager of a business may be legally liable for using his or her authority to request and accept bribes.

Anti-Unfair Competition Law of the People's Republic of China

The Anti-Unfair Competition Law of the PRC protects the "healthy development of the socialist market economy, encourages and protects fair market competition, prohibits unfair competition, safeguards the legal rights

177

and interests of managers."[23] The term *manager* refers to the legal authority, and other economic organizations and individuals who deal with commercial businesses or profitable services. The law specifically states that "Managers shall not use money or properties to bribe others in order to sell or purchase commodities."[24]

It is unlawful to pay a bribe in order to sell or purchase commodities, but if a bribe is paid then normal accounting records must be maintained of that payment. Any discounts or commissions paid to a middleman must be accounted for correctly in a company's books and records. Failure to properly account for such payments is a crime. In addition, the middleman must also correctly book the payment. The Act's books and records provisions are similar to that of the FCPA. A bribe that is not properly disclosed on the company's books and records is clearly a violation. That includes bribes that are disguised as discounts, commissions, consulting services, donations, rebates, or other language intended to be deceptive and hidden.

Invitation and Submission of Bids Law of the People's Republic of China

This law was enacted to "standardize bid invitation and bid submission activities, to protect the interests of the State, the public interests, and the lawful rights and interests of the parties involved in the bid invitation and bid submission activities, to increase economic benefits and to guarantee project quality."[25] It outlaws bribery in the submission of bids for contracts and covers activities by both government officials and those outside of government. This includes employees of companies doing business in the PRC. There are both civil and criminal penalties for violations. There are a number of relevant articles of the law that pertain to collusion, corruption, and fraud including:

- *Bidders may not collude on the bid price, may not preclude fair competition from other bidders or prejudice the lawful rights and interests of the bid inviting party or other bidders.*

- *Bidders and the bid inviting party may not collude in the submission of bids in order to harm the interests of the State, the public interest or the lawful rights and interests of a third party.*

- *Bidders are prohibited from bribing the bid inviting party or members of the bid evaluation committee in order to have their bid accepted.*

- *A bidder may not submit a below cost bid price in competing for a project, or submit its bid in the name of a third party or use other fraudulent means to have its bid accepted.*[26]

178

Interim Provisions on the Prohibition Against Commercial Bribery Acts

The Interim Provisions on the Prohibition Against Commercial Bribery Acts was enacted to prevent the occurrence of commercial bribery and preserve fair competition. The Act criminalizes commercial bribery to buy or sell goods in violation of the Anti-Unfair Competition Law. Of significant importance, "the acts committed by an employee of an operator for selling or buying goods for the operator by means of commercial bribery shall be deemed as the acts committed by the operator."[27] Similar to the FCPA, the acts of one lone employee can affect the entire organization and hold the organization liable.

CHINA ENFORCEMENT AGENCIES

China has a number of national law enforcement agencies responsible for the investigation and prosecution of its laws, especially those around anti-corruption.

Commission for Discipline Inspection of the Communist Party

The Commission for Discipline Inspection is a Chinese Communist Party organization charged with enforcement of the Communist Party rules. They have the authority to investigate and arrest party members in violation of PRC laws. The Commission has its own investigative arm and with their strong powers of enforcement, they are not an organization to be taken lightly. Corruption and bribery are main areas of focus. They have been very active in the last few years and have made examples of party members who have broken the law, especially around bribery. No Communist Party member is immune from the long arm of the law, from the lowest level member to the highest echelon, but most of their focus is on senior leaders of the party. Completed investigations requiring prosecution are turned over to the Supreme People's Procuratorate.

Supreme People's Procuratorate of the People's Republic of China

The Supreme People's Procuratorate of the PRC is a government agency at the highest national level responsible for both investigation and prosecution of a wide variety of crimes. It is similar to the U.S. Department of Justice in scope and authority. They have instituted hotlines and actively encourage whistleblowers and informants to report violations of law. The use of hotlines in the PRC has proven very effective and they are known to receive many calls. The Supreme People's Procuratorate also conducts a large number of investigations due to the many criminal and civil statutes they have responsibility over.

Ministry of Public Security of the People's Republic of China

The Ministry of Public Security is the principal police agency in the PRC. It is a national police force responsible for the day-to-day enforcement of laws throughout the PRC. The Ministry investigates and prosecutes commercial bribery that does not involve PRC government officials and public servants. Governmental corruption and bribery cases are generally left to the Commission for Discipline Inspection.

State Administration for Industry and Commerce of the People's Republic of China

The State Administration for Industry and Commerce is responsible for drafting and enacting legislation pertaining to industry and commerce. Their responsibilities include anti-monopoly, unfair competition, consumer protection, market regulation, registration of foreign-invested enterprises, and advertising regulations. Advertising, marketing, and other related fees that are disguised as bribes can be prosecuted. While their authority is generally civil in nature, they have been known to refer allegations of corruption and bribery discovered in their investigations to the above-mentioned agencies for further investigation and prosecution.

THE DANGERS OF DOING BUSINESS IN CHINA

On July 5, 2009, China detained four employees of the British-Australian mining company Rio Tinto on suspicion of corruption and bribery. The employees stood accused of bribing Chinese steel executives to get access to confidential information that would give it an edge in business negotiations with Chinese steel mills. On the surface, these arrests reflect China's anti-corruption efforts and its efforts to reduce bribery. However, upon closer inspection this case is far more complex and troubling than it appears. It illustrates why China is such a hotspot for FCPA violations and the major difficulties of doing business there.

Alleging that foreign executives have utilized bribery to gain a competitive advantage in negotiations is not unusual. But how China responded and the context in which the arrests occurred are unusual. The four, including one Australian national, were detained on suspicion of espionage, stealing state secrets, and harming the nation's economic interests and security.[28]

The incident created an international furor, with Australian and American representatives meeting with Chinese officials and strong statements from the Australian Prime Minister Kevin Rudd and others calling for fairness and transparency. China dismissed Australian concerns as "noise" and criticized the Australians for interfering with Chinese judicial sovereignty.[29] Rio Tinto strongly denied the allegations, saying that its employees acted at all times in compliance with its strict policies against bribery.[30]

A Chinese newspaper reported that all 16 Chinese steel mills participating in price talks had been bribed into handing over confidential industry data; had they refused, Rio Tinto would have cut their supplies.[31] Chinese media also reported that authorities found detailed information on Chinese steel mills on seized Rio Tinto computers. According to the report, the information was more detailed than even the presidents of the steel mills would usually have.[32] There is widespread speculation that the arrests were in retaliation for Rio Tinto's calling off of a $20 billion deal that would have given a Chinese state-owned company a large stake in it. Chinese steel producers are also unhappy with the high prices of iron ore, which is more difficult to pay in a global recession. The detained Australian national Stern Hu led the very contentious price negotiations which failed to reach a price agreement for 2009's contracts. There has been speculation his arrest was payback for his role in the negotiations. Whether or not this is true, the timing of the arrests has raised questions.

After the arrests, China released few details of the case, though some came out through Chinese media. It is difficult to speculate on whether the allegations have merit. Hu is well-regarded but corruption is rampant in the iron ore trade. China's insistence on secrecy and well-deserved reputation for using its judicial system to achieve political ends leads one to be more than a little skeptical.

For several weeks, the employees languished in prison without being charged. The fear was that they would be charged with espionage. As the companies involved are state-owned, their commercial secrets fall under the definition of state secrets and thus their theft would involve charges of espionage. Under Chinese law, those accused of stealing state secrets cannot meet with a lawyer until they have been formally charged.

Perhaps responding to heavy international criticism or perhaps reflecting internal disagreement in the Chinese government, China charged the

181

four with commercial bribery and trade secret infringement. These are serious charges to be sure but not as heavy as espionage. Legal experts and Australian officials criticized China for its behavior and in particular its application of its vague state secrets law. "China's state-owned companies make up a significant portion of its economy, and the case has raised fears among multinational corporations doing business here that information they have access to could make them vulnerable to similar prosecution."[33]

It is unknown what the exact repercussions of this incident will be and whether it will affect international trade. The fear of being arrested and fighting a confounding judicial system could very well chill the enthusiasm of businesses keen on expanding into China. The great difficulties foreigners face in the Chinese judicial system is a risk for foreign companies. It is likely that the reaction may well depend on the resolution of these charges. If the employees are innocent, as Rio Tinto vociferously maintains, it will be a major wake-up call, particularly as the arrests will be seen as political payback for a failed business deal. Even if the allegations turn out to be true, and China acted in a lawful manner, the lack of transparency raises concern.

CENTRAL ASIA

Central Asia, which includes countries like Kazakhstan, Azerbaijan, Uzbekistan, and Afghanistan, is another region that suffers from autocratic governments and heavy corruption. The autocratic government structure lends itself to graft among the political elite due to a lack of accountability and many opportunities for self-enrichment through state-run industries. Tying into that point, several of these countries have large oil and natural gas deposits. These resources often figure into the FCPA cases emerging from the area.

"Mr. Kazakhstan"

The strange case of James Giffen illustrates the reach of the FCPA and its limitations. James Giffen, the chief executive of Mercator, an investment bank in New York City, allegedly bribed senior officials in Kazakhstan to obtain lucrative oil contracts in the former Soviet Republic.[34] After the fall of the Soviet Union and the subsequent establishment of Kazakhstan as an independent state, Giffen began to work as a middleman for the Kazakh government, brokering deals between the state and the oil companies eager

182

to access its rich natural resources. Between 1995 and 2000, he arranged deals with Mobil Oil, Amoco, Texaco, and Phillips Petroleum, giving them valuable oil and natural gas rights.[35] He had personal access to all major Kazakh figures; he received the title of "Counselor to the President of Kazakhstan," a semi-official title that allowed him to negotiate the deals.[36]

This indictment alleged that Giffen transferred more than $78 million in cash and gifts to the officials. The gifts allegedly included paying off $36,000 of the former Kazakh Prime Minister Nurlan Balgimbayev's debt, millions of dollars in jewelry and fur coats for the family of the Kazakh president Nursultan Nazarbayev, tuition for the family members at exclusive private schools and colleges, and an $80,000 speedboat for the Kazakh president. These bribes allowed Giffen to stay in his position of power and benefit both him and the Kazakh leadership. Giffen would receive large fees for brokering deals. He would place the funds in Swiss bank accounts and then divert them into various offshore accounts, to conceal their source, and finally transfer funds into Swiss accounts maintained by Nazarbayev and Balgimbayev.[37] Giffen is a colorful individual, even being nicknamed "Mr. Kazakhstan." The character quoted at the opening of this book pontificating on the value of corruption was based on none other than Giffen himself.

At the time of Giffen's arrest in 2003, this was considered the largest FCPA case in history, and the most far-reaching use of the statute. The original indictment also alleged violations of the mail and wire fraud statutes, under the theory that he deprived the citizens of Kazakhstan of the honest services of their government. While this theory is often used to attack domestic government corruption, it is too much of a stretch for these statutes to be applicable to foreign citizens. Giffen claimed that all of his activities were done as an agent of the Kazakh government and that American courts could not pass judgment on the official acts of foreign powers.[38] At the time of his arrest, Giffen carried a Kazakh passport. When this defense failed to encourage a judge to dismiss his indictment, he moved on to a different defense: all of his actions were approved and encouraged by the U.S. government and he was working for the CIA. Of course, proving this defense would require access to classified CIA material.

This case also shows some of the difficulties involved in combating foreign bribery, particularly as it involves vital U.S. interests, that being oil. While the government indicted Giffen, Nazarbayev remains a U.S. ally. The government would be unlikely to dramatically upset a country that supplies

183

oil and hosts numerous military bases critical to military actions in Afghanistan and Pakistan. "Giffen's lawyers have called him a patriot who helped ensure that Kazakhstan's reserves of oil and natural gas would be controlled by American rather than Chinese or Russian companies."[39]

Perhaps these competing interests may explain why this case is still ongoing. Even before Giffen's indictment, American attorneys on behalf of Kazakhstan requested the DOJ to drop the probe.[40] It is widely suspected that diplomatic concerns and reticence by the Bush administration to release CIA documents have put this case on the back burner. Much of the evidence, including the indictment itself, remains sealed.

However, some progress has been made. In June 2009 a judge ruled that Giffen's lawyers can examine documents handed over by the CIA; Giffen himself cannot read them, unless the CIA grants specific permission document by document.[41] Does this mean that some of Giffen's story is true? How will this case be resolved when so much of the evidence is classified? Only time will tell.

Head in the Azeri Sand

An executive need not be directly involved in the bribery, or be proven to have direct knowledge of it, in order to be prosecuted as the saga of Frederic Bourke and Victor Kozeny showed. The case was one of the furthest reaching uses of the FCPA and one of the most difficult cases to prosecute. Bourke "was on trial for investing with Mr. Kozeny knowing that he gave Azeri leaders millions of dollars in cash and a secret two-thirds interest in a venture formed to buy the state oil company, known as Socar."[42]

This prosecution was one of 2009's three high-profile FCPA cases, the others being William Jefferson and the Greens (discussed in Chapter 13). Bourke refused a plea bargain and went to trial. In his defense, his lawyers argued that Kozeny stole $180 million from Bourke and his fellow investors and who had no knowledge of the bribes. They also argued that he was not close with Kozeny, in contrast to the prosecution's portrait of them as close confederates. Bourke, who was once married to a member of the Ford family of automaking fame, also got former Senator George Mitchell to invest money in the venture. A jury found him guilty of conspiring with Kozeny to pay bribes to the former president of Azerbaijan, Heydar Aliyev, and other leaders.[43]

During Bourke's trial, prosecutors used a "conscious avoidance" theory: there was a high probability of bribery and that Bourke consciously avoided learning about their existence.[44] Some commentators have criticized this tactic, pointing out that the United States is likely the only country in the world that would have prosecuted under these sets of facts and argued the knowledge requirement as it did. Of course, students of white-collar crime should be well aware of the "ostrich defense" and know full well that it does not work.[45] Nevertheless, this case was the first time the DOJ litigated to trial a willful blindness theory. The government also produced two cooperating witness who both testified that they each told Bourke about the payments. The judge allowed the prosecution to proceed under both knowledge theories: proving either actual knowledge or conscious avoidance would be sufficient.

Kozeny himself is a fugitive from justice living in the Bahamas. Bahamian courts have refused so far to extradite him. He has not yet been charged. He admitted making the payments but said the FCPA does not apply to him. He further admitted bribing Azeri leaders and investors knew of these payments, but denied stealing any of his investors' money.[46] According to the jury foreman, "the panel believed Bourke learned of the bribes after investing and then should have gotten out. By then Kozeny was known as the 'Pirate of Prague' for allegedly stealing money from investors in his native Czech Republic."[47] Bourke had ignored so many red flags along the way and not done the proper due diligence that the jury had no choice but to agree that he knew or should have known about the illegal actions.

Baker Hughes

Another widespread bribery case involved the oil services company Baker Hughes. The company made illegal payments to win oil contracts in Kazakhstan. It also was involved in similar behavior in Angola, Indonesia, Nigeria, Russia, and Uzbekistan.

In 2000, Baker Hughes submitted a bid to develop a large gas and oil field in northwestern Kazakhstan. Baker Hughes received unofficial word that it would be the winning bidder, but it had to hire a certain consulting firm to secure approval of the contract and pay the firm a commission based on the contract's revenue. Baker Hughes paid approximately $4.1 million to the consultant, knowing that much of this money would be transferred as bribes to officials of Kazakhoil, the state-owned oil company.[48]

Baker Hughes had to pay a $10 million penalty to the SEC, a $23 million profit disgorgement, and an $11 million criminal penalty.[49] At the time, $44 million was the largest penalty ever assessed for an FCPA violation.

This, perhaps more than anything, set the trend of very large penalties for violating the FCPA, as seen with Halliburton and Siemens. Alice Fisher, then assistant attorney general said, "The record penalties leveled in this case leave no doubt that foreign bribery is bad for business. By enforcing the FCPA, we are maintaining the integrity of U.S. markets and leveling the playing field for those companies that want to play by the rules."[50]

This was not Baker Hughes' first brush with the FCPA. In an action filed on September 12, 2001, which understandably got little attention at the time, Baker Hughes admitted to bribing government officials in Indonesia and agreed to cease and desist such practices. The agreement, however, had little impact on Baker Hughes' day-to-day activities. Payments "in Kazakhstan and Angola went on from 1998 to 2003, while those to an agent involved in securing business in Russia and Uzbekistan went on from 1998 to 2004, and payments in Indonesia went on from 2000 to 2003."[51] The Nigerian payments continued from 2001 to 2005.

A 2002 lawsuit filed against the company by a former executive alleged a pattern of bribery and corruption. Alan Ferguson, the former region operation manager in Nigeria for the Baker Hughes Inteq drilling systems group, claimed the company paid bribes to win an important contract with Royal Dutch/Shell. When Ferguson refused to go along with the arrangement, his suit claims the company wrongfully dismissed him.[52] Baker Hughes eventually settled the lawsuit in 2003.

INDIA

India faces significant problems with corruption. Like many other rapidly expanding economies, corruption blunts the full extent of economic growth. Many government officials are amenable to receiving bribes, much to the consternation of corruption fighters and average citizens. Corruption and bribery is so pervasive and institutionalized that "it has almost become a way of life," according to the executive director of Transparency International India.[53] Governmental and business corruption has long been entrenched in the country leaving many people with a feeling of helplessness and embarrassment. "Our government is our identity, and if your identity is clouded, it is a shame," said a manager of the *Hindustan Times*, based in Mumbai.[54]

India's approach to fighting corruption is a two-pronged attack. While enforcement authorities are going after high-level officials for bribery, they are also arresting the "little guy" to send a message that corruption will be fought at the top and at the bottom. "The drive coincides with the government's pledge to spend hundreds of billions of dollars on infrastructure projects and welfare programs—funds that officials fear could be wasted if controls aren't tightened."[55] Like China, India is turning to the public for help in exposing corruption. Citizens are being asked to report any public servant who demands a bribe to perform his or her official duties.

The U.S. government prosecuted Westinghouse Air Brake Technologies (Wabtec) Corp. for bribing government regulators in India. India-based subsidiary Pioneer, which manufactures brakes for railway cars, paid government employees approximately $137,000 to obtain and retain business with the Indian national railway system. The Indian Railway Board selects vendors through a sealed bidding process. The Board solicited bribes from Pioneer during the period when it was evaluating bids, in order for it to approve Pioneer's contract price, and solicited further bribes to ensure that its bids would be considered. To cover up the transactions, Pioneer created fake invoices in collusion with outside marketing agents and maintained separate books to record its unlawful payments, which it frequently destroyed.[56] Pioneer also paid off regulators to deal with inspections, issuing needed product delivery certificates, and avoiding tax audits.

Wabtec discovered the payments and, to its credit, conducted a full investigation with outside counsel, voluntarily disclosed the results to the DOJ, and cooperated fully. The deferred prosecution agreement (DPA) called for a $300,000 penalty and the institution of rigorous internal controls. The company also settled with the SEC, disgorging $288,000 in profits and $89,000 in civil penalties.[57]

The case presents a conundrum frequently encountered when doing overseas business such as this. An American company owns a foreign subsidiary, which of course is expected to generate revenue. The subsidiary is approached for a bribe in connection with a bidding process; the company knows that if it refuses the bribe, its bid will be rejected and it will lose the contract. If it chooses to pay, it will get the business but it will have to suffer the consequences, which here included disgorging profits and financial penalties, not to mention the cost of the investigation and instituting internal controls.

ASIA PACIFIC

China and India are not the only countries with FCPA issues within the Asia Pacific region. Other countries are also prone to bribery and corruption.

Indonesia

Indonesia has a long history of corruption and FCPA prosecutions, tied at number four in the number of cases over the last ten years. Since the end of President Suharto's 32-year reign in 1998, Indonesia has made strong progress in fighting corruption. The progress can almost completely be attributed to the Corruption Eradication Commission, popularly known as the K.P.K. The K.P.K. has taken down corrupt individuals of all stripes, from businessmen to police officers to lawmakers. The commission uses aggressive tactics to make its cases, and these coupled with its success has won it many admirers, but also many powerful enemies. Relations between the K.P.K and police and prosecutors have grown strained as the commission has relentlessly pursued its mission. The police, in retaliation, arrested two senior K.P.K. officials on corruption charges. After much public outcry and press criticism, the charges were dropped and the officials reinstated to their positions.[58]

Though the K.P.K. emerged from this struggle victorious, it still has many enemies who seek to impede the fight against corruption. The Indonesia Parliament and the police, both of which are among Indonesia's most corrupt institutions, have attempted to weaken the K.P.K.'s power. New regulations were proposed that would severely limit the K.P.K's wiretapping ability and limit who it would be able to target.[59] While adding greater oversight and accountability to the K.P.K would be a laudable goal, any decision to weaken or demolish it smacks of nothing more than corruption itself.

Vietnam

As the United States continues to enforce the FCPA, it will investigate incidents in countries it never has before. The first case based on violations occurring in Vietnam was seen in 2008. Nexus Technologies sold various types of high-tech equipment to Vietnamese government agencies, including underwater mapping equipment, bomb containment equipment, helicopter parts, chemical detectors, satellite communication parts, and air tracking systems.[60] Nam Quoc Nguyen, Nexus' founder and president, allegedly spent at least $150,000 on "commissions" to members of Vietnamese government agencies in order to obtain lucrative contacts. These bribes allowed him and his fellow defendants to establish relationships with what were termed his "supporters." In exchange for the bribes, the officials allegedly gave Nexus "business by providing confidential information, rigging bids, and other means."[61] As is typical, the bribes were paid to a separate company which then funneled the money back to Vietnam, according to the indictment. The indictment charged the defendants with one count of conspiracy and four counts of violating the FCPA.[62]

Nguyen pleaded not guilty to the charges. Due to the complexities of the case, the court has waived the speedy trial requirements on time limitations to allow for a full review of all the evidence. While this case will likely not be resolved quickly, expect to see other prosecutions coming out of Vietnam and other unexpected places.

South Korea

South Korea has had a long history of corruption scandals. Numerous government officials and corporate executives have been implicated in very public bribery probes. In 2008, the former chairman and several executives of Samsung Group, South Korea's largest conglomerate, were convicted of tax evasion in a case that called into question the company's corporate governance. The criminal investigation started after a whistleblower alleged that Samsung "created secret bank accounts to stash funds used to pay bribes to influential South Koreans."[63] In addition, American corporations, including Tyco and Schnitzer Steel, have also been subjects of FCPA investigations as a result of their activities in South Korea.

A sad commentary on the state of politics in Korea is that every former South Korean president since the 1980s has either been the subject of corruption and bribery allegations or has been convicted and sentenced to prison for such activities after leaving office.[64] Yet, even South Korea had not previously witnessed what occurred on May 23, 2009. For that was when former South Korean President Roh Moo-hyun committed suicide by jumping off a cliff. News reports linked the suicide to allegations of corruption. Roh had the reputation of a reformer and an honest politician but in the months before his suicide, he and his family were caught up in a growing bribery investigation. In April 2009, prosecutors questioned Roh for 13 hours regarding allegations that while president, he received more than $6 million in bribes from a South Korean businessman. Roh denied the allegations but said at the time "I have no face to show to the people. I am sorry for disappointing you."[65]

Roh had previously admitted that "A businessman who supported him had given more than $6 million to his wife and son and his brother's son-in-law while he was in office but he denied they were bribes."[66] Roh characterized the money as either helping to pay a debt or an investment. Nonetheless, a number of Roh's former aides and associates were also under investigation for bribery. The businessman who gave the $6 million was convicted on unrelated bribery and tax violations. Roh's brother was convicted and sentenced to prison earlier in May 2009 for his involvement in another bribery scandal.[67]

Roh did not come from wealth. He was the son of a farmer and never attended college. He taught himself the law and was able to pass the country's bar exam, becoming a human-rights attorney. He was fond of quoting Abraham Lincoln. Roh liked to say that in governing "the main principle you have to respect is never to lie."[68] He was praised as a champion of the underprivileged and a corruption fighter. He left office in 2008 purportedly to a life of leisurely retirement that was not to be.

Taiwan

Even in countries with a low perception of bribery, the threat of corruption still exists. Taiwan, for example, is considered to have a low risk of corruption with a ranking of 37 out of 180 countries in TI's 2009 Corruption Perceptions Index. Yet, both governmental corruption and commercial bribery occur. A court in Taiwan convicted the country's former president Chen Shui-ban on corruption charges in 2009. Chen, along with his wife, had embezzled over $3 million from a presidential fund, received at least $9 million in bribes connected to a government land deal, and forged documents to cover up his crimes. Both received life in prison. This sentence is Taiwan's harshest yet meted out for official corruption.[69]

NOTES

1. Don Lee, "Avery Dennison Case a Window on the Pitfalls U.S. Firms Face in China," *Los Angeles Times*, January 12, 2009, http://articles .latimes.com/2009/jan/12/world/fg-avery12.
2. Department of Justice, "AGA Medical Corporation Agrees to Pay $2 Million Penalty and Enter Deferred Prosecution Agreement for FCPA Violations," press release, June 3, 2008, www.usdoj.gov/criminal/pr/ press_releases/2008/06/06-03-08_fcpa-violations.pdf.

3. Department of Justice, "DPC (Tianjin) Ltd. Charged with Violating The Foreign Corrupt Practices Act," press release, May 20, 2005, www.usdoj.gov/criminal/fraud/press/2005/dpcfcpa.pdf.
4. Lee, "Avery Dennison Case."
5. Ibid.
6. Ibid.
7. Ibid.
8. Ibid.
9. Ibid.
10. Securities and Exchange Commission, "SEC Files Settled Charges Against Avery Dennison Corporation for Violating the Books and Records and Internal Controls Provisions of the Foreign Corrupt Practices Act," litigation release, July 28, 2009, www.sec.gov/litigation/litreleases/2009/lr21156.htm.
11. David Barboza, "The Corruptibles," *New York Times*, September 4, 2009, B1.
12. Shai Oster, "Sinopec Ex-Chief Convicted of Graft," *Wall Street Journal*, July 16, 2009, A8.
13. Jane Macartney, "Ex-Sinopec Boss Wins Reprieve from Death Row," *Times Online* (London), July 15, 2009, http://business.times online.co.uk/tol/business/industry_sectors/natural_resources/article 6714359.ece#cid=OTC-RSS&attr=1185799.
14. "China Food Safety Head Executed," *BBC News*, July 10, 2007, http://news.bbc.co.uk/2/hi/asia-pacific/6286698.stm.
15. Anita Chang, "China Milk Scandal: 2 Get Death Penalty for their Role," *Associated Press*, January 22, 2009, accessed via www.huffing tonpost.com/2009/01/22/china-milk-scandal-2-get-_n_159908.html.
16. "China Executes 2 for Defrauding Investors," *ABC News*, August 6, 2009, http://abcnews.go.com/International/wireStory?id=8263887.
17. Ibid.
18. Richard Cassin, "China's Runaway Bribe Takers," FCPA Blog, May 29, 2009, www.fcpablog.com/blog/2009/5/29/chinas-runaway-bribe-takers.html.
19. Charles Hutzler, "Income Gaps Fueling China Riots," *Associated Press*, July 16, 2009, accessed via www.chinapost.com.tw/commen tary/ap/2009/07/16/216501/Income-gaps.htm.
20. Barboza, "The Corruptibles."
21. "More Anti-Corruption Officials Needed," *China View*, August 7, 2009, http://news.xinhuanet.com/english/2009-08/07/content_11839 744.htm.

22. "Company Law of the People's Republic of China," April 17, 2006, www.chinadaily.com.cn/bizchina/2006-04/17/content_569258 .htm.
23. "Anti-Unfair Competition Law of the People's Republic of China," September 2, 1993, www.lawinfochina.com/law/display.asp?id=648.
24. Ibid.
25. "Invitation and Submission of Bids Law of the Peoples Republic of China," September 27, 2008, http://en.cnci.gov.cn/Law/LawDetails2 .aspx?ID=6029&p=1.
26. Ibid.
27. "Interim Provisions on the Prohibition Against Commercial Bribery Acts," November 15, 1996, www.apeccp.org.tw/doc/China/Decision/ cndec03.html.
28. David Barboza, "Rio Tinto Gave Bribes to Many, China Says," *New York Times*, July 16, 2009, A4.
29. David Barboza, "Concerns On Rio Tinto are 'Noise,' China Says," *New York Times*, July 17, 2009, A6.
30. Enda Curran, "Rio Tinto Case Tied to Price Negotiations," *Wall Street Journal*, July 20, 2009, A7.
31. Zhang Qi and Tony Hao, " 'Bribery is Widespread' in Rio Case," *China Daily*, July 15, 2009, www.chinadaily.com.cn/bizchina/2009-07/15/content_8429852.htm.
32. "Secrets of Chinese Steel Mills Found in Rio's Computers," *China Daily*, July 14, 2009, www.chinadaily.com.cn/china/2009-07/14/ content_8427743.htm.
33. Barboza, "Concerns On Rio Tinto."
34. *U.S. v. Giffen*, 326 F. Supp. 2d 497, 499 (S.D.N.Y. 2004).
35. Department of Justice, "American Businessman Charged with $78 Million in Unlawful Payments to Kazakh Officials in 6 Oil Transactions; Former Mobil Corp. Executive Indicted for Tax Evasion in Kickback Scheme," press release, April 2, 2003, www.usdoj.gov/ usao/nys/pressreleases/April03/giffenwilliams.pdf.
36. Marlena Telvcik, "Kazakhstan: United States v. James H. Giffen," International Eurasian Institute for Economic and Political Research, May 31, 2004, www.positiontoknow.com/S-11/html/JamesGiffen_ Kazakhstan.htm.
37. *United States v. Giffen*, 326 F. Supp. 2d 497, 500 (S.D.N.Y. 2004); Department of Justice, "American Businessman Charged with $78 Million in Unlawful Payments to Kazakh Officials."

38. *U.S. v. Giffen*, 326 F. Supp. 2d 497, 504-6 (S.D.N.Y. 2004); Daniel Biegelman, *Recent Decision: United States v. Giffen, New York International Law Review*, volume 18, Winter 2005, 217.
39. Peter Maas, "The Fuel Fixers," *New York Times*, December 23, 2007, www. nytimes.com/2007/12/23/magazine/23wwln-phenomenon-t.html.
40. "Letter Indicates That Attorneys for Kazakhstan Were Concerned About President's Possible Indictment in US Corruption Case," April 8, 2003, www.eurasianet.org/departments/insight/articles/eav0408 03.shtml.
41. Steve Levine, "Giffen Watch: Former Kazakhstan Consultant Cannot Examine CIA Documents," Oilandglory.com, June 17, 2009, http:// oilandglory.com/2009/06/giffen-watch-former-kazakhstan.html.
42. "Executive Guilty of Conspiracy in Foreign Bribery Case," *Bloomberg News*, July 11, 2009, via *New York Times*, B2.
43. Ibid.
44. David Glovin, "Bourke 'Stuck Head in Sand,' on Oil Bribes, U.S. Says," *Bloomberg News*, July 6, 2009, www.bloomberg.com/apps/ news?pid=newsarchive&sid=aiIE96f0_bys.
45. For more information on the ostrich defense, see Martin T. Biegelman and Joel T. Bartow, *Executive Roadmap to Fraud Prevention and Internal Control: Creating a Culture of Compliance* (Hoboken, NJ: John Wiley & Sons, Inc, 2006), 8–9, 15.
46. David Glovin, "Bourke 'Stuck Head in Sand,' on Oil Bribes, U.S. Says."
47. David Glovin, "Bourke Convicted of Bribery in Kozeny's Azerbaijan Oil Deal," *Bloomberg News*, July 11, 2009, www.bloomberg.com/ apps/news?pid=newsarchive&sid=aXO.vHLdvbcM.
48. Department of Justice, "Baker Hughes Subsidiary Pleads Guilty to Bribing Kazakh Official and Agrees to Pay $11 Million Criminal Fine as Part of Largest Combined Sanction Ever Imposed in FCPA Case," press release, April 26, 2007, www.usdoj.gov/opa/pr/2007/April/ 07_crm_296.html.
49. Securities and Exchange Commission, "SEC Charges Baker Hughes With Foreign Bribery and With Violating 2001 Cease-and-Desist Order," press release, April 26, 2007, www.sec.gov/news/press/2007/ 2007-77.htm; DOJ, "Baker Hughes Subsidiary Pleads Guilty to Bribing Kazakh Official."
50. DOJ, "Baker Hughes Subsidiary Pleads Guilty to Bribing Kazakh Official."

51. Floyd Norris, "Baker Hughes Admits to Overseas Bribery," *New York Times*, April 27, 2007, www.nytimes.com/2007/04/27/business/worldbusiness/27settle.html.
52. Neela Banerjee, "Ex-Executive Sues Baker Hughes; Kickbacks Cited," *New York Times*, March 26, 2002, www.nytimes.com/2002/03/26/business/ex-executive-sues-baker-hughes-kickbacks-cited.html.
53. Niraj Sheth and Jackie Range, "Bribery—and Charges of It—Run Rampant in India," *Wall Street Journal*, July 24, 2008, A8.
54. Ibid.
55. Peter Wonacott, "India Tries New Tack in Drive to Curb Corruption," *Wall Street Journal*, July 13, 2009, A6.
56. *SEC v. Westinghouse Air Brake Technology Corporation*, Civil Action No. 08-CV-706, Complaint, United States District Court for the Eastern District of Pennsylvania, February 14, 2008.
57. Department of Justice, "Westinghouse Air Brake Technologies Corporation Agrees to Pay $300,000 Penalty to Resolve Foreign Bribery Violations in India," press release, February 14, 2008, www .usdoj. gov/opa/pr/2008/February/08_crm_116.html.
58. Camelia Pasandaran and Heru Andriyanto, "Suspended Deputies Cleared to Officially Rejoin KPK," *Jakarta Globe*, December 8, 2009, http://thejakartaglobe.com/home/suspended-deputies-cleared-to-officially-rejoin-kpk/346116.
59. Norimitsu Onishi, "Corruption Fighters Rouse Resistance in Indonesia," *New York Times*, July 26, 2009, A10; "SBY Approves KPK's Wiretapping Authority, *Jakarta Post*, December 9, 2009, www.thejakartapost.com/news/2009/12/09/sby-approves-kpk039s-wiretapping-authority.html.
60. *U.S. v. Nam Quoc Nguyen, et al.*, Indictment, Criminal No. 08-XXX, Dist. Ct. E.D.P.A., September 4, 2008, http://media.philly.com/doc uments/Indictment+-+Nam+Nguyen+et+al.pdf.
61. Ibid.
62. Ibid.
63. Evan Ramstad, "Former Samsung Chairman Found Guilty," *Wall Street Journal*, July 17, 2008, B6.
64. Choe Sang-Hun, "Leap Kills S. Korean Ex-Leader," *Seattle Times*, May 24, 2009, A15.
65. Associated Press, "Ex-S. Korean President Jumps to His Death," Msnbc.com, May 23, 2009, www.msnbc.msn.com/id/30894701.
66. Choe, "Leap Kills S. Korean Ex-Leader."
67. Associated Press, "Ex-S. Korean President Jumps to His Death."

68. Barbara Demick, "Tarnished Politician's Suicide Setback for Democracy," *Seattle Times*, May 30, 2009, A3.
69. "Life in Prison for Taiwan Ex-President Chen Shui-bian and Wife," *Taiwan News*, September 11, 2009, www.etaiwannews.com/etn/news_content.php?id=1054680&lang=eng_news&cate_img=83.jpg&cate_rss=news_Politics_TAIWAN.

CHAPTER 8

BAE Systems: Past
Behavior Haunts
the Company

In the 2006 movie *Inside Man*, the character played by actor Clive Owen commented that "Fact is, all lies, all evil deeds, they stink. You can cover them up for a while, but they don't go away."[1] That sums it up pretty well, as the evil deeds of fraud and corruption usually surface at some point and wreak havoc, no matter how hard the attempts to hide them. That is also the predicament that British defense contractor BAE Systems found itself in.

For years, BAE faced allegations that it maintained a multimillion-dollar slush fund to pay bribes to members of the Saudi royal family to obtain lucrative contracts. Contrary to the approach that the great majority of companies today are taking when faced with Foreign Corrupt Practices Act (FCPA) and other corruption violations, BAE took a different path and denied involvement in bribery and corruption. This is the story of a most unusual case of corruption with many twists and turns.

BAE Systems is a global corporation focused on defense, aerospace, as well as security systems and solutions. In fact, BAE is one of the top defense contractors worldwide in terms of revenue. As of 2007, only Lockheed

Martin and Boeing had more revenue. BAE traces its origins in Great Britain to the year 1560, when it manufactured gunpowder and explosives. The modern day firm is the result of numerous mergers and acquisitions over the years with the BAE name coming in 1999. The UK company has over 100,000 employees with customers and partners in over 100 countries. BAE has particularly strong market positions in the United Kingdom, United States, Australia, South Africa, and Saudi Arabia. The latter market would eventually prove extremely problematic for the company.

AL YAMAMAH DEAL

In 1985, the British government entered into negotiations with Saudi Arabia on an ambitious oil-for-arms contract that would run for almost two decades. Britain, through British defense contractors, would supply the Saudis with large numbers of sophisticated fighter jets, helicopters, and other weapons in return for a much needed steady supply of oil. British Aerospace, as BAE was then known, would supply the majority of the armament orders. This unprecedented deal that would eventually total more than $80 billion came to be known as Al Yamamah, which means "The Dove" in Arabic. What was not publicly known at the time was that as part of the deal, BAE would funnel tens of millions of dollars to Prince Bandar bin Sultan, a member of the Saudi royal family and a very well-connected diplomat. He is the son of Prince Sultan, the crown prince of Saudi Arabia as well as heir to the throne. Prince Bandar is a very rich and influential member of the Saudi royal family with significant political connections in Washington, DC, including close ties to the Bush family.

While there were whispers of bribes and payoffs over the years as well as very discrete probes, nothing really came of this until a September 2003 story in the *Guardian* exposed the sordid matter. The *Guardian* is one of the foremost newspapers in the UK with a long history and a reputation for award-winning investigative journalism. The paper obtained internal documents from the UK's Serious Fraud Office (SFO) that reported that senior executives at BAE, including the then chairman, were personally aware of and/or involved in maintaining a slush fund used to bribe Saudi officials. The *Guardian* was "able to put together a picture of a covert BAE operation allegedly stretching over 15 years, claimed to have poured extraordinary amounts of money into the cause of 'sweetening' officials in the Saudi regime in London connected to the big Al Yamamah fighter and warships deals."[2]

The newspaper story also detailed gifts of expensive sports cars, yachts, exclusive club memberships, gambling trips, procurement of prostitutes, and even the purchase of a home for a woman connected to a Saudi royal family member. The internal report obtained by the paper also detailed BAE's use of a front organization where money was funneled for the entertainment of "top Saudis."[3] Even more disturbing, it was reported that the "Serious Fraud Office said the refusal of BAE to pursue the internal fraud claims might be because 'this is a means of covering up corruption.' "[4]

Just a few months after the *Guardian* story ran, federal agents in Washington, DC were beginning to look into some very suspicious money transfers. In November 2003, Riggs Bank in Washington, DC submitted a Suspicious Activity Report (SAR)[5] to the U.S. Treasury Department after finding unusual funds activity in the millions of dollars related to an account at the bank. Of particular concern, the bank found that over a four-month period, $17.4 million was disbursed from the account to a person in Saudi Arabia. The account was controlled by Prince Bandar, the longtime Saudi ambassador to the United States.[6] Initial investigation by Riggs Bank found that millions of dollars were being sent to an architect in Saudi Arabia for work on one of Prince Bandar's palaces. It was subsequently discovered that over $2 billion in Al Yamamah funds had been deposited in the Saudi account at Riggs Bank and was the source of the money transferred to Saudi Arabia. A second SAR was then submitted to the Treasury Department in January 2004. Compliance Insight 8.1 is the SAR dated January 30, 2004.

COMPLIANCE INSIGHT 8.1: SUSPICIOUS ACTIVITY REPORT, JANUARY 30, 2004

Concern arose over quarterly payments of approximately $4 million made to Mr. Shorbatli from the Saudi Ministry Account. The auditors were unable to determine the purpose of the quarterly payments. Riggs investigations queried World-Check for Ibrahim Shorbatli with negative results. Riggs investigations contacted Mr. Sami Nassar, Vice President of Embassy Banking at Riggs Bank. Nassar reported that Mr. Shorbatli coordinated home improvement and construction projects for Prince Bandar in Saudi Arabia. Nassar stated that the large quarterly payments to Mr. Shorbatli are for the construction of a new

(continued)

(*continued*)

Saudi palace. Large sums of money are being sent from the Resa account in Washington and are being cashed by an individual in Saudi Arabia. Nassar provided a possible explanation for the destination of the funds. However, Riggs' investigation was unable to determine the exact destination and purpose of those funds.[7]

FBI SCRUTINY

The FBI eventually received the SARs from the Treasury Department with an eye toward possible terrorist connections. The FBI reviewed the SARs and conducted an in-depth analysis of more than 20 Riggs Bank accounts. These were both official Saudi Embassy accounts as well as related personal accounts. The focus was on where the deposited funds were going. There were suspicions around commingled funds and the transfers of large sums of money but ultimately no evidence of terrorist financing was found. The FBI never came to learn the source of the funds transferred into Riggs Bank. What the FBI did not know at the time was that in the years to follow, newspapers in the United Kingdom would allege that BAE was the source of the funds that went into the Riggs Bank accounts.

In 2001, Dennis Lormel was a FBI Special Agent and Section Chief of the Financial Crimes Section in Washington, DC. After 9/11, he developed, implemented, and directed the FBI's comprehensive terrorist financing initiatives which evolved into a formal division of the FBI known as the Terrorist Financing Operations Section. As chief of this unit, Lormel was witness to the strong Congressional concern over whether the Saudi government was involved in terrorist financing. "Our mandate in reviewing the Saudi accounts was specifically focused on the outflow of funds to determine if those accounts funded terrorists. Under those circumstances, we were not concerned about the source of the funds. However, I questioned the reasonableness of transactional activity and believed at a future point in time, someone should assess such activity," Lormel recently stated.[8]

BAE's DENIAL

In May 2004, Sir Richard Evans, BAE's former chairman and CEO, testified before a Parliament committee looking into the allegations and denied any corrupt activity at the company. Evans said "I can certainly assure you that we are not in the business of making payments to members of any government."[9] BAE then released a statement stating "categorically that there is not now and there has never been in existence . . . a 'slush fund.' BAE Systems operates in accordance with the laws of the United Kingdom and all other countries in which it operates."[10]

The *Guardian* story and the Parliament inquiry opened the floodgates to further reporting by other organizations. The BBC aired a documentary in October 2004 where former BAE executives and contractors confirmed the existence of the slush fund and the bribery scheme. This dirty secret was apparently known to many people. BAE's chief internal investigator stated on the program that he discovered the slush fund but was told by a senior executive to end his investigation.[11]

SERIOUS FRAUD OFFICE INQUIRY

In July 2004, the SFO began a formal inquiry into the allegations of bribery. The SFO is a highly skilled investigative organization focusing on the most serious and complex frauds in the UK. The SFO has an excellent reputation worldwide and is part of the UK criminal justice system. It was clear that the SFO was making progress in its corruption probe. In a leaked report from the SFO obtained by the *Guardian* in January 2007, several senior BAE executives were named as suspects. In the document from 2006, "BAE's chief executive, Mike Turner, is named along with the former chairman, Sir Dick Evans, and two other executives, in a document dated June 26 last year."[12]

The leaked document detailed a mutual legal assistance request from the SFO to South African authorities regarding a multibillion-dollar aircraft deal. The document alleged secret payments to South African agents "through a BAE offshore front company" and "a highly secret unit within BAE" that handled marketing.[13] The leaked document also included the comment "There is reasonable cause to believe that all the above-named persons and company have committed offences of corruption."[14]

TONY BLAIR QUASHES THE INVESTIGATION

The SFO would never get the chance to complete their investigation because in December 2006, the highest levels of government in the United Kingdom stepped in and stopped the investigation cold. The reason given was that the investigation of BAE, the Saudi government, and connections to corruption imperiled national security. The British government said "Saudi officials had warned the SFO's questioning and potential revelations could damage UK-Saudi relations" and "the Saudis threatened to cancel a giant new defense contract with Britain and to curtail cooperation fighting terrorism."[15]

In a personal and secret memo from then Prime Minister Tony Blair to then UK Attorney General Lord Peter Goldsmith entitled "Al Yamamah: Serious Fraud Office Investigation" and dated December 8, 2006, Blair outlined his reasons why the investigation of BAE needed to cease. The memo was subsequently released to the public as a result of a February 2007 court case. Key points of the memo are as follows:

In light of recent developments, I would be grateful if you would consider again the public interest issues raised by the Serious Fraud Office's ongoing investigation into the possibility of corrupt payments being made by BAE Systems in connection with the Al Yamamah defence relationship with the Kingdom of Saudi Arabia.

It is my judgement on the basis of recent evidence and the advice of colleagues that these developments have given rise to a real and immediate risk of a collapse in the UK/Saudi security, intelligence, and diplomatic cooperation. This is likely to have seriously negative consequences for the UK public interest in terms of both national security and our highest priority foreign policy objectives in the Middle East.

The issue, in Saudi eyes, is not so much about the specifics of any elements of the investigation, but one of cumulative damage to overall confidence in their relationship with the UK. I am advised in strong terms that we are now at high risk of a serious collapse in that confidence.

Article 5 of the OECD Convention on Bribery prohibits you from being influenced by considerations of the national economic interest or the potential effect upon relations with another state. As you know, I strongly support our commitment to the Convention and am proud of this Government's record on putting bribery issues onto the agenda and into law. While this letter is not primarily concerned with the serious damage being done to our bilateral relationship by the investigation, it is of course of concern to me, not least because of the critical difficulty presented to the negotiations over the Typhoon contract.

My primary duty is however to UK national security and it is on this basis that I must urge you to consider the public interest in relation to the pursuit of this investigation.

In summary, it is in my judgment very clear that the continuation of the SFO investigation into Al Yamamah risks seriously damaging Saudi confidence in the UK as a partner. It is also my judgment that such damage risks endangering UK national security, both directly in protecting citizens and service people, and indirectly through impeding our search for peace and stability in this critical part of the world. This letter, and the attached papers, I hope help to explain those judgments. The Defence Secretary endorses what is said earlier in this letter about the impact on Defence interests and both he and the Foreign Secretary share my overall view, expressed here, on the damaging impact of the SFO investigation. This assessment is formed on the basis of advice from the Government's most senior national security official advisors.[16]

Subsequently, on December 14, 2006, Attorney General Goldsmith publicly announced the ending of the SFO corruption investigation due to national security interests. As expected, there was an uproar from a number of sectors. The media, including the *Guardian*, continued its cutting-edge reporting and continuing disclosures. There was criticism from the Organisation for Economic Co-operation and Development (OCED). The Campaign Against Arms Trade and other groups lobbied for the investigation to continue. United States officials also protested to the UK Foreign Office that the decision to stop the investigation would send the wrong message.

The protests fell on deaf ears as Britain's House of Lords ruled in July 2008 that the SFO acted lawfully in halting the corruption inquiry. A British government official upset by the ruling stated, "The unscrupulous who have friends in high places overseas willing to make such threats now have a 'Get Out of Jail Free' card and there is nothing the public can do to hold the government to account if it abuses its national security powers."[17]

That did not end BAE's issues. Although the SFO ended its inquiry into the Saudi contracts, it has continued to investigate bribery allegations in Tanzania, Romania, and Chile.[18] Austrian prosecutors are continuing their investigation of bribes paid by BAE to win aircraft contracts in Austria and the Czech Republic. In September 2008, police searched the Austrian home and office of a person who is alleged to have used his influence to steer contract selection away from other defense contractors and to BAE. The search warrant affidavit alleged that this person "is suspected of receiving commission payments from BAE as a consultant and passing some of this money as bribes to unidentified third parties."[19]

DOJ's HARD-LINE APPROACH

In June 2007, the U.S. Department of Justice (DOJ) began its own inquiry into BAE's dealings in Saudi Arabia, specifically the Al Yamamah deal. In an indication of the more aggressive approach that the Justice Department is taking on FCPA investigations in general and with BAE in particular, in May 2008, the FBI detained then CEO Mike Turner and a BAE board member upon their arrival in Houston. Their laptops and cell phones were forensically examined and documents in their possession were copied. At the conclusion of the questioning, both men were issued Grand Jury subpoenas. Other executives have also received subpoenas. There have also been news reports that several U.S.-based BAE executives had their homes searched at the same time. A UK government official at the time stated "It is very clear that the US authorities will not let this go. If there is any question of illegality on American soil they will investigate fully, and they are putting the British government to shame."[20]

BAE RESPONSE

Besides a number of public pronouncements that the company did not maintain a slush fund, pay bribes, or violate any law, BAE did take a number of positive steps to improve their corporate governance and compliance. In 2007, the BAE Board appointed Lord Harry Woolf, the former Lord Chief Justice of England and Wales "to establish an expert independent committee to study and report on our ethics policies and processes and make recommendations aimed at achieving a leadership position in ethical business practice amongst corporate industry peers."[21] BAE stated that they wanted to provide assurance to their customers, investors, employees, and communities that the company's "policies are subject to continuous improvement and set the pace for the international defense community."[22]

As detailed in their Corporate Responsibility Report 2007, BAE reinforced a commitment to meet the "highest standards of conduct" and "incorporate robust internal and external governance."[23] BAE also documented areas for improvement including increasing the reporting of violations of business conduct and a heightened visibility of senior leadership around ethics and compliance. They also published details on disciplinary actions including the number of employees dismissed for violations related to unethical behavior, including the general categories of violations such as accounting charges practices, company ethical practices, conflicts of interest, international business issues, procurement, trade and marketing, and contract compliance. While this is a good display of transparency, there is no category that specifically lists dismissals for bribery or corruption issues although they could be included in some of the preceding categories. Including such a specific category would have further increased transparency. Yet, since BAE is denying any involvement in such corrupt activity, it is understandable why they haven't specifically called that out for reporting.

BAE also reported on trends resulting from calls to their Ethics Helpline. The number of calls and inquiries decreased in 2007 to 327 from the 410 calls in 2006. In addition, there were many more calls by U.S. employees as compared to those in the UK. BAE attributed the higher number of calls to increased training of U.S.-based employees on ethical business practices and the need for increased training in the UK. By 2008, the number of calls to the ethics line increased to a total of 507 with 425 calls coming from the United States and 82 coming from the UK and the rest of the world.[24] For a company with the size and worldwide reach of BAE, the number of calls is small. This may very well be the result of the corporate culture that may discourage the reporting of business conduct violations, especially in the UK. An indication of this can be seen from Compliance Insight 8.2 that contrasts the types and numbers of calls to the BAE Ethics Helpline in 2008 that resulted in inquiries. Not every issue category has been included in the following chart but only ones that have a potential connection to bribery and corruption issues.

COMPLIANCE INSIGHT 8.2: TYPES AND NUMBERS OF CALLS TO BAE's ETHICS HELPLINE[25]

Issue Type	UK/Rest of World	United States
Accounting charges practices	2	82
Company ethical practices	5	0
Conflicts of interest	2	102
International business issues	0	2
Procurement, trade, and marketing	1	11
Contract compliance	0	3
Management practices	11	69

In January 2009, BAE rolled out a new Global Code of Conduct. They included a graphic of a jigsaw piece to illustrate and ask the question "What does a jigsaw have to do with ethical business conduct?" The answer from the code is "Laws in each country, company policies, and our ethical principles are all part of picture of ethics. We need to understand where each piece fits in meeting our responsibilities."[26] The code addresses bribes, gifts, and entertainment by stating, "We will not offer, give, or receive bribes or inducements for any purpose whether directly or through a third party."[27] This section of the code provides specific information on related areas of concern including issues around gifts and entertainment as well as the use of third parties. This section also provides reinforcement for employees to always seek guidance whenever offering, giving, or receiving gifts and entertainment as they can easily be problematic when related to contracting and corruption.

The code of conduct includes practical examples with questions and answers. Unfortunately, there are no examples around giving bribes and other corruption areas. Considering the investigative attention in this area, practical examples should be included as guidance for employees. The code also takes a strong stand on facilitation payments by stating that BAE does not make such payments. They go one step further by boldly announcing the company will "seek to eliminate the practice in countries in which we do business."[28] A recommended enhancement to this and other codes of conduct is to include guidance around the possible need to make a facilitation payment under duress or threat of imprisonment in a foreign country.

BAE's 2008 Corporate Responsibility Report also listed objectives for 2009 that included senior leadership conducting two employee focus groups discussing the new code of conduct and ethical issues in addition to completing an employee survey on ethical questions. In addition, the company planned to implement the findings of the Woolf Committee.

WOOLF COMMITTEE

The Woolf Committee was an independent committee commissioned by BAE Systems' Board of Directors in August 2007 to conduct an impartial audit of the Company's ethical policies and procedures subsequent to the very public allegations of bribery and corruption. This included a review and determination of adherence to applicable anti-corruption legislation and whether the company's policies and procedures are robust enough to ensure appropriate compliance. The committee was also tasked with making recommendations for remedial action the company may need to pursue. BAE pledged full cooperation and access to the Woolf Committee and the BAE Board agreed to institute the recommendations. BAE's intention was for the committee and its findings to position the company as a worldwide leader in business conduct and ethics. Besides Lord Woolf, other members of the committee included chief executives from business and ethics organizations.

The Woolf Report was issued in May 2008 and contained 23 recommendations for BAE to implement that would serve as a guide "to establish a global reputation for ethical business conduct that matches its reputation for outstanding technical competence."[29] The 23 recommendations mirror the compliance program elements contained in the Federal Sentencing Guidelines for Organizations. In addition to these many recommendations, the report also contains excellent guidance when using third parties to support sales and marketing functions, guidance on acquisitions, facilitation payments, gifts and gratuities, as well as detailed red flags when using advisors to facilitate transactions. For further details on each recommendation as well as the entire Woolf Committee Report, see www.baesystems.com/woolfcommittee.

BAE FOLLOWS A DIFFERENT PATH

The Woolf Committee interviewed then CEO Mike Turner and Chairman Dick Oliver who admitted "the company did not in the past pay sufficient attention to ethical standards and avoid activities that had the potential to give rise to reputational damage."[30] The company accepted certain conditions of doing business that "contributed to the widely-held perceptions that it was involved in inappropriate behaviour." The report further stated that "these perceptions have damaged the Company's reputation" and that they need to take steps to both rebuild that reputation and ensure the compliance lapses are not repeated in the future.[31] The Woolf Committee Report containing these quotes and commentary was released on May 6, 2008.

Interestingly enough, just one day later on May 7, 2008, Turner spoke at BAE's annual meeting and attempted to minimize the comments he made to the Woolf Committee. Turner said, "We have no reason to believe the company has broken the law."[32] Turner subsequently retired at the end of August 2008 and there is speculation that he was forced out when the board decided the company needed a change in the corporate culture. One newspaper article published shortly before he retired opined that his "blind spot has been the issue of ethics . . . . he has failed to appreciate how damaging the constant allegations of bribery and corruption have been. Mr. Turner blamed the media for printing unfounded allegations when the problems were clearly much closer to home."[33]

BAE's strategy of not accepting responsibility for its actions ultimately changed. The FCPA investigation in the United States showed no signs of ending. Bribery allegations related to defense contracts in the Czech Republic, Romania, South Africa, and Tanzania continued to be a focus for UK enforcement officials. In September 2009, BAE was told by the SFO to negotiate a plea agreement or face full prosecution and trial. It was reported that BAE and SFO were negotiating a plea agreement similar in scope to the deferred prosecutions used by U.S. prosecutors.[34]

On February 5, 2010, BAE reached a global settlement with both the DOJ and SFO. BAE agreed with the DOJ to plead guilty to one count of conspiring to make false statements to the U.S. government regarding the creation and implementation of internal controls for compliance with the FCPA. BAE also agreed with the SFO to plead guilty to one count of breach of duty to keep accurate accounting records relating to payments made to a marketing consultant in Tanzania. The company will pay a $400 million fine in the U.S. and a $47 million fine in the UK.[35] BAE was fortunate that it did not receive a business debarment.

The SFO also announced there would be no individual prosecutions and the investigation was now closed. In contrast, the DOJ advised that they were continuing to investigate individuals involved in the matter. The DOJ criminal information "alleges that BAE paid tens of millions of dollars to a Saudi government official and other associates, as well as to intermediaries, as recently as 2002."[36] BAE Chairman Oliver commented in a statement that "the Company very much regrets and accepts full responsibility for these past shortcomings" and "has systematically enhanced its compliance policies and processes."[37]

NOTES

1. *Inside Man* (2006), www.imdb.com/title/tt0454848/quotes.
2. David Leigh and Rob Evans, "BAE Accused of Arms Deal Slush Fund," *Guardian*, September 11, 2003, www.guardian.co.uk/world/2003/sep/11/bae.freedomofinformation.
3. Ibid.
4. Ibid.

5. Banks in the United States are required to file a Suspicious Activity Report (SAR) to report suspicious activity that may relate to the violation of any law or regulation. For instance, SARs are filed when a bank discovers activity that may involve money laundering, financing terrorism, insider fraud, or attempts to avoid reporting requirements, such as multiple deposits just below the reporting figure.

6. Michael Isikoff, Mark Hosenball, and Emily Flynn Vencat, "Bandar and the $2 Billion Question," *Newsweek*, June 18, 2007, www .newsweek.com/id/34112.

7. "Saudi Money Transfers—Suspicious Activity Report," *Frontline*, www.pbs.org/wgbh/pages/frontline/blackmoney/readings/suspicious .html.

8. Dennis Lormel, written comments to the authors, April 30, 2009.

9. David Black, "BAE Faces Fresh Claims of Saudi Arms Bribery," *The Scotsman*, October 6, 2004, http://thescotsman.scotsman.com/business/ BAE-faces-fresh-claims-of.2569857.jp.

10. Ibid.

11. Ibid.

12. David Leigh, Rob Evans, and David Gow, "BAE Bosses Named as Corruption Suspects," *Guardian*, www.guardian.co.uk/world/2007/ jan/17/bae.saudiarabia.

13. Ibid.

14. Ibid.

15. Daniel Michaels, "BAE Probes May Persist, Take Toll," *Wall Street Journal*, May 20, 2008, B2.

16. Prime Minister Tony Blair, "Al Yamamah: Serious Fraud Office Investigation," personal and secret memorandum to then UK Attorney General Lord Peter Goldsmith, December 8, 2006, www.pbs.org/wgbh/ pages/frontline/blackmoney/readings/blair.pdf.

17. Associated Press, "U.K. Ruling Backs Ending of BAE Inquiry," *Wall Street Journal*, July 31, 2008, B2.

18. Ibid.

19. David Crawford and Daniel Michaels, "Police Look for Bribery Evidence in Case Against BAE," *Wall Street Journal*, October 1, 2008, B3.

20. "BAE Bosses Held in US Over Corruption Allegations," *Guardian*, May 18, 2008, www.guardian.co.uk/world/2008/may/18/bae.armstrade.

21. BAE Corporate Responsibility Report 2007, 1, www.baesystems.com/ BAEProd/groups/public/documents/bae_publication/bae_pdf_cr_crre port 2007vii.pdf.

22. Ibid., 14.
23. Ibid., 10.
24. BAE Corporate Responsibility Report 2008, 12, www.baesystems .com/BAEProd/groups/public/documents/bae_publication/bae_pdf _cr08_business_conduct.pdf.
25. Ibid.
26. BAE Systems Global Code of Conduct, 7, www.baesystems.com/ BAEProd/groups/public/documents/bae_publication/bae_pdf_759of 003_001.pdf.
27. Ibid., 28.
28. Ibid., 52.
29. Woolf Committee, "Business Ethics, Global Companies and the Defence Industry: Ethical Business Conduct in BAE Systems Plc— the Way Forward," report, May 2008, 3, http://ir.baesystems.com/ investors/storage/woolf_report_2008.pdf.
30. Dennis Michaels, "BAE Probes May Persist, Take Toll," *Wall Street Journal*, May 20, 2008, B2.
31. Woolf Committee, "Business Ethics, Global Companies and the Defence Industry," 9.
32. Michaels, "BAE Probes May Persist, Take Toll."
33. David Wighton, "Mike Turner Does the Business at BAE Systems," *Times Online*, August 20, 2008, http://business.timesonline.co.uk/tol/ business/columnists/article4569234.ece.
34. Dan Atkinson, Lisa Buckingham, and Tom McGhie, "BAE Told to Plead Guilty on Bribery Charges or Face Trial," *Daily Mail Online*, September 5, 2009, www.dailymail.co.uk/money/article-1211402/ BAE-told-plead-guilty-bribery-allegations-face-trial.html.
35. Daniel Michaels and Cassell Bryan-Low, "BAE to Settle Bribery Cases for More Than $400 Million," *Wall Street Journal*, February 6, 2010, B1.
36. Ibid.
37. Mike Musgrove, "BAE Systems pays $450 million to settle bribery scandal charges," *Washington Post*, February 6, 2010, A14.

CHAPTER 9

Designing an Effective Anti-Corruption Compliance Program

You are only as compliant as the least compliant person in your organization. Remember this insight as it only takes one rogue employee paying a bribe to a foreign government official to bring the full force of the government down on you and your company. In this chapter, and the following one, we will discuss the importance of designing and implementing an effective anti-corruption compliance program. An effective program isn't just an FCPA compliance program but an anti-corruption compliance program. Designing only an FCPA-focused program will not result in a successful program as FCPA compliance is but one element of an overall anti-corruption compliance program. If one is solely focused on the FCPA and fails to consider the impact of anti-corruption laws and policies in other countries, the program is not effective. There are demonstrated benefits of a well-crafted compliance program.

In our previous book on corporate compliance, *Building a World-Class Compliance Program: Best Practices and Strategies for Success*, we wrote about the importance of the compliance program as the engine of compliance:

Knowing the law and following it is only one side of compliance. Compliance goes much deeper than that, true compliance anyway. Simply following the law so that one doesn't get into trouble is not full compliance. State-of-the-art compliance involves a successful blending of compliance—following rules, regulations, and laws—with ethics—developing and sustaining a culture based on values, integrity, and accountability, and always doing the right things. True compliance ensures consistency of actions to eliminate, or at least lessen, opportunities for harm from criminal conduct or other compliance failures. It means going beyond the minimum requirements. More importantly, it involves the ongoing commitment from senior leaders in the organization to promote ethical conduct and compliance with the law. Leading by example and establishing the tone at the top set the stage for every other element of compliance.[1]

Compliance programs can be profoundly significant for a company in reducing fraud and corruption risk. The Federal Sentencing Guidelines for Organizations provides a powerful incentive for companies to have in place an "effective compliance program." An effective program is a program that works to prevent and detect violations of the law. An effective program has an impact on DOJ prosecution decisions and can result in a downward departure in both level of offense and potential penalty. It can even influence a deferral of prosecution.

The U.S. government strongly reinforced the importance of compliance programs in reducing the impact of criminal violations. In the *Principles of Federal Prosecution of Business Organizations*, also called the "Filip Memo" after Deputy Attorney General Mark Filip who issued the memorandum, the government detailed the factors that prosecutors need to consider when determining whether to charge a corporation. Two of the factors specifically relating to compliance program design and implementation are:

- *The existence and effectiveness of corporation's pre-existing compliance program*
- *The corporation's remedial actions, including any efforts to implement an effective corporate compliance program or to improve an existing one, to replace responsible management, to discipline or terminate wrongdoers, to pay restitution, and to cooperate with the relevant government agencies*[2]

The charging factors emphasize the value of a "pre-existing" program as well as ongoing evaluations and improvements in the program to prevent violations and wrongdoing. The Filip Memo cautioned that the existence of a documented program is not enough as words *and* actions are both required:

> *However, the existence of a compliance program is not sufficient, in and of itself, to justify not charging a corporation for criminal conduct under-taken by it officers, directors, employees, or agents. . . . Prosecutors should therefore attempt to determine whether a corporation's compliance program is merely a "paper program" or whether it was designed, implemented, reviewed, and revised, as appropriate, in an effective man-ner. . . . Prosecutors also should determine whether the corporation's employees are adequately informed about the compliance program and are convinced of the corporation's commitment to it. This will enable the prosecutor to make an informed decision as to whether the corporation has adopted and implemented a truly effective compliance program that, when consistent with other federal law enforcement policies, may result in a decision to charge only the corporation's employees and agents or to mitigate charges or sanctions against the corporation.[3]*

FEDERAL SENTENCING GUIDELINES FOR ORGANIZATIONS

On May 1, 1991, the United States Sentencing Commission (USSC) officially promulgated the Federal Sentencing Guidelines for Organizations (FSGO). They were later amended effective November 1, 2004 to provide even greater guidance for organizations. Chapter 8 of the FSGO covering organizational crime has been strengthened over the years, particularly by congressional directives authorizing the USSC to tackle particular issues, such as corporate crime. The amendments in 2004, coming in the wake of repeated instances of corporate scandal and a growing sentiment by the public that the problem must be dealt with, addressed the perceived need for improved compliance by organizations, as well as gave more direct guidance to those organizations which sought to enhance their own compliance efforts to prevent further scandal.

The FSGO emphasizes effective compliance and ethics programs in order to mitigate punishment for a criminal offense. It also requires an organizational culture that encourages ethical conduct and a commitment to compliance with the law. Chief executives and directors are responsible and accountable to ensure compliance. Effective compliance programs must now have adequate resources, appropriate authority, training programs,

reporting mechanisms, risk assessments, and periodic evaluations to promote an ongoing culture of compliance.[4]

The 2004 amendments modified the FSGO, adding an official definition
of an effective compliance program. These revised guidelines specifically
reinforced the importance and need for such a compliance program within
an organization. Since these are the guidelines that will direct federal
prosecutors and judges in evaluating an organization's culpability (or lack
thereof), it is imperative that a compliance program, at minimum, directly
meets these standards.

THE SEVEN STEPS TO AN EFFECTIVE
COMPLIANCE PROGRAM

The "Seven Steps" to an effective compliance and ethics program as
detailed in the FSGO serve as the backbone for building such a program.
They provide clear guidance on how to build it, and give great insight into
the government's expectations. When evaluating a potential criminal case,
prosecutors will be looking for a program that meets the requirements of
the seven steps. If a company's compliance program meets those standards, it can hope for a reduced or suspended sentence, and is at least
assured of more ammunition at the bargaining table. However, if the
minimum requirements are not met, it is a clear indication to the government that the organization does not place a high value on compliance and
ethical conduct. If an organization cannot adhere to the broadly communicated seven steps, why would the government believe that it would
follow more complex and difficult regulatory guidelines?

According to the FSGO, to have an effective compliance and ethics
program, "an organization *shall* exercise due diligence to protect and
detect criminal conduct; and otherwise promote an organizational culture
that encourages ethical conduct and a commitment to compliance with
the law (emphasis added)."[5] Note the inclusion of the word *shall*; this
indicates that this requirement is mandatory for those companies with a
compliance program and that the government unconditionally expects
these requirements to be followed. Even though the government expects
strict adherence to the FSGO, it does recognize that not every violation
will be prevented. "Such compliance and ethics program shall be reasonably designed, implemented, and enforced so that the program is generally
effective in preventing and detecting criminal conduct. The failure to
prevent or detect the instant offense does not necessarily mean that the
program is not generally effective."[6]

The FSGO allows for the possibility that a rogue employee committed the crime. If this is the case, and if the company had an effective compliance program in place, the organization may be allowed to escape unscathed, provided it cooperates in the prosecution of the employee. The FSGO recognizes that even the best compliance programs cannot catch every misdeed, particularly those of an employee operating alone. Of far greater concern are those misdeeds performed by those in power within the company who actively subvert the compliance program for their own ends, or those companies that, upon discovery of the crimes, seek to cover them up rather than respond appropriately.

The Seven Steps of Compliance as mandated by the FSGO require organizations to build and maintain an effective compliance and ethics program by requiring the following actions:

1. *Compliance Standards and Procedures*
    *   *The organization shall establish standards and procedures to prevent and detect criminal conduct and ensure compliance with the law. In other words, an organization's code of conduct must be robust and embed ethical conduct as an integral component of the ethics and compliance program.*

2. *Organizational Leadership and a Culture of Compliance*
    *   *The organization's governing authority shall be knowledgeable about the content and operation of the compliance and ethics program. This would normally be the CEO, CFO, and the Board of Directors.*
    *   *They shall exercise reasonable oversight with respect to the implementation and effectiveness of the compliance and ethics program.*
    *   *Specific individual(s) within the highest levels of the organization shall be assigned overall responsibility for the compliance and ethics program.*
    *   *Specific individual(s) within the organization shall be delegated day-to-day operational responsibility for the compliance and ethics program. The individual(s) with operational responsibility shall report periodically to high-level personnel and, as appropriate, to the governing authority on the effectiveness of the compliance and ethics program.*
    *   *To carry out such operational responsibility, such individual(s) shall be given adequate resources, appropriate authority, and direct access to the governing authority of the organization.*

3. *Reasonable Efforts to Exclude Prohibited Persons*
    *   *The organization shall use reasonable efforts not to include within the substantial authority personnel who the organization knew, or*

should have known through the exercise of due diligence, have engaged in illegal activities or other conduct inconsistent with an effective compliance and ethics program.

4. Training and Communication of Standards and Procedures

- *The organization shall take reasonable steps to communicate periodically and in a practical manner its standards and procedures, and other aspects of the compliance and ethics program by conducting effective training programs and otherwise disseminating information appropriate to such individuals' respective roles and responsibilities.*

- *Training shall be provided to members of the governing authority, other high-level leadership, employees, and, as appropriate, the organization's agents.*

5. Monitoring, Auditing, and Evaluating Program Effectiveness

- *The organization shall take reasonable steps to ensure that the organization's compliance and ethics program is followed, including monitoring and auditing to detect criminal conduct.*

- *The organization shall take reasonable steps to evaluate the effectiveness of the organization's compliance and ethics program.*

- *The organization shall take reasonable steps to have and publicize a system, which may include mechanisms that allow for anonymity or confidentiality, where the organization's employees and agents may report or seek guidance regarding potential or actual criminal conduct without fear of retaliation, such as hotlines.*

6. Performance Incentives and Disciplinary Actions

- *The organization's compliance and ethics program shall be promoted and enforced consistently within the organization through appropriate incentives to perform in accordance with the compliance and ethics program.*

- *The organization's compliance and ethics program shall be promoted and enforced consistently within the organization through appropriate disciplinary measures for engaging in criminal conduct and for failing to take reasonable steps to prevent or detect criminal conduct.*

7. Response to Criminal Conduct and Remedial Action

- *After criminal conduct has been detected, the organization shall take reasonable steps to respond appropriately to the criminal conduct and to prevent further similar conduct, including making any necessary modifications to the organization's compliance and ethics program.*

- *The organization shall periodically assess the risk of criminal conduct and shall take appropriate steps to design, implement, or modify each compliance requirement to reduce the risk of criminal conduct identified through this process.*[7]

In addition to the preceding seven requirements, there are others that must be implemented by an organization. An organization must incorporate and adhere to industry practices and standards of compliance as required by government regulation. Unless this is followed, an organization is not considered as having an effective compliance and ethics program. Courts are required to sentence the company to at least probation if the organization failed to have an effective compliance program in place when one was required and can upwardly depart from the guidelines if a compliance program is not in place. Organizations must remember that the way to avoid or at least lessen the impact of prosecution is through self-reporting, cooperation with the government, acceptance of responsibility, and an effective compliance and ethics program.[8] The seven steps to an effective compliance program must include anti-corruption elements.

DOJ GUIDANCE ON ANTI-CORRUPTION COMPLIANCE PROGRAMS

Over the years, the Justice Department has provided anti-corruption compliance program guidance to organizations through its various DOJ Opinion Procedure Releases. This guidance is an excellent resource when developing and revising anti-corruption compliance programs for further organizational integration. The Appendix provides an overview of many Opinion Procedure Releases. Of note, Opinion Procedure Release 04-02 issued on July 12, 2004, spelled out the elements of a "rigorous anti-corruption code . . . designed to detect and deter violations of the FCPA and foreign anti-corruption laws" as seen in the following 12 points:

1. A clearly articulated corporate policy against violations of the FCPA and foreign antibribery laws and the establishment of compliance standards and procedures to be followed by all directors, officers, employees, and all business partners, including, but not limited to, agents, consultants, representatives, and joint venture partners and teaming partners, involved in business transactions, representation, or business development, or retention in a foreign jurisdiction (respectively, "Agents" and "Business Partners") that are reasonably capable of reducing the prospect that the FCPA or any applicable foreign anti-corruption law of Newco's[9] Compliance Code will be violated

217

2. *The assignment to one or more independent senior Newco corporate officials, who shall report directly to the Compliance Committee of the Audit Committee of the Board of Directors, of responsibility for the implementation and oversight of compliance with policies, standards, and procedures established in accordance with Newco's Compliance Code*

3. *The effective communication to all shareholders' representatives directly involved in the oversight of Newco ("Shareholders") and to all directors, officers, employees, Agents, and Business Partners of corporate and compliance policies, standards, and procedures regarding the FCPA and applicable foreign anti-corruption laws, by requiring (i) regular training concerning the requirements of the FCPA and applicable foreign anti-corruption laws on a periodic basis to all Shareholders, directors, officers, employees, Agents, and Business Partners and (ii) annual certifications by all Shareholders, directors, officers, employees, including the head of each Newco business or division, Agents, and Business Partners certifying compliance therewith*

4. *A reporting system, including a "Helpline," for directors, officers, employees, Agents, and Business Partners to report suspected violations of the Compliance Code or suspected criminal conduct*

5. *Appropriate disciplinary procedure to address matters involving violations or suspected violations of the FCPA, foreign anti-corruption laws, or the Compliance Code*

6. *Clearly articulated corporate procedures designed to assure that all necessary and prudent precautions are taken to cause Newco to form business relationships with reputable and qualified Business Partners*

7. *Extensive pre-retention due diligence requirements pertaining to, as well as post-retention oversight of, all Agents and Business Partners, including the maintenance of complete due diligence records at Newco*

8. *Clearly articulated corporate procedures designed to ensure that Newco exercises due care to assure that substantial discretionary authority is not delegated to individuals whom Newco knows, or should know through the exercise of due diligence, have a propensity to engage in illegal or improper activities*

9. *A committee consisting of senior Newco corporate officials to review and to record, in writing, actions relating to (i) the retention of any Agent or subagents thereof, and (ii) all contracts and payments related thereto*

10. *The inclusion in all agreements, contracts, and renewals thereof with all Agents and Business Partners of provisions: (i) setting forth anti-corruption representations and undertakings; (ii) relating to compliance with foreign anti-corruption laws and other relevant laws;*

218

(iii) allowing for internal and independent audits of the books and records of the Agent or Business Partner to ensure compliance with the foregoing; and (iv) providing for termination of the Agent or Business Partner as a result of any breach of applicable anti-corruption laws and regulations or representations and undertakings related thereto

11. Financial and accounting procedures designed to ensure that Newco maintains a system of internal accounting controls and makes and keeps accurate books, records, and accounts

12. Independent audits by outside counsel and auditors, at no longer than three-year intervals, to ensure that the Compliance Code, including its anti-corruption provisions, are implemented in an effective manner[10]

The DOJ provided further compliance program guidance on December 15, 2008, when Siemens and three of its subsidiaries pleaded guilty to FCPA violations. Included as an attachment to the DOJ's Statement of Offense was the detailed corporate compliance program that Siemens agreed to implement as a condition of its plea agreement. The program was designed to enhance Siemens' internal controls and compliance code incorporating ten elements of compliance program design, as covered in Chapter 5. The DOJ guidance on compliance program design is a critical component to incorporate in any program whether an organization is public or private, large or small, foreign or domestic.

COMPLIANCE PROGRAM DESIGN

In designing an anti-corruption compliance program for an organization, compliance program individuality is a key consideration. Ideally a compliance program should be both industry-specific and unique to the organization. It should be tailored to fit the requirements of the individual organization, particular geographic operating locations, related risks, and the overall compliance requirements of its particular industry. Also reflected should be the compliance requirements imposed on all corporations and the laws that they must follow. The anti-corruption program must be integrated into the overall compliance program. Each organization must ensure that their compliance programs are receiving ongoing and individualized evaluation and modification.

Anti-corruption compliance programs must address the inherent risks when doing business in foreign countries. These risks result from the various aspects and forces that come into play in the global business environment. These risks are particularly problematic to the FCPA and anti-corruption laws in various countries. Many companies prosecuted for FCPA violations over the years either outright ignored or were willfully blind to these risks. Their compliance programs were inadequately designed to recognize and mitigate the risk. The following are key business issues germane to corruption risk:

- Business contracts, deals, sales and marketing
- Business partners and third parties
- Dealing with government officials
- State-owned enterprises
- Sales consultants
- Joint ventures
- Mergers and acquisitions
- Conflicts of interest
- Facilitating payments
- Travel and entertainment of foreign government officials
- Gifts to foreign government officials
- Promotional expenses
- Lobbyists
- Charitable donations
- Country risk as defined by Corruption Perceptions Index and other informational sources

An effective anti-corruption compliance program needs to incorporate the following program elements into the overall compliance program:

- Tone at the top
- Anti-corruption standards and procedures
- Reasonable efforts to exclude prohibited persons
- Training and communication
- Mechanisms for reporting violations and seeking guidance
- Third-party due diligence
- Anti-corruption contractual clauses
- Internal accounting controls
- Monitoring, auditing, and evaluating program effectiveness

- Performance incentives and disciplinary actions
- Response to criminal conduct and remedial action

These program elements come from the FSGO, Filip Memo, and Opinion Procedure Release 04-02 and further guidance on many of them are contained in this chapter. Most of these elements are not anti-corruption program specific, but are interconnected to functions and practices across an organization.

RED FLAGS AND RISK AREAS

Based on recent developments, either ignoring red flags of bribery and corruption or willful blindness is certain to result in a government investigation and FCPA liability. The July 2009 conviction of Frederick A. Bourke, Jr. on charges of conspiracy to violate the FCPA, the Travel Act, and making false statements to the FBI, reinforce that premise. The Bourke case was the first that the DOJ took to trial, and won, on a willful blindness theory. "The case provides a stark reminder that a lack of actual knowledge of improper payments will not shield individuals from FCPA liability if the government can make the case that the defendant's ignorance is deliberate."[11] Red flags provide clear warning signs that something is wrong and attention is required. Now, the courts have given clear notice that the failure to act on red flags will end in liability.

Department of Justice's FCPA Red Flags

A few years ago, the U.S. Department of Justice published a list of potential red-flag indicators of FCPA violations. While this list was in no way comprehensive, it provided some of the many predictors of misconduct and noncompliance. Of note, the DOJ has since removed this red flag list from their web site. Speculation is that the DOJ did not want to issue what some might think is a comprehensive list and thus deemphasize other possible red flags. Monsanto Company, profiled in Chapter 11, provides guidance on red flags in their anti-corruption policy by stating that " 'Red flags' come in all shapes and sizes. Just because a particular fact does not fit squarely within one of the listed 'red flags' does not mean it can be ignored."[12]

Each organization needs to determine the particular universe of red flags they may face. The now-deleted DOJ list included:

- Unusual payment patterns or financial arrangements
- A history of corruption in the country
- Refusal by the foreign joint venture partner or representative to provide a certification that it will not take any action in furtherance of an unlawful offer, promise, or payment to a foreign public official in violation of the FCPA
- Unusually high commissions
- Lack of transparency in expenses and accounting records
- Apparent lack of qualifications or resources on the part of the joint venture partner or representative to perform the services offered
- Whether the joint venture partner or representative has been recommended by an official of the potential governmental customer

Red Flags When Doing Business With Third Parties

There are significant red flags to consider when working with vendors, consultants, distributors, agents, business partners, intermediaries, representatives, and other third parties. The discovery of any of these red flags should open the door for further investigation and due diligence as to whether to proceed with any dealings. A red flag exists if your third party has been associated or linked to any of the following:

- Questionable integrity and character
- Reputation for paying or receiving bribes
- Subject of media scrutiny for misconduct, litigation, or other potentially problematic issues
- Prior legal issues including criminal charges for improper business practices
- Has no physical address for its business operations and instead uses a mail drop or works out of another business address
- Does not have an adequate number or appropriately skilled staff to operate the business and carry out the contract
- Will not disclose the true owner of the operation
- Has not been truthful or cooperative in the due diligence phase
- Lacks experience or expertise in the particular business or industry
- Third party's business is not listed in standard industry directories and is unknown to others already established in that industry

222

- Either no one will provide references or references are questionable
- Uses shell companies
- Questionable business associates and subcontractors
- Unrealistic, exaggerated, or false representations of business results
- Claims to have close relationships with government officials for special favors
- Requests fees that are much larger than the normal market rate for comparable work without providing a reasonable explanation
- Questionable and excessive commissions and expenses for which there is no accounting
- Off-the-books transactions
- Business conducted mostly in cash
- Poor record keeping and financial controls
- Influence and contacts are primary deliverables
- Will not sign an anti-corruption warranty that no corrupt payments will be made
- Family members and close friends who are government officials
- Third party was a former government official
- Third party was recommended by government official
- Has business relationships with government officials
- Requires cash payments or other unusual payments
- Requests payment before agreed upon work is completed
- Request payments be made through shell companies or into foreign bank accounts
- Will not provide written agreements or updates of work to be performed
- Questionable and unexpected requests for additional money
- Side letters and changes to contracts that are not documented
- Either refuses to include an audit clause or is uncooperative during such an audit
- Either provides or requests phony invoices or documentation

Travel and Entertainment

Many FCPA prosecutions have some connection to travel and entertainment payments. The Metcalf and Eddy case, profiled in Chapter 3, involved excessive travel and entertainment expenses provided to an Egyptian government official and his family to secure a government contract. The poster child for travel and entertainment violations is Lucent Technologies. For every case that turns on a technical reading of the statute and falls into a major gray area of application, there are those cases where one cannot believe that the company didn't recognize it was breaking the law.

Between 2000 and 2003, Lucent paid all expenses totaling millions of dollars for approximately 315 trips to the United States by numerous Chinese government officials so they could visit Disney World, Las Vegas, Hawaii, New York City, the Grand Canyon, Niagara Falls, and elsewhere. The officials worked for state-owned telecom companies in China. Spouses and children also went on these trips. Some of the trips were characterized as "factory inspections" and "factory tours," even though by 2001 Lucent had outsourced most of its manufacturing and had no factories to inspect. Lucent admitted that these trips were made with the approval of the most senior Lucent Chinese officials and coordinated with staff in the United States, including at its corporate headquarters. Lucent also paid educational expenses including MBA tuition for a government employee. The tuition was booked as "marketing expenses." Lucent entered into a DPA with the DOJ, admitted its wrong-doing, and agreed to pay a $1 million fine and upgrade its internal controls, and settled with the SEC in December 2007 and paid $2.5 million.[13]

A U.S. company with a UK subsidiary manufactured radar equipment that was sold to customers, including government agencies, throughout the world. Prior to delivery of the ordered equipment to a Chinese customer that is a state-owned enterprise, officials for the customer traveled to the UK to inspect the equipment. After making several inspection trips, the customer asked for first-class tickets and then requested additional perks that became problematic. Since the customer was a Chinese state-owned enterprise, this behavior caused FCPA issues for the U.S. manufacturer.

For compliance purposes, any travel expenses paid for foreign government officials must have a legitimate business purpose. They must be directly related to promoting, demonstrating, or explaining the company's products or services or executing or performing a contract, as well as a reasonable amount in light of the business purpose. They must be in accordance with both the company and government policies. Entertainment must be proportional to the business purpose of a trip. Lavish trips and entertainment are prohibited. Travel should be coach class. A clear and valid business reason should be articulated and documented for any travel and entertainment. Only the associated government officials should be on the receiving end and not family or friends. Expenses should be infrequent in occurrence and appropriately documented in the books and records. Transparency is of the utmost importance. The *Wall Street Journal* Rule applies. If you would not mind reading in the *Wall Street Journal* about the travel and entertainment your company provided to foreign government officials, then you are probably following policy.

Gifts

Gifts, along with travel and entertainment, can be problematic and similar guidelines as for travel and entertainment should be followed. Strong company policies need to be in existence and followed when considering giving gifts to foreign government officials. Always ensure any gifts do not violate the laws or customs of the particular country where the gift is given. There must be a legitimate business need for the gift and any gifts must be approved in advance by the appropriate legal or compliance officer. Gifts cannot be lavish or extravagant. Cash or monetary equivalents are always problematic and should be prohibited. No corrupt intent to influence must exist in giving and receiving the gift. The gift must be properly documented in the books and records of the company and transparency must exist throughout. Again, the *Wall Street Journal* Rule applies.

Mergers and Acquisitions

Opinion Procedure Release 08-01, issued on July 15, 2008, provided due diligence guidance that can be applied to mergers and acquisitions in foreign locations, including when there is foreign government ownership involved. The guidance includes:

- Engage a reputable international investigative firm to conduct a background investigation on the company to be acquired
- Retain a foreign business consultant in the foreign municipality to provide advice on due diligence procedures in the foreign country
- Obtain international company profiles on the target company from the U.S. Commercial Service of the Commerce Department
- Search various databases to determine if any relevant parties to the transaction are on lists of designated or denied persons, terrorist watches, or similar designations
- Contact the U.S. Embassy in the foreign municipality to determine if there are any negative records on file at the Embassy regarding any party to the proposed transaction

- Engage outside counsel to conduct due diligence
- Hire a forensic accounting firm to also conduct due diligence
- Engage a second law firm to further review the due diligence

COMPLIANCE INSIGHT 9.1: INHERENT COMPLIANCE RISK IN ACQUISITIONS AND NEW BUSINESS LINES

Nine years after a large multinational corporation acquired an international division servicing both government and nongovernment clients, the corporation conducted an internal review to assess the feasibility of selling the division. The review identified some potentially problematic expense items for further review. Given the corporation's existing policies and procedures, training and awareness of the FCPA and anti-corruption compliance, it did not expect to find any significant issues. The corporation initiated an investigation expecting it to independently affirm the corporation's belief that the issues were likely anomalous.

During the investigation it quickly became apparent that there was a pervasive and accepted practice within the division of providing entertainment, meals, travel, and gifts to foreign government clients and prospective clients by divisional employees and management, as well as improper cash payments to clients and foreign agents. There were no controls to identify, manage, or track these expenses and cash disbursements were evidenced.

The following real-life case contains compliance failures that a corporation can use to avoid common pitfalls and better detect or prevent similar events:

Acquisition: The division was acquired and retained existing employees, customers, and management with no due diligence surrounding existing culture or review of practices around bribery and anti-corruption. Without proper due diligence surrounding a division's operations including existing culture and business relationships, the acquirer is unable to consider areas where existing business practices may be in conflict with those of the acquirer.

Monitoring and Oversight: The division conducted its operations and customer negotiations without oversight or interaction with

226

corporate headquarters. No formal monitoring or integration of divisional reporting and accountability can result in divisions that do not share the same corporate culture and values. Consequently, most will likely continue or revert to prior business practices without effective oversight and intervention of the acquirer.

Corporate Policies and Training: No formal implementation of new corporate policies and compliance expectations at the division were conducted other than circulating copies of corporate policies and code of conduct. Related training and updates were infrequent and lacked FCPA/anti-corruption content relevant to the division's operations. Changes and updates to corporate policies must be formally implemented and communicated through relevant and timely mandatory training. Employees should also have access to policies and procedures, and anti-corruption compliance resources that they can consult to provide further clarification or guidance.

Corporations need to consider the inherent risks that acquisitions or entering new lines of business pose to its established operations and culture. A corporation must invest in the communication, implementation, and monitoring of its policies, procedures, and reporting throughout its operations to help ensure that there is proper oversight and enforcement of the entire organization.

Autonomous International Business Units

Autonomous international business units afford significant risk especially when there is limited visibility of their day-to-day operations by corporate headquarters. With growth and expansion come opportunities for bribes to secure and retain business with government entities in emerging markets. Does the home office have visibility to the financial information generated in the subsidiary, especially around sales and marketing, discounts, rebates, travel, and entertainment, and other problematic areas? Does internal audit have access to this financial information on an ongoing basis for evaluation? Does internal audit conduct onsite audits in high-risk countries on at least an annual basis?

Don't Ignore Small Payments

There may be a tendency to think that bribes are only made in large amounts of money. This is a wrong assumption and a mistake if followed as a course of action. Bribes and bribe givers know no limits and small amounts may be quite acceptable depending on the situation and the country. For example, India's per capita income was $2,800 for 2008. With that per capita income, a bribe of a few dollars can still be a significant payment. Many of the emerging and high-risk countries have similar per capita incomes and small dollar bribes may be the norm. Small amounts may be overlooked when reviewing books and records for possible corrupt payments.

Facilitation Payments

Facilitation payments, also aptly called "grease" payments, ensure that government officials perform tasks they are supposed to perform as part of their normal job function. This includes obtaining permits and licenses, processing customs shipments and travel visas, garbage pickup, and mail delivery. More and more companies are prohibiting facilitation payments. Those that do generally discourage such payments and require approval before making them. Either way, company policy and training must be provided to employees. For companies allowing facilitation payments, a clear policy must exist that all such payments must be reviewed and approved in advance by an appropriate member of the legal department. In addition, all grease payments must be accurately recorded in the books and records of the company as a facilitation payment. Most countries outlaw facilitation payments so that must also be included in any policy and training.

At times, it may be impossible to resist paying a bribe or facilitation payment especially if it is an extorted payment. For example, what if one of your employees is stopped on the street in a foreign country by a police officer and told that her visa is not in order but that a cash payment will resolve the issue. If not, the employee will be detained. Clearly, the employee should have been previously instructed to comply with the extortion request, pay the amount demanded, leave the country, and then report the incident to legal counsel or other appropriate parties at the company. Do your employees know not only what to do at the time but how to report it to the company? Do you have a policy covering extorted payments? If not, such a policy and procedure needs to be prepared and shared with employees. Such a scenario can also be included in ongoing training sessions.

Corrupt Payments

Corrupt payments, bribes, and kickbacks are given with corrupt intent as a *quid pro quo*. They are usually given in such a way as to hide their true purpose. Often, they are made through third parties. Payments can take many forms including:

- Cash
- Gifts and gratuities
- Travel and other entertainment
- Promises of preferential treatment
- Consulting fees
- Commissions
- Marketing and promotion fees
- Jewelry
- Cars
- Home improvements
- Stock
- Discounts not readily available to the public
- Employment or promises of future employment
- Charitable or political contributions
- Loans at less than market interest rates
- Payment of personal expenses
- College education for children of government officials
- Debt forgiveness
- Medical treatment
- Sexual favors

ANTI-CORRUPTION DESIGN NEVER ENDS

Program modification must be constant to address changes in business models, new markets, discovery of internal control weaknesses, business conduct violations, and other risks. Self-reflection and assessments will determine program changes. Ask questions. Is senior management driving a

THOUGHT LEADERS IN FCPA COMPLIANCE: JOSEPH
SPINELLI, SCOTT MORITZ, AND JAY PERLMAN

Using Technology to Develop a Risk-Based Approach
to FCPA Compliance

Joseph Spinelli is the co-founder and COO of Daylight Forensic
& Advisory (Daylight), a global regulatory compliance, forensic
accounting, and investigative consulting firm advising financial institutions, Fortune 500 companies, law firms, and government agencies
on regulatory and investigative issues worldwide. Spinelli is a leading
authority on white-collar crime with more than 30 years of forensic
experience. Prior to Daylight, he was a principal in a Big Four
accounting firm, founding its forensic practice. He spent eight years
as New York State's first inspector general, leading fraud, abuse,
waste, and corruption investigations for all New York State agencies
and authorities. He also served as a Special Agent for the FBI.

Scott Moritz is an executive director with Daylight. He leads
Daylight's FCPA and Investigative Due Diligence practice and is
widely recognized as an authority on investigative due diligence and
international investigations. Prior to joining Daylight, he has held
executive positions at other major accounting firms and global
investigative firms. For nearly ten years, Scott served as an FBI
Special Agent where he was nationally recognized for his expertise
in money laundering and asset forfeiture investigations.

Jay Perlman is a director with Daylight in its Washington office.
He has more than 18 years of legal, regulatory compliance, and
investigative experience relating to the financial services sector.
Prior to joining Daylight, he was an attorney in the securities
enforcement and regulatory group of a large law firm. Additionally,
he was Associate General Counsel of The Motley Fool and frequently appeared in the media as a spokesman for the company, and
he authored several articles about investor education and securities
fraud. Before entering the private sector, he held various positions at
the SEC and served as a Special Assistant U.S. Attorney in the
Eastern District of Virginia. Here Spinelli, Moritz, and Perlman

provide their perspective on a risk-based approach to due diligence and the use of technology to accomplish this task.

THIRD-PARTY BUSINESS PARTNERS: A CAUTIONARY TALE

Of particular concern to the DOJ and the SEC is whether companies are properly "vetting" their third-party business partners to ensure that those individuals and entities are they themselves not violating the FCPA thereby subjecting their business partners to liability.

Since the passage of the FCPA in 1977, nearly 65 percent of the enforcement actions brought by the government involved bribes or other illegal payments that were not paid by the defendants directly, but involved intermediaries or other third-parties such as freight forwarders, consultants, brokers, and distributors acting on behalf of the defendant company. Typically, these bribe-paying intermediaries interacted with government agencies on behalf of companies, assisting them in seeking some type of government approval, or in situations where the government itself was the customer, often in connection with a large infrastructure project.

In fact, the very thing that makes an intermediary or third party an appealing representative of, or partner with the company, is the very thing that can give rise to FCPA liability, namely political clout, influence, and access. While having high-level access to government officials is a recipe for success in many emerging markets, such access can also be a recipe for disaster. To alleviate this risk, it is imperative that companies conduct comprehensive due diligence on their foreign representatives in order to ensure that they do not trigger FCPA liability for them.

THE CONCEPT OF A RISK-BASED APPROACH TO FCPA DUE DILIGENCE

In today's global economy, multinational companies make payments to and maintain relationships with many thousands of business partners and intermediaries all over the world. The notion of investigating all of an organization's vendors, intermediaries, and other third-party business partners is overwhelming and practically speaking, it would be both inefficient and cost prohibitive to do so. But rest assured, if problems arise, the nature and extent of the due diligence that was conducted on these intermediaries and third parties will be assessed by the DOJ and the SEC.

(*continued*)

231

(continued)

From a historical perspective, the development of effective corporate compliance programs has traditionally been premised on the implementation of a "risk-based" approach. In other words, companies customize and tailor their compliance structures and programs to the specific types and levels of risks posed by their customers, the products and services they offer, and the geographies in which they operate. While this concept has been an essential part of anti-money laundering compliance for years, in 2008, DOJ thrust the idea of "a risk-based approach" to FCPA compliance with the issuance of Opinion Procedure Release 08-02, which in connection with Halliburton's proposed acquisition of Expro, required Halliburton to develop and implement:

> a comprehensive, risk-based FCPA and anti-corruption due diligence work plan which will address, among other things, the use of agents and other third parties; commercial dealings with state-owned customers; any joint venture, teaming or consortium arrangements; customs and immigration matters; tax matters; and any government licenses and permits. Such work plan will organize the due diligence effort into high risk, medium risk, and lowest risk elements.[14]

A risk-based approach is premised on a simple concept: certain customers, vendors, intermediaries, and other third parties represent higher potential risk than others. These risks are based upon a variety of characteristics of the intermediary or third party and may include:

- How they interact with your company
- Geographic location
- Nexus to senior political officials or state-owned enterprises
- The products or services they provide
- The manner in which they receive payment
- The volume of business between the parties
- The competence of the intermediary or third party
- How long they have been in existence
- Numerous other attributes and transactional behaviors

Practically speaking, a Kazakhstan-based customs broker owned by the brother of the country's oil minister, with payments in the millions of dollars which are being directed to an offshore account in Cyprus, represents considerably more risk of corruption than the company that cleans the windows at your U.S. headquarters.

Using Technology to Conduct Risk-Based FCPA Due Diligence

Making those distinctions and parsing them across a global, decentralized vendor system isn't simple however and often requires the use of sophisticated technology. For guidance, one can look to how many of the largest financial institutions in the world effectively comply with the requirements of the USA PATRIOT Act. Specifically, many of them have made extensive use of information technology to identify, analyze, and mitigate money laundering and terrorist financing risk. The critical elements of such programs include: (i) the identification and risk ranking of customers, products, and services and geographies (Risk Scoring); (ii) the performance of Enhanced Due Diligence (EDD) of those customers representing the highest risk; and (iii) the ongoing monitoring of these customers in a manner that is proportionate to their individual risk profiles. Companies seeking to strengthen their FCPA compliance programs need not reinvent the wheel as the same proven techniques that are essential to the success of anti-money laundering compliance can be and are being utilized in some of the more progressive FCPA compliance programs.

Despite the inherent challenges, it's hard to refute the business case in favor of a risk-based approach to FCPA compliance. In order to effectively mitigate risk, you must first know its origin which means understanding that certain third-party relationships, together with their geographies and product mix, represent much more risk than others. Of equal importance to understanding the risk of certain third parties is developing an understanding of how your company interacts with them. Such factors as whether they can act on your behalf with government customers or regulators or if they have the ability to bind the company to agreements should be heavily weighted when risk-ranking these third parties.

Using technology as a means of developing a risk-based approach to organize, review, and analyze these potentially huge volumes of data can assist companies by effectively isolating the number of vendors, intermediaries, and other third-party business partners that need to be subjected to heightened scrutiny, thus allowing companies to assimilate FCPA due diligence into overall vendor creation, and on-boarding process without a huge budgetary impact in a manner consistent with regulatory expectations.

(continued)

(*continued*)

COMPLIANCE AS PREVENTION

FCPA compliance can be an expensive undertaking and the addition of vendor risk ranking and screening procedures will only add to the sticker price. So why do it? Just because the DOJ said so? Actually, there are tangible economic benefits to be realized from performing FCPA due diligence on third parties and intermediaries. The fines, disgorgement of ill-gotten gains, and drop in market capitalization resulting from a company having been implicated in an FCPA enforcement action can total many millions of dollars and can result in closer government oversight including the imposition of a court-appointed monitor, which the company has to fund for a period of several years.

Having thousands of third-party payment recipients requires extensive use of information technology to mitigate the potential FCPA risk. A combination of risk patterning, list matching, and transactional analysis using information technology can analyze millions of lines of data allowing companies to focus their limited compliance resources where they are needed most. "A needle in a haystack" is an age-old metaphor when describing a difficult task. Using information technology to apply a risk-based approach to FCPA compliance is a lot like using X-ray machines and metal detectors against the haystack.

culture of compliance? Is there a robust code of conduct? Is the anti-corruption program integrated with the overall compliance program? Is the communication equally strong both in the United States and in foreign countries? Does an anti-corruption program even exist in the organization? Are there documented policies and controls around travel and entertainment, commissions, payments, and cash? Is there mandatory training and completion certifications? Does internal audit have a seat at the table in program design and corruption risk assessment? Does internal audit conduct FCPA and other anti-corruption audits? An effective compliance program addresses all these issues. In the next chapter, we will explore implementation of various elements of an anti-corruption compliance program.

NOTES

1. Martin T. Biegelman with Daniel R. Biegelman, *Building a World-Class Compliance Program: Best Practices and Strategies for Success* (Hoboken, NJ: John Wiley & Sons, 2008), 2–3.
2. Department of Justice, "Principles of Federal Prosecution of Business Organizations," August 28, 2008, 3–4.
3. Ibid., 14–16.
4. Martin T. Biegelman and Joel T. Bartow, *Executive Roadmap to Fraud Prevention and Internal Control: Creating a Culture of Compliance* (Hoboken, NJ: John Wiley & Sons, Inc, 2006), 98–99.
5. United States Sentencing Commission, *Federal Sentencing Guidelines Manual,*www.ussc.gov/2004guid/CHAP8.pdf, 476.
6. Ibid.
7. Ibid., 476–81.
8. Biegelman and Bartow, *Executive Roadmap to Fraud Prevention and Internal Control.*
9. Please note that the name "Newco" merely represents a generic company.
10. Department of Justice, "Opinion Procedure Release 04-02," July 12, 2004, www.usdoj.gov/criminal/fraud/fcpa/opinion/2004/0402.html.
11. Joseph P. Covington, Iris E. Bennett, and Sean J. Hartigan, "U.S. v. Bourke FCPA Prosecution Highlights Dangers of Turning a Blind Eye to Red Flags," Jenner & Block White Collar Practice Alert, July 17, 2009, www.jenner.com/files/tbl_s20Publications%5CRelatedDocumentsPDFs 1252%5C2553%5CU.S.%20v.%20Bourke%20FCPA%20Prosecution %20Highlights%20Dangers%20of%20Turning%20a%20Blind%20 Eye%20to%20Red%20Flags_072009.pdf.
12. Monsanto Company Revised FCPA Working Group Guidelines, 26.
13. Department of Justice, "Lucent Technologies Inc. Agrees to Pay $1 Million Fine to Resolve FCPA Allegations," press release, December 21, 2007, www.usdoj.gov/opa/pr/2007/December/07_crm_1028 .html.
14. Department of Justice, "Opinion Procedure Release 08-02," June 13, 2008, www.usdoj.gov/criminal/fraud/fcpa/opinion/2008/0802.html.

CHAPTER 10

Implementing an Effective Anti-Corruption Compliance Program

Tone at the top is best defined as the example set by the upper levels of management, especially the C-suite officers, in words and actions for the rest of the company. This is especially important in evangelizing anti-corruption compliance both internally and externally. Fluor CEO Alan Boeckmann is an example of a senior leader implementing strong anti-corruption tone at the top. "The first thing that companies should do is send a message from the top," he says. "Fluor has put its face to the world when its peers haven't."[1] Fluor's compliance program has instituted a number of strong anti-corruption policies and a zero tolerance for violations.

Fluor's head of compliance spent well over a year traveling to their worldwide company offices to speak with employees and learn their challenges in dealing with corruption. The sites included high-risk countries such as China, Russia, and the Philippines. This attorney met with project managers and engineers in these countries. These meetings provided experiences used to design a response to corruption issues. In a Southeast Asian country, local government officials demanded that Fluor hire their security people. Fluor refused and faced the consequences. The government changed the dirt road that ran to the company mining project into a one-way street so traffic could not reach the operation. In addition, company employees were arrested as a means of harassment. Fluor refused to pay the extorted bribes and appealed to the regional government for help and that resolved the issue. Fluor then built this experience into their worldwide training program to train employees about the many ways that corruption can occur, and how it can be mitigated.[2] The message is that one can play without paying.

ANTI-CORRUPTION STANDARDS AND PROCEDURES

An organization must establish specific standards and procedures to prevent and detect corruption and bribery, and ensure compliance with the FCPA and other country-specific anti-corruption laws. The company's code of conduct must incorporate these standards and policies as well as guidance for facilitation payments, interactions with foreign government officials, reporting violations, and how to ask related questions.

The following are recommended anti-corruption policies that must be in place in an organization:

- Anti-Corruption Policy that includes:
  - Clear policy defining bribery and prohibiting it in any shape, manner, or form including public and commercial bribery
  - Definition of foreign government officials, third parties, and associated corruption risks
  - Description of the FCPA and other relevant anti-corruption laws
  - Identification of red flags and associated risks
  - Holding employees accountable for disregarding or not reporting a red flag
  - Prohibition or restrictions for facilitation payments
  - Business partner and third-party due diligence
  - Transparency in business dealings with government officials
  - Guidance on anti-money laundering, lobbyists, charitable donations, influence of government officials in hiring decisions, and related risks

- Maintaining accurate books and records
- Training and communication for anti-corruption prevention and detection
- Annual anti-corruption training and certification of compliance with policies and procedures by all employees
- Mechanisms for reporting of violations and requesting guidance
- Nonretaliation policy
- Associated policies, procedures, guidance, and prohibitions regarding:
  - Travel, Entertainment, and Gifts for Government Officials
    - Guidance and restrictions when providing things of value to U.S. or foreign government officials. Included must be how and when travel, entertainment, and gifts may be provided, limitations in size and value, documentation and prior approval, and avenues for seeking guidance. Scenarios should be included detailing real-world examples of providing travel, entertainment, and gifts as further guidance and understanding of the policy for employees to follow.
    - Guidance for travel or lodging of foreign government officials should include the following six points:
      1. Travel is for a legitimate business purpose
      2. Expenses are reasonable
      3. No friends or family members are included in the travel
      4. No side trips to vacation sites or other non-business-related locales
      5. No per diem, petty cash, or travel expense reimbursement is provided to the official
      6. Prior approval from both the company and the government official's management
  - Influence of Government Officials in Company Hiring Decisions
    - Foreign government officials may attempt to influence hiring decisions to benefit a friend or relative, or their future employment, as the *quid pro quo*, so a strong and detailed policy is required.
  - Currency Reporting Policy
    - Guidance around U.S. federal currency reporting requirements and restrictions on how much currency one may carry into or out of the U.S. and similar restrictions when traveling in foreign countries. The inference is that cash and other financial instruments exceeding allowable amounts could be used for bribery.

- Charitable Donations Policy
  - Charitable donations may be a conduit for corrupt payments and clear policy around when and how such donations may be made. For example, a government official in negotiations with a company employee may disclose that he is on the board of a charitable organization and request a donation made to the charity. Strong policies and training around this and similar scenarios are necessary for a full understanding and mitigation of this risk.
- Negotiating with Government Officials
  - Clear policy when negotiating with government officials including restrictions on verbal contracts, nonstandard agreements, side letters outside the four corners of the written contract, delayed billings, channel stuffing, vendor prepayments, prohibited transactions, and other transactions that are not transparent or within policy.
- Relationships with Business Partners and Third Parties
  - Clear policy when using business partners, sales consultants, lobbyists, and other third parties including knowing their background, experience, expertise, and deliverables. The policy must include a detailed listing of the various red flags related to third parties, a requirement for vetting of third parties, requiring them to follow the company's anti-corruption policies and ethical standards, and annual compliance certifications.

One Fortune 500 company supplemented its anti-corruption compliance program by preparing a comprehensive booklet for its sales and marketing employees. Generally, sales and marketing employees have numerous touch points with government officials and are more at risk for involvement in corrupt practices. The booklet reinforces the company's commitment to its values and the importance of integrity and honesty in all business dealings, including those involving government officials and business partners. The guidebook includes:

- Information
- Definitions
- Frequently asked questions
- Dos and don'ts
- Scenarios around deal making and pricing
- Conflicts of interest

- Dealing with government officials
- Giving and receiving gifts
- Travel and entertainment
- Handling confidential information
- Obtaining competitive intelligence

There are links to additional policies, forms and instructions, and resources for more information. In addition to the guidebook, sales and marketing employees receive annual anti-corruption training with various scenarios employees may encounter. This is an excellent best practice for communicating the organization's commitment to anti-corruption compliance.

TRAINING AND COMMUNICATION

Preventing corruption and bribery from occurring is the best defense to an FCPA or other corruption violation. There is a good reason that training and communication is one of the seven steps of the Federal Sentencing Guidelines for Organizations (FSGO), as effective anti-corruption training is a critical component in protecting an organization. Some of the best training programs are found in companies that have had FCPA violations. While that is expected, companies should not wait until after a prosecution to implement a best-in-class program.

Employee training is a required element for a compliance program being deemed "effective." Training must cover antibribery laws, as well as the books and records requirements, and the company's policies, procedures, standards, and requirements related thereto. Recent FCPA enforcement actions illustrate the perils of nonexistent or inadequate training programs. In the February 2008 SEC enforcement action against Westinghouse Air Brake Technologies Corporation (Wabtec), detailed in Chapter 7, the government found that Wabtec "did not have a FCPA policy or provide training or education to any of its employees, agents, or subsidiaries regarding the requirements of the FCPA."[3]

In a June 2008 DOJ settlement with Faro Technologies, the DOJ found that "Faro offered no FCPA training of any kind to its employees, including sales people and managers in China and other countries where there is an increased risk of improper payments."[4] Faro Technologies' Chinese subsidiary made improper payments to government officials between 2004 and 2006. A high-level executive authorized employees of the Chinese subsidiary to make the payments through third-party intermediaries to avoid detection. The company made a voluntary disclosure to the DOJ and SEC. On June 5, 2008, the SEC and DOJ announced settlement of the enforcement action against Faro. There was a total of $1.8 million in disgorgement of profits and a $1.1 million fine as well as a nonprosecution agreement and a two-year monitorship.

Anti-corruption training should cover the FCPA's antibribery, and books and records requirements, and all associated company policies, procedures, and standards. Training should stress the importance of FCPA compliance to the company's culture, reputation, and ethical standards. Companies need to cover more than just the FCPA and other U.S. laws. Be sure to discuss the existence of and compliance with anti-corruption laws that apply in the countries they operate in. At minimum, training should be provided to all persons within the organization who have government touch points as well as the organization's governing authority and managers who provide oversight. Remember that the FCPA is an unknown quantity to most employees and they have no idea of the potential consequences.

A more costly but a more effective approach is to train all employees and anyone who acts on the company's behalf. For example, Monsanto's anti-corruption training is given to employees as well as third parties, including vendors and contractors, who interact with government employees. The training policy is broad so almost all employees are trained worldwide. A strong recommendation is for more detailed and specific training of salespeople with government touch points, senior managers, country managers, and finance employees such as subsidiary controllers, and controls and compliance managers outside the United States and in high-risk countries.

Training should adopt both a rules-based and a values-based approach. Remember that gifts, business travel and entertainment, and charitable donations can be appropriate business tools if used legally and within corporate policy boundaries. A risk-based approach will focus increased education on certain employees involved in the process of obtaining or retaining business in foreign countries, as well as high-risk business sectors and countries. In looking at risk, be mindful of perceived corruption concerns in countries where business is sought to be acquired or maintained. As a result, consider focusing on countries with high risk such as China, India, Nigeria, and Indonesia but remember that bribery can occur anywhere. Training tailored to the specific organization including industry sector, risks, and culture as well as factoring in Transparency International's Corruption Perceptions Index is recommended.

Red Flags Training

It is especially important to provide training on the many red flags of corruption that may occur whether it pertains to third parties, travel and entertainment, or other high-risk areas. Employees must understand what a red flag is and what to do if recognized. Train employees on red flag identification and how to report them. Training around red flags must include real-life examples of these red flags. This includes guidance on the organization's responsibility for dealing with third parties and agents who may be conduits of bribes to government officials. Other red flag training should include due diligence steps, anti-corruption clauses and audit provisions in contracts, prohibition on side letters in contracts, and lavish travel and entertainment, gifts, and special treatment expenses for government employees.

Train employees in specific business lines who deal with government officials in any form. State-owned enterprises abound especially in countries like China and Russia. It is critical to be able to identify government officials when engaging in business transactions. Ownership arrangements are not always clear. For example, doctors in China may be government officials if they are employed in the government-run health care system. Provide training around distributor agreements and arrangements, distributors selected by government officials or sales consultants, distributors who are simply pass-through entities or shell companies.

Other red flag training should include:

- If the business uses agents, foreign sales representatives, consultants or other intermediaries
- Consultants retained by government customers may be considered government officials
- Corporate policy and approval requirements
- Guide to sponsored conferences and promotional expenses
- Guide to FCPA permitted "grease payments" and whether or not they are permitted by corporate policy as well as a clearly defined facilitation payments policy
- Guide to foreign charitable contributions
- Abnormal credit terms
- Define what slush funds and off-the-book transactions are and that they are prohibited
- Travel for government officials, especially around contract signing or renewals

- Policies and restrictions on hospitality, gifts, and entertainment
- Other key aspects of training from recent DOJ/SEC enforcement actions
- Extend enhanced training beyond senior managers and compliance/ legal staff (Many cases show that those in lower/middle management make the decisions that lead to violations.)

Anti-Corruption Training Best Practices

Subject matter experts (SME) from the legal and compliance departments should provide ongoing onsite training to the organization's employees in addition to online training. Anti-corruption SMEs have experience and expertise in fighting corruption and bribery and intimate knowledge of case studies that can be shared with employees. Be sure to train the trainer so that they are well-versed in both the organization policies and current developments in anti-corruption activities.

Subsidiary leadership and employees must be trained to reinforce knowledge around anti-corruption, the company's policies and procedures, and enhancing tone at the top. Local jurisdiction anti-corruption rules should be included in training. Subsidiary company employees have numerous contacts with government officials and provide the greatest risk of corruption and related ramifications. In many countries there is a high turnover of employees and leadership and that reinforces the need for ongoing anti-corruption training.

Training should include frequently asked questions and examples drawn from the company's business operations and experiences. Frequently asked questions help employees apply the anti-corruption policies and procedures in real-world situations. Include time for questions and answers from attendees. That is the benefit of live training but it is also possible with online training that has chat tools. Ensure that all important topics are covered by training. Advanced, business-cycle, or other topic-intensive training can be prepared and provided as necessary to address specific issues. Train in the native language as needed.

Training must be mandatory with attendance documented by sign-in sheets. If possible, require 100 percent completion of online and in-person training. There needs to be consequences for noncompliance such as loss of bonus payment or other discipline. The full attention of all attendees is required during the training. That means no open laptops with employees reading and responding to e-mail or texting on cell phones while the

244

training is in session. Any time anyone leaves and returns from the room, that too must be documented. The missed sections of training will need to be repeated. The presenters should also document the training with their names, titles, dates, times, location, and subject matter presented. Training should be tracked, documented, and periodically refreshed. Be sure to create a living record to demonstrate that employees were appropriately trained. Have someone take notes during the training session. Document the questions asked, and then build the answers in future classes.

These procedures will be beneficial if and when the government needs proof of the effectiveness of your training program and overall compliance program. Remember to train your internal investigators and compliance staff on anti-corruption subjects and have them become subject-matter experts.

COMPLIANCE INSIGHT 10.1: DRIVING HOME THE IMPACT OF CORRUPTION

Jane Wexton has had a long career in the legal profession and corporate compliance. As a partner at a major law firm, followed as chief compliance officer and chief global anti-money laundering officer for Fortune 500 companies, and now in private practice, she has focused on the challenging issues of corruption, money laundering, conflicts of interest, fraud, and competition violations. Wexton has extensive experience conducting due diligence and internal investigations and has worked in over 100 countries. Additionally, she is a frequent speaker on the FCPA, anti-corruption, and compliance issues.

Wexton has developed a unique way to emphasize corruption's impact, especially when speaking before audiences in bribery-prone countries. Rather than show slides of corruption statistics or the specifics of anti-corruption statutes, Wexton simply shows pictures. But not just any pictures. They are photographs that scream out the old adage that a picture is worth a thousand words. There are photos of children drinking filthy water from mud puddles because there is no running water, dilapidated buildings that serve as hospitals for the poor and the infirmed, unpaved roads that hinder transportation and commerce, and partially completed schools sitting empty. These

(continued)

(*continued*)
images touch the heart and soul and more than words could say, vividly demonstrate the impact and cost of corruption. Once these compelling images set in and she has the audience's attention, Wexton drives home the message of what needs to be done to stop corruption and bribery.

Delivery Methods for Training

Both traditional in-person and online training should be employed for anti-corruption training. In-person training allows for greater interaction and provides the opportunity for the instructor to answer specific questions as they arise. It fosters discussion of key issues to reinforce their importance. A group setting can also include role-playing exercises that gauge the understanding of issues important to employees. Online training is growing in popularity and can reach large audiences in a very cost-effective manner. In addition, it allows for customization by location, language, employee function, and subject matter. Employees can decide when they want to complete training and how much they want to complete at one time. Tracking of employee attendance and course completion can be easily accomplished with online training.

A company should try to successfully balance in-person versus online training. Mitigating factors include costs and coverage. With online training, an organization can cover more employees and geography quicker. In-person training should be used for high-risk roles and regions as well as for reinforcement as necessary. Whether in-person or online, employee training hours must be recorded. Consideration should also be given to having a minimum requirement of training hours completed per year. Training programs can be developed in-house and there are vendors that can help an organization prepare robust online training with dramatized scenarios followed by a short quiz for employees to take to test their knowledge of the material. Note that basic training is a minimum; more may be needed depending on any number of factors.

Specific Anti-Corruption Reporting Mechanism

Create a specific anti-corruption alias e-mail address within the organization so employees can easily communicate questions or concerns about the anti-corruption policies, red flags disclosures, FCPA, possible violations, or other related issues. This dedicated anti-corruption e-mail address should be separate from the organization's hotline or helpline.

For hotlines to be effective, companies need strong policies and training on whistleblowers and nonretaliation. If you build it right, they will call and report violations. So, communicate the existence of hotlines and helplines. Remember that when you encourage voluntary disclosure, employees need to see the results and know that management is responding.

Communicating the Compliance Program

Ongoing communication of the anti-corruption compliance program is essential to success. Use the company intranet, e-mails, posters, table tents in cafeterias, and other ongoing communications for constant reinforcement of the program and the engagement of employees. One best practice is to create a Quarterly Ethics and Compliance Newsletter that is delivered in electronic form to all employees worldwide. This newsletter can have links to anti-corruption and other company policies, new policies or changes in policies, the hotline number, an investigations section, policies and procedures, news on corruption and violations by other companies, and other information.

Publicize ethical lapses within the company. All organizations, no matter how good their compliance programs, will have ethical lapses by their employees. It is human nature, but these personal failures can be turned into learning opportunities for the betterment of the entire organization. Thus, communicate the impact of noncompliance. This communication is especially important when a significant compliance lapse or public event occurs such as the arrest of an employee for a criminal offense involving company assets. Senior leaders need to inform the organization about the event, how it happened, the compliance failures involved, and what to do to ensure it does not happen again. These events, while painful, can be used as learning opportunities from which to grow and improve.

Use an ongoing communication such as an "Integrity Corner" in internal communications to employees where ethics lapses and disciplinary actions are publicized. While specific information about the employees and others who were disciplined is not recommended to be used, the facts of the case can be used for learning and prevention. Some companies actually list on their web sites the number of investigations conducted into compliance failures, the number of related employee terminations, hotline referrals, and other related information. One company uses a well-publicized reward system offering up to $25,000 to employees who report violations of their code of conduct. While very few companies offer cash rewards, it has proven very effective for this particular company. Of course, as with any hotline or reporting mechanism, due care must be given to protect against the receipt of false allegations.[5]

Evaluating Your Anti-Corruption Training Program

Evaluating the success of an organization's anti-corruption training is important to demonstrate that it is effective. It is an element of the ongoing evaluation of overall compliance program effectiveness. Evaluation and continuous improvement is a requirement of the FSGO and ongoing evaluation of compliance training is part of that. Included are the time, money, and resources that an organization puts into building and improving a compliance program. There are the outcomes from training including the impact that compliance efforts have on an organization's level of compliance. These outcomes include employee awareness and understanding of FCPA compliance program, laws, regulations, and policy requirements, a decrease in violations and noncompliance, and creating a culture of compliance.

Training content, objectives, evaluation metrics, and indicators should be relevant and specific to the organization. In preparing training content and goals, consider using the SMART approach. SMART stands for:

Specific: clear and concise training that is understandable by all
Measurable: quantifiable by clear measurements such as a pass rate
Achievable: realistic, practical, and reasonable results such as training attendance
Relevant: indicators measure expected or desired change of behavior
Timed: provide a realistic time frame for completion

Evaluate the delivery methods and determine the most effective platform. Review frequency of training and the number of employees who completed training by job function and risk level. Determine if all senior management and board members completed training. Do the same for vendors, contractors, agents, and other third parties if they are trained by the organization. If not, determine the level of training they receive from their respective companies and encourage the development of specific training.

Review confirmation of attendance documentation and training completion statistics for business leaders and hold them accountable for completion in their organization. Consider a competition among company organizations to complete training first. Identify those not attending training. Review documentation showing discipline for those not completing training or other explanation. Determine if handout materials were provided for ongoing reinforcement. Review attendee feedback and evaluations of training. Also review the credentials of the trainers.

A best practice is to measure employee awareness and their understanding of laws, policies, and procedures as part of the evaluation process. Look for an increase in helpline calls. Was there a spike after training? Was there a decrease in violations and noncompliance? Use employee surveys and consider three to five possible questions to assess the impact of training. Some possible questions include:

- What does FCPA stand for?
- Do you know what a facilitation payment is and whether it is allowed by the company?
- Do you know how to report FCPA misconduct and/or ask for guidance?
- Can you provide examples of improper conduct with respect to anti-corruption that would require reporting?
- Do you know the name of the company's compliance officer?

Determine if there was an assessment of training content and effectiveness with regular updating to reflect changes in law, red flags, best practices, case studies, and other content. An important element of assessment is tone at the top and a commitment at the executive level. Ask these questions:

- Have senior leaders completed the required anti-corruption training before everyone else?
- Have senior leaders handled compliance matters including anti-corruption issues appropriately when they have occurred in their organizations?
- Have senior leaders communicated the importance of the code of conduct and related policies and procedures throughout their organizations?
- Have senior leaders set the appropriate "tone at the top" and is it widely communicated and practiced?

Maintain evaluation metrics for both program evaluations and worst-case scenarios to demonstrate to the government your program effectiveness. The DOJ looks closely at program effectiveness in determining whether to charge a corporation for FCPA violations as evidenced in the Wabtec and Faro Technologies cases.

M&A DUE DILIGENCE

The vetting process during mergers and acquisitions can uncover significant information that may determine whether the deal goes through. An unintended consequence of the vetting process has been the discovery of FCPA violations. "FCPA issues had not historically been at the top of acquirers' due diligence checklists, but in the wake of several FCPA actions that stalled or even shattered deals, buyers are paying more attention to potential violations and the risk of successor liability."[6] Mergers and acquisitions have resulted in FCPA investigations as corrupt activity was discovered either during the due diligence phase or later when the business is being integrated. This can impact whether the transaction closes or not. Titan Corporation's planned merger with Lockheed Martin fell through after the discovery of FCPA violations resulting in Titan's disgorgement of profits and a $28.4 million fine. Disclosures and government investigation will continue as this is a focus of DOJ and SEC enforcement.

A recent example is eLandia's acquisition of Latin Node, a telecommunications services company, which led to a discovery of pervasive corrupt payments. Between March 2004 and June 2007, Latin Node funneled $1,099,899 to third parties that were to be passed to government officials in Honduras. Between July 2005 and April 2006, the company paid $1,150,654 to third parties to be passed to government officials in Yemen. eLandia learned of the violations after the acquisition of Latin Node and self-disclosed them to the government. On April 7, 2009, Latin Node, a privately held Florida corporation, pleaded guilty to FCPA violations of improper payments made in Honduras and Yemen. They paid a $2 million fine. "Due diligence during mergers is going to be a fruitful source of these [FCPA] cases," commented a former SEC enforcement official.[7]

In conducting effective due diligence and determining the risk assessment for M&A activity, a thorough vetting must be conducted. The following is an M&A due diligence checklist of best practices to consider in the vetting process:

- Does the company do international business?
  - What is the extent of international sales?
  - What countries is business conducted in?
  - What is the industry?
  - Nature of sales–use of consultants or distributors?
  - How much business is government related?
  - Amounts of retainers, commissions, and expenses paid to consultants in connection with sales?
  - Sales through foreign subsidiaries or joint ventures?
- Does the company have FCPA compliance controls?
  - Is there a code of conduct and FCPA compliance policy which is distributed to all employees and consultants?
  - What FCPA training is conducted, how frequently, and which employees and consultants are trained?
  - Is due diligence performed on consultants?
  - Is due diligence documented?
- Does the company have written agreements for every international consultant?
  - FCPA/antibribery representations and warranties?
  - Provisions for short-notice termination without cause and the right to terminate for cause upon reasonable belief that a violation of the FCPA representations and warranties may have occurred?
  - Prohibition on the use of subagents without the prior written approval of the company?
  - Requirement of payment in the country where services are performed, that is, a prohibition on payments to third countries?
  - Audit rights?
- What is the percentage of commissions paid to international consultants?
- Records of disbursements?
  - What level of approvals?
  - Audit trail of payments tied to invoices and approvals?[8]

RISK ASSESSMENTS

Organizations are required to periodically evaluate their compliance programs, assess the risk of criminal conduct, and modify their programs

251

THOUGHT LEADER IN FCPA COMPLIANCE:
LESLIE McCARTHY

The Role of Technology in Third-Party Due Diligence

Leslie McCarthy is a director at The Steele Foundation, where she is a subject matter expert in the area of third-party due diligence for global FCPA compliance. Over the course of two decades, Steele has executed due diligence functions in more than 120 countries on behalf of more than 500 multinational companies, including nearly half of the Fortune 100. Prior to her work at Steele, McCarthy was for 15 years a New York-based national correspondent and investigative reporter for The Associated Press covering news events domestically and abroad. McCarthy is a three-time Pulitzer nominee, Headliner Club award winner, and former Nieman Fellow at Harvard University. She holds a BA from Columbia University and early in her career worked for the Organisation for Economic Co-operation and Development in Paris. Here McCarthy provides her expertise in using the power of technology in third-party due diligence.

Just as many companies have turned to online technology to implement training, establish hotlines, and disseminate ethics policies to employees, many multinationals have also found it helpful to deploy reliable FCPA-customized software tools to manage their due diligence caseloads and associated workflow.

Automating the process of vetting third parties overseas drives consistency, efficacy, and transparency across the enterprise. A robust platform enables a company to effectively and efficiently manage a decentralized program. The result is an organization that has one system that everyone is using.

So, what constitutes a robust "reasonable" FCPA third-party due diligence review? The process of "on-boarding" an overseas intermediary may involve several steps, including completion of a standardized due diligence intake questionnaire, issuance of corporate documents and anti-corruption declarations and, finally, some level of field or database investigation into that prospective third-party partner's background and reputation. We find many of our clients struggling with a patchwork endeavor, utilizing different processes from region to region and department to department.

In one business unit, due diligence may be conducted internally and recorded in a spreadsheet stored on a sales manager's desktop. Elsewhere, there may be a series of PDF questionnaires circulated among would-be intermediaries, faxed, and then stored perhaps randomly at some centralized compliance department. But where are these reports stored subsequently? It is the equivalent of file folders stacked here and there, full of information, but none of it securely retained or readily accessible. It does not have to be this way. Centralizing these various functions is critical to averting an administrative nightmare.

By using an automated case management system, companies establish an end-to-end process that does not vary or drop valuable information. You can systematically avoid doing business with intermediaries who have been rejected or "red-flagged" and at the same time enhance anti-corruption measures to prevent any confusion among those with whom you consider doing business.

Each due diligence investigation should be independent and attached to a discrete case folder, which contains the third-party's overall corruption profile and other data relevant to a company's due diligence compliance process. Each case folder should contain information confirming the chain of communication, notifications, declarations, investigative findings, remediation actions, education, representations, and certifications between the company and its agent/partner/distributor/third parties.

What does this process look like and how do you accomplish it efficiently and cost-effectively?

- *Deploy a technology platform that drives and encapsulates your process. There are simple web-based options that require no training or infrastructure investment.*
- *Establish a protocol, which might include:*
  - *Automated issuance of a standard corporate due diligence intake questionnaire to be completed by all current and prospective third parties.*
  - *Automated issuance of a corporate FCPA policy and accompanying anti-corruption agreement letter to be signed by current or prospective third parties.*

(continued)

(continued)

- *Review of a "reject list" to ensure third party has not previously been associated with corruption risk or activity.*
- *Engage a basic due diligence investigation at the level of scrutiny appropriate to the subject. This is determined through a comprehensive risk inventory to establish types of intermediaries, identify levels of exposure, and define appropriate degrees of investigation. Levels of investigation might include:*
  - *Tier I: Global Database Investigations—basic overview of third-party history limited to review of watch and sanctions lists and range of relevant media.*
  - *Tier II: Enhanced Due Diligence—field investigation that provides site visits; validation of corporate, criminal, and civil records; review of public documents, social networking sites, and interviews to establish third-party history and relationships. This option is particularly recommended for targets of joint ventures, and intermediaries associated with especially high volumes of business, a high-risk industry, or geographic region.*
- *Analyze any red flags and determine whether or at what level of business relationship in which to engage.*
- *Review completed investigation and reject, request additional information, or accept.*
- *Automate third-party agreements, including relevant warrants and representations.*
- *Optional: offer automated online training module*
- *Retain all cases and accompanying documentation in a secure, encrypted archive that provides easy accessibility allowing for:*
  - *Review of due diligence caseload metrics, such as budgeting across departments, regional investigative activity, timelines, and completed reports.*
  - *Repository for paper chain to demonstrate effective compliance programming should your program come under scrutiny of regulatory authorities.*
  - *Secure vault for date- and time-stamped records that may provide a clear evidentiary chain should litigation of any type occur.*
- *Customize timeline for renewal of vetting process (usually cycles of every 18–24 months).*

- *Automate a system-generated notification to reengage with third-party intermediaries in a way that provides consistent messaging and up-to-date investigation cost-effectively and consistently.*

Putting a credible third-party due diligence program in place is understandably daunting, particularly for companies with limited knowledge of legacy relationships, complex joint-venture activity, or idiosyncratic business practices and customs that may be industry- or country-specific. The backlog alone may be unwieldy and potentially costly enough to make even the most proactive compliance officer want to stick his or her head in the sand.

But keep in mind that there are technology tools, flat-fee FCPA-specific investigation services, and practical timelines/roadmaps to help minimize the first wave of cases. Compliance enhancements become easier as your program matures and becomes progressively more familiar, well-practiced, and established.

When it comes to avoiding the multimillion-dollar fines, prison time, and reputational damage that go with increased DOJ and SEC enforcement activity, self-policing is important, and a thoughtful compliance program is the best preventive strategy for ensuring effective FCPA compliance.

---

as appropriate. This includes documenting the risk of corruption and bribery within the organization and identifying the potential magnitude and likelihood. Consider who your customers are, the nature of your operations, whether you have a centralized or decentralized business model, whether you operate in high-risk geographies that are corruption-prone, the sophistication of your compliance program, and your history of compliance failures. Assess the risk of doing business with government officials and state-owned enterprises, business partners and third parties, sales and marketing employees, supply channels, joint ventures, mergers and acquisitions, lobbyists, and charitable donations.

Internal controls and mitigation strategies need to be tested and revised for compliance. Build robust risk profiles by business lines and locations. This includes reviewing the red flags related to each risk. Internal audit can drive this risk assessment and audit planning process to ensure compliance with corporate governance. Use examples from the many FCPA prosecutions for various scenarios of corruption that can impact the company. This is especially valuable when looking at companies within your industry that operate in the same geographic areas, as they potentially can have the same corruption issues that your company faces. Make sure you know the local anti-corruption laws as well as the frequency of bribery prosecutions in the various countries you do business in. As detailed in Chapter 7, China is taking a more aggressive stance in fighting corruption and other countries are following suit.

Risk assessments should include detection and prevention controls; surveys of employees and management in the various subsidiaries; interviews with employees in management, legal, finance, and sales and marketing who interact with government officials; reviews of reports from the regional compliance committees on corruption incidents and policy violations; and anti-corruption certifications.

INTERNAL ACCOUNTING CONTROLS

Role of Internal Audit

Internal audit departments can add great value in antifraud and anti-corruption compliance. As a result of Siemens' prosecution, the company has significantly ramped up both the number of personnel in internal audit and their level of skills and qualifications. Internal audit at Siemens regularly audits their compliance program with a specific focus on internal controls, antitrust, and anti-corruption program elements. "Internal auditors can assist in the deterrence of fraud by examining and evaluating the adequacy and the effectiveness of the system of internal control, commensurate with the extent of the potential exposure or risk in the various segments of the organization's operations."[9]

An anti-corruption compliance component should be added to internal audit to ensure linkage and continuous interaction with the auditing function. Adding qualified professionals to the internal audit team, training and empowering them in anti-corruption expertise, giving them direct reporting to executive leadership, and high visibility to the audit committee, are steps that should be considered.[10] The internal audit function should designate and train auditors as FCPA and anti-corruption subject matter experts.

Dedicated FCPA and anti-corruption audits should be conducted with proactive testing programs built into audit work plans. Internal audit involvement in both anti-corruption risk assessments and audits is an important component of an overall compliance program. There should be a specific focus on high-risk locations and industries. The company

256

should use the power of technology to identify and test high-risk business transactions. In addition, a strong, ongoing partnership between the internal audit, compliance, and legal functions is a requirement.

The FCPA requires that the organization's books and records accurately and fully reflect all transactions, including corrupt payments. Since few people will correctly document a bribe in a company's books and records, the disguised payment opens the door to an FCPA accounting violation. More enforcement actions are brought under this FCPA provision than the antibribery provision. Effective audit programs should address compliance in this area.

Anti-Corruption Audit Program

Robust audit programs should be used to ensure compliance and detect violations.

The controls that should be in place and tested include accounting controls, training completion details, annual anti-corruption certifications, due diligence, anti-corruption contract clauses, and issue escalation and mitigation. Internal audit should review the general ledger for suspicious payments. Wrongdoers have been known to hide corrupt payments on the balance sheet. Effective accounting controls can determine how gifts, travel and entertainment, rebates, refunds, commissions, charitable donations, and other high risk expenses have been booked. Transaction testing should be conducted using the following keywords, as well as others, in various business accounts:

- Advisor fee
- Bonus
- Bribe
- Charitable
- Commission
- Conference fee
- Consultant fee
- Contribution
- Customer commission
- Customer relations
- Discounts
- Donation

- Entertainment
- Facilitation
- Finder's fee
- Foreign official
- Foundation
- Gift
- Government official
- Gratuity
- Hosting
- Incidentals
- License fee
- Lobbyist
- Lodging
- Marketing
- Miscellaneous
- Processing fee
- Professional fee
- Promotion
- Public official
- Rebate
- Referral fee
- Refund
- Sales commissions
- Slush fund
- Sponsorships
- Transfer fee
- Transportation
- Travel

In transaction testing, auditors should look for the common red flags. They include:

- Even dollar amounts
- Expense reimbursement just under the receipt submission requirement amount

- One-time payments to vendors and third parties
- Duplicate names, payments, or invoice numbers
- Sequential invoice numbers
- Payments in countries where the company does not do business
- Business addresses that are also home addresses of company employees
- Businesses using mail drop addresses
- Advances to employees where no reimbursement is requested

This is not an all-inclusive list and each organization should determine the specific transactions to review.

The following are other audit best practices:

- Review employee expense reports for employees in high-risk roles including those in sales and marketing, subsidiary management, and others who interact with government employees. Also review expense reports for employees who work with lobbyists, public sector sales consultants, government policy consultants, and other third parties.
- Review expense reports for employees who have excessive travel and entertainment expenses. Test for gifts, travel, and entertainment given to government employees.
- Add a field to expense reports confirming whether any of the expenses relate to government officials. If employees acknowledge such an expense, more information can be asked to determine whether the expense is in compliance.
- Audit third parties to determine that due diligence took place.
- Audit to determine that third-party contracts have been prepared and approved by company attorneys.
- Determine that third-party contracts and agreements are in writing and contain anti-corruption language including anti-corruption compliance and certifications, audit clauses, termination rights.
- Review third-party contracts and agreements and test a sample of commission payments. Verify that these commissions relate to sales activity. Verify that commission rates are in line with what is specified in the contract. Verify that commissions have been approved by an authorized person.

- Audit any time a business unit has an issue with a government entity.
- Audit regional compliance committees.
- Any anti-corruption finding in an audit report is a potentially serious issue and needs to be thoroughly followed up. Create a culture where such a finding will be something that any business leader will do everything possible to avoid.
- Ensure that any such findings reach all the way to the CEO, CFO, General Counsel, Chief Compliance Officers, and Audit Committee.
- Conduct dedicated anti-corruption onsite audits in subsidiaries in high-risk countries.[11]

Internal auditors need to review potentially problematic business relationships, especially those involving distributors, resellers, and other third parties. One example is when the government customer selects the distributor and then conducts price negotiations directly with that distributor. The third party may have agreed to pay a bribe to secure the deal. Or, the third party could be a shell company operated by a government official. The shell company will then inflate the price point in merchandise or services provided to the government with the extra money going into the pocket of the corrupt government official.

OTHER COMPLIANCE PROGRAM BEST PRACTICES

Field-Based Compliance Officers

There are different standards of business practices, cultural sensitivity issues, as well as legal and employee requirements in foreign countries, and all have to be understood and dealt with. Each of these is potentially a compliance minefield. One way to address this and increase the breadth and depth of the compliance program is to assign field-based compliance officers in the countries and regions where the organization operates. They can be the face of compliance and provide a local connection to all aspects of the program with a special emphasis on anti-corruption compliance. These field compliance officers can be a resource to local subsidiary management, answer questions and share compliance information with management and employees, discuss best practices with human resources and legal departments, and provide compliance awareness and education.

260

FCPA Enforcement Database

Maintain an FCPA database containing DOJ and SEC criminal and civil enforcement actions and recent trends in enforcement, DOJ Opinion Procedure Releases, as well as trends and prosecutions in other countries. There is increased anti-corruption enforcement and legislation that companies must be up-to-date on. The new Bribery Bill being considered in the UK that will significantly increase enforcement activity is but one example of the need for knowledge in this area. This information should be maintained in the database and will be useful in preparing risk assessments and training content.

Benchmarking

A best practice to consider is benchmarking your anti-corruption program against other companies, including those with FCPA compliance issues. Companies that have had FCPA violations have had to build very strong programs and there is much to be learned from them. Sharing experiences around compliance program design and implementation is an excellent way to advance compliance. Consider hosting a compliance summit with other companies, both from your particular industry and from other industries, to share red flags, best practices, and training techniques, and other related issues. Engage qualified consultants for program reviews and improvements that have a wealth of experience from their work on behalf of clients with FCPA violations. Be sure to document these benchmarking and consultant sessions as another element of an effective compliance program. Compliance Insight 10.2 is a sample compliance activities checklist to evaluate anti-corruption program compliance.

COMMITMENT TO ANTI-CORRUPTION COMPLIANCE PROGRAMS

Change takes time but by all appearances, anti-corruption compliance programs are taking hold and becoming more robust. "FCPA compliance has risen up near the top of the compliance totem pole. I've seen many companies avoid doing business and walk away from lucrative opportunities because of FCPA considerations. Overall, there are fewer governments that still adhere to the pay-for-play arrangements," said attorney Timothy Dickinson whose law practice focuses on the FCPA.[12] Businesses are realizing that as well. Siemens is developing one of the best anti-

261

COMPLIANCE INSIGHT 10.2: SAMPLE COMPLIANCE ACTIVITIES CHECKLIST

	Strategies in Practice	Yes	No
Compliance Training & Monitoring	Maintain a compliance hotline and past records	X	
	Conduct mandatory FCPA training seminars	X	
	Require FCPA certification for senior employees		X
Compliance Procedures	Conduct due diligence reviews		X
	Pre-approve all agents, consultants, JV partners , etc.	X	
	Include FCPA compliance clause in written agreements		X
	Review existing contracts	X	
Internal Audit Procedures	Pre-approve all facilitating payments	X	
	Conduct accounting & bookkeeping audits at foreign sites	X	
	Conduct thorough operational audits at foreign sites		X

Source: General Counsel Roundtable Research, Compliance and Ethics Leadership Council Research, 2009, The Corporate Executive Board Company. Reprinted with permission. All rights reserved.

corruption compliance programs in existence today. The company likes to say that it is critical "to have an adequate compliance system in place and a corporate culture that stands for clean business."[13] It's not just companies like Siemens who greatly enhanced their programs. One company that reported a possible bribery issue in a European subsidiary started sending compliance professionals to some of the 100 countries it operates in to train its employees in anti-corruption requirements and policies.[14]

The undeniable fact is that prevention is far better than the cure but it is still costly. Experienced consultants in FCPA matters are not cheap. One global investigative firm "starts its billing at about $7,500 for each employee a company wants to scrutinize" and costs "can quickly rise if the employee works in multiple countries."[15] The cost of compliance is the cost of doing business legally and with integrity and accountability. The government will not accept the defense of "I couldn't develop an appropriate compliance program because I didn't have the budget" when a corruption violation is discovered. "FCPA compliance will become a top corporate governance issue leading to more rigorous FCPA compliance and self-monitoring programs. The onus—and the expense—will continue to be placed upon companies to dedicate greater resources to anti-corruption initiatives, including due diligence, during mergers and acquisitions."[16] Effective compliance is not an option today. Those companies that have best-in-class programs have lessened the risk of bribery while protecting their employees, shareholders, customers, and partners.

NOTES

1. Mina Kimes, "Fluor's Corporate Crime-Fighter," *Fortune*, February 9, 2009, http://money.cnn.com/2009/02/05/news/companies/Fluors_crime_fighter.fortune/.
2. Ibid.
3. *Securities and Exchange Commission v. Westinghouse Air Brake Technologies Corporation*, Civil Action No. 08-CV-706, February 14, 2008.
4. U.S. Department of Justice letter to Gregory S. Bruch, Willkie Farr & Gallagher, LLP, attorney for Faro Technologies, containing Statement of Facts as part of nonprosecution agreement, June 3, 2008. www.law.virginia.edu/pdf/faculty/garrett/faro.pdf.
5. Martin T. Biegelman with Daniel R. Biegelman, *Building a World-Class Compliance Program: Best Practices and Strategies for Success*, (Hoboken, NJ: John Wiley & Sons, 2008), 193–94.
6. Joan Harrison, "Does Your Foreign Target Have Clean Hands?" *Mergers and Acquisition Journal*, July 2007, www.bdoconsulting.com/resources/thought-leaders/m%20and%20a%20(mich).pdf.
7. Richard Grimes (former assistant director, Enforcement, Securities and Exchange Commission), comments at an FCPA Conference, November 2004, www.lavca.org/lavca/web.nsf/pages/pastpresentations-pdfs.html/$file/2008summit%20Gregory%20Swinehart.pdf.
8. Ed Rial and Wendy Schmidt, "Foreign Corrupt Practices Act: Why Heightened Vigilance Can Be Critical" (webinar presentation, Deloitte Financial Advisory Services, November 14, 2007).
9. American Institute of Certified Public Accountants, Fraud and the CPA Self-Study Course, http://fvs.aicpa.org/Resources/Antifraud+Forensic+Accounting/Fraud+Detection+Investigation+Prevention/Interviewing+Skills+and+Guidelines/Fraud+Prevention.htm.
10. Martin Biegelman with Daniel Biegelman, *Building a World-Class Compliance Program*.
11. Rial and Schmidt, "Foreign Corrupt Practices Act."
12. PricewaterhouseCoopers, *Corruption Crackdown: How the FCPA is changing the way the world does business*, July 27, 2009, 27.

13. Dionne Searcey, "U.S. Cracks Down on Corporate Bribes," *Wall Street Journal*, May 26, 2009, A1.
14. Ibid.
15. Ibid.
16. PricewaterhouseCoopers, *Corruption Crackdown.*

CHAPTER 11

Monsanto: Fighting Corruption for a Better World*

Even great companies make mistakes. It is not necessarily the mistake that is the critical issue, but how a company handles that mistake once it is found. It's the adage that we cannot change the past but we can surely influence the future through our actions, integrity, and accountability. That was the decision facing Monsanto when it discovered financial irregularities in its Indonesian affiliates in 2001. Monsanto's culture and values ensured there was no question what the company would do in this challenging situation. The company immediately took the right path and started an internal investigation, which was initiated at the direction of the Board of Directors. Monsanto subsequently self-disclosed the results of its investigation to the Department of Justice (DOJ) and Securities and Exchange Commission (SEC), including FCPA books

---

*The material in this chapter was graciously provided by Monsanto Company and we have adapted this profile of their anti-corruption compliance program from that material.

and records violations and compliance issues involving the Indonesian affiliates.

Today, Monsanto has a global FCPA compliance program that is second-to-none, winning praise from independent experts and earning cover story profiles in leading industry journals. They hired thought leaders in compliance with an ongoing focus for improvement and world-class practices. The commitment of senior leaders made this a reality, from the Chairman and CEO on down. In this chapter, we tell the story of how Monsanto successfully responded to serious misconduct and in the process created and implemented a best-in-class FCPA and anti-corruption program that is a model for other companies.

A COMMITMENT TO AGRICULTURE

Monsanto Company is a leading global provider of technology-based solutions and agricultural products that improve farm productivity and food quality. It is headquartered in St. Louis, Missouri and has locations around the world. Monsanto is the world's leading producer of the agricultural herbicide Roundup and other products used by farmers, consumers, and lawn-and-garden professionals. Monsanto is also the world's leading producer of genetically engineered seeds.

Monsanto considers itself first and foremost an agricultural company. They apply innovation and technology to help farmers around the world produce more while conserving more. They help farmers to be successful, producing healthier foods, better animal feeds and more fiber, while also reducing agriculture's impact on our environment. The company's global seeds and traits business and genetic technology platforms produce leading seed brands in large-acre crops like corn, cotton, soybeans, and canola, as well as small-acre crops like vegetables. The agricultural productivity segment consists primarily of crop protection products and residential lawn-and-garden herbicide products. The Monsanto of today is focused on agriculture and supporting farmers around the world in their mission to feed, clothe, and fuel our growing world.

DOJ AND SEC FCPA INVESTIGATION

On January 6, 2005, Monsanto resolved a DOJ and SEC investigation related to Monsanto's discovery and voluntary disclosure of improper payments and financial irregularities related to the company's Indonesian affiliates. The DOJ charged the company with FCPA violations in

266

connection with a bribe of $50,000 to a senior Indonesian Ministry of Environment official and falsely documenting the illegal payment as "consultant fees." The SEC filed related civil enforcement actions that Monsanto violated the antibribery and books and records provisions. Monsanto agreed to cooperate with any further investigation, received a deferred prosecution agreement (DPA), paid a $1 million fine, and agreed to retain an independent compliance monitor to review and evaluate the company's policies and procedures to ensure compliance with the FCPA and the DPA.

In describing the details of the FCPA offenses, the DOJ wrote the following in its January 6, 2005 press release:

> Monsanto hired an Indonesian consulting company to assist it in obtaining various Indonesian governmental approvals and licenses necessary to sell its products in Indonesia. At the time, the Indonesian government required an environmental impact study before authorizing the cultivation of genetically modified crops. After a change in governments in Indonesia, Monsanto sought, unsuccessfully, to have the new government, in which the senior environment official had a post, amend or repeal the requirement for the environmental impact statement.

> Having failed to obtain the senior environment official's agreement to amend or repeal this requirement, in 2002 a Monsanto employee responsible for certain activities in the Asia-Pacific Region authorized and directed the Indonesian consulting firm to make an illegal payment totaling $50,000 to the senior environment official to "incentivize" him to agree to do so. The Monsanto employee also directed representatives of the Indonesian consulting company to submit false invoices to Monsanto for "consultant fees" to obtain reimbursement for the bribe, and agreed to pay the consulting company for taxes that company would owe by reporting income from the "consultant fees."

> In February 2002, an employee of the Indonesian consulting company delivered $50,000 in cash to the senior environment official, explaining that Monsanto wanted to do something for him in exchange for repealing the environmental impact study requirement. The senior environment official promised that he would do so at an appropriate time. In March 2002, Monsanto, through its Indonesian subsidiary, paid the false invoices thus reimbursing the consulting company for the $50,000 bribe, as well as the tax it owed on that income. A false entry for these "consulting services" was included in Monsanto's books and records. The senior environment official never authorized the repeal of the environmental impact study requirement.[1]

267

In the SEC's press release also issued on January 6, 2005, the agency commented:

> In addition, the Commission charged that, from 1997 to 2002, Monsanto inaccurately recorded, or failed to record, in its books and records approximately $700,000 of illegal or questionable payments made to at least 140 current and former Indonesian government officials and their family members. The approximate $700,000 was derived from a bogus product registration scheme undertaken by two Indonesian entities owned or controlled by Monsanto.[2]

ACCEPTANCE OF RESPONSIBILITY AND REMEDIAL ACTIONS

Monsanto learned of the financial irregularities in its Indonesian affiliates in 2001 and quickly initiated an extensive internal investigation. The matter was escalated to the Board of Directors who then directed the investigation. The self-disclosure to the DOJ and SEC followed along with full cooperation with the government investigation. Throughout the government investigation, Monsanto continued to disclose additional information that it developed from internal compliance reviews. It also severed the relationship with the employees involved in the improper activities as well as the outside consultant.

> "Monsanto accepts full responsibility for these improper activities, and we sincerely regret that people working on behalf of Monsanto engaged in such behavior," said Monsanto's General Counsel Charles W. Burson at the time of the settlement. "The Company has taken remedial actions to address the activities in Indonesia. At every stage of this process—beginning with our voluntary disclosure and throughout the governmental investigations and settlement process—Monsanto has been fully cooperative, and has made clear that improper activities will not be tolerated by the Company."[3]

Monsanto acknowledged that its internal controls were insufficient to detect or prevent the corrupt payments and it did not conduct internal audits of the Indonesian affiliates. The company began a robust review and compliance enhancement to fix the problem. It corrected the accounting treatment of the subject transactions, restructured its Indonesian affiliates, appointed a new Director of Business Conduct, and implemented an improved and expanded FCPA compliance program worldwide, and much more. Compliance Insight 11.1 is an overview of the Monsanto Compliance Program.

COMPLIANCE INSIGHT 11.1: MONSANTO COMPLIANCE PROGRAM OVERVIEW

Monsanto's FCPA program includes the following elements:

- Awareness/communications
- Training
- Internal audit
- Internal controls
- Review of promotions to certain levels or positions within the company
- A due diligence process that covers:
  - Contracts with government officials or their relatives
  - Contracts with a government entity
  - Contracts with any third party dealing with a government official on behalf of Monsanto
  - Any proposed gifts, meals, lodging, or transportation to be provided to government officials
  - Political or charitable donations
  - Entering into a joint venture
  - Membership in trade associations
- A process for review of proposed facilitating payments

The program also includes due diligence and business conduct/FCPA integration for acquired companies.

TONE AT THE TOP AND A REVAMPED CODE OF CONDUCT

When faced with the challenge of corruption violations, tone at the top quickly kicked in and Monsanto did the right thing by disclosing the FCPA violations. That is integrity in words and action. The cornerstone of an effective compliance program and culture of compliance is a strong value system based on integrity. These values can best be reflected in a code of conduct or ethics to ensure that employees, vendors, contractors, and other related parties know what is expected of them so as to make the right decisions.[4] Monsanto embraces this and revamped their code of conduct to better convey it. Chairman and CEO Hugh Grant reinforces both his commitment and that of the company to fostering a culture of compliance in the introduction to the code of conduct when he states:

An unwavering commitment to integrity in all business operations is at the core of our corporate behavior. We must never take this commitment for granted. In fact, we must reconfirm this commitment every day. By building integrity into all we do, we will earn and retain the trust of all of our stakeholders.

We must strive to maintain and increase that trust every day. With it we can accomplish our vision of abundant food and a healthy environment; without it, we can face nearly insurmountable barriers to our freedom to operate.

Earning that reputation means more than observing the letter of the law. It means doing what is right even when we are faced with situations not governed by any specific law or regulation. Sometimes the right thing to do is not clear, but at Monsanto our job is to seek and find the right answer in every business situation. To help us pursue the best course of action this Code presents guidelines for appropriate business conduct. Our Code will help us deal responsibly with the range of complex business practices that affect our reputation.

Each us will be expected to live up to our Code in all we do.[5]

The code includes guidance on bribes and kickbacks, gifts and entertainment, accurate books and records, and the FCPA. Here are select passages from the code:

Bribery and Kickbacks
Bribes and kickbacks are illegal and prohibited. Bribes and kickbacks severely damage the fabric of trust that must be created in order to foster a healthy environment for our business to grow. No funds or assets of Monsanto shall be paid, loaned or otherwise disbursed as bribes, kickbacks, or other payments designed to influence or compromise the conduct of the recipient. No employee may ever solicit or accept a bribe or kickback.

Gifts and Entertainment
At Monsanto, part of our commitment to competing fairly means not seeking any improper or unfair advantage that can be obtained by providing gifts

or entertainment. Nor will we allow any company to gain an improper or unfair advantage when dealing with us. On occasion, the provision or exchange of items of modest value such as gifts, meals, and entertainment is a permissible way to establish goodwill and trust in business relationships. Employees will neither offer nor provide any gift that could be perceived as an attempt by Monsanto to improperly influence anyone with whom we are doing business. In that same light, no Monsanto employee may accept any gift that would give the impression that the employee or Monsanto can be influenced by the gift. Special care must be taken with relationships that involve suppliers to Monsanto.

Accurate Books and Records
Honest and accurate recording and reporting of company information is extremely important. Investors rely on us, and the law requires us to provide accurate information about our business and to make informed business decisions based on reliable records. Business transactions of all kinds are to be executed only by employees authorized to do so. Business transactions must be recorded promptly and accurately in order to permit the preparation of accurate financial and other records, and in order to reflect clearly the responsibility for assets and liabilities. No unrecorded funds may be established or maintained for any purpose. Records shall not be falsified in any manner. No entry may be made that intentionally hides or disguises the true nature of any transaction. Monsanto employees with supervisory duties are responsible for establishing and maintaining an effective system of administrative and accounting controls in their areas of responsibility.

Assisting in the Fight Against Corruption
In the course of their duties, Monsanto employees may from time to time come into contact with government officials. It is vital that all such contacts be open and above board. Monsanto employees and agents shall comply with the FCPA and similar anti-bribery laws.

Facilitating payments shall not be made without the prior approval of the general counsel unless there is an emergency situation. No payments, gifts, services, or any other item of value may be offered or given to any government official, anywhere in the world, if that payment, gift, service, or item is intended to or could even have the appearance of being intended to influence the actions of a government official to win or retain business for Monsanto.[6]

Messages from Senior Leaders

Monsanto created specific FCPA compliance training and incorporated strong messages from senior leaders. In one from 2007, General Counsel

Dave Snively opened the computer-based training video with the following words:

Welcome back to Monsanto's training on our Pledge from the aspect of compliance with the Foreign Corrupt Practices Act or FCPA, as it's widely known. This is a U.S. law, and it criminalizes bribery of foreign officials. It applies to Monsanto's employees throughout the world.

As you are aware, Monsanto is committed to doing business with integrity. This is really the heart of our pledge. It is a commitment we all must make every day, now and in the future.

The FCPA and similar international laws are really about winning business the right way. And in this context of Monsanto's pledge, it means earning our business in the environment globally, ethically—and through the appropriate channels of approval and regulation. Therefore, it is extremely important that we avoid even the appearance of improperly influencing government officials. To provide you with guidance, assistance, and a process for making sure we act with Integrity and comply with the FCPA, we have instituted Monsanto's FCPA Best Practices program.

Please understand the importance that each of us plays every day in Monsanto's pledge and in doing business the right way. I'd like to thank you personally for your time and attention.

Other executives also put their imprint on FCPA and code of conduct training with similar messages of reinforcement. These communications from senior leaders support Monsanto's promise of words and actions in living the company values.

BUSINESS CONDUCT OFFICE

Monsanto created the Business Conduct Office (BCO) to implement and manage the new Business Conduct Program (Program). The duties of this office include providing guidance and advice on the code of conduct and any business ethics issues. The BCO has responsibility for the FCPA compliance program and functionally resides within Monsanto's global law department.

The Audit and Finance Committee of the Monsanto board provides oversight and direction for the Program. The Public Policy and Corporate Responsibility Committee of the board is also kept apprised of ongoing developments in the Program. The general counsel is responsible to the Audit and Finance Committee for overall management and implementation of the Program.

272

A Director of Business Conduct was appointed to oversee day-to-day operations of the Program including the development of the necessary elements, organization, and structure to effectuate and implement the Program. The BCO director reports to the general counsel and meets regularly with the board committees for Audit and Public Policy and also with the company's senior executive team. Vision, structure, connectivity, empowerment, resources, and personal commitment are essential to the BCO's successful design and implementation of the company's global compliance effort. The BCO's team effort uses global personnel and corporate resources far beyond those in the law department to assure that its successful business conduct program continues ad infinitum beyond the term of any DPA or compliance monitor.

A Business Conduct executive committee (St. Louis Committee) was also created. The St. Louis Committee, which consists of Monsanto senior leadership, assists the BCO Director in the performance of their duties and in reviewing executive-level-related expenditures involving ex-U.S. government officials. In particular, the St. Louis Committee, which has the authority to replace members and appoint new members, has the following responsibilities:

- Approving the policies and reviewing the procedures established to carry out the Program
- Providing a forum for the discussion and resolution of Monsanto Company business conduct issues as necessary

Monsanto Company holds managers accountable for creating and maintaining a working environment conducive to ethical conduct, and expects the same from all employees. In particular, Monsanto managers are responsible for taking appropriate measures such that their direct reports comply with the Program and the code.

TRAINING

Training for Monsanto employees is given in two formats: online and in person. In consultation with its FCPA attorney, regional law leads, and others, a dedicated employee annually devises what are called "business rules" that dictate which employees must receive and complete the online training. "These rules are deliberately made broad so as to capture almost anyone in the company, worldwide, who might be involved in any process that could put us at risk for an FCPA violation," commented Alfredo

Avila, Monsanto Assistant General Counsel. Online training is managed by the BCO through a project manager and is provided by a third-party vendor and is customized to fit the program. Employees receive training not only on the law itself, but also on the compliance program, its scope, the working group system, and how and where to raise issues or questions.

In-person training is generally given by company attorneys, either the BCO Director or BCO FCPA attorney, or by the law leads and their attorneys in each region in the language(s) of that region. "Our philosophy is that no computer-based training can substitute for the in-person communication provided by our subject matter experts. Visiting sites, listening to questions, understanding the specific challenges in adhering to the policies in specific countries, helps us adjust our program, our message, and our communications to make sure we have more than a paper-tiger. We need a vibrant, practical approach that all our employees worldwide believe in and that is consistent in dealing with external challenges," noted Avila. In-person training utilizes slide decks approved and generally created by the BCO, but regional law leads are strongly expected to add information about anti-corruption laws in their regions as well as local "war stories" to bring the information closer to home. Some of the training decks are placed on the BCO web site, while all of them are available to working group members on the Business Conduct TeamSpace. TeamSpace is a proprietary database that Monsanto uses to manage and monitor internal information.

REGIONAL WORKING GROUPS

Monsanto created compliance committees, or working groups that have been tasked with the responsibility for the Business Conduct Program including the FCPA Program in their respective regions. In order to ensure that each region benefits from the skills and experiences of different functions and senior leaders, each working group includes as members the region's business lead, law lead, finance lead, human resources lead, government affairs/regulatory affairs lead, manufacturing lead, and others identified by the BCO. This responsibility cannot be delegated to a subordinate.

The working group charter specifies that this group will provide guidance and assistance in the day-to-day running of the Monsanto Business Conduct Program and Monsanto's FCPA Policies in the particular region of the world for which this group is responsible. Each working group member is tasked with utilizing his or her unique experiences and functional knowledge in carrying out the working group's responsibilities. In addition, each member communicates the importance of compliance to their reports and the company's third parties, and monitors those parties for compliance with the company's policies. The importance of localized knowledge cannot be substituted; these are senior leaders who have spent their careers understanding the local markets and the inherent challenges in the industry.

With respect to Monsanto's FCPA Policies, the working group evaluates and determines the appropriateness of company-sponsored travel and related costs for foreign officials, gifts above nominal amounts for foreign officials, and meals and entertainment above nominal amounts for foreign officials. It is involved in reviewing the suitability for retention of foreign government officials, or a company in which a foreign official has an ownership or other beneficial interest, and third parties. Those third parties include but are not limited to agents, consultants, subcontractors, contractors, representatives, and joint venture partners likely to have interactions with foreign government officials.

The regional working group, along with the St. Louis Committee as necessary, works with the sponsoring employee to perform and evaluate due diligence, determines in writing if retention is appropriate, and determines the amount and type of training the official or third party should receive. In two regions where the size of business warrants, Asia/Pacific and Europe/Africa, Monsanto has created Business Conduct/FCPA working groups at the country level. These country-level groups report to their regional working groups and consist of the country business lead, country finance lead, and the country human resource lead at a minimum. Often, members of the technology, manufacturing, and commercial departments are incorporated into country working groups as well.

FCPA WORKING GROUP GUIDELINES

Monsanto created a voluminous handbook entitled the FCPA Working Group Guidelines that details every aspect of the FCPA compliance program. It offers guidance to the regional working groups regarding their responsibilities and obligations in fulfilling the code of conduct, the BCO Program, and other policies and procedures. It also instructs employees in how they are to interact with their particular regions and regional working groups. The guidelines and subsequent revisions are introduced to the regional working groups by the BCO Director in training sessions.

Monsanto also realized that employees are often the first to recognize a corruption issue and need assistance in what to do. The company created employee guidelines to help individual employees understand the FCPA, the reason Monsanto created and maintains such a robust compliance program worldwide, and especially the workings of the Monsanto FCPA compliance program and each employee's role in meeting compliance obligations. The employee guidelines have been translated into well over 20 languages and are available to employees from the Monsanto BCO web site. This special web site is one of the many channels, along with a global Guidance Line and Web-based e-mail system, by which employees and others can bring concerns to the BCO's attention. Compliance Insight 11.2 is the Monsanto Business Conduct Policy Employee Guidelines.

COMPLIANCE INSIGHT 11.2: MONSANTO BUSINESS CONDUCT POLICY EMPLOYEE GUIDELINES

Compliance with the FCPA and Similar Antibribery Provisions

POLICY

Monsanto will conduct its business in compliance with applicable laws and regulations, including the U.S. Foreign Corrupt Practices Act ("FCPA") and similar antibribery laws of other countries, including laws implementing the OECD and OAS conventions. All persons subject to this policy, as noted below, are strictly prohibited from offering, paying, promising, or authorizing any bribe, kickback or other thing of value to any "foreign official," directly or indirectly through a third party, to secure any contract, concession, or other favorable treatment for Monsanto. In addition, all such persons are required to adhere to the Company's policies and procedures designed to ensure compliance with these laws. Finally, Monsanto shall comply with the accounting and recordkeeping provisions of the FCPA.

SCOPE

This policy applies to Monsanto businesses and subsidiaries worldwide and applies to all Monsanto officers, directors, and full-time and part-time employees. Additionally, this policy applies to all affiliates

---

and joint ventures controlled by Monsanto. For affiliates and joint ventures not controlled by Monsanto, the Company will proceed in good faith to use its influence to the extent reasonable under the circumstances to require the affiliate or joint venture to implement an FCPA compliance policy similar to this policy.

All third parties representing Monsanto (such as consultants, agents, sales representatives, distributors, and independent contractors and sub-contractors), who may interact with "foreign officials" (as defined by the FCPA) on behalf of the Company, shall agree in writing to follow all applicable portions of this policy. Those third parties will be bound by the same provisions that apply to Monsanto employees.

DISCUSSION

The Company and individual officers or employees may be liable for payments made by a third party, such as a sales representative, consultant, agent, contractor, sub-contractor, joint venture partner, or others, if the Company makes a payment or transfers other value to that third party when the Company knows or has reason to know that the payment will be used in whole or in part to make a payment to a "foreign official." Liability can arise if the Company is aware of facts that suggest a "high probability" that the third party will pass through all or part of the value received from the Company to a "foreign official." Accordingly, the Company must approach relationships with third parties with caution and satisfy itself that third parties will comply with Monsanto standards and policies.

As noted, in certain circumstances, gifts and entertainment, and other expenses incurred on behalf of foreign officials, can give rise to violations of the FCPA and parallel antibribery laws. Accordingly, all Monsanto directors, employees, and representatives shall comply with the Company's policies on the provision of and reimbursement for gifts, meals, entertainment and travel.

Monsanto employees or third parties acting on the Company's behalf may be asked to make facilitating or expediting payments to a "foreign official" to expedite or to secure the performance of routine governmental action by that official. The FCPA recognizes a narrow exception for such payments. It may be difficult, however,

(continued)

(*continued*)
to distinguish a legal facilitating payment from an illegal bribe, kickback, or payoff. Moreover, such payments may violate local law. Accordingly, Monsanto policy strongly discourages the offering or making of facilitating payments. Where such payments are necessary, they will be made only following the prior approval of the General Counsel or his designee. The only exception to this prior approval requirement is in an emergency—when, for example, personal safety is involved. Payments made in such circumstances must be reported to the General Counsel as soon as possible after the payment. All facilitating payments shall be recorded as such in the accounting records of the Company.

Directors, employees, or third parties who make improper payments to foreign officials are subject to appropriate disciplinary action by the Company, as well as the legal consequences of applicable laws. Appropriate disciplinary action equally applies to all employees who:

- Know that conduct prohibited by these Guidelines is contemplated by other employees and fail to report it to the Business Conduct Office or their Working Group
- Know that conduct prohibited by these Guidelines has been engaged in by other employees and fail to report it to the Business Conduct Office or their Working Group

GIFTS, ENTERTAINMENT, AND OTHER PROMOTIONAL EXPENDITURES

The Monsanto Employee FCPA Guidelines and Corporate Controller's Policy set out the company's policy regarding promotional activities that involve foreign officials. The FCPA Guidelines separate these activities into three types of expenses: (1) gifts, meals, and entertainment; (2) travel and travel-related expenses; and (3) Monsanto-sponsored events (e.g., an agricultural conference organized by Monsanto). Each of these types of expenses calls for some level of working group involvement.

The FCPA Guidelines permit company payment of certain gift, meal, and entertainment expenses provided that the expenses satisfy certain criteria.

278

In addition, any gift over $25 and any meals or entertainment expenses greater than nominal value require the prior approval of the Business Conduct working group for the country or region wishing to incur the expense.

All requests for hosting official travel require the prior written approval of the working group for the country or region wishing to incur the expense. Any exceptions from Monsanto's travel policies, including any expenditures for a foreign official to attend a Monsanto-sponsored event, where that attendance includes air or long-distance travel or per diem payments, requires advance approval by the St. Louis Committee. It is the responsibility of the working groups to vet requests from the business units and ensure all information relevant to these approval requests is obtained prior to going to the St. Louis Committee. The following sections offer guidance:

- Expenditures to be incurred on behalf of a foreign official before whom any decision relating to the company is pending
- Unscheduled or special trips made to accommodate a foreign official, such as a ride on a chartered jet
- Payments of per diems to foreign officials regardless of whether the foreign officials' government permits the payment of the per diem
- Expenditures for a foreign official's attendance at company-sponsored events that include air or long-distance travel

In determining whether to pay or reimburse such expenses, the following factors may be relevant:

- Whether there is a specific, legitimate business purpose that underlies the proposal.
- Whether the expenditure is part (or may be understood at the time or in hindsight as being part) of an exchange in which the company will receive something of value.
- Whether the nature and/or value of the items or activities covered by the expenditure seems inappropriate or unreasonable.
- Whether local law, regulations, government ethics policies, or local practice govern the expenditure. Working groups should maintain current, accurate local law advice regarding interactions with officials for countries within their region.
- Whether the company (or the industry) has an established practice with regard to the proposed expenditure.

- Whether the foreign official is acting primarily in a governmental or in a commercial context.
- Whether the company is negotiating or renegotiating specific contracts or sales with the particular government or government-owned or operated company.
- Whether a third party would perceive the proposed action, if taken, as corrupt, unethical, immoral, or illegal.

PER DIEM PAYMENTS

Monsanto guidance is that per diem payments are the least preferred method of covering official travel and lodging costs, since they leave the most room for the official to use the money for purposes other than to cover actual travel expenses. The provision of per diems in lieu of expense reimbursement increases the FCPA risk, particularly when such per diems pay substantially more than the reimbursement of actual expenses. Unless mandated by local law, such payments are avoided. Merely being permissible under local law may not satisfy the local law affirmative defense. The FCPA Guidelines require advance approval from the St. Louis Committee for any payment of per diems to foreign officials.

It is important to remember that all payments or reimbursements of expenses must be properly recorded in the company's or its joint venture's books and records. This requirement places a premium on obtaining the proper documentation of all expenses and payments to cover them.

FACILITATING PAYMENTS

The FCPA Guidelines and Corporate Controller's Policy require prior written approval from the General Counsel for all facilitating payments, with the narrow exception of facilitating payments made under exigent circumstances implicating the health or safety of an individual (e.g., paying an official to secure safe passage through an airport or police roadblock). Where exigent circumstances make it impossible to obtain preapproval, the FCPA Guidelines require company employees to report the payment to the General Counsel as soon as possible after making the payment. It is the responsibility of working groups to assess the merits of requests to make facilitating payments and to forward appropriate requests to the General Counsel for approval.

The regional law lead should consider the local law implications of any potential facilitating payment. Although the payment may fall within the exception to the FCPA, under local law it may still be a bribe and, therefore, prohibited. This local law sensitivity is one of the primary reasons that all facilitating payments are subject to prior approval. The regional finance lead should coordinate with the company employee to ensure that, at minimum, the payments fall within the facilitating payments exception. Facilitating payments can be recorded as such or otherwise in sufficient detail to make clear that the payment was made to facilitate or expedite a routine service (e.g., payment to expedite scheduling of routine fire safety inspection of offices).

POLITICAL DONATIONS

The Monsanto Code of Conduct prohibits contributions to political parties and candidates outside of the United States without prior approval of an appropriate Monsanto official. The FCPA Employee Guidelines designate the working groups and the BCO as the appropriate entities to review requests to make political contributions. The working groups are responsible for conducting the initial review of the proposed contribution. Recommended contributions must be referred to the BCO, which will review the working group's assessment, and refer appropriate requests to the executive vice president of commercial acceptance for ultimate approval.

CHARITABLE DONATIONS AND DONATIONS TO GOVERNMENTS

In many countries, Monsanto contributes to charities in order to foster goodwill and promote issues that are important to the company. In addition, Monsanto, from time to time, provides goods, services, or monetary donations to government instrumentalities that lack adequate resources and funding to carry out their duties. These payments present FCPA risks and the FCPA Employee Guidelines therefore direct employees to refer requests to donate to charities or government instrumentalities to the working groups.

Monsanto policy is to refer requests to make charitable or governmental donations to the Monsanto Fund and assist them with their due diligence process. For requests remaining with the working groups for review, the following steps are recommended:

- Conduct due diligence to confirm that the donation will be appropriate and consistent with the needs of the recipient and will not be diverted to individual officials.

281

- Require the government entity to provide an official written request seeking the donation.
- Determine whether the donation is consistent with local law.
- Obtain a written receipt from the entity receiving the donation.
- Make payments to purchase equipment or services directly to vendors.
- Avoid cash payments. Monetary donations must be deposited in an authorized bank account of the governmental entity or charity.
- Consider additional safeguards such as requiring the recipients to sign FCPA certifications and provide Monsanto with audit rights regarding the use of the funds.
- Accurately record donations.
- Contact the BCO for additional guidance in assessing any requests to make a donation to a charity or government instrumentality.

TRADE ASSOCIATIONS

Monsanto is a member of several industry associations that advocate positions common to Monsanto and other companies in the agricultural and biotechnology industries. In promoting issues, these associations may interact with officials and government agencies. Although interacting with officials on their own behalf instead of specifically for Monsanto, the associations could still subject Monsanto to FCPA liability if improper payments were made to officials with Monsanto's "knowledge." It is therefore important that the working groups carefully vet membership in associations as follows:

- Perform due diligence and confirm that the association's objectives are consistent with Monsanto's business goals, values, and the Monsanto Pledge.
- If membership is governed by a contract between Monsanto and the association, include relevant contract clauses (e.g., prohibiting improper payments, termination, audit rights, etc.) where feasible.
- Where the association is governed by a charter or bylaws, encourage the association to include anti-corruption language in the governing document and to adopt anti-corruption policies, including due diligence procedures for the retention of third parties to interact with officials.
- Avoid cash payment. Dues must be deposited into an authorized bank account of the association.

- If the association requests Monsanto to contribute additional funding beyond the dues for activities involving officials (e.g., travel expenses for officials), submit those requests through the normal working group approval process.
- Monitor the activities of the association to ensure they are consistent with the FCPA and local laws.

Furthermore, employees are advised to always object to improper payments, even if the objection will not affect the outcome, and to record the objection. Employees should also not ignore rumors or concerns about "red flags" suggesting potential wrongdoing and should report them as appropriate.

DOING BUSINESS WITH FOREIGN OFFICIALS AND THEIR RELATIVES

Given the potentially significant risks posed by direct business relationships with foreign officials, company policy requires that business transactions with foreign officials, close relatives of a foreign official, companies in which foreign officials or close relatives of foreign officials hold some financial or beneficial interest be reviewed and approved in advance by a working group under the procedures set forth in the Business Conduct Policy. The working groups have the discretion to decline to review such relationships, where the official's governmental position, responsibility, authority, and influence have no intersection with Monsanto's interests. When reviewing transactions with a relative of an official, the working group should assess the risk of pass-through payments to the official. In particular, they should be wary of an official who recommends Monsanto do business with a relative or any other third party.

DEALING WITH THIRD PARTIES

Under the FCPA, a company may be held liable for improper payments or offers made by third parties—such as consultants, agents, contractors, or joint venture partners—even if the third party is not subject to the FCPA. The risk of vicarious liability is great and requires that company policies, procedures, and preventive measures be followed to protect against potential liability.

The company must: (1) conduct due diligence in advance of any relationship or transaction with a third party who will interact, on the

Company's behalf, with "foreign officials" exercising discretion that affects the Company's business; (2) follow up on any red flags raised to ensure that they are resolved and appropriate safeguards imposed; and (3) monitor the relationship for any red flags that may arise later, including through audits, certifications of continuing compliance, and general vigilance regarding the third party's activities.

All third parties who may have contact with "foreign officials" in the course of performing their obligations for the Company must be vetted through the due diligence process set out in the FCPA Guidelines and Monsanto Business Conduct Policy. There are no exceptions.

Monsanto recognized that there are different categories of third parties interacting with foreign officials and each present different levels of FCPA risk. Category 1 third parties are parties interacting with "foreign officials" on behalf of the company. These include lobbyists, parties responsible for registering the company's products in foreign jurisdictions, customs brokers, law firms representing the company in disputes or claims between the company and a foreign government, and third parties interacting with foreign officials who are paid success fees.

Category 2 third parties are all third parties interacting with foreign officials on behalf of the company that do not fall into Category 1. These parties include research scientists retained to perform studies that are in turn provided to foreign governments, tax advisors, companies assisting with the immigration requirements for expatriates, and companies retained to conduct due diligence on other third parties.

Once it has been determined that a third party is covered by the Business Conduct Policy, due diligence must be conducted. Although the following steps are generally the same for both Category 1 and 2 parties, the due diligence review of Category 1 parties should be expected to take more time and effort because of their greater risk profile and activities:

- Establish lines of communication between the business sponsors working with the third party and the appropriate working group.
- Perform due diligence regarding all potential third parties to identify any business risks and any red flags that suggest possible FCPA issues or other legal or business risks:
  - For Category 1 third parties, consider additional due diligence, including interviewing the prospective third party or retaining a company specializing in due diligence to gather additional information on the third party.

- The working group should assess the red flags and accompanying risks uncovered in the due diligence, and determine the type and amount of training the company should provide to the third party to ensure compliance with the applicable laws and to protect against liability.
- The working group reviewing the proposed contract must consider both the requested compensation and payment terms for the third party. In assessing compensation, the working group should consider industry standards and, if necessary, request information from the business sponsor and/or third party justifying the compensation.
- The working group negotiating the contract should negotiate contract provisions to ensure that the third party complies with the FCPA antibribery rules and its accounting and record-keeping requirements. The character, substance, and relative importance of individual provisions will vary somewhat depending on the issues uncovered by due diligence, whether the third party is Category 1 or 2, and on the nature of the relationship.

Company policy requires the business sponsor to request that the proposed third party complete the Third-Party Questionnaire. If the third party refuses to complete the questionnaire, the working group should coordinate with the business sponsor to determine the reasons for the refusal. If the refusal is simply based on an objection to filling out a form (for example, the third party may have a company policy against such questionnaires), the refusal may not itself be a red flag. In such cases, the business sponsor should use the questionnaire as an outline of the information that must be gathered from the third party.

If the third party continues to refuse to provide some or all of the information requested, however, the refusal or incomplete response constitutes a red flag for FCPA purposes. The working group should coordinate with the business sponsor to determine the reasons for the refusal and to evaluate the importance of the missing information. In addition, the due diligence process should be expanded to include efforts to obtain the missing information through other means. Under these circumstances, the company's evaluation of the due diligence results will include an evaluation of the information gathered as well as of the seriousness of the red flag raised by the refusal or incomplete response.

Training Third Parties

The company's risk of vicarious liability for the acts of third parties and joint ventures can be reduced if the company effectively trains the third parties with whom the company does business. This training can be adjusted to fit particular situations. In presenting the code of conduct to the third party, the working groups highlight the existence of the Guidance Line and inform the third party that it can use the Guidance Line to ask questions about the FCPA or anonymously report any concerns about any past or proposed behavior. The Memorandum on the FCPA can be translated into the native language of the third party in order to maximize its educational value.

In addition, particularly where Category 1 third parties are involved or significant red flags have been raised, the working group may dedicate a face-to-face meeting with the third party to explain the FCPA, the company's commitment to compliance, and the consequences to the third-party relationship of noncompliance. These discussions can also be guided by the FCPA training presentations found on the Business Conduct web site. The regional working groups have also leveraged supplier conferences to provide an overview of the FCPA program. It is one of the advantages of having the supply chain and other business leads involved through the regional working group structure.

The initial training of the third party is periodically reinforced during the relationship. Such follow-up training could include meeting with the third party to discuss the FCPA, providing the third party with additional material on the FCPA, and requiring the third party to certify that it has read and understands the material, and that it will comply with the company's FCPA policy. The working groups maintain records evidencing the additional training.

JOINT VENTURES

Joint ventures pose unique risks and responsibilities for FCPA compliance. Accordingly, all joint venture relationships require the prior approval of a working group or the St. Louis Committee. Prospective joint venture partners shall be subjected to the same due diligence requirements for Category 1 parties as mandated by Business Conduct Policy regardless of whether the joint venture partner or the joint venture will interact with foreign officials. The due diligence process should focus on detecting red flags that are more likely to arise in joint ventures than in other third-party relationships. Joint-venture red flags come in all shapes and sizes, such as:

- Due diligence suggests that the partner is a shell company or has other irregularities in corporate structure or operations.

286

- The partner or a principal shareholder has a government affiliation (directly or through close relatives).
- The partner refuses to agree to reasonable financial and other controls in the joint venture.
- The proposed relationship with the partner is not in accordance with local laws or rules, including civil service rules concerning outside interests for any government officials involved.
- The partner has a reputation for bypassing normal business channels, particularly in activities involving the government.
- The company learns that the partner made an improper payment to relevant government officials prior to the company's entry into the venture.
- The partner insists on financial terms that are unduly generous to it in light of its contributions to the venture.
- The company learns or has reason to suspect that the partner has a "silent partner" who is a government official.
- The partner refuses to reveal the identities of its principals or others holding a beneficial interest in the company.

Contractual Safeguards and Oversight

Contracts with the joint venture partners must include certain clauses, which are listed in the FCPA Sample Contract Clauses document. The mandatory terms include terms requiring that the joint venture partner comply with the FCPA and periodically certify to such compliance; the joint venture or joint venture partner obtains the company's written approval, following due diligence, before retention of subcontractors, agents, and representatives for the joint venture; and, the joint venture partner agrees to make its books and accounting records relating to the venture available for auditing. With respect to the periodic certifications, it is the working group's responsibility to set a schedule for requesting such certifications. The certification process can be carried out in connection with providing the partner with additional training.

All joint ventures are subject to the following requirements:

- Prior to retention, the prospective relationship must be submitted to the relevant working group or St. Louis Committee.
- Working in conjunction with the business sponsor, the working group and St. Louis Committee shall complete the due diligence process on the prospective joint venture partner.

- The working group or St. Louis Committee shall ensure that the mandatory clauses are included in the draft joint venture agreement.
- The working group or St. Louis Committee shall determine the amount and level of training the joint venture partner should receive.
- After execution of the agreement, a copy of the file must be posted on the TeamSpace page.
- The working group is responsible for ensuring that the joint venture partner receives periodic FCPA training and certify compliance with the terms prohibiting improper payments to officials.
- The working group is also responsible for approving, after determining that sufficient due diligence has been performed, any subagents, subcontractors, or representatives the joint venture partner wishes to retain on behalf of the joint venture.
- Where Monsanto is the majority owner or has "effective control" of the joint venture, the working group must ensure that the venture has adopted Monsanto's policies and procedures, such as the FCPA policies, accounting and record-keeping policies, internal controls, business expense policies, and code of conduct.
- The working groups shall oversee the joint venture's retention of covered third parties.
- Where Monsanto does not have "effective control," the working group shall use and document its good faith efforts to require the joint venture to adopt Monsanto's policies and procedures.

AUDIT

Assessing adherence to the FCPA program is built into Monsanto's internal audit plans. For each site visited where an FCPA situation could even be a slight risk, the audit team expends time and effort auditing against the requirements and processes of the Monsanto FCPA compliance program. The audit includes an examination of each type of contract covered by the program, gifts to government officials, any travel, meals, or lodging provided to government officials, membership in trade associations, and so forth. The predominant amount of audit time is spent looking at the various third-party relationships that are a part of the FCPA program, making sure that each such relationship has been properly vetted and approved with appropriate documentation kept.

The auditors also interview the managers and employees at a site with questions designed to assess not only the knowledge of the FCPA and compliance program by those managers, but how well the tenets of the program have been implemented and cascaded at each site. This is a very important component of the Compliance Program. Audits and Audit Findings are taken very seriously by the business units.

Audit findings are presented to the Audit and Finance Committee, CFO, Controller, BCO Director, and FCPA attorney, among others, and ulti- mately result in an audit report to the site manager and the employees to whom he/she reports. Management has a short period of time to present its remediation plan to the audit team, senior management, and the BCO Director. Where the remediation plan includes any matter pertaining to the FCPA or Monsanto's compliance program, fulfillment of the remediation plan is reviewed and monitored by the BCO Director and FCPA attorney.

The Monsanto Audit Program also entails monitoring its compliance program, which includes the BCO, the regional working groups, and country working groups. "I think this dimension of our compliance program brings credibility to our mission. The local working groups understand that we are not just creating policy and 'hoping for the best' but rather that we are methodical and efficient. We are going to be evaluated on how effective our policy is implemented into the business. They understand that the BCO will seek their input because our goal is not to create volumes of policies but rather to create a policy that adds value to the company by addressing a gap, setting direction, or strengthening our controls," observed Avila.

OPINION FROM OUTSIDE COUNSEL

Consulting with outside U.S. counsel regarding the FCPA can help the company better identify, evaluate, and address FCPA risks. Where outside counsel's advice comes in the form of a written opinion, the advice may provide defenses to allegations of an FCPA violation. For example, acting consistent with a written opinion from qualified U.S. FCPA counsel may defeat any allegation of "corrupt intent" on the part of the company. In some situations, an opinion from outside counsel can provide protection to the company by demonstrating the company's care in handling potential issues. More importantly, if a company acts in reliance on advice from expert counsel, it could defeat allegations that the company acted with corrupt intent. For this tool to prove useful, the company must disclose all material facts to the outside counsel, and the Justice Department must consider the outside counsel an expert in this area.

LOCAL LAW ADVICE

Local law advice can provide valuable legal protection in many situations, such as:

- Entering into and performance of a particular agreement is permitted under local law (some countries' laws prohibit certain third-party relationships and forms of compensation for third parties having contacts with the host government).

- No host government authorization, approval, or other action, nor any notice, or filing with the host government is required for the due execution and performance of the agreement (some governments require all third parties having contacts with the host government to register with the government).

- Payment of certain expenses on behalf of government officials is permitted under local law.

- An agreement's compensation and payment provisions are consistent with local law and do not raise any issues of currency or exchange violations or evasion of local tax laws.

Law leads are tasked with keeping apprised of local law issues for their respective working groups. Law leads should maintain current and accurate local law advice concerning issues under the working groups' purview.

In some instances, an opinion from qualified local counsel that a particular contract, venture, or transaction is consistent in all material respects with local law may enable the company to avail itself of the "local law" affirmative defense should a potential violation occur. Law leads, pursuant to Law Department procedures, are responsible for determining whether obtaining a local law opinion is required or prudent for a particular issue.

Local law opinions likely will not provide much comfort in cases where the risks stem from a third party's actions after contract formation. Nor will a local law opinion be controlling on the issue of whether a third party is a "foreign official." The Justice Department does not consider the local law definition of "foreign official" binding for FCPA purposes.

Moreover, to support an affirmative defense, local law opinions must meet the standard of U.S. legal opinions. Language barriers and differences in legal systems often make it difficult to meet that standard and frequently require the company to oversee multiple revisions to an opinion. In some instances the time, expense, and effort of obtaining a local law opinion will outweigh the benefits.

RESPONSE TO POSSIBLE VIOLATIONS

A violation of the FCPA can result in serious consequences for Monsanto and the individuals involved. If a member of a working group learns of a potential FCPA violation (or request for a bribe), the working group should:

- Immediately report the potential violation or request to the general counsel or the Director of Business Conduct.
- Instruct any company employees involved not to discuss the potential violation or request with anyone outside the Legal Department, not to share any potentially relevant documents with any person outside the Legal Department, and not to take any further action with regard to the potential violation or request unless instructed to do so by the Legal Department.
- Wait for guidance from the general counsel or the Director of Business Conduct.

INTERNAL AND INDEPENDENT INVESTIGATIONS

Where a serious question arises involving a possible violation of the FCPA, the company may wish to conduct an investigation to evaluate the situation. Such an evaluation may produce recommendations to correct or prevent the deviation from FCPA requirements, thus eliminating or reducing any potential liability under the FCPA. There are two types of investigations: internal investigations, which can be conducted in-house, and independent investigations, which require the company to engage an outside entity. The latter is generally more costly, but conveys the appearance of independence thus providing greater credibility.

INTERNAL COORDINATION AND TRAINING

Members of a working group need to inform and train employees and third parties about FCPA issues, encourage employees to consult with their working group with any questions regarding FCPA compliance, and be alert to circumstances that require immediate attention by a working group, the general counsel, or the Director of Business Conduct.

THE MONSANTO PLEDGE

The Monsanto Pledge is the company's commitment to how it does business and leads responsibly. With the pledge statement that "Integrity is the foundation for all that we do," Monsanto demonstrates that they live their values and are an example to others.[7] Today, Fortune 500 companies reach out to Monsanto for insight on how to work in tandem with a government monitor or how to design and implement best-in-class anti-corruption measures to assure FCPA problems do not arise. This is how one deeply committed company set about to accomplish its pledge to the global community.

NOTES

1. Department of Justice, "Monsanto Company Charged with Bribing Indonesian Government Official: Prosecution Deferred Three Years," press release, January 6, 2005, www.usdoj.gov/opa/pr/2005/January/05_crm_008.htm.
2. Securities and Exchange Commission, "SEC Sues Monsanto Company for Paying a Bribe, Monsanto Settles Action and Agrees to Pay a $500,000 Penalty, Monsanto Also Enters Into Deferred Prosecution Agreement with Department of Justice," Litigation Release No. 19023, January 6, 2005, www.sec.gov/litigation/litreleases/lr19023.htm.
3. Monsanto, "Monsanto Announces Settlements With DOJ and SEC Related to Indonesia," news release, January 6, 2005, http://monsanto.mediaroom.com/index.php?s=43&item=278.
4. Martin T. Biegelman and Joel T. Bartow, *Executive Roadmap to Fraud Prevention and Internal Control: Creating a Culture of Compliance* (Hoboken, NJ: John Wiley & Sons, Inc, 2006), 71.
5. CEO letter introducing the Monsanto Company Code of Conduct, www.monsanto.com/responsibility/business_conduct/ceo_letter.asp.
6. Ibid.
7. Ibid.

CHAPTER 12

Internal Investigations

We live in a time of heightened economic risk and regulatory scrutiny with an unprecedented level of investigations around corruption and bribery. The increased prosecution of the FPCA by the Department of Justice has forced corporations to take unprecedented steps to develop compliance programs and prevent violations. As of 2009, the DOJ had at least 130 companies under investigation, up from 100 in 2008. Reinforcing this aggressive approach, Mark Mendelsohn, deputy chief in the DOJ over-seeing FCPA prosecutions, acutely observed, "If we call them before they call us, it's not where they want to be."[1]

This is why every organization today needs an effective compliance program capable of conducting a professional and objective internal investigation once a possible corruption violation, or any questionable activity, is discovered or suspected. An investigation is required to determine the facts of what happened and what did not happen. Any investigation must establish whether wrongdoing and criminal misconduct occurred and the potential risk and legal exposure. Further inquiry will ascertain required remediation steps and potential government disclosure. An important component of this process is managing the public and customer relations that will invariably result from any public disclosures. In today's media-savvy age, there is bound to be extensive coverage from the press. Managing media inquiries will require an experienced and professional communications department with assistance from external public relations firms.

The organization's response from the onset will have a significant impact on the outcome. Once the Munich public prosecutor made the pervasive corruption violations public, Siemens made the decision to conduct an unprecedented and extremely thorough internal investigation. It was so comprehensive that on the day in December 2008 when Siemens settled with government authorities, the DOJ recognized the company's efforts in conducting an amazingly robust investigation and instituting company-wide changes. This is the investigative standard expected today.

CONSEQUENCES OF FAILING TO ACT

An organization has no excuse for not conducting a thorough internal investigation whether for anti-corruption issues or other violations of policy and law. There is criminal and civil liability for consciously disregarding a FCPA violation. A company faces peril even if the company does not have actual knowledge of corrupt payments but still consciously disregards the violation. As a result of the *In Re: Caremark International, Inc.* derivative litigation, directors and officers can be held liable for breaching fiduciary duties by failing to provide appropriate oversight and compliance with the law. Willful ignorance is an aggravating factor for courts to consider under the Federal Sentencing Guidelines for Organizations (FSGO). It can be argued that failing to conduct an investigation when there is evidence of FCPA red flags and wrongdoing can be considered consciousness of guilt.

The FCPA prosecution of Triton Energy is an excellent example of the consequences of failing to investigate a corruption issue as detailed in the testimony of a then Associate Director of the SEC's Division of Enforcement before a Senate Subcommittee in 1998:

> In this case, the SEC alleged that during the years 1989 and 1990, two former senior officers of Triton Indonesia, a subsidiary of Triton Energy, authorized numerous improper payments to the subsidiary's business agent who acted as an intermediary between Triton Indonesia and Indonesian government agencies, knowing or recklessly disregarding the high probability that the business agent either had or would pass such payments along to Indonesian government employees for the purpose of influencing their decisions affecting the business of Triton Indonesia. The two former senior officers, along with other Triton Indonesia employees, concealed these

payments by falsely documenting and recording the transactions as routine business expenditures. Triton Indonesia also recorded other false entries in its books and records. Although Triton Energy did not authorize or direct these improper payments and misbookings, when Triton Energy's internal auditor notified its management of the violations in a memorandum, Triton Energy's former president ordered that all copies of the memorandum be destroyed, and Triton Energy's management failed to put a stop to the illicit activities. . . . The result in Triton makes clear that whenever senior management becomes aware of FCPA violations, even if it did not authorize them in the first instance, it is liable for failure to investigate and put an end to such violations. [2]

Management's failure to take appropriate action by conducting a full investigation is clear in this instance. The question of whether to conduct an investigation is generally moot as the failure to properly investigate an allegation involving business conduct will weigh heavily in prosecution decisions. Conscience avoidance is a guarantee of future problems. An investigation in every instance allows an organization to learn the facts, determine potential corporate liability, discover red flags and internal control deficiencies, and lessen the risks from reoccurring. More importantly, the government expects companies to conduct effective internal investigations. A final consideration is that an organization may have no idea if the government is already conducting an investigation that may become public at any moment.

The Principles of Federal Prosecution of Business Organizations, previously discussed in Chapters 3 and 9, requires prosecutors considering charging a company for criminal behavior to consider the "corporation's timely and voluntary disclosure of wrongdoing and its willingness to cooperate" as well as the "corporation's remedial actions, including any efforts to implement an effective compliance program." A professional and timely internal investigation, and self-disclosure as appropriate, will help determine the outcome of a federal prosecution. The government can no longer require companies to waive privilege in order to obtain cooperation credit and they will not be penalized by failing to waive privilege.

The SEC's Seaboard Decision, also previously discussed in Chapter 3, provides SEC guidance concerning the treatment of organizations that have violated securities laws. The SEC rewards self-policing, self-reporting, remediation, and cooperation. Like the DOJ, the SEC will consider the steps the company took upon learning of the misconduct, including the thoroughness of the internal investigation, in deciding whether to seek penalties. Whether the results of the investigation were disclosed to the SEC is also another factor.

PREPARING FOR THE INVESTIGATION

Investigative success depends on many factors but the most important are the early steps. Company policies and procedures should be reviewed for a thorough understanding of what is included in them. That includes not only anti-corruption policies but also any company policies around conducting investigations, whistleblower protection, and nonretaliation. If the allegations were escalated through the hotline, intake principles should be reviewed to determine that all appropriate notifications were made and proper documenting occurred. The investigation needs to be an impartial and nonjudgmental fact-gathering process. The confidentiality of the investigation is a consideration, as to how many people are informed of its existence beyond those in the most need-to-know basis. The investigation venues need to be determined as local laws in various countries tend to differ and provide additional risk.

The allegations themselves need to be reviewed. How specific and serious are they? Is there enough information provided to determine a potential basis in fact? The more detailed the allegations, the more an organization can do to quickly respond. Yet, even less specific allegations of bribery and corruption need to be vetted fully. Are the allegations something that the company has experienced before? What is the source of the allegations? Were they made anonymously? A careful review of the allegations is important in preparing the investigative plan and the resources needed to conduct the investigation. The investigative plan needs to be completed and approved by an appropriate legal or compliance department senior leader and/or outside counsel specifically retained for the investigation.

Some organizations have an investigative framework that details the various investigative steps from intake, assignment, assessment of the allegation, creation and approval of the investigative plan by legal counsel, investigation, reporting, disciplinary action, and remedial steps to improve internal controls and policy breakdown. An initial step is to identify all potential witnesses and subjects of the investigation but knowing that the list will no doubt increase as the investigation proceeds. Once additional planning steps are completed, these witnesses will be interviewed. Interview preparation is a critical step in the process as the more information gathered and time spent in getting ready for the interview, the better the result will be.

PRESERVING DOCUMENTARY AND ELECTRONIC INFORMATION

In conjunction with witness identification, the organization needs to gather and preserve all documentary and electronic evidence. This pertains to both people who have data and the sources of that data that may be needed for investigative purposes. A document retention and preservation notice must be issued to all appropriate personnel to put them on notice of the need to comply with the requirement. The notification must be clear that no documents can be destroyed, including e-mail and electronic files on computers and similar storage devices. Any destruction of evidence, especially if it is intentional, will be a problematic issue. The cover-up always makes the initial offense worse, but human nature being what it is tends to cause people to destroy evidence in hopes of concealing their involvement. The usual result is obstruction of justice and far worse criminal penalties.

When collecting data, always err on the side of caution and collect anything even remotely related to the matter at hand. Locate sources of data on desktop computers and laptops. People may have more than one computer so preservation notices need to address that. Employees may have company computers in their homes as well as at their offices. Capture electronic data on servers and network drives. Preservation notification needs to cover backup drives, online and cloud storage, and portable storage devices including thumb drives. If the organization retains instant messages, that should also be captured. The value of e-mail as an investigative tool is undeniable. Yet, the availability of e-mail may depend on the venue. Strict privacy restrictions in certain countries prohibit the capture and review of an employee's e-mail, requiring other means of information gathering.

Although there is a focus on gathering electronic evidence because so much of our communication is done electronically, make sure a similar focus is on collecting hard copy documents. Documentation is especially important in bribery investigations in order to follow the money trail of corrupt payments and how they were accounted for in the company's books and records. An effective investigation must determine if violations of the FCPA's antibribery and books and records provisions have occurred and the paper trail is often the best way to determine that. The internal investigation must evaluate if systemic corruption is present and if the company profited from the illegal payments.

ASSEMBLING THE INVESTIGATIVE TEAM

Determining who should manage and supervise the investigation is a consideration. It can be someone from senior management such as the general counsel, or delegated to a senior legal counsel, or a compliance officer. In some cases, the board of directors or the audit committee will oversee the investigation. Determining who will conduct the investigation is another matter. The trend has been to retain outside counsel to conduct FCPA investigations. That was the case in the Siemens investigation where the company brought in global law firm Debevoise & Plimpton to oversee the investigation. They eventually used 100 attorneys and 100 support staff in conducting a massive investigation. The expense involved in using outside counsel may be a consideration but that should not be a deciding factor by itself. An important consideration in who should conduct the investigations is the severity of the allegations. Bribery and corruption definitely fit in that realm.

Outside counsel with experience and expertise in FCPA and corruption investigations bring a significant advantage. They have the ability to staff a large-scale, long-term, global investigation. They may have specific experience in FCPA investigations and prosecutions in the subject countries and can better guide the company through the minefield of a bribery case. Outside counsel may also be viewed by the government as more independent than investigators from inside the company. Many law firms with dedicated FCPA practices have former federal prosecutors who have experience prosecuting corruption and bribery. They understand how the government conducts investigations and may be able to provide better guidance in the investigation process.

Retained counsel may also better demonstrate to the DOJ and SEC through their presence as outside counsel that the company is taking the allegations very seriously. Outside counsel investigations can potentially be conducted under attorney-client privilege although that is no guarantee that the investigative results will not become public. "Many corporations choose to collect information about potential misconduct through lawyers that may confer attorney-client privilege or attorney work product protection on at least some of the information collected. Other corporations may choose a method of fact-gathering that does not have that effect—for

298

example, having employee or other witness statements collected after interviews by non-attorney personnel"[3]

Attorney-client privilege is not accepted everywhere in the world. Take the example of Akzo Nobel, the Dutch chemical company. Government officials investigating antitrust violations raided the company's UK offices. Among the evidence seized were communications between the company and its in-house counsel. Akzo Nobel sought to exclude this evidence as attorney-client privileged communications. The European Court of First Instance ruled in 2007 that the privilege does not apply to in-house lawyers who "are loyal to their companies and don't offer independent legal advice."[4] To get around this issue, it is recommended to limit communications with attorneys located in foreign subsidiaries to key core team members. This includes documents and unnecessary records related to internal investigations and allegations of noncompliance. An alternative is hiring outside counsel in the EU to whom attorney-client privilege still applies. "What's clear is that companies should take great care not to generate themselves the very dossier that the investigators will use to condemn them," advised a former European Commission official who is now an attorney in private practice.[5]

Internal investigator resources can also be used in conducting corruption investigations. Corporate investigators have knowledge of the company and its operations through their many cases. Those with global experience know that conducting any kind of internal investigation outside the U.S. is problematic. Conducting a corruption investigation is even more demanding. In assembling the team, the knowledge, skills, and abilities of the investigator are critical. Professionally trained investigators with corruption, bribery, fraud, and FCPA investigation expertise is an advantage. Certified Fraud Examiner, Certified Compliance and Ethics Professional, and Certified Public Accountant certifications are also beneficial. Forensic accounting, language skills, country-specific or regional experience, experience in local privacy and privilege issues, and fluency in corporate systems including finance, sales channel, audit, and information technology are additional pluses. While some organizations may have internal investigators with these skills and abilities, many do not have FCPA-specific expertise.

Investigations Code of Conduct

Whether internal investigators are used in bribery investigations, a recommended best practice is to have an Investigations Code of Conduct in place. While almost all companies have employee business conduct codes, very few have specific codes of conduct for their investigative staff. Such a code details how investigation professionals must conduct themselves when engaged in investigation activities. This code should require adherence to company policies as well as the highest ethical and legal standards. The investigations code should address the following requirements:

- Investigators will conduct their investigations with honesty and integrity
- Investigators will use investigative techniques approved by the company and always within the highest professional standards
- Investigators will gather evidence and report facts accurately and completely
- Investigators will not permit any bias, prejudice, or preconceived opinions to interfere with the investigation
- Investigators will not participate in any investigation where they have an actual or perceived conflict of interest
- Investigators will not use subterfuge or use false statements in their investigations
- Investigators will respect the privacy rights of witnesses and subjects of investigations
- Investigators will safeguard all evidence obtained in investigations
- Investigators will ensure that any investigative vendors or contractors that assist in company investigations will adhere to the same standards as this code of conduct
- All investigators and authorized vendors and contractors will comply with annual certification requirements

Whether outside counsel or corporate investigators conduct the internal investigation, they may still need professional consultants to assist them. The major accounting firms have been involved in many of the recent FCPA investigations and have a great deal of foundation knowledge that can be leveraged in other such investigations. They have the needed forensic accounting expertise and can readily provide the staffing for a resource-intensive, large-scale investigation. In the Siemens investigation, Deloitte used 130 forensic accountants. Forensic accounting practices have the tools needed to analyze huge amounts of digital and hard-copy information. They may also have potential conflicts from the other work they perform that might limit their engagement. There are a growing number of professional investigative firms outside the Big 4 that have FCPA practices and they can also be considered to assist in corruption investigations as well as due diligence vetting.

INVESTIGATIVE PLAN

Prior to the start of the actual investigation, an investigative plan should be prepared outlining the anticipated steps of the investigation. The plan should cover the scope and objectives of the investigation and should be in writing, unless determined otherwise by legal counsel. Then determine if the investigation will be conducted in-house or by outside counsel. Identify key business, legal, human resources, audit, and other contacts for assistance in gathering documents, identifying witnesses, and explaining business operations. Consider contacting the company's public relations department so they are alerted to possible external communication issues. Internal investigations need to be coordinated, not only between the company's inside counsel and outside counsel but also with other corporate functions. This includes corporate security, human resources, internal audit, and the appropriate business groups. Also consider whether there is a need to disclose the investigation to the external auditor at this stage or at the conclusion of the investigation.

Identify key contacts in the business, finance, and compliance departments at company headquarters and in the country or region. Review and analyze all gathered documents. Identify in-house or external counsel for legal assistance in foreign venues for an understanding of local employment and criminal laws, especially around anti-corruption. Identify all potential interviewees including witnesses, subjects, supervisors of complainants, and others. Establish if any of the interviewees are nonemployees or located outside the United States, which would require an understanding of local laws for interviews. The issue of any employee indemnifications should be considered as well as a review of the directors and officers (D&O) insurance policy for coverage and limitations. It is always advantageous to prepare a timeline of the issues and events in the case to provide a better understanding of the who, what, when, where, why, and how.

Determine if any advance notice will be given to interviewees. Prepare for the possibility of workplace searches if allowed. Consider privacy and privilege issues. Is the company a union shop requiring the presence of a union representative in interviews? Note that the investigation plan should be approved by the appropriate legal authority. Remember, the course of an investigation can invariably change resulting in modifications to the investigation plan. Therefore, the plan is a living document that should be revised as appropriate through the course of the investigation.

At times, there may be parallel government investigations occurring where both federal prosecutors and civil regulatory agencies are conducting inquiries into the same set of facts. These parallel government investigations may be taking place while the company is conducting its own internal investigation. This may be an opportunity to have a dialogue with the government to learn more about their investigation and how the company is viewed. It is also possible that the government may request the company to share results from the internal investigation.

In planning the investigative steps for any internal investigation, it is a best practice to reflect on the lessons learned from prior investigations, both internally and externally. The lessons, both good and bad, from prior investigations can help advance a professional investigation and avoid repeating pitfalls that create greater risk. One problematic area that arose in prior government investigations was the destruction of documents by the subject company and its employees. This can pertain to subpoenaed documents and other documents not yet under subpoena but may very well have an investigation nexus. The two cases that come to mind are *United States v. Arthur Andersen* and *United States v. Quattrone*. In *United States v. Arthur Andersen*, Andersen was the external auditor for Enron and anticipated being served a government subpoena for Enron-related documents connected to the government's corporate fraud investigation. Ahead of that, an in-house counsel for Andersen recommended that a notice be sent out reminding the Andersen engagement team of their document retention policy. This was a thinly veiled attempt at encouraging destruction of documents related to the Enron engagement that was the subject of the government investigation.

David Duncan, the Houston partner in charge of the Enron audit engagement, met with Enron executives and other members of the Andersen engagement team and after that, organized a wholesale destruction effort to shred documents and delete e-mails. Subsequently, Andersen was indicted for obstruction of justice for shredding documents and deleting computer files in order to protect its client, Enron. Duncan pleaded guilty and was a cooperating defendant for the government at trial. Although Andersen was convicted after trial, the U.S. Supreme Court overturned the conviction in May 2005 on procedural grounds related to jury instructions.[6]

In *United States v. Quattrone*, Frank Quattrone was an investment banker at Credit Suisse First Boston (CSFB) charged by federal prosecutors in April 2003 with obstruction of justice relating to the destruction of subpoenaed documents. Quattrone forwarded an e-mail to his staff containing a reminder of the company's document-retention policy and the possibility of damaging civil litigation based on the government's criminal investigation. The government eventually indicted Quattrone and he was convicted at trial and sentenced to prison. In March 2006, the Court of Appeals for the 2nd Circuit threw out Quattrone's conviction on grounds of improper jury instructions but the court commented that the evidence was sufficient to sustain a conviction.[7] Quattrone was never retried on the charges.

CONDUCTING INTERVIEWS

In conducting interviews of company employees, it is imperative that employees understand the role of corporate or outside counsel and the company's right to use and disclose anything that is said during the interviews. That includes disclosure to law enforcement authorities of any employee statements and evidence obtained. Employees need to understand that attorneys representing the company are not representing them and they may have adverse interests. These cautionary statements to employees are called Upjohn warnings and they need to realize the potential impact of admissions to wrongdoing while employed at a company.

In *Upjohn v. United States*, the Supreme Court decided that, in federal proceedings applying federal law, corporate entities could claim attorney-client privilege and that the scope of the privilege should depend on the subject matter of the communication, not on who was doing the communicating. As long as the communication involves the subject matter of the representation on whatever legal issue counsel is working on for the company, it does not matter if the communication was with management, lower-level employees, or agents. Prior to this, federal courts used a "control group" test to determine privilege and it is still used in some states. The privilege applied only to members of the control group, those senior leaders responsible for the highest level of decision making. The Supreme Court in *Upjohn* extended attorney-client privilege to a wide group of employees beyond the previous control group.[8]

Although the *Upjohn* case was not actually a warnings case, warnings would need to be given in order for companies to retain the discretion to disclose the results of internal investigations to third parties. The result was, these new "Corporate Miranda" warnings have become almost mandatory in internal investigations. In 2008, the White Collar Crime Committee of the American Bar Association's (ABA) Criminal Justice Section created a Task Force to recommend best practices for corporate counsel to follow when advising corporate employees subject to interviews by counsel.[9] The Thought Leader profile that follows provides the ABA's Task Force Model Upjohn Warning for corporate investigators to use during employee interviews. The Upjohn warning provides a clear understanding of what protections are, and are not, afforded to the employee and protects the attorney-client privilege between counsel and the corporation.

THOUGHT LEADER IN INTERNAL INVESTIGATIONS: DAVID Z. SEIDE

Ethical Issues and the Corporate Miranda

David Z. Seide is a partner in the Washington, DC office of Curtis, Mallet-Prevost, Colt & Mosle LLP. He represents companies and individuals who are or may become subjects of government investigations, particularly investigations by the U.S. Department of Justice (DOJ) and the Securities and Exchange Commission (SEC). He has represented a broad array of well-known financial services companies, including hedge funds, mutual funds, broker-dealers, banks, and publicly traded companies, as well as their officers and directors before the SEC, DOJ, and state regulatory agencies.

From 1991 to 2003, Seide served as an Assistant United States Attorney in the U.S. Attorney's Office for the Central District of California. He served as the Office's Securities Fraud Coordinator and prosecuted a multitude of fraud cases including insider trading, bank fraud, insurance fraud, and identity theft. He also handled over 30 criminal appeals. After leaving the U.S. Attorney's Office, he spent a year working in the Los Angeles office of Morgan Stanley's law department and thereafter moved to Washington, DC to practice for four years at Wilmer Cutler Pickering Hale and Dorr LLP.

Seide is a co-chair of the Securities Fraud Subcommittee of the ABA's White Collar Crime Committee, is the ABA's liaison to the National Association of Criminal Defense Lawyers' White Collar Crime Project, and is the principal author of an ABA Task Force Report entitled *Upjohn Warnings: Recommended Best Practices when Corporate Counsel Interact with Corporate Employees.* Here Seide opines on conducting internal investigations and the FCPA. The views expressed herein are not necessarily the views of the law firm or its clients:

FCPA matters pose unique challenges for lawyers, investigators, and clients. By virtue of the fact that FCPA issues are typically fact-intensive, legal procedural rules will affect how to investigate alleged FCPA violations.

When a company receives an allegation involving the FCPA, it is likely to turn to its counsel to undertake a damage and/or risk assessment. Such assessment will inevitability involve an undertaking to learn the facts underlying the allegation. That factual inquiry may be conducted by in-house staff, in-house lawyers, outside investigators, outside counsel, and/or a combination of all these groups.

Ethical issues cannot and should not be overlooked. In particular, lawyers subject to United States rules of practice may be obliged to provide Upjohn Warnings (also know as Corporate Miranda Warnings), to employees who are interviewed. Such warnings are intended to advise employees that the lawyer conducting the investigation does not represent the employee personally; rather, the lawyer represents the company and the company alone. In addition, the warning further advises the employee that the company is the sole holder of the attorney-client privilege, and the company alone reserves the right to waive the privilege—by deciding when and if to disclose what the employee states in the interview to third parties, including government investigators. That option may be especially important in situations where companies seek to reduce their criminal and/or civil FCPA exposure by waiving the attorney-client privilege and producing the interviews to government investigators.

Where the role of counsel conducting the interview is not made clear, the employee may be able to claim that the employee believed that the interviewing lawyer represented the employee, and that the employee, too, has the right to invoke the attorney-client privilege. In that situation, companies lose the sole discretion to decide whether or

(continued)

305

(continued)

not to waive the attorney-client privilege, thereby putting at risk their ability to secure cooperation credit granted through such waivers. It is therefore incumbent upon companies and their counsel to avoid ambiguity when providing Upjohn warnings.

In 2009, a Task Force established by the ABA's White Collar Crime Committee issued a Report on best practices for company counsel to follow when providing Upjohn warnings.[10] The Report provides a history of the attorney-client privilege, a summary of best practices in this area, along with suggested procedures to follow. It also provides the following Model Upjohn warning:

I am a lawyer for or from Corporation A. I represent only Corporation A, and I do not represent you personally.

I am conducting this interview to gather facts in order to provide legal advice for Corporation A. This interview is part of an investigation to determine the facts and circumstances of X in order to advise Corporation A how best to proceed.

Your communications with me are protected by the attorney-client privilege. But the attorney-client privilege belongs solely to Corporation A, not you. That means that Corporation A alone may elect to waive the attorney-client privilege and reveal our discussion to third parties. Corporation A alone may decide to waive the privilege and disclose this discussion to such third parties as federal or state agencies, at its sole discretion, and without notifying you.

In order for this discussion to be subject to the privilege, it must be kept in confidence. In other words, with the exception of your own attorney, you may not disclose the substance of this interview to any third party, including other employees or anyone outside of the company. You may discuss the facts of what happened but you may not discuss this discussion.

Do you have any questions?

If employees who are interviewed request counsel, the company has to decide if they will provide counsel or have the employee retain their own counsel at their own expense. If the company decides to provide representation, they must consider the issue of multiple representation and conflicts of interest. While it might appear simpler and cheaper to have one law firm represent all employees who ask for an attorney, this is a path fraught with peril. The company may have totally different issues than the employee. Employees may have different interests from each other and these interests may change over time creating significant legal issues for the company. The case of *United States v. Stein* is an example of how the interests of a company and its employees can differ.

Employee Legal Representation

In *United States v. Stein*, federal prosecutors indicted 16 KPMG employees involved in a major tax fraud case. In order to ensure that KPMG continued to be credited with cooperation with the investigation, KPMG cut off coverage of legal bills for these employees. The defendants subsequently sued KPMG to force it to cover their legal bills. They claimed that federal prosecutors pressured KPMG to threaten the employees into cooperation. Indeed, KPMG told its employees that they would cut off legal expense payments unless they cooperated with the government. The employees did as instructed and made admissions to prosecutors that would be used against them if any went to trial.[11]

The employees later alleged that the coerced statements violated their Fifth Amendment privilege against self-incrimination and the government deprived them of their right to a fair trial. The court agreed with the employees that "KPMG refused to pay because the government held the proverbial gun to its head."[12] KPMG, by cooperating with the government's investigation, which included not paying the legal fees of defendants, got a deferred prosecution agreement. The court allowed the employees to go to trial against KPMG and required KPMG to advance their legal fees.

The court also chastised the U.S. Attorney's Office for the Southern District of New York for misleading the court about it pressuring KPMG regarding the legal fees. Clearly, the government pressured KPMG into making employees talk to the government. Some statements by employees offered as evidence, which would not have been made but for the pressure, were suppressed as coerced confessions. Subsequently, the court dismissed 13 of the defendants' indictments because the government violated the employees' civil rights. The judge's heavy criticism of the Thompson Memo led to changes in DOJ policy and the issuance of the revised McNulty Memo, the predecessor to the Filip Memo.

The recommended practice in situations with multiple representation issues is for the company to hire one law firm to represent the company, a different firm to represent employees who are determined as witnesses, and separate law firms for employees who may be targets of the investigation. The lawyers can communicate with each other and enter into joint defense agreements but clearly the interests of represented employees can change over time. The government uses the power of prosecution and long prison terms as a strong inducement for employees to plead guilty and cooperate against other defendants. As the U.S. Court of Appeals for the Second Circuit stated so well in the 1973 case *U.S. v. Rosner*, "in human experience, the pressure of imminent incarceration tends to snap the bonds of loyalty."[13]

The possibility of long periods of incarceration has been known to convince even the most-hardened individual to cooperate with the government in the hope of a reduced sentence. White-collar criminals are usually not in the league of organized crime figures who subscribe to the code of "omerta" or the vow of silence. For fraudsters, including corporate executives engaged in bribery and corruption, prison is something to be feared. Fraudsters are not used to prison life and all the harshness and violence associated with it. Factor in the increased penalties for FCPA transgressions that translate to much longer jail time and one can see how cooperation with the government begins to look very appealing.[14]

Overall, the benefits of multiple law firms far outweigh any perceived convenience of using just one firm to represent everyone. This eliminates the possibility that the government will later move to disqualify the law firm due to conflicts of interest. The government will look with a suspicious eye at having one law firm represent the company and all employees. Separate law firms representing the company and employees will better position the company for possible cooperation and a mitigated outcome. Of course, the cost of multiple law firms will be exceedingly expensive if the company decides to pay the legal fees for everyone.

Interviewing and Reporting

When conducting interviews, it is highly recommended that two investigators participate. This provides increased documenting of the interview as one person can take detailed notes while the other conducts the interview. Having two investigators present provides greater protection from allegations of fabricated investigator misconduct by subjects. While this is an infrequent occurrence, it does happen and it is always better to be protected in advance. Taking copious notes is a must for all interviews. At the completion of the interview, the notes should be carefully reviewed for any necessary clarifications and additional recollections. If allowed by company policy and law, consider tape recording interviews. While there are needed protocols around tape recording, this practice removes many issues around what was actually said and what was not. Whether tape-recording or not, interview notes should be formalized in a memorandum of interview.

Develop a working chronology of the investigation and update frequently as the investigation progresses. At appropriate intervals of the investigation, prepare detailed reports of the investigation replete with exhibits. Report writing is a critical skill and takes time and effort to become good at. Always check with legal counsel to determine if written reports are required as there may be a determination by counsel to not prepare a report. Consider using privilege during the investigation and reporting phases. Companies should provide ongoing training on internal investigations, interviewing, and report writing to its investigators using outside counsel and other subject matter experts to ensure a professionally trained investigative group and work product.

Employee Cooperation with Company Investigations

When people are confronted about possible fraudulent activities, admissions and truthfulness are paramount. It's all or nothing when it comes to being truthful; half-truths are not acceptable. Investigator skill and experience play a key factor into obtaining the truth from employees when conducting interviews. Professional interviewing techniques and treating all people with dignity and respect go a long way in getting to the truth.

The cooperation of employees in internal investigations is critical to a successful outcome and determination of the facts of the case. Witnesses will provide great insight into the issues under investigation as well as context for the allegations. The collection of documentary and supporting evidence along with witness interviews may help to prove or disprove the allegations before having to confront the subject employee. An interview with a subject is made easier with this approach, and when an employee is confronted with substantial evidence of wrongdoing, it is easier to obtain an admission.

Therefore, the company code of conduct should include a statement that employees are required to cooperate fully and truthfully with any authorized company investigation. Employees who are subjects of investigations cannot be forced to speak with investigators but the failure to meet and discuss the allegations can be used by human resources and management in a determination of final disciplinary action.

309

International Investigations

Fraud and corruption violations are increasing throughout the world and there is little chance that this will change. Companies with an international reach need investigative coverage in all countries where they operate. Accounting fraud, embezzlements, and bribes to government officials can and do occur everywhere in the world. If a company's operations are based in the United States, it needs an investigative presence at the headquarters office. If there are significant operations outside the United States, investigative units need to be in those regions too. It is important to remember that the manner in which investigations are conducted in one country may differ widely from how they are done in other countries. This is due not only to different cultures, but different labor and employment laws, as well as business practices. Thus, the need for guidance from legal counsel is critical in protecting the interests of the company.

In some countries, the authorities have the ability to detain people for prolonged periods without charging them, while subjecting them to constant interrogation and intimidating tactics. At one company's operation in a foreign country, a large number of its local employees found themselves detained without access to counsel or company resources. The company found itself without critical employees needed to operate its business. More importantly, the company was unable to interview these confined employees in order to perform its own internal investigation. In addition, the authorities seized computers and files, which also had an impact on the business and the company's ability to "get its arms" around the government's investigation. Preparing employees for the possibility of government enforcement activity can be difficult due to the variability in individual and company rights in foreign countries. However, knowing what those rights are, establishing communication protocols, systemic back-up of data, as well as proper document retention policies can prove to be invaluable in such circumstances.

Anti-Corruption Enforcement Trends

The increased cooperation between U.S. and international law enforcement authorities in corruption and bribery investigations has yielded very positive results. Incriminating evidence obtained from the many FCPA prosecutions is being used by anti-corruption agencies all over the world for their own investigations. While the collaboration between the DOJ and

310

German authorities in the Siemens case is probably the best known example, there are others and we can expect to see more.

Thailand began investigating bribes paid to government officials in connection with the sale of high-technology baggage screening machines at the new Suvarnabhumi International Airport in Bangkok after an FCPA investigation of the conduct was settled. In March 2004, GE announced it would acquire explosives detection systems manufacturer InVision Technologies and the subsequent acquisition due diligence uncovered the corrupt payments. InVision voluntarily disclosed the matter and settled with the DOJ and SEC by paying fines totaling $1.9 million and received a nonprosecution agreement.[15] Although the Thai government-appointed investigation committee cleared country politicians and officials, the Thai Senate investigation committee responded by accusing executives at the airport of breaking Thai procurement and anti-corruption laws for accepting bribes.[16]

Just days after Textron, a Rhode Island-based global conglomerate of aircraft, defense, industrial, and finance businesses, settled an FCPA case with the DOJ and SEC, the Indonesian Corruption Eradication Commission began its own investigation of the company. On August 21, 2007, the company received a nonprosecution agreement and agreed to pay a $1.15 million fine.[17] Textron initially got caught up in the Oil-for-Food Scandal and that opened the door to discovery of other bribery. The U.S. government investigation found that employees not only made corrupt payments to Iraqi government officials but also to officials in the UAE, Egypt, Bangladesh, India, and Indonesia.[18]

Siemens Internal Investigation Approach

For complex corruption investigations with systemic and long-standing bribery practices, the necessary investigative approach should be one similar to that undertaken by Siemens. The response to a multi-jurisdictional criminal investigation requires an extremely thorough internal investigation. Financial transactions, bank records, contracts and agreements, and a whole host of other internal and external documents need to be collected and reviewed. The range of document retention and review may cover many years. Forensic accountants and other experts will be needed to address such a large amount of information. The review of books and records will need to be conducted on-site in not only the suspect locations but others to ensure that the full extent of corrupt payments and violations are determined. A thorough analysis and testing of the internal control framework should also be conducted to determine breakdowns in the process that may have failed to detect or deter violations. Interviews of potentially hundreds or thousands of people in numerous locations throughout the world may also need to be conducted. This entire process is convoluted and can take months or years to complete.

DETERMINING SYSTEMIC CORRUPTION AND FCPA VIOLATIONS

Once the investigation has been concluded, there needs to be a determination if there were violations of law, whether it is the FCPA or other criminal statutes and whether self-disclosure is appropriate. If there is evidence of bribery and/or books and records violations, the investigation should have determined how much the company benefited from this misconduct. That is critical, as the amount will figure into whether a company is prosecuted and the subsequent disgorgement of profits. Disgorgements are becoming a key penalty component of FCPA prosecutions along with fines and other penalties. There needs to be a solid understanding of how the company books and records were manipulated and how payments and expenses were incorrectly recorded.

The investigation should have determined not only what happened but also the root cause of any violations. A review of the company's business model should have discovered if any misconduct was caused by a rogue employee or was part of a pervasive culture of corruption. A finding of a pervasive problem may require further investigation and an expansion into business areas and geographic regions that were not included in the initial investigation. Any breakdown in internal controls is also problematic. Depending on the results, the company may face more or less penalties from the government.

If the investigation corroborated the allegations of corruption, remedial efforts must be immediately considered to address compliance program modifications and enhancements. These remedial actions are needed to prevent reoccurrence. If employees have been found to have violated policy and laws, appropriate discipline including termination must be considered. Business relationships with vendors, contractors, and other third parties whose conduct contributed to the violations need to be severed. Also, internal audit may need to conduct further audits to address the investigative findings. Policies may need to be revised or created as appropriate.

312

The investigative findings now need to be reported to senior management. FCPA violations need to be communicated to both senior management and the board. The detailed results can be memorialized in written report form or presented orally. Written reports can end up in the hands of federal prosecutors and government regulators as well as in civil litigation. That should be a consideration, even when the investigation and reports are done under attorney-client privilege. A consideration is to discuss the draft report, disclosure recommendations, and remedial action with senior leadership prior to submitting a final, written report.

SELF-DISCLOSURE OF FCPA VIOLATIONS

Once the investigation has found solid evidence of FCPA violations, a determination must be made whether to voluntarily disclose this misconduct to the government. There are advantages to self-disclosure including the opportunity to shape the presentation to government authorities, eliminate the possible impact of whistleblowers who may have knowledge of the wrongdoing, nonprosecution agreements, and leniency. A very important consequence of self-disclosure is that it reinforces a renewed commitment to a culture of compliance and tone at the top. The disadvantages of self-disclosure are many and include an intrusive government investigation that the company cannot control, the possible discovery of other violations, prosecution by U.S. and foreign authorities such as in the Siemens case, placement of independent monitors, derivative actions, and financial and reputational impact.

In any decision on voluntary disclosure, other factors also need to be considered. The seriousness and extent of the FCPA violations, as well as other related violations, in and of themselves will likely be discovered eventually. It is important to remember that the more serious and more pervasive the crimes, the greater the likelihood that someone will eventually blow the whistle on them. When there are multiple conspirators and large sums of money involved, someone is likely to talk. There is also the potential harm to business competitors from corrupt behavior and there is little doubt that if they learn of the misconduct, they will report it. If the strength of the incriminating evidence against the company is overwhelming, that is one more reason for self-disclosure. Timeliness of the disclosure is also important.

"The majority of companies benefit from self-disclosure of FCPA violations. The DOJ sees the big picture today. They are generally reasonable in how they resolve corruption violations and that has contributed to the large numbers of corporate disclosures," says attorney George Stamboulidis. Stamboulidis should know as he has represented clients who have had FCPA violations and self-disclosed to the government. He has also served as an independent monitor in several cases.

The Sentencing Guidelines reward voluntary disclosure of FCPA and other criminal violations. An effective compliance and ethics program in place prior to the instant violation can reduce the culpability score for penalties that an organization faces upon conviction. This reduction does not apply if certain high-level personnel are involved in the offense, condoned, or were willfully ignorant of the offense. However, self-reporting, cooperation, and acceptance of responsibility can significantly reduce the culpability score. This only applies if the organization discloses the violation prior to knowledge of the government investigation or threat of a government investigation.

If senior management of a company has knowledge of an FCPA violation, they should consider reporting it to the government. Self-disclosure and acceptance of responsibility is a consideration in charging decisions. If the organization is an established company, if they are a long-term listed company on one of the major stock exchanges, and if they had a compliance program in place, there will be little, if any, defense when the government eventually discovers the violations. The government will say the company should have known better and will hold them accountable. FCPA voluntary self-disclosure becomes mandatory when it relates to public companies with Sarbanes-Oxley internal control and CEO/CFO certification requirements. Failure to do so may be a consideration in a charging decision by the government. The government has stated that making examples of violators is preventative in nature.

The DOJ's Mendelsohn has opined on globalization of business and the shrinking world we live in. He reinforced the notion that with e-mail and the Internet, it is almost impossible to hide in plain sight when an organization is doing wrong. Misconduct is now easier than ever to uncover thanks to the increased worldwide attention to anti-corruption activities. His message reinforces the importance to consider self-disclosure of FCPA violations.

Problems in a faraway country are more likely to be learned by us—sitting here in Washington—than ever before. People in Bangladesh can e-mail me directly with an allegation that a company in Bangladesh is paying bribes to a government official there. Information about our work is now known

314

around the world. The media is paying a great deal of attention to corruption issues. There is a lot more English language media reporting around the world. It's more difficult to hide.[19]

If that isn't enough, Mendelsohn also has this to say:

We have come up [with] some creative ways to try to resolve cases involving companies so that we are no longer faced with a binary decision to either charge a company or not charge a company. We have crafted resolutions— non prosecution agreements, deferred prosecution agreements, corporate compliance monitors—we have come up with tools that provide positive incentives for responsible companies to self-disclose, to self-investigate, to remediate appropriately. And that has had an enormous impact on the number of companies that have been willing to come in and talk to us about the problems they are identifying in their operations.[20]

It is highly recommended that a company use experienced outside counsel to make the disclosure to the government. Once you have made the decision to self-disclose, be prepared for the inevitable questions the government will ask. These include:

- The results of the internal investigation
- Extent of the crimes discovered
- The individuals involved and their positions in the company
- The evidence obtained and safeguarded
- The actions to stop the corrupt practices
- Details on the preexisting compliance program
- Compliance program remedial steps already taken

The answers to these questions and the extent of cooperation with the government will determine eventual outcome.

COMPLIANCE EMERGENCY PREPAREDNESS KIT

All companies should have a Compliance Emergency Preparedness Kit (CEPK) when serious compliance failures are discovered. Unlike a regular emergency kit, which contains water, food, and medical supplies, this kit covers what to do in case of a compliance emergency. Companies should be prepared because corruption and fraud can happen at any time. And just like a natural disaster, it can't be avoided but with proper preparedness the damage can be minimized.

Advance preparation is an element of Enterprise Risk Management (ERM). ERM involves identifying and mitigating risk and according to the Committee of Sponsoring Organizations of the Treadway Commission (COSO). ERM is defined as "a process, effected by an entity's board of directors, management, and other personnel, applied in strategy setting and across the enterprise, designed to identify potential events that may affect the entity, and manage risk to be within its risk appetite, to provide reasonable assurance regarding the achievement of entity objectives."[21] A well-conceived CEPK addresses the ERM requirements to identify potential events that can significantly impact an organization.

A CEPK contains a checklist of things to do in case the company discovers a compliance failure. The types of issues and events that would trigger an emergency response must be fully discussed and documented as needing a response. Once defined, the kit will document the roles and responsibilities of the CEO, CFO, General Counsel, Chief Compliance Officer, other senior executives, Board of Directors, and other key personnel. The kit will include staff responsibilities, which personnel will be involved in any investigative response, the role of outside counsel, and even name the official spokesperson who will be responsible for disclosing the violation to outside parties. The names and contact information for outside counsel and other specialists who may be called upon to assist in case of such an emergency should also be readily available. The kit should also include contingency plans for action if the violator(s) is found to be the CEO, CFO, or other key persons. With these step-by-step instructions, a company will not be shocked into inaction and will know exactly how to proceed and handle whatever happens.

It is also highly recommended that the organization create a "compliance resume" and include it in the CEPK. This resume would include a detailed description of prior compliance issues that the company discovered and mitigated, including previous remedial action. A compliance resume is also one of the many recommended steps of the FSGO. In the event a compliance issue or criminal violation occurs, the organization can demonstrate to the independent auditors, DOJ, SEC, FBI, and others that it took every reasonable step to comply with the highest standards of corporate governance. This approach incorporates both an effective compliance program and the tenets of ERM to protect the organization from criminal misconduct, litigation, and enforcement actions.

This kit will help to demonstrate that the company took strong remedial action after the discovery of the instant violation. The FSGO require the company to take reasonable steps to respond appropriately. The reasonableness and appropriateness of the response will, of course, depend on the type of violation, the type of company, the industry that it is in, and the regulations with which it must comply. A major violation in a heavily regulated industry will demand much swifter and decisive action than a minor violation in a less heavily regulated one. These considerations should go into the kit, with different checklists depending on the type of violation uncovered. With appropriate action and preparedness, the company can prove that it took every reasonable measure to comply with the highest standards of corporate governance.[22]

NOTES

1. Dionne Searcey, "U.S. Cracks Down on Corporate Bribes," *Wall Street Journal*, May 26, 2009, A1.
2. Paul V. Gerlach (associate director of the SEC's Division of Enforcement), testimony before the Senate Subcommittee on Finance and Hazardous Materials Committee on Commerce, September 10, 1998, www.sec.gov/news/testimony/testarchive/1998/tsty1198.txt.
3. U.S. Department of Justice, Principles of Federal Prosecution of Business Organizations, August 28, 2008, 10.
4. Rick Wolf, "EU Court: No In-House Counsel Privilege," The Datakos Blawg, September 21, 2007, http://wolfs2cents.wordpress.com/2007/09/21/eu-court-no-in-house-counsel-privilege/.
5. Ibid.
6. *United States v. Arthur Andersen LLP*, 544 U.S. 696 (2005).
7. *United States. v. Quattrone*, 441 F.3d 153 (2d Cir. 2006).
8. *Upjohn v. United States*, 449 U.S. 383 (1981).
9. American Bar Association, "Task Force To Make Recommendations on Best Practices When Providing Upjohn Warnings," White-Collar Crime Bulletin, August 2008, www.abanet.org/crimjust/wcc/aug08 upjohn.htm.
10. American Bar Association White-Collar Crime Committee Working Group, "Upjohn Warnings: Recommended Best Practices When Corporate Counsel Interacts with Corporate Counsel," July 17, 2009, www.fr.com/news/2009/July/ABA_Upjohn_Task_Force.pdf.
11. *United States v. Stein*, 435 F. Supp 2d 330 (S.D.N.Y 2006).

12. Stephen Taub, "Judge: Feds Forced KPMG to Abandon Employees," CFO.com, June 27, 2006, www.cfo.com/article.cfm/7108196?f= related.
13. *U.S. v. Rosner*, 485 F.2d. 1213 (2d Cir. 1973).
14. Martin T. Biegelman and Joel T. Bartow, *Executive Roadmap to Fraud Prevention and Internal Control: Creating a Culture of Compliance* (Hoboken, NJ: John Wiley & Sons, Inc, 2006), 338.
15. Securities and Exchange Commission, "SEC Settles Charges Against InVision Technologies for $1.1 Million for Violations of the Foreign Corrupt Practices Act," February 14, 2005, http://sec.gov/litigation/ litreleases/lr19078.htm.
16. Terry Fredrickson, "More to Come," *Bangkok Post*, June 14, 2005, www.bangkokpost.com/education/site2005/wnjn1405.htm.
17. Department of Justice, "Textron Inc. Agrees to $1.15 Million Fine in Connection with Payment of $600,000 in Kickbacks by its French Subsidiaries under the United Nations Oil for Food Program," August 23, 2007, www.justice.gov/opa/pr/2007/August/07_crm_646.html.
18. *U.S. Securities and Exchange Commission v. Textron Inc.*, Complaint, August 23, 2007, United States District Court for the District of Columbia, www.sec.gov/litigation/complaints/2007/comp20251.pdf.
19. "Mendelsohn Says Criminal Bribery Prosecutions Doubled in 2007," *Corporate Crime Reporter*, September 16, 2008. www.corporate crimereporter.com/mendelsohn091608.htm.
20. Ibid.
21. Treadway Commission, *Enterprise Risk Management—Integrated Framework*, Committee of Sponsoring Organizations of the (2004), www.coso.org/documents/COSO_ERM_ExecutiveSummary.pdf.
22. Martin T. Biegelman with Daniel R. Biegelman, *Building a World-Class Compliance Program: Best Practices and Strategies for Success* (Hoboken, NJ: John Wiley & Sons, 2008), 211–14.

CHAPTER 13

Past, Present, and Future of the FCPA

The movie *All the King's Men* chronicles the rise and fall of a corrupt politician in the American South in the 1930s. Jack Burden is a newspaper reporter sent to cover a political neophyte running in his first election who has garnered a great deal of local buzz. Burden asked his editor, "What's so special about him?" The editor replies, "They say he's an honest man."[1] Honest men and women can defeat corruption but it is not easy. Society needs more people who are willing to stand up to bribery and say no more. There's a lot of history to overcome to make a better future.

The U.S. Department of Commerce's Good Governance Program estimates that U.S. companies lost deals worth at least $27 billion in 2008 as a result of corruption. "U.S. companies often cite corruption, weak rule of law, the lack of customs enforcement, and poor judicial reform as key impediments to doing business in developing countries."[2] Two foundational factors have helped drive increased FCPA enforcement: "a deeper desire among most developed nations to establish a level playing field for business competitors regardless of their countries of domicile; and the recognition by governments that corruption of any type is a destabilizing force within the international community."[3]

It is interesting and most welcome to note the ongoing attention to corruption issues in the media, by business organizations, and government. During the writing of this book, we observed an almost daily reporting on FCPA enforcement, new bribery prosecutions in other countries, and the need for enhanced anti-corruption compliance. The increased scrutiny and perception of the huge risk of noncompliance is most beneficial. There is no doubt that we will continue to see further enforcement actions both in the United States and elsewhere in the world. Let's conclude this book by briefly looking at the past, present, and future of the FCPA.

THE PAST

When Senator William Proxmire sponsored the FCPA bill more than 30 years ago, he had his concerns about how strongly its provisions would be enforced. He believed the DOJ was being "timid" in going after corporations involved in bribery. "Many companies will continue paying bribes if they can get away with it. . . . Nobody has gone to jail. Only three corporations have fired their chief executive officers. At most there has been some unfortunate publicity. . . . And so we come to a need for a remedy," Proxmire said.[4] Frequent corporate critic Ralph Nader also weighed in at the time and said, "I don't give much credence to the likelihood of companies policing themselves."[5]

In April 1976, Roderick M. Hills, then Chairman of the SEC, was speaking at a town hall meeting in Los Angeles where he made the following observations on the revelations of widespread corporate bribery and the pending FCPA bill:

As so we ask, have we uncovered a cancer lurking at the core of American business that government has the obligation to remove with extensive new civil and criminal laws, or are we naively depriving American corporations and their stockholders of the capacity to do business abroad in the manner it normally is done? In short, whose business is it?

No one can be sure, but results to date suggest that American business has the will to cause a permanent change in methods of doing business.

The major accounting firms now make far greater efforts to verify the accuracy of books and records. Their remedial actions to date are impressive and we will by consultation and rulemaking, if necessary, strengthen their own demonstrated resolve to re-establish the reputation of financial statements.

Independent directors now recognize far better their obligations. They surely know that they have, in effect, an affirmative obligation to question both management and outside auditors on the matter of questionable payments.

More important, there is today a large percentage of publicly held companies that have audit committees of outside directors that meet privately with the outside auditors.

And the business community must know by now that the Commission's Enforcement Division has the capacity and the will to test the depth of disclosures from time to time and from company to company in such a manner as to give us assurances that their disclosures are sufficient.[6]

One month later at the hearings for the FCPA bill, Hills said, "Let me say with some emphasis that I am personally convinced, and I believe the Commission is entirely convinced, that the measures we are taking, aided by this form of legislation, will stop the bribery of a foreign official to get business."[7] In his comments at the town hall and in the Senate hearing, Hills was wrong. American companies were unable to police themselves in preventing corporate bribery. Government enforcement and the new FCPA legislation would not be sufficient, in and of itself, to stop bribery.

What was needed was a confluence of several elements including changes in business attitudes, corporate culture, legislation, and law enforcement approach in combating corruption and bribery. The enactment of Sarbanes-Oxley in 2002 and its requirements for greater transparency and accountability for financial reporting and internal controls, opened the door for the explosion of FCPA disclosures and investigations. The attestation and certification requirements of Sections 302 and 404, the requirement for a code of ethics for senior financial officers, strengthening the oversight role of audit committees, and stronger whistleblower and nonretaliation protections made clear to public companies their obligations under the FCPA.

The revised Federal Sentencing Guidelines for Organizations released in November in 2004 further emphasized effective compliance and ethics programs in order to mitigate punishment for criminal offenses. These compliance program enhancements were required for all companies, public or private, and included anti-corruption and fraud prevention elements. The stage was set for enforcement and compliance.

THE PRESENT

This book opened with the story of Control Components, Inc. (CCI) as an example of how the DOJ is aggressively prosecuting FCPA violations. This case study bears repeating here as enforcement officials are taking a coordinated and impressive approach. CCI's business strategy employed corruption and bribery to drive revenue. The CEO and others devised a sales model euphemistically called CCI's friend-in-camp (FIC) program. The FIC program cultivated relationships with employees of both state-owned enterprises and private companies that included the payment of bribes to obtain and retain business.

CCI's senior management was involved in this decade-long conspiracy along with employees and agents. FICs were primarily people who had the authority to award contracts or at least steer a contract to CCI. Code words such as "flowers" were used to refer to bribes. Consultants were retained whose sole purpose was to funnel bribe payments to recipients. In addition to corrupt payments, bribes were provided in the form of lavish trips to Disneyland, Las Vegas, and Hawaii. College tuition was paid for the children of executives at state-owned enterprises.[8]

In 2004, when CCI's parent company conducted an internal audit of suspect commission payments, CCI executives tried to obstruct the audit. Information was purposely withheld from auditors. False information in the form of phony invoices to conceal bribes was provided to the auditors. When outside counsel was hired to conduct an internal investigation, CCI personnel made false statements to obstruct the inquiry. Incriminating documents were destroyed.[9]

Among the many companies and countries where CCI admitted to paying bribes, one was the China National Offshore Oil Corporation (CNOOC), a state-owned enterprise. CCI admitted that the "payments involved had been wired to personal accounts of CCI staff or friends and relatives of CCI staff" for bribes to CNOOC employees.[10] Even with these admissions and CCI's guilty plea, a CNOOC official denied that any employees received bribes. An internal investigation conducted by CNOOC found no violations of company policy or procedures and "all staff and officials involved in the transactions had vowed, in written pledges, to have violated no rules against commercial bribery."[11] Knowing that bribery and corruption in China is a crime punishable by death, it is understandable why no one would admit to receiving bribes.

In April 2009, six former CCI executives including the CEO; director of sales for China and Taiwan; director of worldwide sales; vice president of worldwide customer service; head of sales for Europe; Africa, and the Middle East; and president of the CCI Korea office were indicted. Two other executives, including the former CFO, have pleaded guilty. In July 2009, CCI pleaded guilty to violations of the FCPA and the Travel Act and was sentenced to three years probation and a criminal fine of $18.2 million. The company will have to retain an independent monitor for three years and implement an effective compliance program.

The lesson that CCI and other organizations learned from the government in this case is clear and simple: FCPA compliance is not an option and violations will be vigorously prosecuted. "The number of individual prosecutions has risen—and that's not an accident," said the DOJ's Mark Mendelsohn. "That is quite intentional on the part of the Department. It is our view that to have a credible deterrent effect, people have to go to jail. People have to be prosecuted where appropriate. This is a federal crime. This is not fun and games."[12] Self-reporting of FCPA violations is the expected norm according to the DOJ. Companies hoping for leniency have no alternative other than to face the consequences of a detrimental prosecution. Remember Mendelsohn's line about calling them before they call us.

THOUGHT LEADER IN FCPA COMPLIANCE: MARJORIE DOYLE

The Hard Part: Implementing an Anti-Corruption Compliance Program

Marjorie Doyle, principal in Marjorie Doyle & Associates, LLC, is an expert practitioner and leader in the field of ethics and compliance. She advises, coaches, and counsels chief ethics and compliance officers, CEOs, boards of directors, and others in designing and successfully implementing effective ethics and compliance programs. As a subject matter expert, a particular focus for Doyle is the FCPA and anti-corruption program compliance.

Doyle led the Compliance and Ethics Solutions practice at LRN where she provided a range of services. She joined LRN from Vetco International where she was Executive Vice President, Chief Ethics and Compliance Officer, responsible for a newly formed organization of compliance officers, directors, and specialists. She directly reported to the Compliance Committee of Vetco's Board of Directors. At Vetco, she built an ethics and compliance function which

(continued)

(*continued*)

resulted in best-in-class practices after the company entered into an agreement with the DOJ resulting from FCPA violations pleas.

Before Vetco, Doyle was the Chief Ethics and Compliance Officer at DuPont, where she founded and led the Ethics and Compliance Central organization, the first dedicated team of compliance officers chartered with furthering the company's global compliance objectives. Earlier in her career, she was a litigation associate with Fulbright & Jaworski in Houston, Assistant U.S. Attorney for the District of Connecticut, and Law Clerk to the Honorable John R. Brown, Chief Judge of the U.S. Court of Appeals for the Fifth Circuit.

Doyle is a frequent speaker on all elements of building ethics and compliance programs, FCPA anti-corruption and antibribery programs, responsibilities of boards of directors, and creating ethical business cultures. She is a member of several ethics and compliance organizations and in 2005 was recognized by the Society of Corporate Compliance and Ethics for her work and contributions to the ethics and compliance community. Doyle is a graduate of Mount Holyoke College and the University of Houston Bates College of Law, where she served as Editor-in-Chief of the Houston Law Review. Here she opines on the best practices to incorporate as well as the challenges when implementing an anti-corruption compliance program.

> *After the law firm you retained has written a memo detailing the increased enforcement of the FCPA, after you purchased all sorts of expensive online courses and other tools, and perhaps even after your company has become the target of enforcement—after all this—now you have to actually implement an anti-corruption program that your employees will take to heart and use.*
>
> *There is nothing intellectually difficult about understanding the FCPA, but to implement an effective program it does require the enthusiasm, persistence, and engagement of all sorts of people within the culture of your company. "Effective" means reducing the likelihood that FCPA violations will occur. I was on the hot seat in one company as the chief ethics and compliance officer after the company pleaded guilty to FCPA violations. I had to lead the creation of an effective program. I have since worked with other companies in*

building strong, practical anti-corruption programs and here I boil down my hard-earned wisdom to the following seven points:

1. IF YOU HAVE A VIOLATION, BE PROACTIVE

Don't sit and wait for the DOJ or the SEC to order you to do something. That could take months and then they would wonder why you sat around with your thumb in your mouth and are not capable of understanding the issue and therefore unable to fix it on your own. You have become the perfect candidate for an independent monitor.

I would encourage you to report violations and do an extensive internal investigation. If you have no compliance program, start building one now. If you have a compliance program, determine what changes need to be made for effective compliance and start implementing them before the DOJ and the SEC require you. The violation could be a one-off rogue employee or it could be part of a systemic problem. In most of the publicized cases, initially discovered incidents are only the tip of the iceberg and many other violations are subsequently revealed. That initial incident is usually the "dead canary in the mine" indicating there are more serious issues.

A company's immediate actions signal to enforcement authorities, shareholders, and employees, that the company is taking this matter seriously: that bribery is not acceptable behavior. Such responsive actions are not only good for the company's future business processes, but it is likely to help in mitigating what the DOJ/SEC ultimately decides in the way of penalties and whether the company needs a monitor.

2. CREATE A STRONG, STAND-ALONE POLICY ON NONRETALIATION

Most companies have a nonretaliation policy, but it is usually part of some other policy, usually an HR policy. Recent studies have shown that the number-one indicator that a company will have ethics and compliance failures that cause serious harm, is if employees do not feel safe to report violations. One reason is a culture of retaliation. The first step is to have a strong, highly visible, stand-alone nonretaliation policy. Then, of course, you have to publicize it, live it, and enforce it.

(continued)

(continued)

3. TRANSLATE YOUR CODE OF CONDUCT AND ANTI-CORRUPTION POLICIES INTO THE COMMON USE LANGUAGES OF THE EMPLOYEES

Some companies resist doing this because of the expense involved and often think they have solved the problem by declaring that English (or whatever other language) is the official language of the company. This reason fails to carry any weight with enforcement or the real world. A company can declare anything it wants, but it doesn't make it so or make it right. If you want employees to really comprehend the message, you must deliver it in their language of comfort. This means making an accurate, cultural translation. I had one DOJ attorney tell me that the first question she always asks of a company in trouble is whether they have made all necessary translations of their policies and procedures.

4. CREATE AN ETHICS AND COMPLIANCE MANAGEMENT STRUCTURE WITHIN THE COMPANY THAT HAS INDEPENDENCE AND POWER

The temptation to bribe or engage in other shortcuts can be very intoxicating and not always clear cut or obvious. It is no accident that many of the companies who have had major anti-corruption failures now have ethics and compliance departments with a high level executive who has direct reporting lines and/or easy access to the board of directors. This arrangement not only allows for a strongly positioned executive to implement a program and report sometimes sensitive problems involving valued employees, but it is also a clear signal to the whole organization that ethics and compliance are taken seriously. Some companies push back by saying that ethics and compliance are everyone's job, but then that would dictate that there is no need for a CFO or General Counsel because making money is everyone's job as is following the law and policies.

5. THERE IS NO SUBSTITUTE FOR IN-PERSON TRAINING OF EMPLOYEES IN HIGH-RISK POSITIONS REGARDING BRIBERY

There are so many modes of communication for training and there is no one way that does it all. Online training is cheaper and can reach many people quickly; the same is true for e-mails, webcasts, and podcasts. The most effective means remains in-person communication, although it can be the most expensive, especially with a global company. The best practice, and that required by enforcement authorities, is to have person-to-person training on antibribery for those employees in bribery-prone, high-risk positions. Not just any live training is effective: gone are the days when a lawyer delivering a dry, legalistic PowerPoint is acceptable. The training must be understandable, engaging, interactive, and focused on likely scenarios in the particular business.

Training sessions are an ideal opportunity to talk about actual compliance failures despite what the attorneys might prefer. Failures are costly and hard-fought lessons so you might as well make the most of them to prevent future damaging situations. DOJ and the SEC will often ask employees if they are aware of the failures to determine if they have learned anything. I have had some employees respond that management discouraged people from talking about bad things that occurred in the past, so many times employees miss out on the lesson.

6. STRONG AND SPECIFIC POLICIES NEED TO BE IN PLACE REGARDING THE SELECTION AND MANAGEMENT OF THIRD PARTIES WHO DO WORK FOR THE COMPANY

The recent strong enforcement of the FCPA has single-handedly been responsible for changing how companies view using third parties. Gone is the attitude—or it should be—that outsourced means out-of-sight, out-of-mind, and not my problem. Many bribery situations involve a contractor or supplier making bribes on behalf of the company to show that they can "deliver." As a result, new best practices have developed in how to handle third parties. Companies should have detailed policies on how third parties should be selected, managed, educated on bribery policies, and audited. Many companies now have teams in their purchasing or sourcing departments who are focused on the red flags that might warn of third-party vendors who might bribe because of their history or function they were hired to perform.

If a third party is responsible for a business process that could be open to bribery, especially in a geographic region that has a high corruption reputation, then, for example, a personal visit to the third party's place of business is a necessity as part of the vetting process.

(continued)

(continued)

A mere desktop vetting is probably not enough. This becomes even more essential when a company does business in a country where it only has a third party representing them. These "new hiring best practices" for third parties are most expensive in the short term but are certainly a fraction of the cost of defending bribery activities. You should treat mergers and acquisitions as you would the hiring of a third party. Make sure that you understand your new acquisition's anti-corruption history and status before you make the deal. It could significantly affect the cost later.

7. LAST, BUT NOT LEAST, MAKE SURE THAT THE MIDDLE MANAGER OR FRONTLINE SUPERVISORS BUY INTO THE IMPORTANCE OF THE ANTIBRIBERY POLICIES OF THE COMPANY

These are the people who control employees' paychecks, evaluations, and advancement. Not surprisingly, then, these are the people who most influence an employee's behavior. Middle managers (the "mushy middle") can make time for a message or not, or can deliver a message with passion and enthusiasm, or roll their eyes in frustration. These are the people who must live the policies every day or be removed, regardless of their sales or production numbers. These are the people who you want to discuss antibribery lessons and scenarios with their employees, to continually deliver compliance and ethics messages, and to be present at the live training to make introductions and lend their support. It is a given that the board, the CEO, and other top managers must take the lead on the policies and code of conduct, but middle management is the ultimate key to the success of the program.

Corporate Ignorance Is Not Bliss

In September 2009, Deloitte Financial Advisory Services released the results of an online poll of over a thousand business professionals from varied industries on how their organizations are responding to the FCPA and corruption risk. The results are troubling given the recent attention to anti-corruption compliance. Seventy-two percent expect an increase in FCPA prosecutions in the coming years. Yet, 34 percent of respondents have no comprehensive FCPA compliance program in place. Twenty-three percent claimed they were unaware of the severity and consequences of the FCPA. More than half are relying on government enforcement to stop corruption; fifty-nine percent of respondents believe that increased enforcement activity will deter FCPA violations. "When it comes to FCPA, corporate ignorance is not bliss," said Ed Rial, leader of Deloitte's FCPA consulting practice.[13]

It's Not Rocket Science

Bribery and corruption are not complex issues to comprehend, especially for juries. All the FCPA trials in the first nine months of 2009 ended in convictions. In fact, there has not been an acquittal in an FCPA trial since 1991.[14] Case in point is the trial of Gerald and Patricia Green, husband-and-wife film executives indicted on charges of bribing Thai officials to land lucrative contracts and projects such as the Bangkok International Film Festival. At their trial in Los Angeles in late August 2009, the prosecutor had this to say: "This case is about greed, it's about corruption, and it's about deceit," the Greens "turned the TAT [Tourism Authority of Thailand] into their own personal piggy bank."[15] The jury came back with guilty verdicts with just a few hours of deliberations. The Greens were convicted of conspiracy, violating the FCPA, and money laundering.

Richard Cassin, attorney, FCPA subject matter expert, and creator of the widely read FCPA Blog had this to say about the FCPA and the speedy convictions of the Greens: "Lawyers are trained to quibble and criminal defense lawyers do it best. After all, their job is to create reasonable doubt. So it's no surprise that when talking about the FCPA, they say it's complicated, technically challenging and obscure, poorly drafted, and badly organized. But don't believe it. There's no evidence in the record that judges or juries have any trouble understanding the FCPA. Just the opposite." Cassin added, "Juries get it. Which means anyone who's completed a typical compliance training program has no excuse for not understanding the FCPA."[16]

Perhaps companies are getting the message. In the wake of disclosing FCPA violations in 2009, aviation and government service provider DynCorp fired its chief compliance officer.[17] The company moved quickly in addressing its compliance failure, and we would hope that it institutes a more dynamic anticorruption program.

ON THE HORIZON

Enhanced FCPA enforcement is only one aspect of the government's renewed war on corruption. In the first year of Barack Obama's presidency, his administration demonstrated that fighting financial corruption, in a myriad of forms, is a high priority. The SEC, DOJ, FBI, among others, have shown an increasing aggressiveness in enforcement and investigation. Among other cases, the government has stepped up insider trading probes, including breaking up a major insider trading ring; pursued tax evaders by going after the Swiss banking giant UBS; and charged 44 people in a major New Jersey corruption, money laundering, and bribery case, including three mayors and five rabbis.

A November 2009 speech by Lanny Breuer, Assistant Attorney General for the DOJ's criminal division, could prove to be very telling for what is on the FCPA horizon. More and more individuals will be in the crosshairs, not just corporations; asset forfeiture may become a common weapon against violators. According to Breuer, "Whether we're talking about kleptocracy or those who benefit from bribery, we're going to pursue and pursue it aggressively. When we can prove the case we're absolutely going to seize their profits and their land and their fancy cars and boats."[18] The DOJ will not shy away from difficult prosecutions, and is willing and able to take on cases in any district in the country. In summary, as he put it, 2009 was "the most dynamic single year in the more than 30 years since the FCPA was enacted."[19]

THE FUTURE

President Obama gave a speech to the Ghanaian Parliament in Accra on July 11, 2009. Reading between the lines, it can be strongly inferred that the United States will not only continue, but step up its fight against corruption and bribery. Early in the speech, he said that "development depends on good governance" and this theme of governance ran throughout the remainder of his remarks. He discussed corruption and that "No person wants to live in a society where the rule of law gives way to the rule of brutality and bribery."[20] President Obama stressed the importance of good governance in telling the people of Ghana and Africa that they must take responsibility for their future and hold their leaders accountable. He also reinforced how America will increase support of good governance and the rule of law. His focus on fighting corruption and bribery is a telling message that the United States is committed to its strong enforcement of the FCPA.

There are clear signals that other countries will have a similar enhanced focus on enforcement. On September 25, 2009, the UK's Serious Fraud Office (SFO) highlighted its fight against corruption with the news of the "first prosecution brought in the UK against a company for overseas corruption and breaching United Nations sanctions."[21] The SFO announced that bridge manufacturer Mabey & Johnson, as discussed in Chapter 6, pleaded guilty to corruption charges and paid £6.6 million in fines and penalties. The SFO commented that "overseas corruption is not a victimless crime" and reiterated that both companies and individuals will be prosecuted as the specific situations warrant.[22]

The U.S. government has given clear guidance that the compliance function is critical and protects customers, partners, employees, and shareholders. Even in the economic downtown, the SEC reminded companies of their obligations to ensure full compliance. "While many firms are considering reductions and cost-cutting measures, we remind you of your firm's legal obligation to maintain an adequate compliance program reasonably designed to achieve compliance with the law," said the SEC in a December 2008 open letter to CEOs of SEC-registered firms.[23]

There have been other new developments in FCPA and anti-corruption enforcement that foretell the future. In September 2009, the Financial Industry Regulatory Authority (FINRA) announced that it would begin examining broker-dealers for FCPA compliance. "This pronouncement will force broker-dealers with international footprints to examine their existing FCPA compliance programs and benchmark them against ever-rising government expectations.[24] The SEC's new FCPA Unit will likely result in increased coordination with the DOJ and even more enforcement actions. If this FCPA-focused unit meets expectations, we can expect:

- More interactions with overseas regulators
- Increased sharing of red flags and lessons learned in corruption and bribery
- More industry-wide investigations
- Faster resolution of cases[25]

Battling the Disease of Corruption

The FCPA and the leadership role that the United States is taking in pursuing enforcement have had a significant influence in the worldwide fight against bribery and corruption. The focus on the FCPA has opened the door for other countries and organizations to follow suit with improved laws and resources to battle graft. There is no doubt that the FCPA has spurred businesses around the globe to seriously look at their compliance programs and make much needed improvements. In the excellent book *Bribes* that details the history and concept of bribery, author John T. Noonan, Jr. very aptly sums up the uniqueness and importance of the FCPA:

> For the first time in the history of the world, a measure for bribery was introduced into law that was universal as far as those subjected to the law were concerned. For the first time, a country made it criminal to corrupt the officials of another country. America's ambassadors—that is, its businessmen—were to show American purity throughout the globe.[26]

Willie Stark, the "honest" politician in *All the King's Men* eventually says to reporter Burden, "Jack, there's something on everybody. Man is conceived in sin and born in corruption. . . . There's *always* something."[27] Willie Stark starts as an honest man but succumbs to corruption and the dark side of power. How did Willie Stark go from being an honest man to a corrupt and cynical human being? Is the answer as simple as "Power tends to corrupt, and absolute power corrupts absolutely" or is it something else? Corruption and self-dealing are always a temptation, so eternal vigilance is a necessity. Embracing FCPA and anti-corruption compliance is the only way to fully protect an organization in today's global environment. Failure is not an option.

NOTES

1. *All the King's Men* (1949), Columbia Pictures Corporation, www.imdb.com/title/tt0041113/quotes.
2. U.S. Department of Commerce, Good Governance Program, www.trade.gov/goodgovernance/.
3. PricewaterhouseCoopers, *Corruption Crackdown: How the FCPA is changing the way the world does business*, July 2009, 3, www.pwc.com/en_US/us/foreign-corrupt-practices-act/publications/assets/pwc-corruption-crackdown-fcpa-2009.pdf.
4. Gerry M. Czarnecki, "Sarbanes-Oxley & Section 404: Old Dog/New Teeth," *World Business Academy Viewpoint*, Volume 19, Issue 6, March 31, 2005, 5, www.nationalleadershipinstitute.org/Portals/0/SOX%20Old%20Dog%20New%20Teeth.pdf.

5. "Gulf Prober, Nader Differ on 'Bribe' Bill," *Pittsburgh Post-Gazette*, April 6, 1976, 12, http://news.google.com/newspapers? nid=1129& dat=19760406&id=N00NAAAAIBAJ&sjid=f20DAAAAIBAJ&pg= 6863,596827.

6. Roderick M. Hills, "Corporate Morality—Whose Business Is It?" (speech, Los Angeles, CA, April 13, 1976), www.sechistorical.org/ collection/papers/1970/1976_0413_HillsLAT.pdf.

7. United States Senate, Ninety-Fourth Congress, Prohibiting Bribes to Foreign Officials, Hearing Before the Committee on Banking, Housing, and Urban Affairs, Testimony of Roderick M. Hills, May 18, 1976, 6, www.archive.org/details/ProhibitingBribesToForeignOfficials.

8. *U.S. v. Control Components, Inc.*, information filed July 22, 2009, CR No. 09-00162, United States District Court, Central District of California, www.usdoj.gov/criminal/pr/press_releases/2009/07/07-31-09control-guilty-information.pdf.

9. Ibid.

10. "CNOOC Denies Involvement in U.S. Firm Bribery Case," Xinhua News Agency, August 15, 2009, http://news.xinhuanet.com/english/ 2009-08/15/content_11888205.htm.

11. Ibid.

12. "Mendelsohn Says Criminal Bribery Prosecutions Doubled in 2007," *Corporate Crime Reporter*, September 16, 2008, www.corporate crimereporter.com/mendelsohn091608.htm.

13. "Deloitte Online Poll: Most Respondents Expect FCPA Violations to Increase in Coming Years," *Corporate Compliance Insights*, September 14, 2009, www.corporatecomplianceinsights.com/2009/deloitte-poll-fcpa-violations-expected-to-increase.

14. Richard Cassin, "We Get It," The FCPA Blog, September 18, 2009, www.fcpablog.com/blog/2009/9/18/we-get-it.html.

15. Associated Press, "LA Trial in Thai Film Festival Bribery Case Begins," *Long Island Press*, August 26, 2009, www.longislandpress .com/2009/08/26/la-trial-in-thai-film-festival-bribery-case-begins/.

16. Cassin "We Get It."

17. Ashby Jones, "In Wake of FCPA Disclosure, DynCorp Top Lawyer Gets Axe," *Wall Street Journal* Law Blog, November 30, 2009, http://blogs.wsj.com/law/2009/11/30/in-wake-of-fcpa-disclosure-dyncorp-top-lawyer-get-axe/.

18. Dionne Searcy, "Breuer: Beware, Execs, The DOJ Will Take Your Fancy Cars," *Wall Street Journal* Law Blog, November 17, 2009,

http://blogs.wsj.com/law/2009/11/17/breuer-beware-execs-the-doj-wants-your-fancy-cars/.

19. Lanny A. Breuer, "Prepared Address to The 22nd National Forum on the Foreign Corrupt Practices Act" (speech, November 17, 2009, Washington, DC), www.justice.gov/criminal/pr/speeches/2009/11/11-17-09aagbreuer-remarks-fcpa.pdf.

20. President Barack Obama (remarks to the Ghanaian Parliament, Accra International Conference Center, Accra, Ghana, July 11, 2009), www.america.gov/st/texttrans-english/2009/July/20090711110050abretnuh0.1079783.html&distid=ucs.

21. Serious Fraud Office, "Mabey & Johnson Ltd. Sentencing," press release, September 25, 2009, www.sfo.gov.uk/press-room/latest-press-releases/press-releases-2009/mabey-johnson-ltd-sentencing-.aspx.

22. Mabey & Johnson Ltd. Prosecution Opening Note, September 25, 2009, www.sfo.gov.uk/mabeyjohnsonltd/SFO-Annex2-Statement-01-250909.pdf.

23. Securities and Exchange Commission, "Open Letter to CEOs of SEC-Registered Firms," press release, December 2, 2008, www.sec.gov/about/offices/ocie/ceoletter.htm.

24. Richard Grime, David A. DeMuro, Jeremy Maltby, George Bagnall, O'Melveny & Myers, LLP, "Financial Services Industry and Individual Investors Face Increasing Scrutiny and Risks Under the Foreign Corrupt Practices Act," FCPA alert, September 25, 2009, www.omm.com/financial-services-industry-and-individual-investors-face-increasing-scrutiny-and-risks-under-the-foreign-corrupt-practices-act-09-23-2009/.

25. Alexandra A. Wrage, "New FCPA Team at the SEC," WrageBlog Anti-Bribery Compliance Blog, September 4, 2009, http://wrageblog.org/2009/09/04/new-fcpa-team-at-the-sec/.

26. John T. Noonan, Jr., *Bribes* (Berkeley, CA: University of California Press, 1987), 680.

27. *All the King's Men.*

APPENDIX

Opinion Procedure Releases

This chapter summarizes a selection of the Department of Justice's (DOJ) Opinion Procedure Releases made public since 2000. The Procedure allows companies or individuals to request an opinion on proposed business conduct or a transaction to see whether it would violate the Foreign Corrupt Practices Act (FCPA). Conduct in conformity with an issued opinion will be granted a presumption of FCPA compliance.

In general, though these Releases are only binding on the requestor, they do contain general principles applicable beyond the exact facts explained therein. They give an idea of the DOJ's stance on particular issues. While the Releases may be specific to the requestor's particular facts, the situation themselves are general enough that they are useful to others.

Note that various opinions have been discussed throughout the preceding chapters. Furthermore, Opinion Release 2004-02 was covered in depth in Chapter 9 and need not be repeated here. That opinion covered the elements of a rigorous anti-corruption code designed to detect FCPA violations. For further information on that opinion, please refer to that chapter.

OPINION PROCEDURE RELEASE 2009-01

A medical device company proposed to donate a number of its devices to the government of a foreign country as part of a program to evaluate the devices for possible mass purchase and government endorsement. The company would sell the devices to the government directly and would not have any input on the specific recipients aside from developing the guidelines used in the study protocols. Criteria would be established to prevent any favoritism or official influence in the patient selection. DOJ noted that this conduct does not implicate the FCPA, as the donation would be to the government directly and not to individual officials.[1]

OPINION PROCEDURE RELEASE 2008-02

This is an important Opinion Release, as it sets out a standard for FCPA due diligence specifically approved by the government. Halliburton targeted a British oil and gas services provider for acquisition. Halliburton's ability to conduct due diligence was restricted by UK legal restrictions regarding the bidding process and thus had insufficient time and inadequate access to information to fully investigate any potential FCPA or corruption issues. The company would only be able to complete due diligence after closing and was concerned about inheriting any FCPA issues from either the target's preacquisition conduct or postacquisition conduct prior to due diligence completion. In spite of this, Halliburton represented that it would institute an extensive due diligence plan after the closing. The plan included:

- Immediately after the closing, meeting with the DOJ to disclose whether the company has any information regarding FCPA, corruption, or related internal control, and accounting issues
- Within ten business days of the closing, presenting a comprehensive, risk-based FCPA and anti-corruption due diligence work plan, which will organize the due diligence effort into high-, medium-, and low-risk elements
  - The work plan addresses, among other things:
    - The use of agents and other third parties
    - Commercial dealings with state-owned customers
    - Any joint venture, teaming, or consortium arrangements
    - Customs and immigration matters

- Tax matters
- Any governmental licenses and permits
- Within 90 days of the closing, reporting the results of the high-risk due diligence, plus progress reports during that period and beyond as appropriate
- Within 120 days of the closing, reporting the results of the medium-risk due diligence, plus progress reports during that period and beyond as appropriate
- Within 180 days of the closing, reporting the results of the lowest-risk due diligence, plus progress reports during that period and beyond as appropriate
- If due diligence continues as needed beyond the 180-day period, completing such due diligence expeditiously and providing periodic reports until its completion
- In any event, completing due diligence, including investigating any relevant issues, no later than one year from the date of closing
- Retaining external counsel and third-party consultants, including forensic accountants, as well as utilizing internal resources to conduct FCPA and anti-corruption due diligence
- Process shall include review of all relevant records of the target company, including e-mail, company financial and accounting records, and interviews of relevant personnel and other individuals
- Requiring associated agents and third parties who are to be retained and do not present compliance issues, to sign new contracts (rather than contract modifications or extensions) with Halliburton that incorporate FCPA and anti-corruption provisions, and audit rights
  - Agents and third parties who will not be retained will be terminated as soon as possible
  - Based on due diligence, Halliburton will take appropriate remedial action if it discovers any corruption-related problems
- Upon closing, immediately imposing its own Code of Business Conduct and specific FCPA and anti-corruption policies and procedures, and communicating the same to the target's employees
  - Within 60 days of the closing, providing FCPA and anti-corruption training to all officers and all employees whose positions or job responsibilities warrant such training, including all employees in management, sales, accounting, and financial controls positions

- Providing all other appropriate employees such training within 90 days
- Disclosing to the DOJ all FCPA, corruption, and related internal controls and accounting issues that it uncovers during the course of the due diligence, and completing any additional steps DOJ deems necessary to complete the plan

DOJ indicated it did not intend to take any action against Halliburton, based in large part on the strength and depth of the due diligence plan and the unique circumstances surrounding the transaction. Halliburton lacked the sufficient time or legal ability to require a specified level of due diligence or insist upon remedial measures until after the completion of the acquisition. Since the company was unable to prevent unlawful payments by the target in the period immediately after the closing, the opinion indicated that DOJ would take no action for any such payments, provided Halliburton discloses such conduct, stops it, and otherwise continues its work plan. Of note, the protection afforded Halliburton is limited to things occurring during the 180-day post-closing period, provided that Halliburton has fully disclosed all relevant issues and continues to take appropriate measures.[2]

OPINION PROCEDURE RELEASE 2008-01

The requestor, an American Fortune 500 company, wanted to purchase an interest in a foreign state-controlled business that was to be privatized. The foreign government owned a majority share; the requestor was concerned that the minority owner with whom it would be dealing would be considered a public official due to the involvement in a state-owned business. The parties came to an agreement whereby the minority owner would buy out the majority, then sell a majority stake in the newly formed company to the requestor.

Before the proposed sale, the U.S. company undertook extensive due diligence and made numerous disclosures to the foreign government. Among other things, the company:

- Commissioned a report on the foreign company and the minority owner by a reputable international investigative firm
- Retained a business consultant in the foreign country who provided due diligence advice

- Did searches on all relevant persons and entities involved in the transactions
- Met with representatives of the U.S. embassy
- Retained both a forensic accounting firm and outside counsel to conduct due diligence and issue a preliminary report, as well as a second law firm to review the due diligence

The company's representatives also met with government officials regarding the sale to discuss concerns and the steps the company had taken involving the sale. The representatives made numerous disclosures to the government, including that it planned to offer a substantial premium in the purchase price, and the business reasons behind that decision. Additionally, as part of the negotiation process, the foreign company agreed to several important compliance obligations and responsibilities.

DOJ approved the proposed transactions, and specifically stated that the approval resulted from the company's reasonable due diligence with special attention paid to FCPA risks and compliance with local laws and regulation, the transparency of its process through adequate disclosures to relevant government entities, and the representations and warranties from the other party regarding anti-corruption compliance.[3]

OPINION PROCEDURE RELEASE 2006-02

A U.S. company sought an opinion on its foreign subsidiary's retention of a local law firm to aid it in matters before a particular government agency which oversees currency exchange. The subsidiary had major difficulties with applications before the agency being rejected for trivial reasons; the law firm was to be hired to prepare the applications. Though the law firm rate was substantial, it was not out of line with the amount and nature of the work to be performed and with the rates of similar firms.

The company performed substantial due diligence on the firm, which had a reputation for competence and ethical conduct, by having the principal attorney interviewed by its general counsel and outside counsel and by speaking with other attorneys in the country who recommended the firm. The representation agreement between the subsidiary and the firm included several provisions to prevent corruption. While this is typically a situation fraught with peril—namely a company having difficulty with a government agency and hiring a local expert to solve it—it appeared as though the company did everything it could to ensure that no improper payments have been or would be made and all parties would engage in ethical conduct, and no action was taken.[4]

OPINION PROCEDURE RELEASE 2006-01

A U.S. company headquartered in Switzerland wanted to start a pilot program in an African county to improve enforcement of local anti-counterfeiting laws. The company's business had been harmed by counterfeiting of its products and the country served as a major transit point for such counterfeit goods. The company wanted to donate $25,000 to fund incentive awards to local customs officials to improve enforcement and increase seizures of counterfeit products. The company also wanted to involve its competitors in the program and planned to establish a number of safeguards to ensure that the money would in fact be used for its intended purpose. Its business in the country was relatively small and would not change based on this program. The DOJ stated it did not intend to take any enforcement action but noted that the release covered only the $25,000 donation and would not be applicable to any future contributions.[5]

OPINION RELEASE 2003-01

During the due diligence phase of an acquisition, a U.S. company discovered that officers of the target company's foreign subsidiary made payments violating the FCPA. The requestor and the target disclosed the results of their investigations to the DOJ and SEC while the target made appropriate public disclosures, took steps to stop the violations, and punished the offenders. The companies wished to proceed with the acquisition but the requestor was concerned with acquiring criminal and civil liability for the past FCPA violations.

The requestor, as owner of the target, represented that it would continue to cooperate with the investigation and the DOJ and SEC and disclose any further findings. The requestor would also ensure appropriate discipline for violators, extend its compliance program to the target, modifying it as necessary, and will ensure that the target implements a system of internal controls and keeps accurate books and records. The DOJ stated it did not intend to take action against the requestor for the preacquisition conduct. However, it did note that an acquiring company may be held liable for any unlawful payments made by an acquired company or its personnel after the date of acquisition.[6]

OPINION RELEASE 2001-03

A U.S. company's wholly owned subsidiary submitted a bid to sell equipment to a foreign government. The subsidiary used the help of a foreign dealer to prepare the bid. The dealer's president made a comment to a company employee that the employee believed indicated the president paid off government officials to accept the bid. The company sought to enter into a new agreement with the dealer.

The company, through its counsel, investigated the comments and found nothing indicating that the dealer made any payments; the dealer has represented that it never offered or made any such payments, and if it did, the requestor had the right to terminate their agreement and withhold any owed payments. The dealer also agreed to allow the requestor to annually audit its books. Based on this information, and the requestor's assurance that it would notify DOJ if it finds any new information, the DOJ declined to take any action.[7]

OPINION RELEASE 2001-02

An American and a foreign company planned to form a consortium to bid on and perhaps enter into a business relationship with the foreign company's home country. At issue, the chairman and shareholder of the foreign company acts as an advisor to senior government officials and is a senior public education official himself. The chairman represented that his duties do not in any way involve him in the potential business of the consortium and he will have no influence over any bidding processes. He will not initiate or attend any government meetings on behalf of the consortium and will recuse himself from any official discussions relating to the consortium. Furthermore, his dual status in government and the consortium is legal in his country. The DOJ declined to take any enforcement action.[8]

OPINION RELEASE 2001-01

A U.S. company planned to enter into a joint venture with a French company but was concerned with possible liability for FCPA violations in connection for contracts the French company contributed to the venture. The requestor took a number of precautions to avoid any potential FCPA liability. The other company represented it did not illegally procure any of its contributions. That company also took substantial steps in regard to its agents.

The French company terminated all agent agreements related to contracts contributed to the venture made before the enactment of the French Law Against Corrupt Practices and liquidated all payment obligations owed to those agents. The joint venture will negotiate new agent agreements in accordance with a rigorous compliance program to avoid corrupt business practices. This program was designed to ensure that no agents known to have engaged in illegal or unethical conduct will be part of the venture. DOJ specifically cited the agent practices as "a significant precaution to avoiding illegal payments to foreign government officials," and while it does not officially endorse such practices, it would seem like they would satisfy the "effective" compliance program requirements of the Federal Sentencing Guidelines for Organizations (FSGO).[9]

OPINION RELEASE 2000-01

A foreign partner of a U.S. law firm's overseas office had been appointed to a high-ranking position in a foreign country's government. The partner took a leave of absence from the law firm to take the position. The law firm sought to provide the partner with insurance and other benefits during his leave. The benefits, which included health and life insurance for the partner and his family, payments based on clients brought to the firm, and interest on the partner's partnership contribution, were typically provided in leave situations and consistent with firm practice. The firm had obtained local counsel who advised that such payments did not violate the law.

The requestor and foreign official both made assurances to the DOJ to avoid any appearance of impropriety. The requestor certified that it would not represent any clients before the foreign official's ministry; it would maintain a list of clients previously represented by the official, and it would not advise such clients in any business or lobbying matter involving that particular foreign government. The foreign official agreed to recuse himself and to refrain from participating or affecting any decisions of his government relating to his law firm, its clients, or on any matter on which the firm lobbied.

The DOJ stated it did not intend to take any action. It also noted that ordinarily a foreign official would not be covered by the FCPA but due to the official's position in a U.S. law firm, he would be treated as a domestic concern.[10]

PAYING FOR TRAVEL: OPINION PROCEDURE RELEASES
2004-01, 2004-03, 2004-04, 2007-01, 2007-02, 2008-03

Numerous opinions have dealt with the issue of paying for travel and expenses of foreign government officials. As these six opinions deal with the same topic, they will be covered at the same time. Two of the opinions, 2004-01 and 2004-03, deal with nearly identical issues and appear to be requested by the same law firm.

The facts of each are as follows:

- 2004-01: Sponsorship and presentation of a seminar on labor and employment law to be held in China, in conjunction with a Chinese government ministry; law firm paying for travel and hotel accommodations of government officials and some costs of seminar itself[11]

- 2004-03: Sponsorship of a trip to the United States by Chinese government officials to meet with U.S. public-sector officials, to discuss U.S. regulation of employment, labor unions, and workplace safety, lasting for ten days and including stops in three different cities; law firm paying for travel, lodging, meals, and insurance for the officials and a translator[12]

- 2004-04: Funding a study tour for foreign officials who are members of a committee drafting a new law on mutual insurance to meet with company officials, insurance industry groups, and other insurance companies; company paying for economy airfare, hotels, local transportation, modest per diem, and occasional additional meals and tourist activities[13]

- 2007-01: Organizing a four-day trip to the United States by a six-person delegation from a foreign government to an educational and promotion tour of one of the requestor's sites, intending to familiarize the delegates with its operations and establish its business credibility; company paying for domestic economy airfare, local transportation, and meals, with the international airfare paid by the foreign government[14]

- 2007-02: Trip to company's U.S. headquarters for foreign government officials attending internship program in the United States for foreign insurance regulators; paying domestic economy airfare, lodging, local transportation, and modest incidentals including a four-hour sightseeing tour, for approximately six days' stay[15]

- 2008-03: TRACE, a membership organization specializing in antibribery initiatives, compliance benchmarking, and due diligence reviews, sought to pay expenses for 20 Chinese journalists to attend a press conference in Shanghai coinciding with an international anti-corruption conference; journalists based in Shanghai would receive a stipend to cover local transportation, one meal, and incidentals while journalists outside Shanghai would receive a larger stipend to cover those expenses[16]

DOJ approved all of these requests. The overall rule is that all expenses must be reasonable and connected directly to the event; nothing should be paid or organized that would give the appearance of impropriety. The company sponsoring the event cannot select who will attend; that should be left to the foreign government. The agency or ministry involved should not have any actual or pending business before it from the company. Souvenirs and gifts should be avoided, but if they are given out they should be of nominal value and connected to the company (i.e., branded with its logo). All costs should be paid directly to the provider and reimbursements should be reasonable and only given with presentation of a receipt. The company should only pay for the officials themselves and other necessary personnel such as translators and should not pay for spouses, family, or other guests. As the DOJ noted, promotional expenses must be reasonable and directly related to promotion, demonstration, or explanation of products or services.

NOTES

1. DOJ, FCPA Opinion Procedure Release 2009-01, August 3, 2009, www.usdoj.gov/criminal/fraud/fcpa/opinion/2009/0901.html.
2. DOJ, FCPA Opinion Procedure Release 2008-02, June 13, 2008, www.usdoj.gov/criminal/fraud/fcpa/opinion/2008/0802.html.
3. DOJ, FCPA Opinion Procedure Release 2008-01, January 15, 2008, www.usdoj.gov/criminal/fraud/fcpa/opinion/2008/0801.pdf.
4. DOJ, FCPA Opinion Procedure Release 2006-02, December 31, 2006, www.usdoj.gov/criminal/fraud/fcpa/opinion/2006/0602.html.
5. DOJ, FCPA Opinion Procedure Release 2006-01, October, 16, 2006, www.usdoj.gov/criminal/fraud/fcpa/opinion/2006/0601.html.
6. DOJ, FCPA Opinion Procedure Release 2003-01, January 15, 2003, www.usdoj.gov/criminal/fraud/fcpa/opinion/2003/0301.html.
7. DOJ, FCPA Opinion Procedure Release 2001-03, December 11, 2001, www.usdoj.gov/criminal/fraud/fcpa/opinion/2001/0103.html.
8. DOJ, FCPA Opinion Procedure Release 2001-02, July 18, 2001, www.usdoj.gov/criminal/fraud/fcpa/opinion/2001/0102.html.

9. DOJ, FCPA Opinion Procedure Release 2001-01, May 24, 2001, www.usdoj.gov/criminal/fraud/fcpa/opinion/2001/0101.html.

10. DOJ, FCPA Opinion Procedure Release 2000-01, March 29, 2000, www.usdoj.gov/criminal/fraud/fcpa/opinion/2000/0001.html.

11. DOJ, FCPA Opinion Procedure Release 2004-01, January 6, 2004, www.usdoj.gov/criminal/fraud/fcpa/opinion/2004/0401.html.

12. DOJ, FCPA Opinion Procedure Release 2004-03, June 14, 2004, www.usdoj.gov/criminal/fraud/fcpa/opinion/2004/0403.html.

13. DOJ, FCPA Opinion Procedure Release 2004-04, September 3, 2004, www.usdoj.gov/criminal/fraud/fcpa/opinion/2004/0404.html.

14. DOJ, FCPA Opinion Procedure Release 2007-01, July 24, 2007, www.usdoj.gov/criminal/fraud/fcpa/opinion/2007/0701.html.

15. DOJ, FCPA Opinion Procedure Release 2007-02, September 11, 2007, www.usdoj.gov/criminal/fraud/fcpa/opinion/2007/0702.html.

16. DOJ, FCPA Opinion Procedure Release 2008-03, July 11, 2008, www.usdoj.gov/criminal/fraud/fcpa/opinion/2008/0803.html.

About the Authors

Martin T. Biegelman has been fighting fraud and corruption for more than 35 years in various roles in law enforcement, consulting, and the corporate sector. He is currently the Director of Financial Integrity at Microsoft Corporation. In 2002, he joined Microsoft to create and lead a global fraud detection, investigation, and prevention program based within internal audit. In addition to focusing on preventing financial fraud and abuse, his group promotes financial integrity, fiscal responsibility, and compliance in a COSO framework of improved business ethics, effective internal controls, and greater corporate governance. He works closely with Microsoft's executive leadership, the Office of Legal Compliance, Internal Audit, and others in protecting Microsoft from financial and reputational risk.

Prior to joining Microsoft, he was a Director of Litigation and Investigative Services in the Fraud Investigation Practice at BDO Seidman, LLP, an international accounting and consulting firm. He is also a former federal law enforcement professional, having served as a United States Postal Inspector in a variety of investigative and management assignments. As a federal agent, he was a subject matter expert in fraud detection and prevention. He retired as the Inspector in Charge of the Phoenix, Arizona Field Office of the Postal Inspection Service.

Martin is a Certified Fraud Examiner as well as an adjunct faculty member, Regent Emeritus, and Fellow of the Association of Certified Fraud Examiners (ACFE). He is a Certified Compliance and Ethics Professional and an adjunct faculty member of the Society of Corporate Compliance and Ethics. He is also a member of ASIS International and the High Technology Crime Investigation Association.

He serves on the Board of Directors of the ACFE Foundation, the Board of Advisors for the Economic Crime Institute at Utica College, and the Accounting Advisory Board for the Department of Accounting and Law in the School of Business at the University at Albany, State University of New York. In 2008, he was appointed by Washington State Governor Christine Gregoire to serve on the Washington State Executive Ethics Board.

Martin is a sought-after speaker and instructor on white-collar crime, corruption, the FCPA, identity theft, fraud prevention, and corporate compliance. He is the author or co-author of several books including *Building a World-Class Compliance Program: Best Practices and Strategies for Success*, *Executive Roadmap to Fraud Prevention and Internal Control: Creating a Culture of Compliance*, and *Identity Theft Handbook: Detection, Prevention, and Security*. He is a contributing author to *Fraud Casebook: Lessons from the Bad Side of Business*.

He is the 2008 recipient of the Cressey Award bestowed annually by the Association of Certified Fraud Examiners for lifetime achievements in the detection and deterrence of fraud. Martin has a Bachelor of Science degree from Cornell University and a Master of Public Administration from Golden Gate University.

Daniel R. Biegelman is an attorney with the law firm of Baker Hostetler. He is a member of the Litigation Practice Group in their New York office. Baker Hostetler is a Top 100 law firm with over 600 attorneys around the world, representing many major corporations, including 10 of the Fortune 25. Prior to joining Baker Hostetler, he worked on a wide range of litigation, including criminal, securities, employment, and pharmaceutical cases.

Daniel is admitted to practice in New York and California. He is also a Certified Compliance and Ethics Professional and a member of the Society of Corporate Compliance and Ethics. Daniel is a contributing author to *Building a World-Class Compliance Program: Best Practices and Strategies for Success* and co-author of "Building Compliance Programs: Ethics and Compliance Will Always Matter" published in the July/August 2008 issue of *Fraud Magazine*. He also worked with Martin Biegelman on *Executive Roadmap to Fraud Prevention and Internal Control* and *Identity Theft Handbook*.

Compliance and Ethics Magazine, a publication of the Society of Corporate Compliance and Ethics profiled Daniel in a cover story in the June 2009 issue.

Daniel has a Bachelor's degree from the Barrett Honors College at Arizona State University and a law degree from St. John's University School of Law. The FCPA has been a topic of interest for him dating back to law school, when he wrote an article on *United States v. Giffen* for the *New York International Law Review*.

Index

351

356